BORDERLAND BEAT

BORDERLAND BEAT

Reporting on The Mexican Drug War

September 29, 2019

ISBN: 9780359595884
Copyright: Alex Marentes
(Standard Copyright License)
Edition: 11th Edition
Publisher: Lulu Publishing
Published: April 16, 2019
Language: English
Product: ID24067205

505-672-8447
buggs2001@gmail.com
www.alexmarentes.com
www.borderlandbeat.com

SBN #: 978-0-359-59588-4

Content ID: 24646190

Book Title: Borderland Beat

Contents

Author

Alex Marentes (Buggs) resides in Albuquerque, New Mexico. He was born in Ciudad Juarez, Chihuahua, Mexico, and came to the U.S. at the young age of 10 years old. While living in Ciudad Juarez, his father commuted daily to El Paso while working for Tony Lama making cowboy boots. His father eventually moved to Albuquerque with his family after getting terminated for going on strike. Alex joined the United States Marines and was honorably discharged after eight years of active duty service. He also served three years in the United States Marine Corps Reserve after his active duty. Alex joined the Albuquerque Police Department in 1986 and retired after 30 years of service to his community. Alex spends his retirement as a professional photographer, one of his lifetime passions. He is also an avid adventurer and motorcycle rider. Alex has traveled extensively to Mexico, has family and friends there and has always had an interest in the political and social life of Old Mexico. Going under cover using the pseudonym name of "Buggs," that was derived from his love of the Looney Tunes Bugs Bunny cartoon, Alex is the founder and owner of the Borderland Beat Project that gathers information about the Mexican Drug Cartel War and shares the information in the popular, internationally renowned blog.

From the Author

I want to thank all the contributors from Borderland Beat Project and the loyal readers, who are among the most knowledgeable about the drug cartels in Mexico. I also want to thank all the people who at one point or another helped me along the way and guided me through the uncertainty. I want to thank all of the law enforcement officers on both sides of the border that have gone above and beyond their duty to make a positive impact on society and have kept us all safe. I want to give my appreciation to the officers of the Albuquerque Police Department, who provide service to my community and are like a family to me. I specifically want to thank the officers who have made the ultimate sacrifice fighting the narco war. I want to thank my family and friends who have supported me in this effort. I want to thank Susan Gomez for the art on the cover and Unek Francis for the banner. I plan on touring Mexico in the near future and visiting the hot zones covered in this book, and documenting the area and situation, mostly through photographs, and touching base with old contacts.

Know that my only purpose in life is to "Live and Learn."

I dedicate this book to my mother,
Bertha Saucedo Marentes

Preamble

Mexico's drug war diary: borderlandbeat.com
By Conor Fay

"It is an arcane website, something reminiscent of about 2005. When I first checked out Borderland Beat I paused, sneering at the ugly beige tone of its homepage. No interactive menu obeys the whims of my hovering mouse.

Then I read some of the posts. Borderland Beat is something of a pin board, or a newspaper scrapbook, where anonymous writers contribute the content, with stories about a drug war that rages on in Mexico.

That anonymity is what makes Borderland Beat so arresting; its contributors are talking about the kingpins of Mexico's multi-billion-dollar drug industry.

These are men who don't have limits, murder is not a consideration for them but a gut reaction. Exposing them online without the barrier of anonymity could mean death for the writers. Death has been doled out to thousands in the region for far less.

The evidence is splattered all over the walls of the website. You could pick a page at random and you'll see some post with a "WARNING EXTREME FOOTAGE". That post could feature pictures of a gang member shot to bits, or a school teacher with her head cut off, or a whole excruciating video of a poor soul being beaten to death with baseball bats in a torture room.

Like the crack cocaine pedaled by these gangs, the effect of Borderland Beat is scarily addictive. The blunt depiction of graphic violence draws you in, but you're eventually hooked by the stories. They tell the tale of Mexico's slow death. Border cities like Juarez were the first to go. Thousands die there now each year directly as a result of the gang violence.

They tell the tale of the brave who try to sever the limbs of the gangs, that seems an impossibility though.

The media have largely failed also, and those who have tried were swatted away. In 1996 Gary Webb published a series of articles, "Dark Alliance," criticizing the CIA for their role in the drug crisis with Mexico. He was immediately labeled a fraud and was vilified by all mainstream American media outlets, culminating in Webb's own suicide.

Borderland Beat rises above this; it feels like something more than news, it is a diary. The contributors cannot be attacked because they are many and they are largely anonymous, and because they do not fear it.

While the stories of mass grave discoveries and corrupt officials are endless, the fact that the locals continue to publish en masse documentation of their collapsed country and the bandits who rule it offers some respite. These people are defying the torturers; they just need an audience.

The Borderland Beat is an English language blog that reports news about the Mexican Drug War. The blog was started in April 2009 by an anonymous individual using the pseudonym Buggs, who remains the sole owner. The blog has been referred to and quoted in the New York Times, Small Wars Journal and the Houston Chronicle.

In an article published in May 2012, the journalist, Gary Moore, described Borderland Beat as follows: "An English-language digest Web site called Borderland Beat forms a lonely watchtower on the Mexico battlements, manned by a small cadre of Mexican-Americans (my work has appeared there as well), who set themselves the vital mission of archiving any available news on Mexico's meltdown."

From National Mexican Magazine
"El Semanario"

That dangerous information gap is being filled, for better or worse, by blogs. A former Texan policeman and former Marine, who conceals his true identity under the pseudonym "Buggs" (madman, in underworld jargon), is the founder of Borderland Beat (borderlandlandbeat.com), popular blog that almost censors nothing and that mixes videos and macabre photographs with hard information from recognized sources. On the weekend he uploaded the photos of the alleged assassins of San Fernando that the Mexican press did not risk spreading. For American cybernauts, it has the appeal of being written in English, unlike Blog del Narco. Borderlabd Beat become a mandatory source if information for police, justice enforcement officials, and the general public, particularly in the border states. In his presentation, Borderland Beat says that the blog seeks to "give perspective" to the issues that determine the complicated neighborhood with Mexico under the understanding "that the activities on one side affect the other." Blog reporters, identified as El Viento, Tianguera, Huero, RiseMakaveli, Ovemex, Pancho and La Adelita, operate in Texas, California, Chihuahua, Tamaulipas and even Colombia. Its sources include local authorities.

How to Interpret this Book

The Borderland Beat Project is collaboration from a group of people of different backgrounds located in the U.S. and Mexico that gather information related to the Mexican drug cartels and presents it in English through the internet, publications and presentations.

Almost all content in this book comes from the result of reporting in the Borderland Beat blog and the personal experience and research of the author. It primarily covers a time frame when the author was an active contributor between the last part of 2008 and when he stopped getting directly involved around 2013. Information from this book is a reflection of the Borderland Beat blog that is derived from research, open media sources, informal official authorities and people on the ground, all of which has been gathered by collaborators from Borderland Beat Project. This represents the most extensive and comprehensive source of information between the years 2008 and 2013 covering a very wide range of topics related to the Mexican cartels and the Mexican drug war in Mexico and along the US/Mexican border.

Almost all material covered can be found at www.borderlandbeat.com.

The author has created a website that contains more information and media sources, to include some of the videos mention in the book. To seek further extended information beyond what is contained in this book visit www.alexmarentes.com.

This book in essence gives a perspective of issues related to the complicated issues of both neighboring countries and how the activities from one side impact the other. It is important for both sides of the border to understand how mayhem and ruthless violence from organized crime touches

the people on the borderland and the misery it brings to every day social conditions we sometimes call civilization.

Consider this a huge source of information related to crime on the borderland.

Knowledge is power.

Most of the information and content is derived from open source media, unconfirmed individual sources and personal viewpoint of author. The content is for information purposes only, and in most cases is not derived from direct official sources. In fact, sometimes the information has not been formally confirmed. Most information coming out of Mexico is fluid and always changing on a daily basis. And frankly, no one really has the market on credible information to form a sense of clear-cut validity or formal confirmation, so thread lightly.

Because crime in Mexico is extremely violent, this book depicts large amount of very graphic material. The need to present graphic source material is vital in showing a true representation of the extent of violence generated by the Mexican drug cartels upon the people of Mexico and the U.S.

The Mexican Drug War is an ongoing armed conflict taking place among rival drug cartels that fight each other for regional control (plazas), and Mexican government forces, which seek to combat drug trafficking. Although Mexican drug cartels, or Drug Trafficking Organizations (DTO's), have existed for a few decades, they have become more powerful since the demise of Colombia's Cali and Medellín cartels in the 1990s.

Again, while reading the content, keep in mind that this book covers the DTO's that were active during that periods of 2008 and 2013. The main cartels included are:

The powerful Sinaloa Cartel or Cartel de Sinaloa (CDS) that dominated the Golden Triangle in the states of Chihuahua, Sinaloa and Durango; the Beltran Leyva

Organization (BLO) made up of the Beltran brothers mainly concentrating in Guerrero; the Juarez Cartel fighting to protect its turf in one of the deadliest border cities in Mexico from the Sinaloa Cartel; the Gulf Cartel fighting its own break-away armed wing known as Los Zetas on the gulf coast that turned towns in the state of Tamaulipas into ghost towns; La Familia Michoacana (LFM), which is trying to make a presence in the lands of Tierra Caliente of Michoacan, and which has morphed into the Caballeros Templarios, or The Knights Templar.

Toward the end of this book you can find more detail references to these individual Mexican Cartels for reference.

The general definition for the term "plaza" is mostly a downtown public square, but in narco terminology a plaza is a village, town or city controlled by a cartel boss. They control everything related to drug trafficking and cartel activities in their turf. The cartel leader in a plaza is known as a "plaza boss," and runs all business in the plaza for the cartel. When you hear this term throughout the book it refers to the narco meaning.

A "sicario" in the Mexican cartel sense is a cartel member that is paid to enforce the will of the organization and to battle other rival cartels. A sicario is usually a paid professional who has some training with weapons or tactics. In most cases, they are people who have deserted from the military or are active or former police officers. Although, in most cases, most cartels will often employ anyone as a sicario that can pull a trigger. You will find other reference information at the end of the book that can be helpful with putting the pieces together as we maneuver through the rocky road of the cartel world.

Some of the content in this book is directly quoted from Borderland Beat. These entries are usually followed with a date and the name of the collaborator who posted the content, which is also shown in parentheses and in italic. I understand that this can be confusing, especially since the material that is covered is from 2008 through 2013, and because a lot has changed since then. Keep this in mind as you read through the passages.

The information in this book is fast-paced, with a lot of DTO information thrown at you at once. It's filled with sicario activity and the Mexican government's attempt to intervene, but it also contains a lot of direct, behind-the-scenes information from the author. This particular information is the involvement of the author from his early stages when he started to formalize his plan to bring to life the Borderland Beat Project.

Follow Buggs as he sets the stage and takes you on a wild ride into the dark shadows of the violence and chaos of the Mexican drug cartels. A narrative, as told in the deep dark pages of the Borderland Beat blog.

Glimpse of Hope

I can't really recall exact dates and times, but it must have been sometime around 2008. I was working as a School Resource Officer for the city of Albuquerque at Jefferson Middle School. That is where I met an 11-year girl named Alicia. She was a pretty little girl who was always dressed in real nice new clothes. Although she appeared to come from an affluent background, she was very humble in nature. She was born in the U.S. but had a distinctive Spanish accent. She touched my heart one hot day when I had been playing basketball with some of the boys on the school's basketball court.

I was exhausted and overheating with sweat. She came over to talk to me and I asked her if the snack bar sold water. She said yes and I told her I needed to go to the office to get money to buy myself some water. But as things happen from time to time, I got distracted for a few minutes. I saw Alicia return after a while and she handed me a cold bottle of water. I asked her how much I owed her for the water and she said, "nothing." I was not necessarily touched by the fact she bought it for me (as money was not an issue with her), but that she thought of me when I needed water.

So, I got to know Alicia a little better while at school. I met her mother one day during a school visit and noticed her mother dressed in real nice clothes too. She was a Mexican national who spoke very little English. She also appeared to wear a lot of expensive jewelry and drove a luxurious brand-new white Escalade. They also lived in a brand-new two-story house in an upscale neighborhood known as Ridgecrest. The thought of how they got so much money did cross my mind a few times.

Little Alicia had mentioned that her mother did not work, and that they got their money from her father. I asked Alicia where her father worked, and she replied that she did not know because he lived in Ciudad Juarez. She said they visited him in the summers during school breaks.

Summer came and went, and school started again, but Alicia did not return. I became concerned and went to do a home visit but did not find anyone at home. So, I asked her cousin at school about Alicia and I was not prepared for what I heard. I was told that her mother, father and her 3-year-old little brother were killed in Ciudad Juarez during the summer. The cousin told me that Alicia had moved to San Antonio, Texas, with her aunt from her mother's side. I was able to get a phone number for Alicia's aunt in San Antonio and I was able to verify the story I was told.

I never heard from Alicia again, although I always wondered how she was doing. The times I had contact with her while at the school were very pleasant and I always knew her to be very polite and willing to be helpful. She was always smiling. That made a good impression on me and planted a promise of hope with our youth no matter where they came from.

So, I started to do research about the incident on the internet and for the first time ever I started to learn what was happening in Mexico. There was a real wave of violence engulfing Mexico, and Ciudad Juarez was the main battle ground for feuding drug cartels. While researching, I started to dive deep into the dark side of Mexico's drug war.

In 2008 the Sinaloa cartel was attempting to take the plaza from the Juarez cartel and both cartels were in a fierce battle in the city of Juarez. Juarez is a popular hub for drug trafficking into the U.S. In 2008 Juarez, which is on the border with El Paso, Texas, was considered to be the most dangerous city in the world.

I did find the brief article about Alicia's parents on the internet in the Juarez newspaper.

On the date in question, Alicia's father was driving a golden sedan, and her mom was in the front passenger seat. Her little brother was on the right rear seat behind his mother and Alicia was on the left rear seat behind her father. While the car was stopped for a traffic light, two vehicles blocked their path from the front and rear. Two men armed with assault rifles came up to the car from both sides and opened fire on the dad, mother and little boy. They were killed instantly. The man on the driver's side that had just shot and killed the father was supposed to shoot Alicia, but he didn't. He pointed his gun at her and at the last moment did not shoot. Perhaps he had a little girl himself and felt compassion, who knows. The killings took place at mid-day on a crowded street, and many people witnessed the executions. No one was ever brought to justice for the murders.

It was just another day in Juarez.

They eventually found a cache of weapons in the trunk of the car and a substantial amount of U.S. currency ($30,000). Mexican authorities suspected that the father had ties to the Juarez cartel and that the shooting was a matter of "ajuste de cuentas," or "settling of scores," a phrase I would later hear often after reading about an execution. Alicia's father was known to be a lieutenant for "La Linea," the armed wing of the Juarez cartel.

Up until then I had never heard of La Linea.

Living in the comfort of my home, I did not have the slightest idea what was happening in Mexico. But I soon learned that crimes such as gangland-style murders and kidnappings were at record levels, making Mexico one of the world's most dangerous countries in the world. I learned that kidnapping was a multi-million-dollar industry in Mexico.

I soon realized that Mexico's murder rate was topping all others in the Western Hemisphere. All this despite the fact that Mexican President Felipe Calderon's tough new war on drugs had sent thousands of Mexican Army troops into the countryside, while a record number of drug warlords were extradited to the United States for trial.

I learned that crime had been on the rise in Mexico throughout the last decade, as drug cartels battled each other for control of lucrative smuggling routes. And it wasn't just the violence, but the extent of it. I saw that Mexico's violence was often spectacular and lurid, with tales of street shootouts, decapitations and bomb blasts filling Mexico's news pages and airwaves.

No place was immune, and Ciudad Juarez, our back yard, was the worst. As I continued to read the news every day, the bloodbath continued unabated and everyone here in the U.S. had no idea what was happening right across the border.

I did not know it at the time but this was a nasty storm that was just beginning.

The violence and mayhem just multiplied over the months and years. I bought books about the Mexican drug war, saw the daily news, read the Mexican newspapers, and glued myself to the internet while learning about the Mexican cartels.

Everyone around me went about their business as usual without any inclination or idea of the misery and devastation that was ravaging a country that shared a border with us. I myself would not have known about it if it had not been for the tragic fate of a little girl named Alicia.

The real important issues about Mexico have been lost on the U.S. side with the debate of issues such illegal immigration and the origin of weapons in the hands of Mexican cartels. I have seen some real heated confrontations on both sides of the aisle. We have Mexicans blaming the U.S. for creating a demand for drugs through their vile habit, and Americans blaming Mexico for permitting a drug industry through corrupt practices. I do not want to sound cliché when I repeat the saying, "drugs go north while money and guns go south."

There is a big connection between Mexico and the U.S., and it's more than just a border or the cultural history that sometimes bind us. It is a shared common interest to stop the flow of drugs and the misery of the tragic and violent consequences it brings with it.

The bottom line is that the sale of illegal drugs is just a business decision and it exists for two reasons: product is very good, and profit is very high. Nothing on Earth can stop something that generates billions of dollars and is desired by millions of people. The sad part of all this is that when you try to stop it, it fuels a wave of violence like what's happening in Mexico and which could very easily transform that nation into a failed state. That is why we will never totally eradicate illicit drug trafficking, the temptation it brings, and leaves in its wake the worst violence one can possibly fathom.

Now here we are, the violence has not subsided, it is relentless and more shocking with every passing day. I knew someone had to record it and bring it out, because the violence is not about merely interchangeable parts, but about real people. This is more than just statistics, or about nameless decapitated bodies thrown into the middle of the street with a "manta" attached to them, (a narco manta is a written message that is left on a cardboard placard or banner at the scene of an execution, or displayed in public to warn other cartels or government officials). It's about real people like that little girl named Alicia who had a heart to give, if only just to give someone some water. Despite the fact that Alicia's father was colluding with the Juarez cartel in crime, drug trafficking and murder, Alicia was just an innocent child with a good heart. She was an innocent of circumstances who found a way to do a good deed. It was in her nature, and was a glimpse of hope, despite all that is bad in this world.

Ciudad Juarez, a Mexican city that borders El Paso, Texas, was one of the most violent cities in the world. The Sinaloa Cartel was disputing the territory, trying to take the plaza away from the Juarez cartel. It was making Juarez a playground for shootouts, assassinations and the most horrific violence anyone can imagine. The homicide rate was spiraling out of control. Yet, the U.S. was blind to it all. It was around this time that I started reading a lot about organized crime in Mexico, and I was shocked at the amount and extent of violence on the other side of the U.S. border.

Rocky Point - Sonora

The same summer of 2008 when Alicia's family was executed in Ciudad Juarez, my brother and I were planning a motorcycle trip to Puerto Penasco (Rocky Point) in Mexico. I still had not been aware of the tragic incident involving Alicia when we made our trip. We would be traveling in our larger street motorcycles, my brother had a large Harley Davidson and I had a 2006 GL1800 Honda Goldwing. The plan was to travel along the border on the Mexico side to see the countryside.

We crossed in to Mexico at the Santa Theresa point of entry on the Texas–New Mexico state border. We then took Rural Road 2 that runs along the border through the Mexican state of Sonora. We were to stay in Agua Prieta, Nogales, a town sharing a border with Douglas, Arizona.

I did not know it then but the state of Sonora was very active with cartel activity. There were shootouts where multiple people were being killed. Many of the police officers from different municipalities were also killed. There was an intense fight over the plaza of Sonora, one of the main points of drug trafficking in to the U.S. Sonora is known for its narco tunnels into the U.S., primarily funded by the Sinaloa Cartel. There were a lot of executions and most of the town lived in fear of the drug cartels. Sonora for the most part was being ignored by the federal authorities that were focusing most of their resources on Ciudad Juarez and Tijuana.

We entered Agua Prieta toward the end of the day. I immediately started to look for a motel. I saw a few on the outskirts of town, but they appeared to be in the industrial district and they did not look very inviting to me. In the middle of town, I saw a brand-new beautiful motel that seemed like a very safe place to stay. We pulled in and I thought that perhaps it was still under construction as there were no cars in the parking lot. The sign on the office window read "Vacancies."

The man in the office told us he did not have any vacancies, and also something about not being open for business. I tried to get him to recommend a motel and directions, when a late model luxurious SUV pulled up. Two beautiful ladies who were well dressed came in and told the man behind the counter to give us a room.

The man got us a room.

The two ladies were really friendly to us and I assumed they were probably the owners or managers of the motel. My brother started a conversation with the lady driver and invited her for some drinks in town. She politely declined and said that she hoped we enjoyed our stay.

We went to eat at a little restaurant that was within walking distance of the motel and I asked the server about the motel. I also told him about how the two ladies had ensured we got a room. His eyes lit up when I told him about it.

He cautioned us to be very careful and refrain from talking to people we did not know. "You can't trust anyone here, it's very dangerous," he told us, almost whispering and looking around as if he was looking for someone. He said that the motel was owned by a cartel boss who went by the name "Dos Mil" who lived in Cananea, just west of Agua Prieta. He owned a large, beautiful mansion, modeled after the architectural preferences of Amado Carrillo Fuentes (a former Juarez cartel capo), a hacienda-style home complete with cupolas.

He said that the motel, like many other businesses he owned around Sonora were fronts to launder large amounts of money. He told me that "Dos Mil" was very dangerous, drove around with a large armed escort and could kill anyone at will without any consequences.

He told us that the lady driving the SUV was one of Dos Mil's girlfriends and that the cartel boss didn't like anyone talking to her. He told a story about a man who asked the girlfriend to dance at a local nightclub when Dos Mil was in the bathroom. Dos Mil also owned that particular nightclub. He came out of the restroom and saw the man talking to his girlfriend. Dos Mil went in to a rage and shot the man 20 times right in front of everyone. The whole thing was swept underneath the rug. He said most local police were on Dos Mil's payroll.

He warned us that my brother had placed our lives in danger by asking the ladies for drinks. Back in our rooms in the motel I suddenly did not feel real safe.

I heard a knock on the door at around 9 p.m. that frankly scared the hell out of me. It turned out to be a man who was asking if he could wash our bikes in the morning for a donation. Relieved, I said yes. I can attest that I did not sleep well that night. The next morning, I picked up my camera that had a long lens attached to it and was going to load it on the small trunk of my bike. The man washing my bike looked up at me, saw me holding my camera, and I guess he must have thought that I was holding a firearm. He screamed, put his hands up and head down. He started pleading for me not to kill him. I had never seen such fear in a man like I did at that moment.

We made it to Puerto Penasco and had a very good time with no issues whatsoever. On our way back to Albuquerque, we drove the U.S. side of the border.

In 2008, there were a lot of Mexican cops that were killed or caught actively colluding with organized crime in the state of Sonora.

Later, while I tried to do some research of the so-called Dos Mil, who was mentioned on our trip I got an idea of who this person might be. It was none other than Francisco

Hernandez Garcia alias "El 2000," or "El Panchillo," who was at one time a drug lord for the Beltrán Leyva Brothers Organization Cartel (BLO).

It is said that "El 2000" allied himself with Los Zetas after he felt betrayed by the BLO. The Zetas had a feud with the BLO who at one time sent one of their Lieutenants, Édgar Valdés Villarreal "La Barbie" to the state of Tamaulipas to help the Gulf Cartel take over the gulf region. There is a video that went viral on social media where La Barbie is seen torturing and executing four members of Los Zetas. Suddenly "El 2000" felt that he needed to control his turf, specifically police officers working with and for Sinaloa and BLO.

In 2008, they found the head of a local cop wrapped in silver duct tape. They had used a knife to pin a note with a message in his chest. As a final touch, they left a hand grenade by the corpse—a calling card, of sorts.

The note read:

"Miren ojetes, la pelea no es con el gobierno, es con Arturo Beltrán y La Barbie (Édgar Valdés Villarreal) –capos del cártel de Sinaloa– Todos los judiciales y municipales que estén con ellos se van a morir: Carlos Bojórquez, Andrés Sánchez (PJE), Manuel Ángel Barrios Mo PJE."

On the back it read: "Policías Municipales... Urrea... Almaraz... tienen 24 horas para salir del estado, todos los policías que estén con la maña morirán Att El 2000 y aliados."

Somewhat it translates: "Listen here assholes, our fight is not with the government; it's with Arturo Beltrán Leyva and La Barbie of the Sinaloa Cartel. All the state and city police who are with them will die."

It contained at least 10 names of police officers from around the state of Sonora who were targeted for execution, and it was signed "El 2000 and allies."

Cananea narco-trafficker Dos Mil had risen to power by eliminating the established Sonoran narco-families and could kill a person just for looking at him the wrong way. He controlled the Sonora region and ruled with total impunity. That is who my brother risked his life for, just for flirting innocently with the girlfriend of a bad hombre.

The Curse of Cusarare

December 24, 2008

There would be another event that would eventually prompt me to get involved in some way. It involved my love of photography and motorcycles

I am an avid motorcycle rider who likes to travel to remote areas with an enduro/dual sport type motorcycle that's modified to travel long distances. I have traveled in remote areas all over the southwestern U.S. and Mexico. Every Christmas, friends and I used to ride our bikes to the Copper Canyon area to enjoy the beautiful remote mountains of Chihuahua. So, in December of 2008, I traveled to Creel, Chihuahua with an American friend named Everest to ride our motorcycles through the desolate back country of Copper Canyon. It is Sinaloa territory, and the hills of the Sierra Madre are where they plant their marijuana crop and poppy fields, and poppy is what they turn into heroin. I had a dilemma, and that was whether I should tell Everest of the sleeping giant—the drug cartel violence—that was starting to wake up. I made the mistake of not telling him because I didn't want to scare him away. I wanted him to enjoy the trip and relax without having to worry at every turn in the road. I had been looking forward to the trip all year and I didn't want him to get scared and cancel the adventure.

It turned out that not warning him was a grave mistake on my part and something that I would later regret.

The Chihuahua state highway from Creel is a well maintained paved road that winds through beautiful Ponderosa and pine trees. It had snowed the day before, but on this day when we were on the road it was all sunshine and blue skies. The smooth asphalt was already dry from the melting snow, and as I accelerated, I thought to myself that that particular road was made for motorcycles.

As I leaned my bike to the right on another twisty curve, I could hear the knobby tires of my DR650 dual sport bike squeak a bit in protest as the rubber met the pavement. I was careful not to lean too much because I figured it was too early to chance an accident. We each had our own bike and we were riding to the bottom of Copper Canyon on our journey to reach Batopilas, a town of 1,200 people. I was following Everest, who was keeping a good speed. I looked down at my speedometer and saw that I was just below 50 mph while pulling out of the wide curve. I had to remind myself not to push myself too hard because, after all, we were there to relax and do three full days of riding the Tarahumara back country.

Christmas was the next day and I was glad to be away from all the commercialized propaganda of a holiday that no longer seem to mean much to me. I took a deep breath, taking in as much fresh air as possible and was glad to be there, riding my bike on Mexico Highway 25.

I saw a blue a sign to the right announcing our approach to Cusarare, a small Indian town on the side of the road. I could see that we were approaching another curve and I downshifted to a lower gear in preparation to enter the curve at a decent and safe speed.

Everest was a much better rider than I was and he tended to pull away from me on the curves, so I had to accelerate to catch up to him on the straightaways. I saw Everest disappear on a turn ahead of me, so I leaned my bike to the right to start into the curve while trying to maintain the same speed.

When I came out of the curve, I could see that Everest had pulled away a bit and I immediately started to accelerate to ensure I kept a good, close gap between us. As I started to gain distance and get closer to him, I noticed that another curve was coming up fast, but this time it was a left turn. I still had some time to accelerate a bit more and gain a little more distant toward Everest before I had to slow down for the upcoming curve.

As Everest approached the curve, I noticed that he had moved to the center of the lane because there was a person in a yellow jacket riding a bicycle on the right side real close to the edge of the steel guardrail. Everest approached the curve with his motorcycle on the center of the yellow line of the road and he was gaining on the bicyclist. As he accelerated and leaned into the curve, he came side-by-side to the person on the bicycle. Suddenly the bicyclist made a quick left turn toward the middle of the road and right into the path of Everest and his motorcycle.

Everest didn't have time to react and t-boned the bicyclist straight on. There was a loud crashing sound, and the bicyclist flew 20 feet through the air as a result of being hit by a motorcycle at full speed. Everest and his bike went down on the right side. The impact and momentum of the crash propelled Everest over his bike and he slid on the pavement about 15 feet in front of his motorcycle.

I immediately started to look for a safe place to park my bike. It seemed like everything was in slow motion; every movement was fluid as I stopped my bike, placed the kick stand down, turned the key to shut off the engine, dismounted, and took off my helmet and placed it on the ground.

Everest's motorcycle was on its right side, still in the middle of the road, and Everest was on the ground on his side facing away from me. He was the first person I was able to reach. He still had his helmet on but his face shield was gone.

I called to him but got no response. He was not moving at all. I got really close to him, called out his name about four times but still got no response. I opened one of his eye lids and noticed that his eye was also not responsive. I immediately started to feel for a pulse on his right wrist but I wasn't certain there was one. My own heart was racing fast and I was breathing hard because I had run to get to Everest.

I was excited, and that wasn't helping me. I was a trained first responder and I knew I had to calm down if I was going to be of any help. The problem is, a crash or catastrophe is never easy when it involves someone you know. Somehow, I calmed down and was finally able to detect a pulse from Everest.

Then I ran toward the other person and realized that he was a small Indian boy about 10 years old. His whole body was shaking in spasms and his eyes were wide open and fixed up to the top of his head. His mouth was open and he looked like he was going into shock. Blood streamed down his face and I knew he had some sort of head trauma. Both the boy and Everest were in the middle the highway and I knew I had to do something.

I looked behind me to see if there was any traffic coming but there was only the empty highway and another blue sign announcing the approach to Cusarare.

I saw that Everest was starting to move around and moan. I got closer to him and told him not to move. He didn't listen. He tried to stand up and fell back down. I was concerned about oncoming traffic, especially about vehicles coming from the south and around the curve. Vehicles traveled fast on that road, and there were two people lying in the middle of it. A driver speeding around that curve probably would not have seen us and probably would have hit us. I helped Everest move to the side of the road and asked him if he was okay and if anything hurt. He looked at me and asked what had happened. At that point he couldn't remember anything about the accident. I sat next to Everest and was trying to talk to him when I saw the boy Everest had hit crawling to the side of the road.

"Well at least he's moving," I said to myself, feeling a bit relieved.

I went to the boy and he actually stood up. He was wobbly but was walking away. I sat him down next to Everest. He had abrasions to his arms, but the bleeding from his head had stopped. I inspected his head. He had a big lump to the top left forehead and a small cut to the top of his head. I asked him if he was okay and he said he was. I asked him if his head hurt, he said a little bit. I asked if his legs hurt, he said a little bit.

A Mexican couple passing by in a car stopped and they tried calling for help on their cell phone, but there was no signal. The boy asked the couple if they could take him home, but the male driver said he didn't think that was a good idea.

The male driver got out of the car and looked around as if he was nervous. He told us it was best if we left before the police showed up. "It's never good when the police show up," he said while looking around as if someone was right around the corner. I asked if he could go somewhere and get us help. He walked back to his vehicle and said he didn't want to get involved. The couple drove away as fast as they had arrived.

I turned and saw that Everest was already moving his motorcycle to the side of the road. He couldn't remember anything about the accident, but some of his memory about what happened just before the crash was starting to come back. He had a huge abrasion on his right hip and a tooth had been knocked loose.

It was remarkable that both Everest and the boy appeared to be only slightly injured. I rode my bike a few miles to Casarare where a lady from the local clinic agreed to help. She got into a pickup truck, drove to the accident scene, picked up the boy and drove him back to the clinic. Everest and I rode our bikes to the clinic and saw that the boy had sustained minor injuries: scrapes to his arms and legs, a lump on his forehead and a small cut and scrape to the top of his head. The lady assured us that everything was okay and that they were going to take the boy home.

Everest was little sore but wanted to continue with the ride.

We ride!

Deep in the Sierra Madre Mountains we rode the switchbacks down the Copper Canyon into Batopilas. Every so often we would see crosses on the side of the road. Sometimes there were multiple crosses staggered in a cluster—probably a place to mark the spot of some cartel execution. We got a room at Marys Motel for 250 pesos (about 21 U.S. dollars), ate dinner at the same hotel and bought a cup of corn from the corn lady at the corner stand.

We decided to go to a bar next door and have a beer. The lady at the motel gave us directions to the little bar but also cautioned us not to wonder off at night, not to stay out too late and to be very, very careful.

To say the bar was small was an understatement; it had room for only three tables. The owner cleared a bunch of empty bottles from an empty table and greeted us very politely. As soon as we sat down, a very drunk man came over to us and asked if we would buy him a beer. We did. He sat at our table and started talking loudly, but we just wanted to relax and not be bothered. The friendly owner, who was also the bartender, came over to tell the drunk man to leave us alone. The owner apologized and I immediately noticed he had a handgun strapped to his waist—a Colt 1911, .38 caliber with a fancy grip.

We eventually retreated to our room for a well needed rest and sleep.

It was Christmas eve.

The Motel Mary is in the heart of Batopilas, right across from the town's main church. The sounds of children singing

Christmas songs from a loudspeaker serenaded us late into the night

It had been a long day and the next day we were going to try to reach Urique.

The Encounter with the Drunk Sicarios

We woke up in Batopilas on Christmas day. I saw that Everest was getting ready for the day, cleaning his helmet. It's amazing how one day he was lying in the middle of the road breathing his last breath and the next day he was full of life waiting to ride out of the Copper Canyon.

We ate a quick breakfast in the motel restaurant and headed out on our way to Urique, a mining town of 1,100 that had been established by the Spaniards more than 300 years earlier. On our way out we stopped at the Cathedral of Satevó where I tried to get directions out of the Copper Canyon from there. No one seemed to know how to get out. So, we went south on a dirt road, and when we came upon a fork in the road, we weren't sure which direction to go. We asked a young man in an old, beat-up truck. He pointed to the right and up a huge mountain.

We could see the road winding its way up the top of the crest. As we were climbing, we came to another fork and decided to go left, but after a while the road was getting really rough. We realized we were going the wrong way and had to backtrack. The dirt road up the mountain was very good, rocky in some areas, but not bad. We continued on the road, and eventually made a left turn and continued through a few small towns reaching a small town of Rodeo where we stopped for a break. Some kids came out to greet us and I bought them some candy at the small, local store.

We continued on some very interesting roads and scenery. It was a nice day, it was Christmas and we were having a blast riding in some of the more interesting roads in Tarahumara country. The accident from the day before was still fresh in my mind and I attempted to forget about it but, I couldn't. I had a strange premonition that I couldn't explain or understand.

It started to get warm and Everest wanted to stop to shed some clothing. Suddenly the road took us to a river that had no bridge to cross. It was maybe knee-deep but was lined with a lot of large-grade gravel—large rocks, actually. I thought Everest would stop to talk about how to enter the river, but he stood up on his bike and accelerated right into the water.

Everest went down right on the middle of the river. The current was strong and I was trying to find a good place to set down my side stand on the huge rocks. Somehow Everest was able to pick up his bike and push out of the water. He was soaked. I placed my camera and clothes in a plastic bag and rode through the river at a slower pace.

We continued to ride, it was starting to get late and we were not sure how far we were from Urique. As we came around a bend and started to climb a hill, I saw a large white truck coming down the hill. I also could see that there were several Indian men in the back of the truck. There was a narrow gap between some trees just enough for the truck to fit. Everest managed to cross the gap before the truck made it through. He sped up the hill and I had to wait for the truck to make it through the gap so I could pass.

But the truck stopped in the middle of the gap and blocked my path.

There were two men inside the truck's cab. Suddenly, the driver, who was wearing a military jacket and blue plants, got out and started walking toward me. He was carrying an AR-15 style assault rifle.

I did not like this a bit and knew it was extremely dangerous. We were deep in the vast empty mountains and the whole scene was not right. I started to look around, hoping to find some options that would get me out of there.

I tried to back up to turn around fast, but the driver was moving too fast toward me. Before I knew it, he was right in front of me. I then saw that the passenger had also exited the truck and he also was armed with an assault rifle. I became afraid of what they might do, and for a second, I thought of ditching my bike and running as fast as I could. But I knew I didn't have time to do anything.

Off in the distance I could see that Everest had reached the top of the hill kicking dust in the distance.

I thought to myself, "Stop, don't panic. Think." I focused my attention on the two men who had quickly approached me, trying to see signs or red flags. The driver had his trigger finger extended on his weapon while the passenger had his finger resting on the trigger of his rifle. As the driver got closer, I saw that the hat he was wearing said "Urique police." Out here that did not mean shit. Most municipal police were actively colluding with organized crime.

I knew that I easily could have been killed right there and my body not found for days. It would not have mattered because I would have been just another casualty of the violence that was sweeping the country.

The driver reached me first, but he was laughing and that made me relax a bit. One thing you never want to do in these kinds of situations is show fear. He stopped right in front of my bike and asked where I was going. I told him Urique and he asked where I was from. I said the U.S.

I told him we were just doing a motorcycle ride to see the country. He was holding two cans of Tecate beer in his hands, and he reached out and offered me one, saying, "Here cabron have a beer." I said, "No thanks," and could see by the change in his facial expression that he did not like my response.

He stood there looking at me and I could tell he was intoxicated as he swayed in his stance. His friend pointed his rifle at me and said, "Did this cabron just say no?"

The passenger seemed unsteady on his stance and he pulled a folded piece of paper out of his pocket, unfolded it and started snorting the content inside. There is nothing more dangerous than an armed sicario high on coke.

I tried to reason with them, if it was at all possible, but I knew that what I said in the next couple of seconds could determine whether I lived or died.

"Listen guys, I would be happy to join you for a beer, but it is getting late and we are trying to reach Urique before it gets dark," I told them. "Otherwise, I would be honored to join you for a drink."

"We?" the driver asked as he started looking around. I pointed up the hill toward Everest and said, "Yup. Up there."

I pointed to the hill up front to the north of us. Everest had reached the top of the hill and had stopped far up the distance looking at our direction.

"That is my friend up there and he is waiting for me, so I need to go," I said trying not to sound too alarmed. But my heart was beating a hundred miles an hour.

They both looked up and they could see the tiny figure of Everest waiting for me to come up. The driver came around the bike and looked at me closely. He could not really tell who I was, as I was wearing my helmet and sunglasses.

"Are the gringos in the bicycles up ahead your friends?" he asked.

He kept playing with his rifle and now had his finger on the trigger. I saw that there were two more ammo magazines sticking out of his jacket pocket.

"No," I responded.

He started to laugh out loud.

"Well, we scared the fuck out of them, not sure where they went," he said while both he and his friend laughed together.

The driver waved me off and joked with his partner, "Ah deja a este guey (leave this fuck be)."

They both turned around, still laughing, and walked toward the truck and got inside. They had a hard time keeping their balance as they walked away and I figured they were highly intoxicated, and probably coked out too. The driver grinded the truck gears as he shifted to first gear and drove past me, and even the men in the back of the truck were laughing.

I started to ride up the hill and met Everest halfway. He had been coming down to see what had been holding me up. I motioned him to keep going. We stopped at the top of the hill and I told Everest what happened. I cautioned Everest that if we ever encountered problems like that again, and if we got separated, not to rejoin. Everest was starting to get concerned and told me we needed to get the hell out of the area as quickly as possible. I agreed, but I also knew that we still had at least two days of riding before we got out of the Sierra Madre mountains.

We traveled another hour or so and we came to a "T" in the road. We turned left to reach a small town down the hill called Tubares, which had a small church that was falling down. I told Everst to stop so I could take pictures of the church. He argued with me, saying it was best that we keep going, as it was starting to get dark. I told him it would not take long. I parked my bike a short walking distance to take some pictures. As I was taking pictures, I could detect movement underneath a pile of wood inside the dark shadows of the church. There was someone inside, apparently hiding underneath a pile of wood.

I called out to Everest and I saw two blond men come out of the shadow with their eyes wide open. They were bicyclists—both in their late 20s or early 30s—from California and they told us they were hiding from two drunken armed Mexicans that were making them drink beer. One of the cyclists was limping and said he had been shot in the toe, as two armed men were making him dance while shooting at his feet. I looked around, trying to hear any sound of anyone approaching.

It was dead silent.

The cyclists asked me if it was safe to stay there for the night, and I said I didn't think it was a good idea. On my way into the town I had seen several houses with a bunch of pickup trucks and SUV's parked in the front. I also noticed lots of men drinking beer outside the houses. It was narco country and I didn't feel safe here. I told the cyclists that they should ride out and find a secluded hidden area to sleep for the night. They had intended to ride to Batopilas, but It had taken us all day to reach the small town we were in from Batopilas, and so they had a long way to go. We gave them some snacks and water. They were scared to death, and in that part of the country it gets very cold at night. I cautioned them not to make a fire in order to avoid detection. They had warm clothes on the bikes. We saw them mount their bicycles and head out.

I felt really bad, and I didn't like the idea of leaving them behind on their own. But under the circumstances, we didn't have much of a choice.

It was starting to get dark and we still had many miles to go before reaching Urique.

Everest and I decided that we would ride to Urique even if it took all night. As we watched the bicyclists ride out, I wondered if they would be safe. We mounted our own motorcycles to try to reach Urique in the dark of night. I was starting to miss my home in the USA. I stood there for a while, almost in a trance and deep in thought until Everest yelled at me to get going.

As we rode away, I could hear gunshots in the distance, echoing on the walls of the far away canyons. A reminder that

Tarahumara country had changed and perhaps it was no longer safe to travel in this beautiful remote country of Mexico.

We reached Urique around 11:30 at night. We had just ridden through some of the most beautiful country in Mexico, but we did not see any of it. That's because it was dark and because we were weighed down with stress, worry and concern. We checked in at the only motel in town. We were able to park our bikes right next to the door of our room, right in the lobby.

During the rest of the nigh, we would wake up to any sound outside our door. What would happened if a heavily armed commando stormed inside our room, abducted us (called a "levanton" in Mexico), took us to an unknown location to torture us to confess to things we knew nothing about and then slowly start cutting our limbs with a knife?

The feeling of insecurity was deafening to anything else that at the moment did not seem to matter much.

The next day, early in the morning, we went for breakfast in the restaurant right next to the motel. We sat down and saw three officers in uniform sitting at a table next to us. They were eating breakfast and drinking beer. It was eight in the morning. All three had long guns slung on their shoulders and they were laughing and talking about something funny. One of the officers had sergeant insignia on the sleeve of his shirt and the words "Urique Police" on his cap. He looked at me and walked over to our table.

"How you doing friend? Where are you guys from?" he asked. He seemed really friendly and pleasant.

"We are from the U.S., just riding our bikes through the beautiful country," I replied. "We are on our way back to Creel."

He sat at the table with us and started talking about how he also had a motorcycle and how he enjoyed hiking in the mountains. Since he seemed very approachable and a person with a nice side, I decided to tell him what had happened to us the day before. I detailed how we had met the two sicarios and the American bicyclists, and that they were still out there somewhere. He suddenly became quiet. I was wondering why he wasn't taking notes or asking for me to elaborate with more detail.

Then he abruptly stood up and said, "Listen Amigo, I think is best for you to leave. I would be very careful telling people such things. I will pay for your meal and I am kindly requesting that you leave now." He said all this while smiling and still with a friendly tone, but the content was hardly friendly. We left having just eaten part of our meal.

Back home in Albuquerque, New Mexico I was an active police officer for the city. I would eventually serve a total of 30 years for the Albuquerque Police Department and this instill in me a brotherhood with other police officers, not just with my own department, but with other members from other departments in the states. And in my case, this extended beyond my country where I live, especially when I travelled abroad.

I always had some degree of respect for police in Mexico. I guess it was a common bond that police have, and sometimes it extends universally. Yes, I knew they took bribes, but I always thought that because of the low wages they made, it was a necessity for them to provide enough for the families.

I had learned to accept this as a norm and accepted it. But what we had just seen and heard was totally different. I thought back to the sicarios we had met on the mountains, and I was starting to think that perhaps both, or at least one of them, might have been a police officer. Even maybe from Urique. From that point on, I saw them differently. Perhaps they could not be trusted, perhaps they were dangerous and a threat to anyone that happened to come across them in unfortunate times.

In 2015, the village of Urique was left without any police protection after all 18 members of the police department resigned amidst threats from organized crime. The resignation was a response to the execution of three of their officers in the mountains surrounding Urique. Perhaps things got so bad in the mountains, that they could no longer be part of the corruption or risk be killed if they resisted. It was easier to just quit.

As we rode out of the small town, we saw that we had descended a huge canyon with narrow switchbacks on narrow dirt roads. Just thinking we had ridden down this in pitch darkness made me feel very lucky that I had actually survived. Honestly, I was ready to get back home. As we rode our motorcycles forward toward our destination to Creel, we would see an occasional vehicle behind us, or one coming from in front, and this made us worried, and nervous, and bad feelings all together.

We came to a little town called Bahuichivo and decided to stop to get something to drink at a little stand next to the small plaza. We both got a soda and sat at the plaza to rest for a little. There was an old man sitting on a bench next to us who looked sad and spent. I asked if he was okay and he responded that he wasn't. I noticed a large brown stain on the concrete with traces of dried matter.

I asked what had happened there. He said their two local police officers had been executed and their bodies had laid there for almost two days before the federal police and military came in. He said that most of the people in town were very scared. We decided to get on our bikes and try to get out of that desolate country. It just did not seem safe anymore.

We reached Creel at around 4 p.m. We were to pack up, load our bikes on the truck and head back home. We would drive straight north until we reach the border through the night.

Many tourists were visiting the shops and walking around, laughing and enjoying a nice day in Mexico. But I knew something was very wrong. Underneath all the curious shops and restaurants catering to tourists, some underlying violent threat was brewing. I wondered if the American bicyclists made it out alive of the Sierra Madre Mountains, something that would haunt me for a long time.

Every time I saw a state police officer walking around the crowded street of Creel and waving at us with a smile, I wondered if he held a dark secret. Was the friendly act a front to deceive us from thinking everything was okay in Mexico, or was there a more sinister motive behind the hidden narco life of organized crime? I was very suspicious and could no longer trust the very ones that had a duty to protect us.

Creel in the Sierra Tarahumara Country

We had been traveling to Creel, Chihuahua, for many years during the Christmas season and we always felt safe. We could ride in the beautiful countryside, mostly in the forested mountain region. Creel (Spanish pronunciation: [kril]) is a town in the Sierra Tarahumara (part of the Sierra Madre Occidental) of the Mexican state of Chihuahua. It is the second-largest town in the municipality of Bocoyna. It is located 109 miles to the southwest of the state capital, Chihuahua City. Tourism had become the primary job source over the last 20 years because it is close to the Copper Canyon as well as Basaseachic Falls, one of the highest waterfalls in Mexico. There are many hotels, restaurants and a number of tours down into the canyons and throughout the surrounding area.

At the time, little did I know, that a narco war was escalating. The region was the backyard of the powerful Sinaloa cartel, where they hid form authorities, grew marijuana and poppies. It was also a main transport route of drugs to the U.S. I would eventually end up posting cartel events in Creel on the blog, Bordeland Beat.

In the year of 2010 a large convoy of sicarios, mostly from the Sinaloa cartel, took over the town and massacred a family that was suspected to have ties to the Juarez cartel. I posted an article on Borderland Beat in April 11, 2010 titled "Video of Massacre in Creel."

Here's the article:

The suffering felt deep in the stomach is an epidemic in the Palace.

The television news caster of the Mexican program "Punto de Partida" on Televisa, Denisse Merker, presented a chilling narcovideo that lasted seven minutes that has been seen around the world.

In the video recorded by the Command Center of Cipol (Cuerpo de Inteligencia Policíal) in Creel, a dozen gunmen arrive at the village, and with total impunity, massacred nine members of the family of an employer, including a 14-year-old child.

The incident was recorded in the early morning of March 15 in Creel, where there have been previous major killings.

For over two hours heavily armed sicarios took over the town in a large convoy of trucks blocking streets and setting up roadblocks. The video clearly records the faces of the thugs, even when they are snorting cocaine, almost at handfuls, from a plastic bag. You can also see how they beat and terrorize passing drivers who happened to drive by the crime scene in their vehicles.

Another portion of the video shows two gunmen intercepting a car and sequestering the driver. Later in the video, the men shoot two people in an SUV.

In the video, gunmen are shown approaching the passenger side of a vehicle to receive what appears to be an order for the killings. A man holding a large gun in the passenger seat also is seen taking a pinch of a white substance and putting it in his nose several times.

In some of the most shocking footage, armed men are seen running across a field before reaching the doors of a housing complex and opening fire into the doors and windows of the residence.

All the details of the killing of tens of mercenaries on board a dozen trucks were recorded by the State Police, and for good reason Denisse Merker questions why the authorities did nothing to pursue the murderers. The state authorities are moving and zooming the video cameras for 90 minutes while the sicarios walked around with long rifles and proceeded to terrorize the public and target people for execution, in the meantime the authorities watching all this did nothing to stop them.

"We don't know what group these hitmen are part of, but here in Chihuahua there are two warring groups: the Sinaloa Cartel and Juarez Cartel," said Carlos Gonzalez, a spokesman for the state Attorney General's office. "We're working on trying to figure out which group was responsible."

Gonzalez said there is no evidence to suggest that the victims were involved in drug activity, adding that the motive for the shootings is unclear.

He said the video—captured by a state public security camera—is "important" evidence in the investigation.

"This is evidence to identify these people and it's part of the ongoing investigation to find them," said Gonzalez, who is the lead investigator in the case.

"There are very few authorities in this area to police this kind of activity," Gonzalez said.

The images of the gunmen operating freely in the mountainous northwest part of Chihuahua highlight just how lawless rural parts of Mexico have become as the country works to combat an increasingly violent drug war.

Governor Reyes Baeza has remained silent on this case that illustrates the savage and brutal lawlessness of the state of Chihuahua.

There were follows up on the events, primarily out fear and hopelessness. On April 17, 2010, I posted a follow up titled, "Questions of Impotence in Creel."

Creel Residents expressed their repudiation of the way a convoy of gunmen arrived to town in plain daylight hours and also question how it's possible for the police authority station in the area not to be able to see the caravan of 16 trucks that arrived to execute seven people with no regards that some of victims were young girls or women. This was the exact same scenario that was played out in the massacre of 13 people in Creel in August 16, 2008.

For his part, Father Javier Avila Aguirre lamented about the residents of the area saying they need to prepare and to get used to the violence. He was unwilling to elaborate further on the subject but said that he talked with some residents of Creel and that the incident happened so fast that it has yet to sink in.

On that dreadful day that the sicarios planted fear among anyone they came in contact with in the usually busy main street in Creel, no one dared to venture out of their homes, not to mention the tourists; they were nowhere to be seen. With a tinge of sadness in his voice, "El Padre Pato" pointed out that everything is forgotten almost immediately as life has to go on.

After the bloody events of that early morning, residents of San Juanito and Creel continue with their lives. "El Padre Pato" said that despite what happened, everyone has to continue with their normal lives, going to school, working, shopping, and perhaps the town will be again calm and feel just a bit safer.

Why didn't any of the active checkpoints operating in the outskirts of the towns stop them? Where was the Cipol who are stationed in the area? These are the questions locals from San Juanito are asking, but they still declined to give their name for obvious reasons. The entire town could hear the burst of gunfire from the gunmen for at least 10 minutes while they were executing people. The 10 minutes of loud gunfire echoing in the walls of Creel seem to last an eternity, but no police authority came to the aid of the victims who were being mowed down. This is part of the suspicious reality that is prevalent in the community.

Meanwhile, the injured survivors of the massacre remain fearful in a hospital in Cuauhtémoc because there was a rumor circulating in the city that a commando wanted to abduct or finish off the rest of the wounded, said the mayor of the city, Gerardo Hernández Arzaga.

At times there was fear among the staff of the hospital where the survivors were receiving medical care and where there has already been one execution. At this point this is just a rumor, said the mayor, and fortunately we have not had any recent violent acts in the clinic.

It was finally decided for security reasons that in such cases where patients of gunshot wounds were brought in, such as the ones from Creel, they would be transported to the hospital in the state capital where they have the adequate security in their hospital.

On May 11, I posted the last follow up of the event in Creel in an article titled, "Failure to Act and Protect in Creel."

"They did not act against the sicarios in Creel because there were only seven officers," said Saul Hernandez, director of CIPOL.

Saul Hernandez, director of the Police Intelligence Centre (UNCLE), acknowledged that the day the sicarios took the town of Creel hostage and terrorized the residents while going on a killing spree were being monitored through video by authorities, but the police did not intervene because it was only seven of them, and the closest military installation was in Cuauhtémoc.

"We did react but the problem is ... there were only 7 officers who immediately contacted the Mexican military, but the truth is they can't get from one point to another just like that. I mean they have to get their equipment, they must get organized and they have to leave from where they are, from Cuauhtémoc which is a good few kilometers way," said Saul Hernandez.

He added that in this situation they (military) could not get to the town in three minutes, and he highlighted that he wishes they could do it in three minutes but logistically they can't.

At the same time, he rejected any responsible to the monitors of the video for failure to take any action against the sicarios because they immediately alerted the state police but that logistics problem already mentioned prevented them from intervening.

The wide range of worldwide attention the broadcast the video of Creel made had all the levels of government in a defensive position trying to justify the lack of law enforcement intervention.

I started to realize that Mexico was changing, and for the first time in a long time, I did not feel safe in Mexico. That 2008 trip would be the last time we traveled to Creel and Copper Canyon to ride our bikes like we had done for many years during the Christmas holidays.

Sometime around 2008, while reading some of the news in Mexico, I learned that Mexico's top policeman, Edgar Millan, was executed outside his home in Mexico City. He was the highest-ranking policeman in the federal police and a friend of Mexican President Felipe Calderon.

It was the equivalent of killing the head of the Metropolitan Police in London, or the director of the FBI in the U.S. If organized crime could assassinate him, a person that had one of the best security details protecting him, organized crime could kill anyone. It was established that the Beltran Leyva Organization (BLO) had ordered the hit on Millan, for payback for having been involved in the arrest of Alfredo Beltran Layva, El Mochomo. The incredible thing was that the assassination had not made the news in the US. People in the U.S. had no idea what was happening in Mexico. This started to bother me. I felt like I needed to do something.

I needed to report on these events and let people know in the US what was happening in Mexico. It could have been an unfortunate family that day we met the drunk sicarios, I hate to think a possible tragic outcome.

The Blog and the Contributors

So, one day I started a blog called Borderland Beat (also known as BB), so I could shed some light on the dark side of Mexico to the people in the U.S. and all the English speakers. I knew that it would have to be real, a true manifestation of the reality of Mexico of the so-called drug war. I took the time to translate the stories and load up the pictures and videos.

How did I come up with the name Borderland Beat? It was because the borderland is a place in the corridor of the international border between Mexico and the U.S. I wanted to create a place where anyone could find extensive information about the drug war on the borderland and the beat police walk every day. I wanted to show the chaos and mayhem of the Mexican drug cartels and the law enforcement authorities who seek to destroy them or chose to get on the cartel's payroll. A beat is a specific place where law enforcement has maintained a common jurisdictional path of responsibility, and I wanted readers to join us as we followed the beat on the borderland.

I had been posting some articles I had translated around mid-2008, but then I realized that I should not be posting these Mexican Drug Cartel stories on my personal blog. I had been mainly using my personal blog to post personal pictures as I was a serious amateur/professional photographer. I felt I needed to create a blog specifically for Mexican Drug Cartel material. I soon started a blog using the platform from Blogger that is owned by Google (Google owns everything). I paid for a private domain name and decided to use the name Borderland Beat.

I kept all the information of the domain private.

It was during this time I decided that I would use a nickname to protect my identity. Buggs was a nickname that I had used on occasions, but most people in the internet world had no clue who the true Buggs was. My only interest was to share information related to Mexican Drug Cartels.

For five years I live in the pages of Borderland Beat (BB) only known as Buggs, no one knew my identity. The blog became really popular among law enforcement in the US and there were many times officers I met would recommend that I follow BB. Sometimes I would tell a fellow police officer friend that I was planning a trip somewhere in Mexico, and they would warn me. "Brother, it's not safe to travel to Mexico, if you haven't, you need to read Borderland Beat online," they would tell me. Very few people in my circle knew I was the man behind the Borderland Beat Project.

I started translating material from Spanish to English. There were many. Some were from Mexican news, or stories sent to me from people in Mexico and some material came from Spanish legal court documents I was able to get. It seemed like I spent a lot of my time just translating document after document. My first article on the new Borderland Beat blog was on January 17, 2009, that was titled "Los Capos." It listed all the names of top cartel bosses from the cartels in Mexico that were wanted, and a bounty of up to 30 million pesos (about 2.4 million U.S. dollars) was offered for the capture of each. It listed all the top bosses for each of the cartels: Beltrán Leyva Cartel, La Familia Michoacana, Gulf Cartel, Los Zetas Cartel, Juárez Cartel, Pacific Cartel (a.k.a Sinaloa Cartel) and the Tijuana Cartel.

I learned that crime had been on the rise in Mexico throughout the last decade as drug cartels battled each other for control of lucrative smuggling routes. It wasn't just the violence, but the extent of it. I saw that Mexico's violence was often spectacular and lurid, with tales of street shootouts, decapitations and bomb blasts filling Mexico's news pages and airwaves.

There were times I would ask myself why am I doing this? I just focused on adding content, and soon others eventually joined me, like Illiana, Maka, Gerardo, El Viento, Ovemex, Smurf and Chivis (just to name a few). The readership grew, with many collaborating in the comment section. The comment section and the forum became real popular place for readers to comment, provide information, share their opinion or correct a fact they felt needed to be corrected. The Borderland Beat readers are some of the most knowledgeable sources of the Mexican Drug cartels. Soon we would be averaging 50,000 hits a day. It would bring out people from both sides of the border, both sides of the fence, both sides of the issues.

With the help of other collaborators, we were very active posting articles on a daily basis. There were never times that we did not have something to report, something that was news breaking. Another capo had been captured or killed, groups of people had been found executed, corrupt police or politicians had been arrested.

Borderland Beat collaborators and staff devote a lot of personal time and effort to provide vital information about the Mexican drug cartels to loyal readers without earning a cent. We never monetized the project, although our reach was far and huge.

I have never personally met any of the contributor's face to face, although I became good friends to some of them. Some I knew better than others. Everyone's identity was hidden using nicknames. No one knew who was who. This was important to keep them and their families safe. A lot of them lived in Mexico and it was very dangerous to live in ground zero where organized crime could killed with impunity and would kill anyone that dare to report on cartel activity. But it was important that no one, including other collaborators, know anyone's identity. Cartels do not just execute people; they abduct them, tortured them first to get information, then they cut their bodies in pieces. That is the nature of the Mexican cartel. Who would not talk under these circumstances? No one can blame them, a proactive approach is the key here.

Some of the collaborators had confided in some of their personal information and I knew a little bit about them.

For example, I would talk to Illiana, mostly about the drug cartels, but sometimes about our happiness and fears. I remember when she covered a story where the military had shot at a family that went through a military checkpoint and killed two little boys in the state of Tamaulipas. They were on a vacation travelling to the beach to spend Easter ("El Día de la Coneja" for Two Little Boys). I remember her taking it real hard, and she did because it was personal. Illiana lived in the area where the incident occurred. She started her article by saying, "I cried today." She went on to say:

"Well damn, it turns out the boys were actually killed by Mexican military forces, the same ones who are supposed to be here to protect us from the bad guys.

This whole thing is so sad, especially because we are talking about innocent children, who were just looking forward to going to the beach to hide eggs for Easter. How can this be happening?

This is not the first time Borderland Beat has covered the death of innocent bystanders killed by military forces, last month the Editor of this blog wrote a report entitled "The Mexican Drug War's Collateral Damage." I really don't want to repeat a lot of what has already been said, but really, something needs to be done.

Just so you know, La Jornada and El Milenio, which are national media sources, ran with the story, but the local media outlets did not publish shit, nada! They totally suck, who are they working for? The people should stop buying their worthless newspapers or watching their lame news on TV.

God receive these two young boys in heaven because they have already been in hell for Easter Sunday!

Today they are in the garden of God hunting for eggs on el día de la coneja.

Shit!"

Illiana started organizing protests against the government. I cautioned her not to get too personally involved and to focus on just reporting on the story. I know sometimes that is hard, especially when you live there, and it involves children. But she was so passionate about the incident that I started to get worried. I did not know much about her, other than she lived in a city in the state of Tamaulipas and might be a journalist. She suddenly stopped corresponding with me and stopped posting on Borderland Beat. She just vanished from the Borderland Beat community. I had no way to find out what happened to her. I didn't even have her name. I have always wondered what ever happened to her.

Then there was RiseMakaveli who had a lot of knowledge of Los Zetas and the Gulf Cartel. He knew the names of people in both cartels and who was who. He had so much detailed information that some people were starting to wonder if he was actually a sicario in one of the cartels. I asked him once, but I really never got a straight answer. He eventually left Borderland Beat and left us wondering who he was and what happened to him. Someone once sent me a long email saying he knew that RiseMakaveli was a lieutenant with the Gulf Cartel and that he had died in a shootout with Los Zetas. I was never able to confirm it, and we might never know what really happened to him. I rather believe that he is out there somewhere enjoying life, and moving on to more positive, meaningful things in life.

I did an interview with RiseMakaveli in March 26, 2010 in a post in Borderland Beat titled, "The Rise of Makaveli - Interview on the Gulf and Zetas."

The Interview

RiseMakaveli is a person who lives in Mexico and is in the middle of the waging war of the two cartels, as are many people living in the border towns of Mexico. Because of his geographical location, RiseMakaveli has personal knowledge and has known some of the principles. He is not involved in any drug cartel activity (as far as we know) but has known some of them as a matter of living among them. He has a vast knowledge of what is going on, almost like an insider look of what is happening.

Because of his present situation and we that follow these matters know that these things can be dangerous, he has chosen to remain anonymous to protect himself and his family.

Borderland: "How have the people (el puebo) managed to interact with the Gulf cartel?"

RiseMakaveli: "At first, people were skeptical. People did not know if it really was for the better, but so far, it seems like the CDG has been doing a good job at earning the peoples trust and respect...

You see, it's hard to believe that this war will end anytime soon. The plague of Los Zetas has pretty much injected itself into the very arteries of Mexico. These guys are everywhere, politics, small businesses, restaurants, newspapers, media.

Literally, Zetas are cops. It used to be that you got stopped by city police and some of them were bought by the group, but others where legit but still had to respect their "commandante" who was and always has been bought by los Zetas...

But now it's not like that, the Zetas where the cops. And I speak in past tense because now with the CDG things will have to change, that is why cops are ending up dead all over the place. All of them, literally. As scary as it may sound, it was true.

Cops where actually doing the kidnappings. I don't know if you saw this video of a guy that was scared shitless by some cops in I think it was NL, not sure don't remember but here is the link

Ok, now we do have to admit, this video is sort of funny... But at the same time scary, because it's true. You can't trust cops. I mean you get stop, and if you got the right Código, they'll just let you go.. See for a long time the way things have worked is this way.

If you where someone high in society and you paid for protection, or someone involved in the drug trafficking or whatever, you paid a fee for x amount of time and they would give you your own personal CODIGO (CODE). They would issue you this special password, and whoever stopped you had to let you go, or they would have penalties for withholding you. The officers and Zetas kept a list, updated daily of Codes.

See, it was all commercialized in a way... You have to understand one thing, these are people who were born into this life, they were born in a society which did not provide them with as many freebies as the one we are in now. People who live here in the US are blessed.

Yes, we do have a lot of poverty and crime as well, but there is no comparison. Here, in the US, a lot of people who are broke, is simply due to the fact that they don't want to work. I mean Ociel Cardenas before he became what he was, he used to work as a mechanic and wash cars in Matamoros.

And I've met people who would always say, "oh he thinks he's all that, he used to wash my car in the old days". And I would remind them "yeah but he made millions, and you're still working in the same old deadbeat job" ...

I mean, it's not trying to make him seem like he's all that, my point is that a lot of these guys are involved in that business simply because they had no choice… Of course, that does not include all of them, but a good amount of them are."

Borderland: "Did they accept them at first? How about now?"

RiseMakaveli: "See, after all this shit, and this years of torture and basically unfairness that people here in Tamaulipas have endured, right now. It's basically like they see the Cartel trucks rolling in with CDG on their back window, and it's like.

Ok, what now. Everyone minds their own business, I mean, it was at the point that if you saw a brand new truck on the street, didn't matter if the truck was driving on the other side of the street, or if the truck was cutting you off or not stopping at red lights, but everyone knew "ohh ohh keep to yourself, those guys are probably running with someone else".. and a lot of the time it was true man, I mean you honked at somebody who thought they were the shit and they had no respect for civilian people they would rush out their truck and either scare the shit out of you at gun point, or literally you'd be in for a beating. If not worse…

Clear example, you have a puppy who you want to learn to stay in this box. He always runs out, and is all playful and doesn't listen to you.

Sure I mean it's a puppy, it will keep doing the same thing over and over. But what happens if every time he leaves the box you beat him in the head with a 2x4.

Eventually he will learn the hard way not to leave the box or he will get hit. That's basically what happened to a lot of people here. They lost their own will to fight, they just live life as it is, and a lot of them believe the saying, "if you can't beat them, join them."

Up to right now, the CDG came in with the right set of minds. Supposedly, protecting the citizens, by eradicating the "Sicarios Zetas! " It's all good business, it's good marketing. It's good campaigning. You think the CDG cares for the people? The fuck they do! They don't give a shit.

But they have strong people thinking this shit through. They couldn't care a rat's ass about the people. Back in the day, what did Ociel do while he was locked up? He paid for a party of over 2000 people on the street and got gifts for the children who couldn't afford it. What was that? Good heart? From a guy who killed his friend to take over his business?

You have to always remember this. It is all GOOD BUSINESS. that is all it is.

Those who will prevail will be those who think above the league. You have to stop thinking small time, and start seeing the big picture. You can't take the government full on, but the government can't take on their citizens. Win the people, and you got it made.

The army won't be able to do shit. Bottom line, so far, the CDG is doing a good job, keeping the killing to minimum, trying to sell the image that they are here to save us all, and free us from the KILLERS ZETAS, who for some reason, everyone seems to forget, THEY CREATED THEM."

Borderland: "How are the typical Sicarios for the Gulf or Zetas? Is it the lower class or the middle class? What about the ones that are getting killed, are they from the region?"

RiseMakaveli: "I know, I refer to "IT USED TO BE" a lot. But it's just the way that I feel… It used to be, Zetas where Loyal people, killers. But everyone admired them because they protected the boss man, putting their life in danger, and giving their life for him in a second's hesitation. It used to be that you would recognize a Zeta a mile away. I remember they would all dress in black jeans, black dress shirt and they were all very cautious.

Somewhere along the line everything went to hell. They started hiring drug addicts of the streets, strapping them with an AK, sending them to a boot camp of a couple of days/weeks and put em on the street to handle business. That's when it all turned from Zetas being Elite, to Zetas being "PIEDREROS." Zetas slowly went losing the respect of the people, afterwards, you would see people all trashy, not even dressing right, in work pants, shoes untied strapped with a radio in hand, and he was a Zeta, hahaha.

Somewhere along the way, they got desperate and started to hire people on street corners, who drank all fucking day and got fucked up. How can someone like that be able to handle business? They didn't. That's why shit got stirred. Years ago, you would get in trouble and you'd get stopped. Either police or guardias and depending on the magnitude of what you did, you'd either get a smack in the head with a gun, or end up falling asleep with sour asscheeks (they carried wood sticks in their trucks to smack the shit out of you!)

That's all, and before if they wanted to do something, it was all called in. They'd have you kneed in front of them, and asking you questions. Who are you? Who are you allied with? This, that. And call it in and confirm. Basically, ask permission to either hit you or kill you. Or just let you go.

Now a days, man, you meet the wrong people on the street and you get shot, instantly. Of course, this is not all the time, there's still some sort of restrain in some people, but not all."

Borderland: "Who are the main players currently in the Gulf and Zetas. What is the current status of the Zetas? Have they been put out of commission? I see their leadership is pretty much intact!"

RiseMakaveli: "Well, as to the leadership. It's pretty much the same, Z40 and Lazcano.. I have not known of any updates with that, but none of them have been caught or killed. because be sure of one thing. Once either of them gets killed or captured, they will blow it up on TV.

I'm pretty sure that maybe even the Zetas will make sure that the media finds out. Because it will be a major blow to the company…

Now as much as being out of commission, no, they're not. I mean they have been hit hard and lost some business but they still control major points in Tamaulipas. Only difference is that now everything is falling on them, but they still evade and continue, believe that.

I repeat, they are not just some cockroaches as many people wish to people, they are pretty much a part of the system now. Either people like it or not)."

Borderland: "What place has the most activities currently in your region and what do you see happening here in the next few years? Will they ever get rid of the cartel or will they just realign and change method of operations?"

RiseMakaveli: "It's hard to actually foresee what will happen in years to come, but one thing is for sure. This will not end soon, and I guarantee you man, almost as if it was written on stone. Either both, or one of them will get crucified. This will not end without somebody taking a major hit, and making it seem like it's over. Either Lazcano or Z40, or both. Are going to get crucified. Bad.

People will no longer let this slide, even if the majority of the people know the truth, the media will make it seem like they killed the dragon. Why? Because they are in too deep. It's public now… They made it public that it is MEXICO VS LOS ZETAS.. They are pinning everything bad on them, which is not true.

A lot of the murders that happened where under the orders, or it's wrong to say orders, more like, it was under the contract from CDG.. A lot of the beheadings, fucking bloody massacres where under jobs the Zetas got from CDG.. Or from personal friends of theirs.

See, it is not a fight against drugs. It is a fight against the image they have created on The Zetas. Too bad they turned into the escape goat. Not to say they don't deserve it, they do for being no fucking morale having motherfuckers.

But it's not all the blame on them)."

RiseMakaveli would be an active collaborator by posting stories of events and cartel operations, answering questions in the comment section and clarifying events and names of cartel participants. Around July 2010 RiseMakaveli suddenly disappeared from Borderland Beat (BB) and no one knew what happened to him. There were many speculations from BB readers and some shared information that could not be confirmed. There was a lot of chatter in the BB forum:

Montana: "It was relayed to me from his close sources that RiseMakeveli was mortally wounded and died of his wounds this past weekened. He was wounded by gunfire in a battle against the Zetas on the reynosa-matamoros highway a couple of weeks ago. He was affiliated with the Gulf Cartel and was a commandante under Metro 3, the boss of reynosa. His reporting and editorials will be missed."

Commando956: "I heard the same thing about Rise dying in a battle against the zetas on another site. RIP bro."

Anon: "Rise, if you didnt know is affiliated with the CDG. He is a commandante working directly under Metro-3. Rise was wounded in a shootout with zetas along the reynosa-matamoros highway. He is fine and recovering in reynosa. Hell be back soon on here;)."

quitapuercos: "Risemakaveli was executed for supporting the golfas the brutal Zetas murdered him in tamaulipaZ."

Roffasouth: "I thought he was wounded and recovering in reynosa? Do u have a source? I dont believe it because these idiots are making jokes about it so i dont know whats right... and if its true, i hope these pinches zetas will get a bullet in their head."

Other Contributors

There were many other contributors that I know decided to move on to better things in life, recapturing their personal life, before it got snuffed by the dark side of reporting on brutal, violent narco life in Mexico.

Like many other bloggers that were active on social media and on blogs reporting on cartel events, we got the occasional threat, BB collaborators got their share. Although we did not dwell on them or allow it to stop what we were doing, it was taken serious to the point we took every precautionary step we could.

The longest collaborator to date is Chivis, who has a huge knowledge of the Mexican Drug Cartels. She took over the management of Borderland Beat and is still active running the blog today. She is a fierce defender of BB and has taken good care of the project. BB would not exist without people like Chivis, he/she devotes a lot of personal time to keep the project going, a monumental task.

El Semanario wrote this at the time when things were getting started on BB on the reporting of the narco world in Mexico in an article titled "Uncensored."

"This dangerous empty space of information is being filled, for the good or for the bad, by the blogs. A former policeman and Texas marine, who conceals his real identity under the pseudonym "Buggs" (madman, in the slang of the lower class), is the founder of Borderland Beat (borderlandbeat.com). A popular blog that almost never censures anything and that mixes macabre videos and photographs with graphic information of main stream media sources. This weekend he posted the pictures of the alleged criminals from San Fernando that the Mexican press felts was too risky to report. For the American cyber audience that it has attracted because it's being written in English, unlike the

Blog del Narco that is written in Spanish. (Borderland Beat) has become a source of must-read source for law enforcement, judicial officials, military and in particular the general public."

The ride on working on the Borderland Beat Project had just began and it was going to be a bumpy ride, something that I never expected. But nothing comes easy and nothing ever comes without risk. Like they say when you are playing with fire, sometime you just get burned.

☐

Danger to bloggers reporting on the Cartel violence

Borderland Beat along with other blogs started to grow in popularity and were the "to go" source for news on the Mexican drug cartels. Many journalists were getting killed in Mexico. Some used Borderland Beat as a platform to report cartel activity that they could not report in the Mexican main stream media for fear of retaliation from organized crime.

Reporters would be targeted many times for naming cartels members or for refusing to report specific content requested by cartels. Mexico would become the most dangerous place for journalists. Many were executed by cartels, there is a lot of documentation in BB covering the danger of reporting about organized crime in Mexico.

Around January of 2010 the journalist Bladimir Antuna, of the El Tiempo newspaper based out of Durango was abducted, tortured and strangled. He had been receiving threats, and at one point had been getting police protection, but he continued to report on the cartel violence. He had said that he was not afraid of dying but was afraid of being captured alive and tortured. His killers had written on his body "this happened to me for providing information to the military and writing too much." There were signs of him being tortured while alive following his death. In Mexico it is rare that culprits of these executions get arrested.

The LA Times published an article saying it best:

"Often, the traffickers demand coverage glorifying their exploits, or they may want some of their acts concealed, and they make those desires known to journalists as well.

'If you don't print a narco message from one group, they will punish you. Or the other side will punish you if you do publish it,' said one Durango editor who, like many people interviewed for this story, did not want to be identified. 'Or the government will punish you for printing anything. You don't know where the threat is going to come from.'

'Impunity creates a vicious circle,' said Alberto Brunori, the senior U.N. official in Mexico for human rights. 'You have to break the circle or we do not get out of this. You can't just keep having dead journalists turn up."

Many journalists and media outlets had stopped reporting all together on the cartel violence in Mexico for fear of being killed. But you can't blame them. Some journalists have no choice but to get on the cartel payroll and report on events that the cartels dictate. On March 11, 2010 I published a post on Borderland Beat titled "War on Information in Mexico."

"The U.S.-based Committee to Protect Journalists, or CPJ, said it is aware some journalists are working for cartels.

"We know this is happening. It is a consequence of the huge level of influence these criminals exert," said Carlos Lauria, the committee's senior coordinator for the Americas.

Desperate to spread news of the new outbreak of violence, people in Mexico have turned to social networking sites like Facebook, Twitter and YouTube to post cell phone videos of shootouts and report suspicious activity.

"One of the fundamental human rights has been taken away in some parts of Mexico and the federal government is not speaking out about it," said Alberto Islas, an independent security analyst in Mexico City.

Some honest reporters choose not to report the violence out of fear for their safety. Cartel attacks have made Mexico one of the world's most dangerous countries for the media, the CPJ says, 30 journalists have been killed in Mexico since December 2006 when Felipe Calderon assumed the presidency to the year 2010. Mexico's National Human Rights Commission puts the number of murdered journalists at 66 between 2005 and 2010, in additional to 12 reporters that have disappeared.

So-called narco-reporters may be at an even greater risk of getting caught up in the turf wars. Five reporters suspected of working for the Gulf cartel went missing two weeks ago in Reynosa.

"We don't know who they angered but it wasn't because of their journalism. Two of the reporters hadn't

published anything in months," said a colleague of the missing journalists.

Local politicians say the Gulf cartel, which controls a third of narcotics shipments into the United States, is keeping its war with the Zetas as quiet as possible to avoid provoking army deployments that could disrupt its smuggling operations.

"The Gulf cartel's message is: there's nothing happening here," said a town councilor in Rio Bravo next door to Reynosa. "The hitmen even pick up their dead after gunfights so there's no evidence of what's going on," he added."

Journalists were starting to be afraid of reporting the violence or naming any of the cartel members. This caused many journalists to use anonymity in reporting the violence in Mexico. That is how I started reaching out to them and giving some of them a platform to report on Borderland Beat.

Borderland Beat continued to report on the threats to journalists and bloggers. On November 14, 2011 a post titled

"Mexican Drug Cartel Kills Blogger" that brought to light the dangers of reporting on the drug cartels while living among them.

Mexico's Zetas drug cartel killed yet another blogger, continuing its unrelenting war against persistent citizen journalists fighting the underground organization on social media at any cost.

Zetas' latest victim, a man who moderated the Nuevo Laredo En Vivo whistle-blowing website, was found beheaded at a busy intersection with a nearby note reading, "This happened to me for not understanding that I shouldn't report on the social networks."

The blogger is the fourth citizen journalist in the last months to suffer the same fate as others reporting on Zetas' activities. In September, the cartel posted similar signs next to two men's bodies warning, "This is going to happen to all Internet snitches. Pay attention, I'm watching you."

The Zetas also threatened media outlets with unpleasant consequences unless they report news as directed, prompting citizens to read blogs for more reliable information.

The high cost of speaking out against Zetas online has deterred many from attempting to do so, including Anonymous hacktivists, though some continue to resist.

On November 1, the collective announced #OpCartel, a plan to unmask 100 of Zetas' government collaborators in retaliation for their kidnapping of an Anonymous member in Veracruz.

Security company Strafor, however, warned Anonymous, "Los Zetas are deploying their own teams of computer experts to track those individuals involved in the online anti-cartel campaign, which indicates that the criminal group is taking the campaign very seriously."

Anonymous called off the operation on November 2. Two days later, according to the group's informal spokesman

Barett Brown, the cartel returned the kidnapped hacker with a note saying Zetas would kill 10 people for every one collaborator exposed.

Most Anons decided to back away from the planned attack, but others are still fighting against Zetas. After its moderator's death, Nuevo Laredo En ViVo posted, "Let's continue denouncing them, now that we've seen it burns them, hurts them. We have to continue. We can't give in."

Others share the same sentiment, like Borderland Beat, a reputedly reliable website that functions like a terrorist cell to prevent its members from learning each others' identities for safety purposes.

Blog del Narco, a popular citizen journalist page, has survived because it doesn't take sides, even allowing Zetas members to post murder videos on its site.

The online fight against corruption continues, albeit more clandestinely than Anonymous' planned #OpCartel. But with such high risks, more bloggers may die before Zetas ever topples.

Mexican Drug War Blogger Risks His Life Daily

There was a piece that had been reported and published by the Daily Dot, it had also been reposted on BB on November 17, 2011 by yours truly. It was a piece on Ovemex, an administrator and contributor for BB who was at the time living in the dangerous Gulf Coast region of Mexico.

When a fourth person turned up dead earlier this month in the Mexican border town of Nuevo Laredo for posts made online about drug cartels, Ovemex was one of the first to report it.

He was also very aware that his actions could put him grave danger: He might be the next social media reporter to be brutally killed by Los Zetas, the cartel suspected in the four brutal murders.

"Of course I am" concerned about my own safety, said Ovemex, who is an administrator of Borderland Beat, a blog that is considered a leading source for news on the Mexican drug war. "But my fear of living life under these conditions indefinitely and my fear of never seeing change—unless we actively participate in the pursuit and creation of it—is much greater."

Ovemex, who asked that only his Twitter handle be used when he spoke to the Daily Dot, is part of a network of faceless citizen journalists sharing information about drug cartels.

Many mainstream media outlets in Mexico have had their drug war coverage silenced, either through threats or bribes, forcing people to Twitter and blogs like Borderland Beat for news about the cartels.

Unlike the Arab spring uprisings earlier this year, information shared on sites like Borderland Beat in Mexico is mainly about day-to-day survival and navigating the most violent cities safely. Ovemex, however, is holding out hope that the grassroots, citizen journalists movement will build into a means of enacting change and put an end to a war that has claimed more than 43,000 lives since 2006.

"A person on Twitter who retweets info is helping," Ovemex said. "A person who simply reads everything they can get their hands on is helping."

Much as they did with traditional journalists, the cartels have started killing administrators of the crime blogs in hopes of silencing them. In addition to three people killed in September, Rascatripas, an administrator on another crime news site, was killed in November.

His decapitated body was found with a note saying he was killed for "failing to understand I must not report on social networks."

"I don't think these killings and threats will have their desired effect—not in the long run," Overmex said. "Mexico is awakening and wants to speak. We want the truth known. They cannot silence us all, especially on the Internet where fragments of information are continuously and anonymously passed forward over and over again."

The anonymous nature of the information-sharing network presents problems as readers try to determine what information is accurate and what information is false.

As originally reported by the Daily Dot, the cartels have been posting false information on social networks to divert law enforcement away from where they are operating.

Ovemex said determining which information is accurate and should be passed on is an acquired skill based on trust.

"There is no science to this—no immediate, definite way of knowing the absolute truth," he said. "On the Internet you cannot rely on traditional social skills. Trust is a key issue. You cannot see who you are 'speaking' or 'listening' to, there are no body movements or facial expressions to give hint to their character. Over time you will find those you trust, as well as learn to read signs.

"You learn to read and comprehend what IS communicated by media, as well as what is NOT. And then you start putting the pieces of the puzzle together," Ovemex said.

The better known crime blogs haven't dipped too far into stories about #OpCorrupcion, a movement by Anonymous to hack Mexican government Web sites as a way of protesting suspect cooperation and corruption. Part of the problem is there is often conflicting information coming from different members of Anonymous, and it is often hard to verify what is accurate and what is not.

Ovemex declined to speak about Anonymous specifically, other than to say he has been watching their actions in Mexico closely.

"They are us, we are them. Their power is in anonymity and their numbers," he said. "We all work, for the most part, with the same idea mind—to create awareness and hopefully change—but that is all we know about them. To me what is important and necessary is for Mexico to unite in this battle."

"Everybody knows something," he said. "The information and truths are out there, you just have to know where to look and how to put it together."

A need for Blogs

There is no more freedom of expression in Mexico. Not only is there risk from the cartels, but also from the government which controls any information about violence. And in the U.S., we do not see what is happening across the border. In most of Mexico most of the important news is not being covered, and the American press isn't covering Mexico the way it should be either.

Many reporters are not ashamed to say they have backed off their coverage of the violence for their own safety. "We just don't cover the violence anymore; it's just too dangerous for us," said one reporter from a Tamaulipas news outlet. He has reason to fear for his safety, Mexico is the most dangerous country in the world for reporters.

In essence, the cartels are killing information by killing the messenger. Social media has played a huge role in reporting on the cartel violence in Mexico. This has resulted in cartels targeting bloggers as well as those who try to remain anonymous for their safety. Borderland Beat has led this fight in reporting about cartels, and the contributors have for the most part remained safe by being anonymous. There were some bloggers from other blogs that were identified by the criminal element and ultimately executed in Mexico. This became an issue for some bloggers, especially the ones living in the Mexican crime regions. This was an item with some of the contributors on Borderland Beat:

After the discovery in Nuevo Laredo, Mexico on November 9, 2011 of the body of the fourth blogger to be killed in the space of a month, for posting online information about drug cartels, The Daily Dot, MSNBC and Der Spiegel each produced an article outlining the dangers such internet activity posed. For comment, The Daily Dot and MSNBC turned to Borderland Beat administrator "Overmex," while

Der Spiegel interviewed Borderland Beat contributor "Gerardo." In the interviews, the two bloggers reiterated their determination to continue reporting on the ongoing drug war, and not to be intimidated by the drug cartels' threats.

Quoting from an article in Bloomberg Businessweek: "To protect contributors, the editors of the blog Borderland Beat, which has a reputation as one of the most reliable sources of information on Mexico's drug violence, say even they don't know the identity of some of the site's major contributors. Posts are often passed through intermediaries to protect secrecy. "They could be journalists, cops, politicians, maybe even cartel members themselves," says one of the blog's editors, who uses the nickname Buggs."

For me personally, being the founder and main contributor of Borderland Beat, it was extremely difficult to maintain my anonymity. I was a little bit concerned, but for me it was not very personal or direct, like it was for the collaborators reporting from Mexico. For one, I lived in the U.S., although the cartels could very easily reach out and touch me in the U.S. if they really wanted to. Except that for me, it was a little more complicated than that. I was an active law enforcement officer in the U.S. and was armed 24/7. There was one time, during the time many bloggers were receiving threats, when I did an interview with a media outlet that had discovered my identity.

My decision to come out of the shadow of Borderland Beat was by design rather than by choice. Someone had to confront the logistics necessary to maintain the project. Also, someone had to talk to people in order to spread the mission of the BB Project. The mission of BB was to report on the cartel war through the internet, print and presentations (interview requests from media). For the first time ever, a collaborator of BB made their presence known on the internet. My thought was if the mainstream media has a source of contact from BB, they will not pursue other members to try to discover their identity.

It was the first time I did an interview and came out of hiding, primarily because my cover had been blown. I had received a phone call from a reporter from Texas that knew my real name, place of residence and my profession. It was reported by KRGV News from the Rio Grande Valley in Texas, and ultimately published in Borderland Beat on September 16, 2011 titled, "Cartels Threaten Social Media Users in Mexico."

"Bloggers and social media users in Mexico aren't letting the cartels intimidate them. They continue to blog, tweet, and post information about the drug war. Two people were found hanging from a bridge this week in Nuevo Laredo with a warning to social media users.

Alex Marentes, the blogger who runs a website called Borderland Beat, knows he and his bloggers in Mexico could be the next target. He says his mission is more important than the risk.

The pictures are brutal. The words are brazen. They're a warning to social media users and bloggers. The note mentions three blogs and signed with a Z, perhaps for Zetas.

"This is the first time we've seen a direct possible tie to cartels targeting bloggers," says Marentes.

A man and woman were apparently killed for posting something the Zetas didn't like. Marentes and his Mexican bloggers know they could be targets, too. He says the deaths of these two people are sending fear through the social media community.

"I get threats here and there," says Marentes.

Marentes started the Borderland Beat blog more than two years ago.

"It was intended to fill a voice that the media wasn't reporting," says Marentes. "A lot of the narco cartels were targeting the media."

Mutilated corpses, murdered people, specific names and places where cartels are doing their dirty work, his bloggers know things like who's taking over control of the plazas. You'll find all that on some of the blogs.

"How we get our information, a lot of it is translating from news that doesn't reach out. We have people on the ground that give us info," says Marentes.

They take great risks to be the eyes and ears.

"We had one contributor; her name was Illeana. She was very active posting a lot of information and all of a sudden she just stopped," says Marentes.

Marentes doesn't know if Illeana is dead or alive. The cartels killed a woman last year for talking about cartel activity on a highway.

"The cartels reach deep," says Marentes.

Not deep enough to silence Facebook, Twitter and the bloggers.

"People don't know what's going on over there; that's why I do it," says Marentes.

They know knowledge is power. They want to be the change they want to see in the world.

Marentes says some Mexican blogs act as propaganda machines for the cartels. He says he won't let that happen to his. He says he can't verify the information he's getting from the bloggers because sometimes official information doesn't exist."

Some of the BB readers did not waste any time to chime in with concern that I had went public:

Anonymous: All I know is that with technology now a days, I wouldn't be surprised if zetas found who there looking for. Especially targeting antizeta blogs, like this one.

DD: Buggs, Good Story!!! It shows that the initials "BB" could also refer to Big Balls. You and Sr. Marentes have them and I am proud to be able to be able to be an occasional poster on the Forum section of your website.

Anonymous: I am an American who lives in one of the border states. Borderland Beat is an invaluable source of information for people in the Frontera states to know what's really going on in Mexico. I commend all of you reporters at BB for having the courage to continue to dig out the stories and post the truth.

Anonymous: Is it wise to publish Manteras' [Marentes] name or even Illiana? Haven't you learned anything? Smh

Request for Content

Soon a full team of contributors were keeping a fast pace posting stories on the drug cartels. Some were stories translated from open sources media in Mexico, some stories were provided to us by journalists in Mexico who were afraid to post them on their media outlet, and some were stories from people on the ground with direct knowledge. I was using a Google email to solicit material or for anyone that wanted to communicate with us.

I was starting to get Mexican court legal documents of proceedings that had been requested by public sources from Mexico. I started to translate some of these documents and posting them on BB. I also took some calls from anonymous sources with tips and information, but it was hard to determine the validity of the information coming in. It was almost impossible to get confirmation on the information coming in, unless it made it on main stream media. Keeping the integrity of the project was important, we did not want to convert our blog in to another narco blog, but a source for information that had a degree of legitimacy. Boots on the ground in Mexico was extremely important, and we certainly wanted to ensure the anonymity of everyone involved for safety reasons.

We started to get a lot of videos of executions that were taken with cellular phones. There was a dilemma if we should publish these videos. I wanted people to see the extent of what some of these cartels were capable of, but I also did not want to give these animals a platform to post the graphic brutal killings. We started to be selective with our sharing of the videos. We decided that if they had a news significance value, we would post them, but we would not post some of the videos just for the sake of posting them.

Along with Borderland Beat another blog, "El Blog del Narco (BDN)," started reporting on the Mexican drug cartels and they too were getting a lot of execution videos and graphic pictures. At times, it seemed that BDN was posting gory pictures and videos to lure viewers to their blog. The pictures of people getting dismembered, people getting beheaded, we would see it all day, every day. I saw my share of these videos and they started to take their toll on me. Even today I have a vivid memory of some of the more brutal executions; they are forever embedded in my brain. I did not enjoy viewing these videos, but somehow, I felt I needed to see what was happening in Mexico so that I had knowledge of what had happened.

I remember one of the first videos was when two men were beheaded alive. On one of men they used a chain saw and on another they used a knife to cut his head off. They were shown sitting down on the ground leaning on a wall, and talking about being careful not to betray the cartel, which in this instance was the Sinaloa cartel. Soon, after we published the video, the video went viral and many downloaded it. We soon started to get information on what exactly happened, and the story behind the gruesome execution.

The Execution of Two Chapos

A video of the execution of two alleged members of the Cartel de Sinaloa was brought to my attention, but Initially I chose not to show it. Two grim looking men, whose luck ran out, are butchered while still alive in the most brutal way imaginable, "chainsaw massacre" style. Other narcoblogs have uploaded the video after we eventually made it public on BB and started making its round around the internet.

One of the men is identified as Felix Gamez Garcia, who admits to trafficking drugs to the United States and the other man is identified as Barnabas Gamez Castro, who is the uncle of the first man. Despite their bad decision to become halcones and collaborate with one of the most powerful drug cartels in Mexico, the Sinaloa Cartel or CDS, they are foremost human beings and no human being deserves to die in this manner.

Both men are sitting against an adobe wall, they have no shirt on, and seem renounced to their fate. They answer the questions posed to them by sicarios dressed in military uniforms, and they talk, but deep inside, they must know that no matter what they say, they will not make it out alive this time. You can hear it in their voices, worn, beaten, tired and left without hope. The hope not just to live a wealthy life as they must have thought when they joined the cartel, but now just a basic right to just live.

The men admit to working for Joaquin El Chapo Guzman himself. They describe their duties as halcones or at one time riding in the convoys when they were asked to do so. The sicarios who are holding them for nearly six minutes in the video, are the typical sicarios that have been seen in previous videos of this kind. No remorse, with a full intent of doing a job that is beyond imaginable, that when seen if you dare, it truly shocks the conscious. No one can truly say who they are, or what criminal organization they belong to, perhaps we may never know.

The uncle has a message for those who might decide to enter the dark side of the drug cartels, "Think next time you decide to give the "finger" (being a rat), think about it very carefully, because it's not easy being here, and you never return back. With these people you don't play around, the people of El Chapo are not how they say they are," he says with a broken voice.

When both men are finished talking, it's time to pay the piper. Both men then appeared frozen in time, staring in to the distance, as if in a trance, living but already dead. Perhaps they were heavily drugged, so they didn't kick and scream during the brutal nightmare. Fear itself will not numb anyone enough to face this level of evil directly in the eye. Even the sound of the chainsaw does not break their trance.

The uncle is first; he grimaces as the chainsaw spews blood, flesh and bone, as it tears through his throat, separating his head from his body. The chainsaw accidentally cuts the arm of the nephew sitting right next to the uncle during the violent massacre, but he doesn't flinch.

The second man, the young nephew, is decapitated with a knife. While the knife is cutting through his throat, he makes a last attempt to scream out, but his vocal cords have been severed, and all one can hear is a faint whimpering sound, the last breath of a man that was way too young to die.

The ghastly chilling gurgling sounds coming out of his perforated windpipe, followed by the grinding sounds as the knife breaks through the spinal cord, finally frees his head from his body, ending the most repulsive, heinous and gruesome act witness on video. In a normal world one would say, wake up it's only a dream, but this tangible, repeating itself every day somewhere in old Mexico.

The uncle, Don Gamez Castro, had said that the drug cartels did not pay much, in fact he mentioned that the last work he did for them, they paid him 300 pesos ($21 USD), not nearly enough to die for.

By the way, a BB reader posted information about the younger man, that had been arrested in Phoenix Arizona for the distribution and transporting of illicit drugs on June 17, 2011 and gave his name as Paulino Gomez-Garcia. There is a huge resemblance of the mug shot to the pictures of them in the video. Instead of serving time, he was deported back to Mexico, a life sentence.

It was later confirmed that Gomez-Garcia was in fact the same man in the execution. He had elected to be deported instead of being prosecuted, he in fact had signed his death warrant.

Guys on the forum give a good hypothesis on why he was executed. Perhaps because he had lost a load or perhaps, he gave information to authorities when he was caught in the US, or perhaps both. All good points and nice research from the BB peeps, who are usually very knowledgeable when it comes to cartel crime in Mexico.

The executions are so many that in Mexico people get desensitized to the brutal violence, it's just another day in Mexico. For us too, watching these videos every day, it takes away a little bit of your soul, a coping mechanism used to keep us from going insane.

El Diablo

In 2012, at the peak of reporting on the violence in Mexico, we were getting a lot of execution videos by someone that went by the name of "Comandante Diablo." He was seen executing anyone that was colluding with Los Zetas at any level. He was said to be Plaza boss of Monterrey, a strong hold of the Gulf Cartel (CDG). I posted a few of the videos, primarily to show the savagery that he was capable of. One was on May 8, 2012 titled "Sowing Terror in Ciudad Victoria."

Hooded (encapuchado) sicarios appeared in a video with a young man in the back bed of a truck. They question him, and he states that does not belong to any criminal group, but is merely a drug user.

The face of the victims reflects pure fear, at the same moment one can see the one of the hooded sicarios in a white t-shirt carrying a knife, a handgun, and a rifle on a sling.

The sicario sends a message on behalf of the King of Kings (El Rey de Reyes) and Commander Diablo (Devil). "For all those assholes that are getting involved in Victoria, the only person in command is Commander Diablo under the orders of the King of Kings," says the sicario.

The young man is forced to apologize, and continues to mention that he only buys "pot" as the sicario tells him he has his wife.

Moments later the masked men are seen leaving the victim lying on the ground on the side of the road, and one shoots the victim again with the handgun. It is apparent that they have also executed the wife of the young man and possibly more family members.

The sicrios are then seen again, this time holding another young man who is wearing a white shirt with dark stripes, he is also questioned.

This other victim is also a drug user. The sicario that is wearing the white shirt and shows the camera a bag containing small amounts of marijuana. The victim is then executed (shot in the head).

On May 15, 2012 I posted another execution video in a post titled "The Savagery of El Diablo."

On May 14, 2012 a video was uploaded on Youtube by a user with the name of "anim trent" and was immediately removed by Youtube due to its graphic violent content. The video was titled "Comandante Diablo y Rey de Reyes Acabando con los Zetas" or "Commander Diablo and King of Kings finishing Los Zetas." The video starts with a female decapitating a male while the man is still alive. The man is then dismembered. It is very hard to watch. At one point one of the sicarios carves the letter "Z" on the stomach of the victim.

Two older men are executed. One is shot before being beheaded and dismembered. The other man is beheaded while alive and the head is displayed toward the end of the video. It has not been clearly established who Commander Diablo and Rey de Reyes is, but they have targeted victims that are alleged by this group to have links to Los Zetas.

In the last two weeks a video and several pictures surfaced of members with the same exact name that executed several men, it is not certain if the events are related.

This video gives of clear cut indication of the atrocities these groups are capable of. The extent of violence from these groups that is seen on a daily basis and with multiple horrific consequences is appalling, cutting to the core of the very fabric of the Mexican society.

On July 8, 2012 BB reporter Chivis posted another article titled "Zetas Decapitate "El Diablo's" Mother, Brother, Sister and Sister In Law." This appears to be retaliation on

Comandante Diablo by the Zetas who execute members of Diablo's family.

A grisly video appeared on the Mundo Narco website, of a savage Los Zetas execution of four persons.

As typical with execution videos, each captive is interviewed individually. The doomed group consisted of 3 women and 1 man. As they kneel with their hands bound behind their back, several sicarios are standing in the rear, and one who appears to be in charge is in front to the right. The sicarios are uniformed which bear a "ZETAZ" emblem.

What is far from typical in the video is the captives declare they are relatives of "El Comandante del

Diablo," his mother, sister in law, sister, and brother. They state their name, "Banderas Padilla", Diablo's full name is said to be Hugo Alberto Banderas Padilla. After the brief period of interviewing, the heads of each, in turn, are sealed with duct tape.

A couple of the captives seem hesitant of the answers they give, it impossible to know why. Perhaps they were given a "script" before the execution, or perhaps they were naturally frightened out of their minds anticipating of what is about to happen.

"Look Comandante Diablo, here is your shit family" says the savage in command as the head taping is being conducted. The audio is permeated by the taping sounds making it difficult to define what is being said. The video quality also leaves much to be desired. However, the video is peppered with the usual threats such as, "Hey fucking Diablo, this is what happens to your people, asshole."

After their heads are sealed, the victims are subjected to skillful blows to the back of the skull. The powerful blows are delivered with a 2x4.

Each one falls instantly after one blow from the board, and are rendered unconscious. Unconscious is exactly the best scenario when one is about to be decapitated alive.

At the videos ending a message was displayed:

"Fucking vulgar cartel, they only kill people to heat things up, they don't have balls to confront those who are in this matter.

Attn: The one who gave them the power"

If in fact the executed people are the family of El Diablo, Tamaulipas will truly become hell with the devil on a mission of vengeance.

On July 25, 2012 Chivis posted an execution video retaliating against Los Zetas titled "Diablo Confirms The Executed Were His Family-Sends Message With Decapitation Video."

The video depicts the interrogation and decapitation of at least one man who in his interrogation states he works for the Zetas cartel. The video is the work of "El Diablo" the leader of a brutal group of sicarios in the NE Mexican state of Tamaulipas.

It was two weeks ago that Zetas released an execution video that showed the decapitation of four members of Diablos family, his; mother, brother, sister and sister-in-law. At the time, bloody revenge was anticipated by all that follow the Narco war. However, if one is to believe Diablos message with respect to the execution of his family, he states the executions were "not a problem," it illustrates the psychopathic nature of the man known for his exceptionally monstrous executions.

This execution is of a "halcon" Halcones (Hawks) are lookouts for organized crime organizations. They are hired to follow the movements of the police agencies and military. They are at the bottom of the organizational order. Often Halcones are teens. For sicarios (hit men) to capture a halcon for execution is an easy feat, far from hiding, their jobs require they are out in the open and they are easy to spot.

It would seem such a pitiful statement to the brutal execution of his family, as to pick up a lowly halcon, and execute him to send a message. In this case however, though the victim says he is a halcon, he also states he is the brother of a Zetas sicario, one that his executioner refers to in the video as "El Pelon".

The video is of very poor quality, however it has enough clarity to know the execution was brutal. The sicarios used a large folding saw to behead the man, he was subjected to the severing and removal of his tongue prior to being decapitated.

The video was filmed in Cd. Victoria, Tamaulipas

The video begins with the message in the photo above which reads:

Ya chingaron a mi familia no hay pedo todos sabemos en lo que andamos.

Van a llorar sangre vamos a ver quien es mas verga culeros y los va llevar la verga a todos los mugrosos "Z" con todo y familia ya me lo hicieron a mi ahorra va la mia.

Translation:

"You already fucked my family up but no problem we all know what we are into. You will cry blood and we'll see who's more of a badass fucking asshole and all the dirty motherfuckers "Z" are gonna get fucked up along with all their families you already did to me so now it's my turn."

On September 2, 2012 Chivis posted the arrest of comandante Diablo in a post titled ""EL DIABLO" Captured CDG Boss of NL.

"Federal Police arrested David Rosales Guzman, Comandante

Diablo , identified as the head of the Gulf Cartel plaza in Monterrey, said Luis Cardenas Palomino, head of the Regional Security Division of the Ministry of Public Security.

Rosales Guzman has been linked to killings, kidnappings, extortion and attacks at various bars in Monterrey, including Makiavelo bar that left three dead on August 8, and the bar Matehuala, where nine people died on 14 March.

Also, it is related to the killing of two men who were hanged on a pedestrian bridge in Monterrey limits and San Nicolas de los Garza,

"He was in charge of coordinating and ordering the killings of members of rival groups, conducting extortion bars and nightclubs and drug distribution" in Monterrey, said Palomino. "provided weapons to the members under his command, which operated in Monterrey , it is known that drugs and weapons were brought from Reynosa, Tamaulipas, where other members of the Gulf Cartel, and were coordinated with David Rosales for such activities, it is known also with ties to the municipal police of Nuevo Leon" he said."

Just as recent as December 15, 2018 BB reporter Yaqui posted that Diablo had been sentenced; "El Comandante Diablo" Sentenced to 53 Years."

This is just an example of the savagery that takes place in Mexico with the most horrific heinous violence anyone can inflict upon its people by some of these criminals, truly a heinous act that shocks the conscious.

The Narco Corrido Culture

I was born in Ciudad Juarez, Chihuahua. We used to live in a poor neighborhood called La Cuesta in the outskirts of the city. There was no paved roads and we lived in a small house made of adobe. There was no water, we had to get the water brought in. My father used to commute daily to El Paso while working for the company Tony Lama making cowboy boots.

Life was rough. I remember working on the side shinning boots and selling candy apples in the neighborhood to help my mother buy food.

When I was ten years old, the workers at Tony Lama went on strike and my father was fired.

My uncle who worked for the city of Albuquerque told my father to join him working alongside of him. My father had a visa to work in the US and came to Albuquerque to work for the city. He later was able to make arrangements to bring us all to Albuquerque. I would eventually graduate from High school, join the Marines and retire as a police officer from the city of Albuquerque.

La Cuesta would eventually become an area infested with crime, they would always find bodies buried in this remote neighborhood. Some of the women that were killed in large numbers in Juarez were found buried in La Cuesta. I have never visited that place since I left when I was a child. In the US, I grew up watching my older brother play his Mexican music. One of the music bands I listened a lot while growing up was Los Tigres del Norte. They sang narco corridos. One of their songs "la Banda del Carro Rojo" was one of my favorites.

Dicen que venian del sur En un carro Colorado
Traian cien kilos de coca
Iban con rumbo a Chicago

Asi lo dijo el soplon
Que los habia denunciado
Ya habian pasado la aduana La que esta en El Paso, Texas.
Pero en mero San Antonio
Lo estaban esperando
Eran los rinches de Texas
Que comandan el condado.

The story talks about driving from the south in a red car loaded with 100 kilos of coke on their way to Chicago. They were intercepted in San Antonio by the Texas Rangers and they got in a shootout that resulted in the casualty of four traffickers and three lawmen. One of the traffickers Lino Quintana was arrested but refused to testify. No one knew who they were or where they came from, as no one came to claim their bodies.

I can't say for certainty if this story is true or not, but many of the narco corridos sing about true events or famous traffickers. The narco corrido is deeply embedded in the Mexican culture. Some of the most popular bands and singers in Mexico sing narco corridos.

I never really gave it too much thought when I was young, I just grew up listening to the music. It became almost normal, glorifying the traffickers, seemed almost like they were portrayed as heroes in the corrido. It was not until later, that I really understood the true meaning of what this whole thing actually signified.

A Narco corrido (Drug Ballad) is a type of Mexican music and song tradition which evolved out of the norteño folk corrido tradition. This type of music is heard on both sides of the US–Mexican border. It uses a danceable, accordion-based polka as a rhythmic base. The first corridos that focused on drug smugglers has been dated to the 1930s. Other music critics have compared the narco corrido music to Gangster Rap.

Between 2006 and 2008, over a dozen prominent Mexican musicians, many of them connected to the narco corrido genre, were murdered. The violence came in the midst of the Mexican drug war. Experts and musicians themselves say that the murders can be explained by many Mexican musicians' proximity to drug traffickers.

The most popular musicians killed were Valentín Elizalde and Sergio Gomez, the lead singer of Chicago based Duranguense band K-Paz de la Sierra. On December 2007, both men were nominated posthumously for Grammy Awards in the banda category.

In the third season of The Shield, the episode entitled "Safe", a narco corrido is found. It was a song about an unrequited love, and the man killed her. However, several bodies are found, from meth lab exposure. Later evidence proves that she is alive and living with the boyfriend, so the narco corrido turned out to be fake. In real life detectives have used corrido lyrics to close cases from stories that are found to be true. But many times, it is hard to establish if a corrido is a fable or something related by a narco from true accounts.

Even my all-time favorite television series Breaking Bad that was filmed in and around Albuquerque had Mexican cartel themes in some of their episodes. The second season episode, Negro Y Azul of Breaking Bad, opens with a narco corrido about events within the show's story played by Los Cuates de Sinaloa.

"The cartel's running hot
Because they weren't getting respect
They talk about some 'Heisenberg'
Who controls the market now
No one knows anything about him
Because they've never seen him
The cartel's about respect and they never forgive

But that guy's dead already, he just doesn't know it yet."

The Mexican government has made attempts to change the narco corrido culture, in which they feel it contributes to the problem of narco violence. Mexican youth grow up listening to the corridos of men making a lot of money, having beautiful women by their side and driving expensive cars. They look at it as a possible way out of poverty and misery. The songs paint a picture of romantic adventures in trafficking drugs as a means to be the boss of bosses.

In November 24, 2010 The Smurf published a story about narco corridos related to Los Tucanes de Tijuana.

"Since last November, Los Tucanes de Tijuana, one of the most recognizable bands in the Mexican norteño regional genre, are banned from playing in their hometown and namesake, the border city of Tijuana.

The ban is a result of a 2008 concert in which the band's lead singer sent his regards from the stage to the city's most notorious and wanted men, "El Teo and his compadre, El Muletas." The city's get-tough police chief, Julian Leyzaola, was outraged.

Leyzaola pulled the plug on shows by Los Tucanes as they prepared to perform at the city's storied Agua Caliente racetrack in November. Leyzaola said the band's polka-driven narcocorrido songs glorify drug lords and their exploits and are therefore inappropriate to play in a city that has suffered soaring drug related violence in recent years. The band, with millions of record sales and a fan base as broad as the international border, hasn't been allowed to play in Tijuana since.

Authorities in Mexico widely disapprove of norteño bands that sing about the drug trade, banning their songs from radio airwaves and even threatening jail time for narcocorrido producers (link in Spanish). The effort is especially vigilant in Tijuana, as Marosi reported in a story in 2008.

Last year, another iconic norteño band, Los Tigres del Norte, was banned from performing a popular song titled "La Granja" at an awards ceremony in Mexico City. The song's allegorical lyrics are critical of the government's strategy against the drug cartels. Los Tigres del Norte pulled out of the show, inevitably boosting the song's profile among fans.

Narcocorrido singers walk a fine line between merely commenting on the larger-than-life figures in Mexico's drug war and singing their praises -- sometimes at their own risk. Several norteño performers have been hunted down and killed, such as Valentin Elizalde and, in June, Sergio Vega. Some of the most well-known narcocorridos describe news events in coded details, such as the song Los Tucanes de Tijuana released about Joaquin "El Chapo" Guzman, Mexico's most wanted man.

On March 27, 2015 DD posted this

"A brief history of early attempts at censoring narcocorridors from the book Narcocorrido: A Journey into the Music of Drugs, Guns, and Guerrillas, by Elijah Wald.

'While both drugs and crime cause real problems for society at large, and for many individuals, I am extremely dubious about the purposes of such censorship. It seems to me to be a attempt by politicians to get publicity as defenders of public morals and safety without doing any of the difficult things that would be necessary to genuinely deal with the problems, such as providing poor people with other ways to improve their economic situation.'

I am not a fan of narco-corridors, but I think attempts at censorship, which is a form of prohibition, will be just as unsuccessful as the prohibition on drugs has been. If you think they have not become part of the culture both in Mexico and to a fast-growing extent in the US, just go to YouTube and do a search "narco-corridors" and you will get

217,000 results which suggests Mexico has no hope of pulling the plug on the music."

On June 20, 2009 a story was posted on the execution of narco corrido singer Valentin Elizalde titled "The Strange and Tragic Story of Valentin Elizalde."

"Now you know who you're dealing with, come and test your luck." - from "To My Enemies."

Nicknamed "The Golden Rooster," Valentin Elizalde, 27, was well known in Northern Mexico for his brass based traditional "banda" music: polka-inspired and with gritty lyrics. Musicians like him along the Mexico-Texas frontier have long documented the trials of border life and have turned the region's drug lords into living legends.

In August 2006, on the popular video-sharing Web site YouTube.com, someone posted a photo slideshow depicting a succession of bullet-riddled bodies set to Elizalde's song "A Mis Enemigos" ("To My Enemies") as the soundtrack.

The gory collection had a partisan theme: it was taunting the Gulf Cartel, showing only victims aligned with it and its enforcement arm, known as Los Zetas. And just so nobody missed the point, the screen name of the person who shared the gloating documentary was "matazeta," or Zeta killer.

Volleys of foul-mouthed insults soon began to be posted to the site, resulting in a strange dialogue between self-described supporters of the Sinaloa and Gulf cartels, which are locked in a turf battle over lucrative smuggling corridors into the United States.

On the YouTube site, the rhetoric escalated in the days before Elizalde was slated to play in Reynosa a border town in the heart of Gulf Cartel territory. "Videos like this cause the death of Chapitos," warned a Gulf supporter in a posting one day before the concert, using a slang term for El Chapo's followers.

On November 25, Elizalde played his set in Reynosa, opening and closing it with "To My Enemies."

As he left the fair, two vehicles chased his Chevrolet Suburban and opened fire with automatic weapons in front of dozens of onlookers. Elizalde, his driver and manager were killed. Elizalde had been hit 28 times and died on the scene. As many as 70 cartridges were found.

A cryptic message was posted on YouTube almost immediately after the shooting. "Just because of this video, they filled the Rooster with lead, hahahaha. He cried like a bitch," another poster who sided with the Gulf Cartel wrote.

When Elizalde was gunned down, he was in the passenger seat, his limp body slumped toward the door.

These details are clearly visible in another video posted on YouTube, a 50-second clip of the crime scene.

Meanwhile, the comments on the videos continued. Some comments referred to the ousting of Gregorio "El Goyo" Sauceda from the Gulf Cartel leadership after a rift with other bosses. El Goyo's fall had not been reported anywhere, but matched intelligence that U.S. authorities had gleaned from contacts in Mexico.

If there were other nuggets of truth buried among the poorly spelled curses, they are now lost. YouTube yanked the video and comments Nov. 27, citing violation of terms of service.

But other versions of the Elizalde video surfaced immediately on YouTube, one opening with machine gun fire and closing with a video clip of an execution.

In the territory disputed by the Gulf and Sinaloa cartels the names of cartel leaders are mentioned only in whispers, if at all. But under the anonymity bestowed by the Internet, whispers became pronouncements.

It wasn't the first time an assassination was foretold on the Internet. On a Weblog in August, in a similar vitriolic back-and-forth, a threat to kill Monterrey investigator Marcelo Garza y Garza became reality just weeks later.

Last Wednesday, Norteño singer Javier Morales Gomez of the group Los Implacables del Norte was gunned down in the plaza of Huetamo in Michoacan state. Three days earlier, singer Lupillo Rivera was shot at as he drove in Guadalajara.

On Sunday, a large crowd awaited the arrival of Elizalde's body at the airport in Ciudad Obregon. Two police cars then escorted Elizalde's body to his hometown of Jitonhueca, about 60 miles southeast, where a memorial service was to be held at his mother's home, the government news agency Notimex reported. Along the way, the funeral procession was greeted by the strains of norteno music. Some fans applauded from the side of the road. Others tossed flowers or laid out votive candles.

The song in question, framed as a tribute video:

It's not surprising that there's violence when you're talking about drug cartels, but besides the obvious unfortunate fate of Elizalde (who's survived by his three daughters), I thought this was notable just because of how odd this was."

In Search for La Linea

Albuquerque is a sister city of the city of Chihuahua, Mexico. The Mayor of Albuquerque at the time was Martin Chavez who was said to have an amiable distant relationship with the Mayor of Chihuahua, Mayor Juan Blanco. For the most part, the alliance of the cross-border mayors was a good thing, it allowed both side of the border to collaborate in constructive projects and forged a spirit of cooperation between both cities. Albuquerque Police used to provide some support to the Chihuahua police in training and equipment. I remember our department delivering expired ballistic vest to the police of Chihuahua.

Most of this training by some of the Albuquerque police officers took place in the city of Chihuahua. But some of the Mexican officers who participated in the training were officers from the whole state of Chihuahua, including Ciudad Juarez. There was a police officer with the City of Albuquerque who had been police chief of Sunland Police Department. Sunland is a community right outside the city limits of El Paso, Texas. This officer had a lot of contacts with officers and politicians in Chihuahua and assisted many officers abroad with coordinating with training.

It was during this time that a met several police officers from the Ciudad Juarez municipal police. I would not say they were close friends of mine, but I knew their acquaintance. Some were ranking members of the police department and we had a distant amiable friendship. I felt this might be an opportunity for me to find out more about the so called Línea.

Ever since I had found out that the father of little Alicia had been a ranking member of La Línea, I could not get it off my head. I really wanted to know more, I had this deep craving to learn about who they were and how they operated

99

relative to the Juarez Cartel. I knew Ciudad Juarez was saturated with thousands of military and federal police. How did they move in the city and operate in the open? At the time not many people had heard of La Línea, except for the people in Juarez.

I started to focus on the cartel violence in Ciudad Juarez, being the closest proximity to where I lived. The federal police were suspected of cooperating with the Sinaloa cartel in efforts to destroy the Juarez Cartel. The state and municipal police forces were accused of colluding or joining forces with their hometown Juarez Cartel.

What is certain is that La Linea had suffered much more damage from federal police forces in Juarez than the Sinaloa cartel cells. I had heard a rumor once that the Linea was primarily made up of Juarez police officers. I just did not have enough information to form any type of conclusion.

I had to go to the source.

Back in 2007 I was introduced to an active ranking police officer from Ciudad Juarez that might be willing to talk to me about La Línea or at least facilitate someone to talk to me freely about it. This commander, that I had actually met in Albuquerque, was going to be my point of contact. He indicated that I would have to make a trip to Ciudad Juarez, the most dangerous city in the world at the time. I was not very comfortable travelling to Juarez and meeting with someone to talk to me about criminal organizations.

Although I somewhat trusted this commander, I also knew that may times you will have operatives working for both cartels and leaking information, perhaps to someone that might have an interest to do you harm. People had been killed for much less. I would not be armed, so I would be totally dependent on others for my safety. Some of the videos I had seen posted on social media of people being tortured and executed flashed across my mind. I was not naive of the high risk this trip posed.

I was nervous, but my contact had questioned me if I truly trusted him, and the ultimate test would be if I truly trusted him with my life. "I will make sure nothing happens to you. You have to trust me as I trust you."

In the night of darkness, I made my visit to Ciudad Juarez.

I crossed the international bridge as it was starting to get dark and I was picked up on the Mexico side to be taken to a hotel. An older gentleman picked me up, but he did not talk much. I sat quietly, looking out the window and wondering if this was wise.

I remember staying in this motel in a seedy part of Juarez, not armed, feeling vulnerable, insecure and looking over my shoulder expecting the unexpected. I was not armed, and I was always used to being armed, all the time. The rare times I did not have a weapon on me at home, I always felt vulnerable. Well here in Mexico, I felt terrified.

By the time I settled in the motel, it was completely dark. I looked out the door, and by the entrance to the parking lot of the motel, I could see two parked police cars. I was not sure if the officers were inside their cars or where they were. I saw people walking on the sidewalk, just going about their business, it seemed like a normal night in Juarez. I then realized, normal in Juarez was constant violence and mayhem.

I was harmless, not interested in naming anyone, just telling the story in a general overall view. My intention was not to inject myself in the activities of organized crime in Mexico, or play games with anyone, I just wanted to know more. My only interest was to understand, to know the how, when and why, without worrying about the who. I had no interest to piss anyone off, I just wanted to know more about the armed wing of the Juarez cartel.

I met with what I assumed was an active police officer of the Juarez Police. I was truly expecting him to have his face concealed, but he was not. He seemed like he was in his 30s, clean cut and very friendly. There was a noticeable bulge on the right side of his waist that was covered by his shirt, evidence that he was armed. Every once in a while, through the remainder of the interview, I could hear people walking right outside the door. I was watching him real close, for signs of anything that might be wrong, any red flags that might give me cause for concern.

He told me to call him Hector, but I suspected that was not his real name. He had indicated to me that his identity was not important but keeping his name secret was necessary to keep him and I safe.

The ground rules were easy and simple, do not ask anything personal about him or who he knows. No names, just the names of organizations and events.

So, I started to learn about La Línea.

La Línea did not operate in the cover of darkness, they were very open about it. The word started to spread and soon most of the people in Juarez knew what they represented. It was not kept as a secret. "I am in La Línea," cartel bosses would announce and suddenly they seemed to easily avoid any problems with police or were able to pass through checkpoints with no problems. "I have joined La Línea," young men who joined the organization would bolster to friends. They would point to a nice truck driving by and say, "in that truck are traveling members of La Línea." It was common especially to people who were familiar with the name.

Hector summed it up really easy.

"Initially I do not know what it was," said Hector. "I joined the department two years ago, and I had never heard the word. Until one day during a check point a man from a van said: I'm from La Linea, and a colleague told me that we had to let him go. We let him pass unchecked. "

Hector had asked his companion what that word meant and was told some mysterious explanation. "They are the bosses of the main plaza. They are called La Línea." Since then officer Hector lets them pass and lets them walk at will all over the city.

"Nobody messes with them. It is impossible. I was told that they are protected and no one can do anything about it," the officer said.

A few months ago, officer Hector learned of an incident that happened to a police friend of his who was humiliated by La Línea. "My friend had arrested some armed men, but later they came back to see him. They took out their AK-47's (cuernos de chivo) and forced him get on his knees. They put the assault rifles to his head and told him never to mess with La Línea. The next time you die. "

Since that day, Hector does not dare lay an eye on them.

"Sometimes I see them arriving by convoy. Sometimes they park and get out armed to the teeth. One can't do anything. The only thing I do is turn the other way, as if I did not see them," says Hector. "You just can't go against them. I wanted to be a policeman and fight crime, but that would require removing all the heads of the command. It must be an initiative from the very top, like from the President of Mexico, because La Línea has people everywhere, "he said.

Many people I know in the city know individual members of La Linea. It may be a cousin or a childhood friend or a long-time school acquaintance. There are so many of them that almost everyone knows someone. La Línea has their networks in gangs like "Barrio Aztecas" who are street thugs, and the municipal police commanders that protect their precious cargo.

Also, the state police that are on the payroll, and even judges and prosecutors. Also aligned (as in La Línea) are the mules who pass the drugs to the other side of the border, the taxi drivers who are the network of information and let's not forget "the poles" (people in street corners who are the ears in the neighborhoods).

A young business professional man said that one of his college friends, joined La Línea. "He was my best friend and was middle class. He then graduated college and disappeared for some time. Later I saw him at a restaurant, and he was very well dressed, wore a gold chain and was driving a new expensive car. He said he had found a very lucrative business," the businessman said. Two or three years later, he saw his friend again at a school reunion. The guy was driving a very luxurious SUV.

"He said I'm from La Línea. I'm doing very well. Soon I will allocate a large sum of wealth"

"I did not say anything, but it scared me. It has been about a year and I have not seen or heard of him. He is no longer seen anywhere here. Maybe he's in jail, or has been executed, or plainly moved to another city."

Most citizens here are afraid of La Línea. After two years as a policeman, Hector also fears them. "They are in charge. They give the orders. It's unbelievable, but that is just how it is.

I got some insight in to the background of the enforcers and sicarios of the Juarez cartel, La Línea. Their job, keep all rival cartels away from the plaza, enforce the code of the cartel, protect the trafficking operation on the Mexico side of the border and settle scores, punish anyone who dares to interfere with operations or betrays the cartel institution.

The Sinaloa syndicate had entered the plaza and have dared to challenge the Juarez Syndicate. It's a battle to ensure Juarez does not fall. La Línea has been tasked to repel their assault on the city and take a few federales with them. This is a business that must be protected, and it will. They will not allow anyone to get in the way.

The Juarez cartel does not employ street gangs to protect their empire. Hector made it clear to me, directly and with no reservation, "the Juarez Cartel employs professionals, sicarios that know how to deploy with weapons and have an understanding of police tactics. This is a real business my friend, the corporation makes a lot of money, they have no time for amateur bullshit!"

I was not naive, I knew that La Línea was sometimes the actual local police. At one point, I asked about police corruption in Juarez and I was corrected, "Corruption? The police are the cartel."

It was really simple I was told. The criminal organization is a straight line. All the drug dealers, hitmen (sicarios), the police who protect them and the mules who carry the cocaine to the U.S. must all be aligned. Straight shooters. The Juarez drug cartel created a new term used to describe their organization. It started as a concept, a method of operation, then it became a group of enforcers. So, they call themselves "The Line" (La Línea) and everyone fears it.

Hector looked me in the eye, "fear it my friend."

A knock on the door announced his signal to say his goodbye, and leave the same way he came in, disappearing to the black cold darkness outside my motel door. To me, he was an unknown person who I will probably not ever see again.

What I heard was hard to swallow and initially I thought there was more of bragging going on here, but later on, through experience researching the Mexico narco life, I knew that what I heard was for the most part true. Perhaps I did not want to believe it. I had a lot of respected for law enforcement in general, including Mexico but this made me see things in a totally different way. I found the level of corruption from police institutions, as explained to me, repulsive and dangerous. Later, I was reassured by another Juarez cop that I should not lose faith in law enforcement in Mexico, as not all cops are corrupt. Many of them die fighting the criminal cartels and make great sacrifices in their life to do the right thing. "Do not lose faith, police work in Mexio is still honorable with some, believe it," I was told.

Later on, Borderland Beat would report, on many occasions, of the life of some of the good guys fighting the fight in Ciudad Juarez and that for the most part many of these good guys made the ultimate sacrifice trying to make a better life for the citizens of a very violent city.

There had been a specific report in El Paso Times sometime around 2011 that remained close to my heart, for the knowledge that I had known and the law enforcement south of the border that had touched my life, teaching me that when there is bad, there is also good.

"A Juárez police captain was gunned down after ending his shift at the Benito Juárez police station, according to the Juárez Department of Public Safety.

Several gunmen shot José Manuel Rivas López, after storming into his home in the 1103 block of Joaquín Soto Mendoza and Teniente Daniel García streets, located in the Oasis Revolución neighborhood.

The victim, riddled with bullets, was found dead in the living room, authorities said. Forensics staff members recovered 64 bullet casings. According to an unconfirmed report, Mexican federal police officers arrested two suspects in connection with this shooting.

Forty Juárez police officers have been killed since Juárez Mayor Héctor Murguía took office on Oct. 10, 2010. Fourteen Juárez police officers have been ambushed just in 2011, according to the Juárez Department of Public Safety."

Yes, I survived that night in Juarez. The next morning, I was outside the streets of Juarez and noticed many federal police and soldiers on almost every corner. I ate some tacos of barbacoa real early in the morning, the streets were bustling with people doing their daily chores, going about their business. Sitting there, among the masses of people, for a minute, I was just another person among many.

Walking back to the international bridge I saw three federal police pickup trucks running lights and siren with three or four federal police officers in the back holding for dear life. They were all in black wearing ballistic helmets, ski masks and all had long rifles strapped to their shoulder. I wonder if they were responding to another daily execution or shootout somewhere in Juarez. It did not seem to faze the public as they seem to go about their normal business, like nothing was happening, just another day in the city.

After 2007, Felipe Calderon sent thousands of military troops and federal police to Juarez, you could see check points all over. It was the military and federal police primarily checking for weapons and drugs. So how was La Línea able to operate freely, move heavily armed, many times in convoys, and openly wage war against the Sinaloa cartel in Juarez?

Simple, collusion from police officers of every agency and a network of boots on the ground in constant communication. Many people on the payroll, a costly operation sustained for long periods of times. Everyone had a motive and everyone took a side.

In this plaza it was federal (black uniforms) with Sinaloa faction and municipal (blue uniforms) with the Juarez faction. It was a game being played out in the streets of Ciudad Juarez.

It was said that President Felipe Calderon sent the military and federal police to Ciudad Juarez to take on the Juarez cartel. This was during the time the Juarez cartel and Sinaloa cartel were in a dispute over control of la plaza.

One example was that of a former Juárez police officer suspected in 18 murders and belonging to a drug cartel La Linea, was one of multiple arrests during the operations of the Mexican military.

Ex-officer Miguel Angel Delgado Carmona, 39, and suspected accomplice Roberto Gonzalez Lazalde, 34, were captured after a vehicle chase following an extortion attempt of a Juárez funeral home, officials with Joint Operation Chihuahua said.

Soldiers with the Fourth Infantry Battalion began chasing the van moments after four men had delivered a note to the funeral home stating "Call today (a telephone number) without excuse, attention La Linea."

Two of the men exited the Dodge Caravan at a street corner and escaped.

But soldiers captured Delgado and Gonzalez, who allegedly confessed to belonging to a cell of La Linea, as the Juárez drug cartel is known. The cell (La Linea) was created to kill rivals from the Sinaloa cartel and would enforce extortion operations from several businesses.

The insights of how cartels operate in Mexico among federal police and military forces opened my eyes. My suspicion of this complicated interaction between narcos and police was starting to make some sense. Not that it was right or even wrong, but just that it was a mechanism that had existed for many years and it was extremely hard to fix. Yes, certainly not right, but perhaps it was a way to survive to live another day and keep your precious family safe among a sea full of potential lethal danger.

As I drove back to Albuquerque, my head was spinning. Too much to digest, I would have to take my time to take everything in.

Heating up the Plaza

In the narco world, a plaza usually means a city or town that is controlled by a particular cartel. The term "heating up the plaza," means the increase of cartel violence activity in a city. Sometimes it could be that a cartel was defending a plaza from other cartels through violent means, or cleaning their turf by conducting executions. It could also mean that the military or federal police were targeting a specific cartel that many times resulted in shootouts or as a way for a cartel to enforce their dominance and settle scores as a method of retaliation.

The third way of heating up a plaza is for a specific cartel to intentionally increase violence in a particular plaza to get the attention of federal authorities. For example; one cartel enters the plaza controlled by another cartel, conduct several executions of low-level cartel members or members of law enforcement, and this forces the federal police to put heat on the cartel in charge of the plaza. These tactics can be extremely violent. There were many times Borderland Beat found themselves front and center reporting on these events.

Police corruption and cartel violence is blatant, and open in other cities that were once safe, like Monterrey.

When gang members opened fire on the Café Iguana in downtown Monterrey in 2011, a squad of eight municipal policemen rushed to the scene.

The police arrived to find four people dead and five wounded. Just as they began surveying the scene another group of sicarios pulled up in a truck and began loading the dead bodies in the back. Rather than confront them, the officers watched as the men stashed three bodies in the truck and briefly searched for the fourth, which had fallen behind some parked cars. They eventually left it behind and sped off.

The officers involved came under investigation, but only one was arrested, the others fled.

Monterrey police have been accused of co-operating with drug cartels. Police corruption was so rampant in this city of four million that government officials believe at least half of the force was on the payroll of the cartels. Low pay, scant resources and an inability to cope with the heavily armed cartels made the police an easy target for recruitment.

Monterrey had been spared much of the cartel violence that has ravaged other parts of Mexico. That allowed the city to continue its remarkable growth, driven by its proximity to the U.S. border, just two hours away, and its status as the country's main manufacturing center.

The city is home to some of Mexico's largest companies, including cement giant Cemex, as well as 2,600 factories belonging to foreign businesses such as Whirlpool, Navistar and Philips. General Motors, Ford, Chrysler and dozens of auto-parts companies also have plants about an hour south in the nearby city of Saltillo.

The North American Free Trade Agreement brought untold prosperity to Monterrey and income levels were among the highest in Mexico. There were sprawling shopping malls, gleaming concert halls, a multitude of museums and the Monterrey Institute of Technology, one of the best universities in the country.

Monterrey had been considered so prosperous and so safe it was considered a potential home for baseball's Montreal Expos in 2004 before the team moved to Washington. Even the cartel leaders used to send their families to live in Monterrey's upscale San Pedro district, considered the richest suburb in Mexico.

All that calm and security was shattered when the Gulf drug cartel and its military-like offshoot, the Zetas, began vying for territory. It was a classic fight to take over a plaza, but not just a plaza, a major modern urban metropolitan city. It was said that if Monterrey fell to the cartels, the rest of Mexico would follow suit, making Mexico a failed state. Just why that turf war spread into Monterrey isn't clear.

Some blame Mexican President Felipe Calderon's war on the cartels, which he launched in 2006. They say that some of the fragmented cartels were driven on to untouched areas such as Monterrey, where they waged a war for control. Others point to the U.S. government's crackdown on the Mexican border, saying that pushed more drugs and cartel violence south on to Mexico from the U.S. border and drove up the number of domestic drug users. Still others blame the Zetas, once the hired guns for the Gulf cartel, who had struck out on their own and were trying to develop their own drug trade.

Whatever the reason, Monterrey was feeling the effect. Murders skyrocketed and the Zetas roamed the streets in caravans with near impunity, battling their Gulf rivals as well as the Mexican army. Monterrey had 828 murders in 2010, a threefold increase from 2009.

El Pozolero - The Stew Maker

It was 2009 when Santiago Meza Lopez, El Pozolero, didn´t care if he was seen crying, nor did he care that tens of news reporters, soldiers and curious people wanted to take his picture, or ask him how he made "el pozole" (the Mexican stew), or how much the Sinaloa cartel paid him.

He only cared about being forgiven by God.

Santiago could barely open his eyes. The beating he had received when he was arrested left his face swollen. Crying was hurtful, but the cocaine dose he had inside made it bearable.

Inside the Tijuana´s military base, the detainee was begging, "Please, forgive me…".

Meza Lopez was asking for forgiveness from the relatives of all the people he dissolved for nine years, first under the orders of the Arellano Felix cartel, then under those of the Sinaloa cartel when Teodoro García Semental, El Teo, switched sides.

The job of Santiago Meza López was to dispose of the enemies of a notorious drug baron by dissolving them in tubs of acid. Over several years he claims to have "disappeared" 300 enemies of El Teo, a former henchman for one of the largest cartels.

Meza, 45, told police that, once their remains had been in the acid baths for 24 hours, he would bury them. In a twisted act of chivalry, he said he only dissolved men, refusing to make women vanish in this way. He said that he was paid $600 a week by El Teo.

His horrific career came to an end on Thursday when he was ambushed by elite Mexican troops, acting on a tip-off, who caught him and two other drugs henchmen as they headed to a party with a prostitute in Tijuana.

Armed with a machinegun, three rifles and two hand grenades, plus body armor, Meza and the two others tried to flee but eventually gave themselves up without a fight.

Some people say Santiago was crying because he didn't believe he was guilty, he thought life put him there and that was the job intended for him. He claimed he wasn't a killer, he wasn't a kidnapper, he didn't see himself as a drug dealer.

Soldiers remember him praying out loud when they were transporting him from Ensenada to Tijuana. He asked God for forgiveness. "Sorry, sorry" he was heard inside the Humvee in which he was being transported to Tijuana.

The Mexican authorities paraded The Stew Maker in front of a nondescript shack where he admitted that he had disposed of the bodies over a period of ten years. Two grave-sized holes had been dug near the walls.

The nickname "Pozolero" came from pozole, a stew local to Mexico and the Southwest US. Its ingredients are normally corn, meat and chilli. Meza told police that his busiest time was in December 2007, when he claimed to have disposed of 32 bodies.

Santiago Meza Lopez talked about his recipe on how to make "Pozole." It involved two large empty oil barrels, several pounds of Sodium hydroxide, also known as lye or caustic soda, latex gloves and gas masks. He was taught how to cook from men brought in from Israel.

In the year 2000, the Arellano Felix brothers of the Tijuana cartel decided to use a new method to get rid of their enemies. Previously, they just dumped the bodies in the sewers or the river, but it was dangerous, or someone could catch them.

Benjamin and Ramon Arellano Felix decided to bring people from Israel who knew how to dissolve bodies in acid. They trained a group of men, including Santiago, who in those days used to take care of drugs that were to be smuggled to the United Stated.

Santiago gave details, he would begin by buying the empty oil barrels, then he dumped about 100 pounds of Sodium hydroxide that he bought in a hardware store in the Mariano Matamoros community on the east side of Tijuana. The Sodium hydroxide costing him roughly $1.50 dollars a pound.

"A lady at the store once asked me why I bought so much Sodium hydroxide, I told her I used it to clean houses," said Santiago Meza.

"The bodies that I was given to make "pozole" were already dead. I dumped them complete inside the oil barrels.

Santiago was assisted by two young men who he identified as "El Chalino" and "El Yiyo", a pair of 25 year olds, who were also born in Sinaloa. Both left Guamuchil and arrived at Tijuana with the dream of making lots of money. They ended up learning how to make pozole.

"The way I would receive the bodies was when El Teo would call me to tell me that at a certain hour, in a certain place, I was to be given the merchandise. He would call me and tell me in which vehicle the bodies were in. They would signal me with a light and delivery the bodies to me," explained Meza.

Santiago said that working with Sodium hydroxide was very dangerous. He said he always wore protection such as latex gloves and gas masks.

The location was also selected well. They used a property located in a road to Tecate, a desolated area called "Ojo de Agua."

They would cook the posole and dump it on pits.

Relatives of 100 missing people came forward saying that they wanted to show photos of their loved ones to Meza in the hope he could find their love's ones fate.

Cristina Palacios, president of Citizens United Against Impunity, which represented missing people in Tijuana, said: "We are here because this arrest gives us a ray of hope."

Rommel Moreno, the state's Attorney-General, said that Meza would be shown the photos to see if he recognized any among his victims. He said that the authorities were considering allowing the victims' families to meet him.

Police searched the shack for human remains and ask US authorities for DNA-testing equipment.

Fernando Ocegueda, whose son disappeared in February 2007, said that eastern Tijuana was a stronghold of the drug lord El Teo García. The Mexican Government denied that parts of the country had become lawless, but Meza's arrest was a rare success story in the increasingly savage drugs war.

Since the start of 2008 346 people had died or disappeared in drugs-related violence, and Tijuana was one of the worst-affected areas.

The revelations were a gruesome chapter in a battle that stands out for tales of torture, brutal killings and mutilated corpses. One cause of rising violence was a split between El Teo García and his former bosses, the Arellano Félix brothers, which ignited a war between two cartels to dominate the drugs trade. The two split after a Tijuana shootout between their followers left at least 14 people dead.

The level of violence had heightened concerns in the Government about the damage it was doing to the country's image abroad. Patricia Espinosa, the Secretary for Foreign Affairs, asked foreign correspondents not to file negative reports about Mexico.

The man who dissolved bodies in acid, the same man that cried that day he was arrested, had apparently been forgiven by God. At least that's what Rafael Romo Muñoz, Tijuana's Archbishop, told the media. "Even if he got rid of 300 bodies, he still has God's forgiveness if he is truly sorry. There's always forgiveness in God, no matter the sin you committed."

Calderon takes on the Cartels Syndicate

On December 1 of 2006 Felipe de Jesús Calderón Hinojosa had become president of Mexico and declared war on the Mexican drug cartels. He could not rely on the municipal police or state police departments around the country of Mexico, so he heavily relied on the military to conduct his operations.

When soldiers tried to halt a suspicious-looking SUV that was being escorted through Monterrey by a state policeman, the police officer radioed for backup. In minutes, police from 40 patrol cars surrounded the military troops, drawing their guns and sending the soldiers diving for cover in an hour-long standoff.

Confrontations like that were happening with increasing frequency in Mexico's wealthiest city, Monterrey, as soldiers fought corrupt police officers helping drug cartels - in addition to taking on the drug dealers themselves.

In 2008 police and soldiers had confronted one another more than 65 times, a growing and dangerous trend in the war on drugs.

Things were so bad, the general in charge of army operations in northeastern Mexico warned police chiefs his men are ready to open fire on police if it happened again.

"The moment they shoot at us, get in our way, use their guns to protect criminals, they become criminals themselves," said Gen. Guillermo Moreno, commander of troops in Nuevo Leon and Tamaulipas states along the Texas border.

President Felipe Calderon had acknowledged that corruption permeates Mexico's low-paid police at all levels and therefore had opted to combat the billion-dollar drug-smuggling industry by relying primarily on the military, which has seen remarkably fewer cases of bribery by traffickers. His administration also had sent in federal police and soldiers, both of whom are higher paid and usually better educated, to go after police on the take.

Mexico's top federal cop, Public Safety Secretary Genaro García Luna, had said that the only way to resolve the problem was to get rid of the low-paid city police forces, many of which had seen little improvement after being purged repeatedly in the past decade.

He wanted to create state law enforcement agencies to oversee Mexico's 31 states and the federal district of Mexico City. The government would raise officers' salaries significantly to deter bribery.

President Calderón revamped the federal police from the ground up to be used to combat the cartels. Much of his funding came from the Merida Initiative, millions of dollars in grant money from the US. Federal police suddenly found themselves with upgraded equipment and all the federal police officers were seen carrying exclusively AR-15s.

President Calderón urged Federal Police officers not to allow crime to infiltrate their ranks or to tolerate complicity or dishonesty among their colleagues.

"We want Mexicans to be proud of their Federal Police and unlike in the past, we do not want them to distrust, fear or underestimate police performance," he declared.

"Let the federal police be an example because of its loyalty, effectiveness, service, capacity for unreserved commitment to the public security of Mexican families," he said.

"One of the goals we wish to achieve in Federal Government is to provide Mexicans with a reliable police force, a strong, well-trained Federal Police force whose technical and organizational capacities exceed those of criminals," he said.

He ordered pay raises for the Federal Police and the Mexican armed forces to avoid more desertions and cut down on bribes. Federal police officers are mostly PFP (federal preventive police) and are specialized in combating organized crime and drug cartels. The police officers dedicated to investigating and prosecuting crimes in the country are the ministerial police at the federal and state level with 26,928 policemen and women for the whole country. They only constitute 6.3% of the total strength of all polices forces.

The remainder of the total strength of all state and municipal police forces are "seguridad publica" (public security). The municipal police have only the most basic education, in other words they are semiliterate at best, and about two thirds of all policemen (state and municipal) in the country earn about 4,000 pesos a month (about $315) or less.

It is estimated that 40% of all municipal and state police in the country have no effective role in law enforcement. They do not fight or deter crime, nor do they protect their communities. These men and women are the most corrupt segment of police forces and many have links to organized crime. Some are active criminal participants. They are tasked with basic law enforcement and deterrence and have no investigative functions.

The military and federal police are moved around the country to participate in operations and they also started concealing their identity with ski masks so that cartels would not be able to bribe or retaliate against them.

Calderón was from Michoacan and naturally he did not waste any time taking on the organized crime in Michoacan. On December 11, 2006 Calderón launched Operation Michoacan to fight the "Familia de Michoacan" cartel, who was growing in power and becoming extremely violent and brutal. Calderón would deploy more than 6,500 military troops in the state of Michoacán to battle drug traffickers.

In the early year of 2006 and in to 2007 Calderón devoted a lot of resources in Baja California, dismantling major operations of the Tijuana cartel. These operations against the Tijuana cartel of the Arellano-Félix Organization boosted the takeover of the Sinaloa cartel in Tijuana.

On April 3, 2006 federal Police arrested suspected drug lord Victor Magno Escobar in Tijuana. This caused the state of Sonora to heat up with numerous battles and executions of sicarios and police.

On May 14, 2006 Jorge Altriste, head of operations for Mexico's elite police forces in Tijuana was murdered. By the end of 2006 the war on the cartels in Mexico was spiraling out of control that also spilled to journalists and musicians. Popular singer Sergio Gómez was kidnapped and killed in December 2, 2006 and Gerardo García Pimentel, a crime reporter, was killed on December 8, 2006. The music bands of popular narco-ballads were taking sides with cartel factions and singing homage to some drug lords that was upsetting the opposite cartels.

And sometime around January 12, 2010 federal troops stormed a seaside vacation home and captured one of the country's most brutal drug bosses. American anti-drug officials had been helping Mexican authorities track down Teodoro Garcia Simental, known as "El Teo."

He was arrested near the southern tip of the Baja California peninsula, where his gang had been bringing in plane loads of drugs to smuggle across the U.S. border. El Teo had initially worked for the Arellano-Felix but eventually turned on them when they were weakened and join the powerful Sinaloa cartel.

Calderón started to take on the corruption of the local police. On December 29, 2006 the entire police force in the town of Playas de Rosarito, Baja California, was disarmed by the Mexican military. Their weapons were taken away after there was suspicion of them collaborating with drug cartels.

Eventually Tijuana would hire a military colonel to be chief of the Tijuana police named Julián Leyzaola.

Authorities of the State Preventive Police (PEP) arrested former municipal police officer Luis Gilberto Sánchez Guerrero "El Gil," an alleged associate of El Teo. This arrest represented a serious blow to the structure of the Tijuana cartel operating in the state, as the suspect admitted that he commanded at least ten criminal cells.

At the time of his arrest he was in possession of two handguns, one known as "matapolicías" (police killer), with 58 cartridges and a bulletproof vest.

In October 2007, while in a municipal patrol car, "El Gil" helped drug trafficker Raydel Lopez Uriarte "El Muletas" escape from a federal raid.

He had also participated in various criminal acts including in the murder of several municipal police officers, and the attempted assassination of Tijuana police chief Julian Perez Leyzaola. During the raid from by the military and police, they were able to seize several cloned Military trucks and sophisticated weaponry.

Information obtained confirmed that "El Gil" was also involved in settling narco accounts, executions, abductions and "protection" to small business shops.

According to the analysis of his profile, it was determined that he had a hierarchy similar to that of Filiberto Parra Ramos "La Perra", one of the operators of Teodoro Garcia Simental and another man identified as "El Tomate" also ex-Tijuana municipal police.

"El Gil" was arrested when he came to his home in Colonia La Moderna Ensenada where he was hiding after he fled Tijuana. His location was obtained through intelligence work of the Special Intervention Group of the PEP while detecting his activities.

Four police chiefs and four uniformed municipal officers were arrested and presented to the Federal Prosecutor of Public Security in Baja California, after being identified by Gilberto Sánchez Guerrero, "El Gil," for allegedly participating in organized crime activities.

Lieutenant Colonel Julián Leyzaola Pérez was hired to reform the police in Tijuana, clean up the corruption within the ranks and take on the cartels head on.

This was how Tijuana would become the first major city under Calderón to hit the cartels hard and hopefully end the corruption. It was seen as fighting the cancer from within.

Julián Leyzaola was from Sinaloa, had a degree in military administration and a post-graduate degree in administration from the School of the Americas in Fort Benning, United States.

In 1983 he graduated from the Military academy as a second lieutenant. In 1999 he was promoted to Lieutenant Colonel of the General Staff.

In December 2008 he took office as Secretary of Public Security in Tijuana.

Leyzaola fired 400 police officers as his first act as chief of police for failing integrity tests and charged 25 of them, accusing them of working for the Arellano Félix and/or the Sinaloa cartel.

Leyzaola was interviewed for the magazine The New Yorker in which he revealed that when he started working as chief of police for Tijuana, a retired military officer showed up at his office claiming to be an official representative for El Chapo Guzmán and offered him $80,000 a month to let the Sinaloa cartel operate in the city. He said he rejected the bribe and that at gunpoint, he took that ex-military man to Mexico City and handed him over to the Attorney General's Office (PGR).

On July 14, 2009 WikiLeaks leaked information that was published by La Jornada that indicated that Leyzaola had made a pact with the adversaries of the Sinaloa cartel drug trafficker Teodoro García Simental, El Teo.

He had supposedly agreed to arrest El Teo.

Leyzaola strategy was that by eliminating El Teo, Arellano Félix would "regulate" the other criminal groups and the violence in the Tijuana plaza would be reduced.

El Teo had been accused of the murder of 47 police officers and of trafficking cocaine. Operations from the state and municipal police along with the Army targeted El Teo. On November 2007 he almost got caught in Playas de Rosarito, but his collusion with the Tijuana police facilitated his escape.

Chief Leyzaola had several assassinations attempts and managed to survive all of them. They have attempted to assassinate Leyzaola with bazookas, he has been ambushed, even with trucks cloned to look like military vehicles, they have tried to take him out with car bombs, and even a sicario infiltrated his close circle of security detail to kill him by all means possible, including poison.

There is a story that circulated around mid-2009, that Chief Leyzaola had an encounter with the druglords El Teo and Raydel López Uriarte, El Muletas.

The two drug traffickers were traveling in the heart of the city escorted by a commando and managed to surround Leyzaola. According to the version of a former state official, El Muletas challenged Leyzaola to get out of his vehicle while tapping on his window. "Let's see, get out! Hurry up, bastard, here I am for whatever you want! Let's see if it's true you want to kill me!" El Muletas had shouted.

According to the version from this former official, Leyzaola did nothing. His escorts left him alone in front of the drug traffickers, who eventually left in the open as they had arrived.

At the time the plaza was controlled by El Mayo Zambada of the Sinaloa cartel. But there was some kind of truce between the criminal groups to keep the violence at a minimum.

However, when Leyzaola was chief of police in Tijuana, the amount of executions linked to drug cartels did not decrease much but reached historical figures: in 2008 there were 882 executions, in 2009 there were 655 and in 2010 there were 812.

On October 20, 2009, several journalists claim to have seen Leyzaola hit the dead body of a sicario that had been killed after a confrontation with the police. The journalists, who remained anonymous, maintained that the Leyzaola approached the body, cursed at it, kicked it, then left.

After Leyzaola left Tijuana, the Mayor of Ciudad Juarez, Héctor Murguía, named Leyzaola as his secretary of Public Security.

Leyzaola got the green light through the governor of Chihuahua, César Duarte; by the Secretary of Defense, General Guillermo Galván, and by the very own President Felipe Calderón. Everyone saw in Leyzaola the best option to "manage" the cartel violence in Juarez, the same way he had done in Tijuana.

On his first day on the job in Juarez, the cartels left a body on the streets with a message to Leyzaola saying "this is what awaits you here." Leyzaola was threatened and told that every day he was in office a police officer will be killed every day until he resigned. A previous chief had resigned under similar circumstances, but not Leyzaola, he took the fight to the streets. He targeted the Juarez cartel, La Linea and the street gang of Los Aztecas aggressively reducing violence in

Juarez. On the other hand, this allowed the Sinaloa cartel to prosper in Juarez, as they had also done in Tijuana.

Julián Leyzaola made some strong statements after learning about the arrest of the four gunmen who executed José Manuel Rivas in 2011, the police coordinator of the Municipal Police station Benito Juárez.

The chief said he was extremely angry about what happened, "let them threaten me those dogs sons of bitches" (Que me amenacen a mí esos perros hijos de la chingada), he said while challenging the members of the Sinaloa Cartel.

Leyzaola decided to work out of the station Benito Juárez, after police officers said that they were afraid to work in this particular police station.

Leyzaola said there was no doubt in his mind that his police agency had bad cops working for organize crime, "That makes us vulnerable to any attack, we cannot have corrupt people in the Police and soon I will fire them."

Leyzaola fired around 800 police officers in Ciudad Juarez and made an attempt to clean up the department.

After he retired from police work, Julián Leyzaola would eventually be shot three times by a hitman in Ciudad Juarez and left paralyzed.

This really piqued my interest in learning of the extent of corruption from the municipal police departments in Mexico. Most had no choice, it was either "plata o plomo," silver or lead. You are with us or against us.

Cartels were known to instill fear in the local police department by threatening families, not to mention the amount of money spent in bribes was a lot more lucrative than their salary. The bribe and corruption activities among the local police is a staple of the Mexican police norm, it has always been like this. Everyone knows this, even the US tourists.

The border between El Paso (population: 600,000) and Juárez (population: 1.5 million) is the most menacing spot along America's southern underbelly.

On one side is one of the safest cities of its size in the United States, with only 15 murders so far in 2008. On the other is a slaughterhouse ruled by cartel bosses where the death toll the same year is more than 1,300 and counting.

"I don't think the average American has any idea of what's going on immediately south of our border," says Kevin Kozak, acting special agent in charge of the Immigration and Customs Enforcement's office of investigations in El Paso. "It's almost beyond belief."

"The majority of the people detained and the bodies found are not from Ciudad Juarez. It is an intense battle between these two groups (Juarez and Sinaloa cartels). The level of violence has reached new levels. Retaliation between the groups has become more violent and terrorizing," said Reyes Ferriz, who is the Mayor of Ciudad Juarez but lives in El Paso.

Dismemberments and beheadings have become a common method of retaliation. A government source told about a case where a relative of a drug cartel member was tied to two trucks and stretched until his arms where ripped apart.

The dead are mostly unknown obscured figures in the underground world of the drug trade but are also innocents caught in the crossfire, make up a long procession of clients for busy coroner and daily material for the media sources and blogs (we can hardly keep up). But the mayor downplayed the effect on the general population.

"The important thing for the population is that the large majority of these cases are criminals. We haven't had many cases in which the general population has been involved," Reyes Ferriz said.

The city's tourism economy is sinking and the recession has cut deeply into border trade, but the death industry here is robust and flourishing. Hell, the police even ran out of crime scene tape. The government can hardly keep up with the rising boom in the business of death and murder, the only thing where production is going up.

Regardless of the political take on the problem and what is necessary to find peace and tranquility in the streets of Juarez, the people of Juarez live a daily life of misery and despair. It is honorable to see that the mayor has a positive outlook in the Juarez' mayhem to the point that he sees light at the end of the tunnel, because the only thing that the town has seen lately is a bullet at the end of a gun barrel.

Juárez looks a lot like a failed state, with no government entity capable of imposing order and a profusion of powerful organizations that kill and plunder at will.

The Juárez Cartel controlled one of the primary transportation routes for billions of dollars' worth of illegal drug shipments annually entering the United States from Mexico. Since 2007, the Juárez Cartel had been locked in a vicious battle with its former partner, the Sinaloa Cartel, for control of Ciudad Juárez. Both sides recruited cross-border third generation street gangs to wage their fight.

The Juárez Cartel recruited Barrio Azteca while the Sinaloa Cartel recruited a rival gang called the Artist Assassins (Double A's) and Los Mexicles.

Barrio Azteca is one of the most violent prison gangs in the United States. The gang is highly structured and has an estimated membership of 2,000. Most members are Mexican nationals or Mexican American males. Barrio Azteca is most active in the southwestern region, primarily in federal, state, and local corrections facilities in Texas and outside prison in southwestern Texas and southeastern New Mexico.

The gang's main source of income is derived from smuggling heroin, powdered cocaine, and marijuana from Mexico into the United States for distribution both inside and outside prisons.

Gang members often transport illicit drugs across the U.S.–Mexico border for DTOs. Barrio Azteca members are also involved in alien smuggling, arson, assault, auto theft, burglary, extortion, intimidation, kidnapping, robbery, and weapons violations.

The Barrio Azteca was founded in 1986 by gangsters Benito "Benny" Acosta, Alberto "Indio" Estrada, Benjamín "T-Top" Olivarez, Manuel "Tolon" Cardoza, Manuel "El Grande" Fernandez, Raúl "Rabillo" Fierro and José "Gitano" Ledesma.

The gang succeeded in attracting thousands of violent offenders who hated the Mexikanemi and Texas Syndicate. The Barrio Azteca's primary goal was to dominate the prison system and gain control of its lucrative drug trade.

Members of this ruthless prison gang are all Hispanic and most from El Paso, west Texas and northern Mexico. The gang has grown to become one of the nation's most dangerous prison gangs and is currently on the FBI and DEA's #1 threat list.

Following their emergence into the prison gang scene, both the Texas Syndicate and Mexican Mafia refused to recognize the Aztecas and declared war on the gang. The outnumbered Aztecas struggle to battle their numerous enemies but somehow managed to prevail by murdering several members of the Texas Syndicate in prisons and jails all over the state of Texas.

Barrio Azteca earned the respect of the Texas Syndicate and Mexican Mafia and a peace treaty was signed on July of 1997. The Aztecas have multiplied and now outnumber the Texas Syndicate. The highly organized prison gang currently operates in both state and federal prisons all over the United States and Mexico.

Symbols: *915, EPT, 21, BA, Azteca theme tattoos*

Territory: *El Paso TX, Ciudad Juarez, Midland TX, Odessa TX, Las Cruces New Mexico, and small chapters across the United States and northern Mexican state of Chihuahua.*

Alliances: *Juarez Cartel*

Members: *2,000*

Ethnicity: *Hispanic*

La Gente Nueva was believed to be the enforcers for the Sinaloa cartel while La Línea was known to be the armed wing of the Juárez Cartel.

The House of Death and Special Agent 913

Lalo use to patrol the federal highways in Guadalajara. He was eventually fired from the police department and decided to join the narco trafficking world. Lalo would say that the only other job any former policemen can get is that of a drug trafficker. Lalo joined the Juarez cartel and started participating in executions. He told of the main executioner, a Chihuahua state police commander by the name of Miguel Loya Gallegos or "Comandante Loya" who was the night commander assigned to Ciudad Juarez and was a leader of La Linea. Lalo read something somewhere that the DEA was looking for informants in Mexico, so he went to the border point of entry and becomes an informant for US Customs. Lalo become special agent 913. Lalo briefed the US agents regularly and many times included members of the DEA, the FBI and ATF.

In 2003, Lalo was caught at a border patrol checkpoint in Las Cruces trying to smuggle 100 pounds of marijuana. Lalo explained that he did not have time to tell US authorities that he was working a case for information, but the DEA did not buy the story and they drop him as an informant. ICE kept using him, saying he was too valuable.

A Mexican attorney by the name of Fernando Reyes was looking for a way to cross a load of weed across the border. Lalo could make it happen for him, he knew all the contacts. Lalo brought Fernando to this little house in the city of Juarez. Fernando doesn't know it yet, but he has walked in to a trap. In the house are also two officers from the state police of Chihuahua.

Fernando is unaware, but they are there to kill him. Suddenly one of the police officers comes out from one of the rooms and puts the gun to his face. Fernando pleads for his life, he knows he is in trouble. They decide not using the gun, it's too loud, they can't take any chances.

This house is located in a middle-class neighborhood and people will call the police if they hear gunshots. Fernando screams in panic. They tape his mouth shut in attempts to stifle the loud screams. Fernando fights back, kicking and swinging his arm, so they take him down to the floor. But it's not easy, Fernando is fighting for his life. Lalo helps to restrain Fernando while one of the officers wraps an extension cord around the neck of Fernando. Fernando knows his death is certain but continues to fight, he does not want to die like this.

The chord snaps.

One of the cops grabs a plastic bag and places it over Fernando's head. Fernando continues to kick and fight, but is futile, he finally lays motionless as his life is snuffed from him. Lalo crosses the street and finds Santillan at the little convenience store on the corner. Heriberto Santillan-Tabares, known to U.S. intelligence as "El Ingeniero," is one of the top bosses in the Juarez cartel. He has thinning dark hair and a mustache.

The officers split $2,000 for killing a suspected drug trafficker known as "Fernando."

The killing was ordered by Santillan, a childhood friend of the victim and a top lieutenant in the powerful Juarez cartel organization.

Fernando is dead and they have his dope. Santillan congratulates Lalo, he tells him that Vicente Carrillo Fuentes will be happy.

The next day Lalo crosses in to El Paso and tells his handler from the Immigration Customs Enforcement what happened. Lalo is an undercover informant for the US immigration enforcement unit. Immigration listens to the recording from Lalo, they write a report and these reports make their way up to Washington DC. Lalo's handler from the US Customs Enforcement tells him he did a good job and sends him on his way, to gather further intel. Lalo participates in 11 more executions in that little house dubbed the House of Death.

Throughout the fall and winter of 2003, the killing at the House of Death continued. The cartel comes up with a code word for the executions that occur there: carne asadas, or barbecues. Lalo is often called to open the house for a carne asada, and when the killing is done, he is responsible for disposing of the bodies, most are buried in the back yard.

In November, two drug mules, "Paisa" and "El Chapo", lose 70 kilos on the Free Bridge (puente libre) in Juarez. The load belonged to Comandante Loya of the state Chihuahua police, Santillan's nephew. So, Lalo takes the two mules to the House of Death. Santillan shows up with Comandante Loya and another killer named "Crooked Fingers." Lalo tells Paisa and El Chapo, "You have to take business with us seriously." The Comandante tells them to lift their shirts over their faces so they don't see the boss, who is going to arrive shortly. He begins wrapping tape over their heads, but they can still breathe. One of the men starts moaning, so the Comandante shoots him in the head, at which point the other tries to break free. The Comandante shoots him in the head too.

On and on it goes.

One arrived DOA in a black plastic bag. Two police officers carry him in. He is so heavy they have to drop him in the kitchen; he doesn't fit under the staircase. Another is brought in with a rope around his neck. There was a third, the cops say, but he crawled under a truck, and so they shot him there and left him in the street.

Each time Lalo is asked to open the house for a carne asada, he will later say, he tells his handlers at ICE.

Everything fell apart on the House of Death when three people were tortured and eventually murdered at the house. One of them gave an address of a house, that happened to be the home of a DEA agent operating in Juarez. The Santillanes crew went to the house, but the occupants, a mother with children was afraid to open the door. She called her husband, and the entire family decided to flee. They were being watched. While driving away they were pulled over by Mexican state police officers in marked police cars. It was comandante Loya's police crew. It was certain that they intended to take them to the house of death.

The driver made a phone call to get some help from one of his colleagues. Both were DEA agents and presented consular ID's to the officers at the scene.

Lalo was able to confirm from his US contacts that they were DEA agents, after making a phone call. They did not want to bring attention by killing two DEA agents, so they let them go.

After the proverbial shit hit the fan and DEA agents' lives were put in grave danger and the out-of-control case sped faster off the cliff, one senior agent had enough. "We had five to six DEA staff members in danger as well as their families," said Sandalio 'Sandy' Gonzalez the retired special agent in charge for the El Paso DEA office.

Eventually, the covers/identities of several DEA agents living in Mexico were blown by people that had been executed in the house. The US government evacuated the agents and their families from Juarez, Mexico, several arrest of cartel bosses were made and the Mexican government excavated several bodies from the back yard of the house of horror.

Comandante Loya and some of the other killers went into hiding. The DEA informed ICE that there were 80 AFI agents from Mexico City on their way to Juarez to help capture Loya and his criminal associates. They would take the police station by force if necessary. Comandante Loya escaped arrest, however, several state police officers were arrested or detained.

Mexican state police Commander Loya mysteriously disappeared. Some people think comandante Loya is probably dead.

Days later an attempt was made on Lalo's life at an El Paso Whataburger.

Lalo arranged to pick up some money at an El Paso Whataburger. Lalo said that the money drop was tied to some work he was still doing for ICE, but federal agents say that's not correct. They suggest the money stemmed from the proceeds of some property Lalo had recently sold in Juárez. While others speculate that it was money owed from the Juarez cartel.

Whatever the case, the ever-wary Lalo sent a friend to the Whataburger to collect the money. Lalo's fill-in was sitting in his car in the restaurant parking lot when a gunman appeared out of nowhere and pumped four bullets into his chest before disappearing.

Lalo's friend, who also happened to be an FBI informant, died instantly.

After that, ICE took Lalo and his family into protective custody. Lalo was put into an undisclosed prison. His family was housed somewhere in the US.

Why send a former U.S. snitch who earned more than $250,000 from Uncle Sam to certain death?

At an immigration removal hearing in Bloomington, Minnesota, in August of 2005, Lalo was asked what would happen to him if he was sent back to Mexico.

"Well, they will kill me or they will torture me and then they will kill me," he says.

"Who will?"

"Yeah, the police, the cartel, the government, it's all the same people."

"Why do you say it's the same people?"

"Because the police work for the cartel."

He testified that the power of the Juarez cartel extends all the way to former Mexico President Vicente Fox, and that the cartel once used ships from the Mexican Navy to transport drugs from Colombia to Mexico, and that the PGR, Mexico's federal police, would then fly the drugs to Juarez.

Lalo became an informant because he always felt he belonged in the law enforcement side, being a former police officer himself. He felt he was doing the honorable thing. He also had a soft heart toward law enforcement and respected the US lawmen in general.

Bill Conroy of the Narco News Bulletin covered many of these events concerning Lalo and the "house of Death" at length.

Lalo's real name is Guillermo Eduardo Ramirez-Peyro.

I heard a rumor that he visits Albuquerque often (he most likely has his family living in or around Albuquerque) and has occasional acquaintances that he has befriended that are retired Albuquerque Police officers (APD). In the past he has always trusted US police officers and has enjoys their company. Over some beers, he has told them about his exploits while an undercover informant for ICE. A retired APD officer told me about his many meetings with Lalo, telling me about drug cartel stories that even I would not believe, if I did not know what I know.

No one believes it, it just sounds too incredible.

Armed to the Teeth

The weaponry used by the cartels in Mexico is extensive and high powered. Mexican police officers who only carry a side arm for patrolling are under-armed in most cases and are essentially in a suicidal mission if they elect to engaged heavily armed sicarios. Most sicarios carry ar-15 or ak-47, if not more power firepower.

Most of the time cartels in Mexico over power the police and at times even the military. Cartels spend millions of dollars from their drug profits to arm themselves to the teeth. Law enforcement faces sicarios that are armed with assault rifles that are fully automatic, 50mm style machine guns and fragmentation grenades. The prospect of confronting armed cartels in Mexico is daunting and extremely intimidating. To give you an example let's look at the operation that was carried out in Michoacan on September 2008 by the military.

An arsenal consisting of 18 assault rifles, 222 handguns of different calibers, 38 grenades and more than 10 thousand rounds were seized. Also seized were drugs, police uniforms and radio communication equipment. This was the result after Mexican military conducted six simultaneous search warrants carried out in Morelia and Zamora, all part of the Joint Operation Michoacán.

According to reports from the 21st Military Zone, the work was carried out after military intelligence received information from anonymous citizens demanding action against organized crime.

Military elements, once they had gathered their intelligence work, designed the strategy to carry out the search warrants simultaneously, five of them in Morelia and one in the municipality of Zamora, where they managed to secure the arsenal.

One of the operations was carried out in the Michoacán capital, where the military found a motor scooter and ten wrapped packages with the drug "rock."

Another operation was in the house that is located in the corner of the streets Caucho y Bambú, located in the neighborhood Jardines del Rincón, where they found and secured 6 assault rifles ar-15, ak-47 and a IMI Galil, in addition to seven super .38 caliber handguns.

On the same location, they recovered nine fragmentation grenades and two gas grenades, along with 455 rounds of ammunition of different caliber, 42 magazines for various weapons and uniforms with logos of different police agencies, bulletproof vests, tactical vests, blue shirts, police patches, police caps, several pairs of military type boots and several sets of handcuffs.

Also, in a house that was located on Juan Jose Escalona Street, in the community of Ejidal Ocolusen, they seized three vehicles, about four kilos of marijuana, in addition to 25 small wrap containers of "rock" and heroin.

Meanwhile, on another operation the military arrived at Sauce Street between the streets of Obispo de Acueducto and Fray Antonio San Miguel, in the Rincón de Ocolusen subdivision, where they recovered 12 assault rifles of different calibers, 12 handguns of various calibers, one addition to a grenade launcher, three grenades for the launcher, seven 40 millimeter grenades, nine grenades fragmentation grenades, eight smoke grenades, 145 magazines for various weapons and 6,850 rounds of ammunition of different calibers.

In the same place the military located two telescopic sights, thirteen loaders for caliber 2.23 rounds, 45 strips of ammunition for 50mm caliber machine gun, eight boxes of rounds for 2.23 caliber rifle, 25 uniforms with FF MM logos, 60 uniforms with federal police logo, ten municipal police uniforms, two telescopic sights, gas masks, insignia, holsters and cartridge belts.

Among Mexican traffickers, the AK-47 it has earned itself the nickname "cuerno de chivo" or "goat horn" because of its distinctive banana-shaped magazine.

Since the federal law banning assault weapons expired in 2004, so-called "straw purchasers" have flooded U.S. gun stores in the Southwest, mostly in Texas and Arizona, sweeping up these and other weapons. Court documents show such purchasers buying as many as 20 AK-47s at a time, paying as much as $11,000 in cash. Typically, the purchaser turns the guns over to a broker who takes them across the border to Mexico, where such weapons cannot be bought legally. The weapons are sold to the cartels, often for three or four times the original price.

Gun rights advocates reject the term "assault weapon" and refers to high-powered guns as "modern sporting rifles." An NSSF survey last year found that 44 percent of owners of these weapons are active-duty or former military or law-enforcement personnel, and the typical owner is 35, married and has some college education.

Once in the hands of cartel capos, however, the modern sporting rifle becomes very much an assault weapon.

Violence in Mexico has claimed nearly 71,000 lives during President Felipe Calderon began a military offensive aimed at overpowering drug cartels.

Military-style weaponry has enabled the drug trafficking organizations to match and sometimes overwhelm the firepower of Mexican law enforcement.

In May 2008, Mexican federal police raided a suspected trafficker house in Culiacan, a long-standing drug hotbed in the Mexican state of Sinaloa. Cartel gunmen armed with AK-47s purchased in Arizona overwhelmed the police, killing eight.

Of 2,921 guns traced, 1,470, or 50 percent, were from Texas. A total of 852, 29 percent, were from Arizona. California, by contrast, accounted for 90 guns, three percent of the total. California gun-control activists credited that state's low total to strict state firearms laws that severely limit sales of military-style weaponry.

Another weapon popular among Mexican narcos is the Colt Super .38 pistol: Colt, based in West Hartford, Conn., is the corporate legacy of Samuel Colt, who popularized the revolver in the years before the Civil War. The "El Presidente" model is popular in Mexico because it is one of the few guns legally available there, according to the Violence Policy Center. It is cheaper at gun outlets in the U.S.

The Colt Super .38 is often found popular with Mexican cartel bosses who plate them in gold or silver and engrave them with fancy grips.

The Highway of Death

During the regime of President Felipe Calderon most of the Cartel activities were focused on different segments of Mexico. One of the most heated regions, from the time I began contributing in 2008 on BB, was the Gulf Coast where the waging battle of Los Zetas and the Gulf cartel was intensifying. The region extends from the Texas border on the north of Mexico and spreads south through the gulf coast, ending at south end on the border with Guatemala.

Shootings, executions, kidnappings and attacks happened every day in Tampico, Altamira, Cd Madero, Nuevo Laredo, Matamoros, Valle Hermoso, Rio Bravo, Ciudad Victoria, Cd Mante, Reynosa, the border "Frontera Chica" municipalities and rural areas of the state.

Highway 101 travels through the state of Taumalipas. The highway was a perilous journey that was used by Zetas to plant their seed of terror. People tell stories of mass killings of immigrants, primitive graves of people buried after being executed and buses getting hijacked only to have the passengers dragged out only to meet their ultimate ending in the most horrifying manner ever imagined. The road was so dangerous that no one dared to travel at night and tourist had to be escorted by police cars.

There are many stories on Borderland Beat of people being killed after they got snatched from their buses and hundreds of decomposing bodies found in the area of Highway 101 in San Fernando, Tamaulipas.

Mexican authorities were constantly extracting bodies from mass graves in the state of Tamaulipas not far from the US. Hundreds of corpses have surfaced following reports of passengers being pulled off buses in the area by gunmen and disappearing.

Most of all the bodies were found in pits along the township of San Fernando, Tamaulipas, where security forces located the graves while investigating reports of attacks on buses blamed on the brutal Zetas drug gang.

During most of 2010, the San Fernando municipality had suffered from constant confrontations between Zetas and members of the Gulf Cartel. General Miguel Angel Gonzalez, Commander of the Eighth Military Zone based in Tamaulipas, said that this isolated town was very important because "it is a node where several highways, strategic for drug smuggling come together."

San Fernando was a neglected area, affected by ongoing droughts that weaken agriculture, without businesses to create jobs and with commerce affected by the violence.

Los Zetas took control of the San Fernando region and imposed their rules. The group's high command, El Lazca and El Z-40, appointed Salvador Alfonso Martinez Escobedo, La Ardilla, as chief of the area. He in turn placed a former soldier, Edgar Huerta Montiel, El Wache, as lieutenant for San Fernando, along with Martin Omar Estrada Luna, El Kilo, who, in practice, acted as the area chief.

El Kilo was one of the best examples of the barbarism that characterized Mexican narcos. He was born in Mexico but lived in the United States. His first "schools" were the gangs in northern California, among them "Los Nortenos.

El Kilo went all over the town openly carrying weapons. He'd get out of his vehicle with his weapon to make purchases in the stores on the main square, where the mayor's office is located. He had 20 of the 34 San Fernando police officers on his payroll.

El Kilo inspected every bus that arrived at the municipality. "A bus would arrive every day, and every day they would make the passengers get off the bus to investigate them, to find out where they were coming from. They would check the messages on their cell phones. They would allow most people who were not involved to leave. The rest we would kill," said El Wache when he was interrogated by the Federal Police. From his paranoid point of view, all the young men who were going to the border could be recruited by the rival Gulf cartel.

The afternoon of August 22, 2010, two freight trucks were traveling on Highway 101. In the trucks were migrants from Central America trying to reach their dream to make it to America. About nine miles north of San Fernando, the hopes of the migrants ended and their nightmare began; they encountered three vehicles blocking the highway carrying armed men with their faces covered.

"We're Zetas," they identified themselves, then asked the migrants to get off the trucks. Then they took them in pickup trucks to the warehouse of an abandoned ranch. There, 58 men and 14 women were taken down off the trucks and placed against the walls in the store room. First, they questioned them to find out where they were coming from and what they did for a living. They all denied they were working for the Gulf Cartel.

Their captors wanted to force them to work for them, but the migrants refused the offer. In the face of such a refusal, they made them lie down on the floor with their faces (facing) down. They told them not to look up and then shot them with bursts of bullets from assault rifles. To make sure nobody was left alive, they fired a gunshot to their heads.

A man from Ecuador who was not hit by the bursts of gunfire and whose intended head shot went into his neck and came out through his jaw pretended to be dead and waited until the executioners left. He left the ranch and walked almost 15 miles until he found some marines and asked for help. "The massacre was a little while ago," he told them, but they didn't believe him.

The incident was reported to their superiors, who ordered an aerial reconnaissance of the area. That afternoon, when the Army helicopter was flying near the store room, they were attacked by criminals who were going back to the site get rid of the bodies.

It was getting dark on August 23 and the Marines withdrew to Matamoros. But they came back to the ranch the next day with reinforcements. There they found the 72 bodies.

El Wache confessed that they had killed the 72 Central American migrants on El Lazca and Z-40 orders, because they thought "they were going join with El Metro 3," the Gulf Cartel boss in Reynosa.

In addition to the massacre of the 72 migrants in San Fernando in August of 2010, authorities also discovered at least 193 bodies in 47 clandestine graves in San Fernando between April and May of 2011, and the discovery of 49 human torsos in Cadereyta in the neighboring state of Nuevo Leon in May 2012. Many other narco graves were found in the Tamaulipas state, so many Borderland Beat collaborators lost count and were unable to keep up. Almost all the body remains found in these clandestine graves were immigrants from Central America, not to mention thousands of Central America people that have been reported missing from 2008 through 2013 in the Gulf coast region of Mexico.

Michoacán – Tierra Caliente

In 2006, La Familia Michoacán (LFM) left their calling card when they threw five heads onto the dance floor of a nightclub, along with the message: "La Familia does not kill for money, does not kill women, does not kill innocent people, only those who deserve to die. Know that this is divine justice."

In an incident that shocked Mexico to its core, a new kind of way of conducting business, a drug cartel introduced itself on that day. A cartel whose ultimate goal was to set the moral compass for society and replace the state within its territory.

This was "La Familia's" maximum demonstration of terror. The group had expanded in the Tierra Caliente region. It seized control of Apatzingán from "Los Zetas" and extended its power in the States of Mexico -- where Enrique Pena Nieto was governor; Guerrero, Jalisco and Guanajuato.

La Familia's origins can be traced to a precursor group known as La Empresa that emerged as a large-scale drug-trafficking operation in 2004 through an alliance with the powerful Gulf cartel, based in northeastern Mexico.

It won local support among low-income sectors by offering loans to peasants, micro-enterprises, schools and churches, and provided other types of social assistance to the needy.

That benevolence allowed the gang to develop an important network of informants and collaborators, while it also began making efforts to infiltrate the local police and government.

La Familia cartel was sometimes described as a "pseudo-evangelical cult" since its leaders, Moreno González and Méndez Vargas, refer to the assassinations and beheadings they conducted as "divine justice" and that they may had direct or indirect ties with devotees of the New Jerusalem religious movement, which is noted for its concern for justice issues.

La Familia's boss and spiritual leader Nazario Moreno González, (a.k.a.: El Más Loco or The Maddest One) had published his own 'bible.' A copy of this 'bible' seized by Mexican federal agents revealed an ideology that mixes evangelical-style self-help with insurgent peasant slogans. Moreno González seemed to base most of his doctrine on the work by a Christian writer John Eldredge.

The Mexican justice department stated in a report that Gonzalez Moreno had made Eldredge's book Salvaje de corazón (Wild at Heart) a required reading for La Familia gang members and had paid rural teachers and National Development Education (CONAFE) to circulate Eldredge's writings throughout the Michoacán countryside. An idea central to Eldredge's message is that every man must have "a battle to fight, a beauty to rescue and an adventure to live."

Eldredge quotes from Isaiah 63, which describes God wearing blood-stained clothes, spattered as though he had been treading a wine press. Then he writes: "Talk about Braveheart. This is one fierce, wild, and passionate guy. I have never heard Mister Rogers talk like that. Come to think of it, I never heard anyone in church talk like that, either. But this is the God of heaven and Earth."

La Familia recruited members from drug rehabilitation clinics and forbid them to consume alcohol or drugs, but must transport and sell them. Advancement within the organization depended as much on regular attendance at prayer meetings as on target practice.

On July 16, 2009, a man by the name of Servando Martínez Gómez (La Tuta) identified himself as the 'chief of operations' of the cartel. In his TV message, the self-appointed spokesman for the group stated: "La Familia was created to look after the interests of our people and our family," La Tuta said. "We are a necessary evil." When the TV presenter interrupted to ask what La Familia really wanted: "The only thing we want is peace and tranquility," came the reply.

Michoacan state police commanders aided La Familia in its operations by permitting cartel operatives to use patrol cars, radio frequencies and police uniforms. Former and active state police officials used patrol cars to block off streets and help sicarios escape from other police. La Familia used state police infrastructure to establish routes and ensure the safety of their armed commandos.

La Familia declared war against Felipe Calderon through a letter which delivered a warning. The following is a segment of the message from La Familia Michoacana, reacting after the death of Nazario Moreno González.

"Beware Felipe Calderón, pray to your holy saint because we come with the blessing of our God. Our God Nazario, may God rest his soul. This will not stop until Familia Michoacana dies. And we will never die; Los Pumas, Los Bravos, Los Leones, La Resistencia, El 5-5, Los Élites, Los LF, Los Chayitos, Los Machitos, Las Fieras, Los X, Los de la A, and many more.

We are going after Calderon and all his fucking family, our groups are already in Michoacán, recognize; Cheran, Capacuaro, Cheranastico, La Arantepacua, La Mohonera, Nuevo Morelos, they are united with us. This is not "narco terrorism", it's a guerrilla, it's war for peace and against the federal troops in Michoacán, Don Juan de Arantepacua has his people and we will give our lives for everything."

La Familia also left a message to the people of Michoacán, cautioning them of the forthcoming violence between them and the federal forces :

"Do not panic, try not to go out on the streets because the pigs federales do not have any respect and this is to avoid stray bullets and more loses. Do not go to the hospitals, do not go shopping, watch TV and stay at home please.

Atte. La Familia Michoacana, El Fantasma 6 y Bravo 6.

On July 14, 2009, the cartel tortured and murdered twelve Mexican Federal Police agents and dumped their bodies along the side of a mountain highway along with a written message: "So that you come for another. We will be waiting for you here." The federal agents were investigating crime in Michoacán state; President Calderón, responded to the violence by dispatching additional 1,000 Federal Police officers to the area. The infusion, which more than tripled the number of Federal Police officers patrolling Michoacán, angered Michoacán Governor Leonel Godoy Rangel, who called it 'an occupation' and said he had not been consulted. Days later, 10 municipal police officers were arrested in connection with the slayings of the 12 federal agents.

By December 2010, the streets of Michoacán were set ablaze, burning vehicles blocked the highways. Black smoke could be seen from miles away, it was a war zone. The smell of burning tires and gun powder permeated the air. As bullets ricochet off the pavement, screams of panic could be heard as helicopters flew overhead.

Outnumbered and out gunned the criminals began to vanish into the hills surrounding Apatzingan, taking their dead with them. It would go down as one of the fiercest battles the drug war had seen, lasting several days. This was to be the last stand of the once mighty La Familia Cartel and their leader Nazario aka "El Chayo" or "El Mas Loco" Moreno Gonzalez.

Moreno Gonzalez, the intellectual and spiritual leader of La Familila Michoacana was supposedly killed during this fire fight in 2010. However, his body was never recovered. It was suspected by the authorities that the reason the gunmen fought so fiercely was to protect someone of great importance. It was widely assumed that this person was none other than Nazario Moreno Gonzalez. To Calderon this was to be a huge success; a validation of his crusade against the cartels, with or without a body. To claim with such certainty that the leader of the feared La Familia was in fact dead without a body was strange, considering the prominence of El Chayo. The people of Apatzingan mourned his death but none fully believed he actually died.

On December 12, 2010 I posted an article on BB announcing the death of Nazario Moreno Gonzalez titled ""El Chayo," boss who brought "divine justice" to Michoacán with AK-47s, killed."

"Mexican authorities said that they believe a top leader of the violent La Familia cartel was killed during two days of pitched fighting in the home state of President Felipe Calderon, Michoacán.

Mexico has struck another blow to the highest levels of ruthless drug gangs with the killing of La Familia Michoacana kingpin Nazario Moreno Gonzalez, a.k.a. "El Mas Loco" (the craziest), a messianic and violent leader who wielded vast control over the western state of Michoacán.

The drug lord's death Thursday came amid an ongoing operation that began Wednesday night in the Michoacán city of Apatzingan and has involved intense gun battles between security forces and cartel gunmen.

Federal security spokesman Alejandro Poire told the media shortly after midday Friday, reading from a prepared statement, that Moreno Gonzalez, alias "El Chayo," was one of 11 people – five federal police, three suspected cartel gunmen and three civilians – who had been killed in the operation to that point.

The operation involving federal police, army soldiers, and marines was launched after an anonymous tip alerted authorities to the presence of armed men in Apatzingan.

The ferocity with which the gunmen defended that cartel stronghold led authorities to presume that they were not only protecting a key trans-shipment point for drugs but also one of their top leaders.

Gunmen used torched and bullet-ridden vehicles to barricade roads even as federal forces pursued them with helicopter support, effectively turning parts of Michoacán into a war zone.

That southwestern state, La Familia's home base, is coveted by drug traffickers because of its marijuana and opium fields and its long stretch of Pacific coastline, ideal for receiving shipments of cocaine and chemicals used to manufacture synthetic drugs."

But something strange happened in 2014. Borderland Beat contributor Chivis posted an article on March 9, 2014 titled "El Chayo Killed. . . Again."

"A few minutes ago, the press office of the Interior Ministry (SG) confirmed a few minutes ago the announcement of the death Nazario Moreno, alias El Chayo, early Sunday in the town of Tumbicastio. He referenced the reported death of the capo in 2010, but said the body was missing. (Since then towns people and autodefensas reported to the government that he was in fact alive.)

Also reported was that armed forces located Chayo who initiated a shootout confrontation which ultimately resulted in his death. Fingerprints were used to identify the capo, but DNA studies are also being conducted. The government credits their intelligence for the capture and gave no credit to the autodefensas that have been directing them to Chayo for over a year, and 300 of them were scouts for the operation that located Chayo.

Although, the government will take all the credit, it was in fact autodefensas who not only directed the forces to Chayo, who was celebrating his birthday, but it was autodefensas who identified the dead man as Chayo. Autodefensas had reported two years ago Chayo had plastic surgery that included his face and chin.

Although the 2010 reported death was during the Calderon administration, the Peña administration continued the fallacy, and never denounced it, in spite of the autodefensas federation insistence that he was alive.

However, on March 4th, journalist Carlos Loret de Mola reported that "government sources" revealed it had 2 recent photos of Chayo and that he is alive. Other reports offer the leader usually wears all white and rides a white horse through the sierras, appearing as the mythical character he is thought to be by some."

To understand why El Chayo may had been still been alive after the report in 2010 one must look at the history of La Familia Michoacana. LFM started out as a faction of Los Zetas who went rouge. They had long standing ties with both Los Zetas and the Gulf Cartel, and received training from Los Zetas. Of all the cartels, President Calderon wanted to destroy La Familia most of all. It was personal, La Familia came from the state where he was from, and they were openly provoking the federal authorities, killing several Federal Police. Furthermore, no other state represented how far the narcos had been able to infiltrate the local institutions better than Michoacán. Some said La Familia were able to put in place a shadow government, one which paralleled the state. So, Calderon's war had a pivotal point here.

According to information received by the PGR through witness testimony, the states of California, New México, Texas, Georgia, Illinois, Atlanta, North/South Carolina and Florida were all important territories and centers of operation for 'La Familia Michoacana' in the United States, a fact that is also recognized by the DEA.

La Familia Michoacana had its principal base of operations in California and Texas, two of the states that were seeing a major influx of immigrants from Michoacán.

Often, the members of the criminal organization met and discussed strategies on improving distribution and sale, as well as the topic of more effective ways to launder money.

A protected witness named "Emilio" gave details to SIEDO that "these meetings were for the discussion of logistical strategies related to the sale of drugs in the U.S. and to leave an understanding that those on the north side of the border needed to charge the correct amount, so all the accounts and figures would end up evenly on both sides."

As had happened with the Gulf Cartel, Los Zetas, the Sinaloa Cartel and the Beltran Leyva Organization, La Familia Cartel fragmented and, triggered a struggle for leadership and control of the business after the heads of the organization were taken down. A new group emerged, a copy of La Familia's tactics and strategies for social and political infiltration:

After the death of Nazario Moreno González, leader of the La Familia Michoacana cartel, the other cartel co-founders, Enrique Plancarte Solís and Servando Gómez Martínez, formed an offshoot of La Familia calling itself Caballeros Templarios. Dionicio Loya Plancarte would also join.

Various objects seized by the police in the Mexican state of Michoacan, revealed that the mysterious 'Knights Templar" drug cartel is more bizarre than most people imagine.

There were four hooded tunics, with a red cross, a metal helmet, and a pamphlet or Templar rule book. This drug cartel claims to draw inspiration from the medieval Christian warriors who fought to protect Jerusalem and the Holy Grail.

The rules in the modern day 'templar bible' call for observance of 'gentleman' like behavior and respect for women – but also state that any disclosure of knights templar activities will result in the death of the person and his whole family, and confiscation by the cartel of the snitch's property.

The cartel is like a secret society.

Like La Familia, the Knights claim to be pious and patriotic protectors of the Michoacán community even as they traffic and murder. When they first announced themselves last spring, they hung more than 40 narcomanteles, or drug-cartel banners, across the state with a message promising security. "Our commitment is to safeguard order, avoid robberies, kidnapping, extortion, and to shield the state from rival organizations," they said. A week later, their first victim was hanged from an overpass with a note claiming that he was a kidnapper.

The Mexican Templars have an initiation ritual, which apparently includes dressing up like knights from the Middle Ages and performing blood pacts.

The cartel recruits drug users and enrolls them in the organization's rehabilitation centers; the process is closely monitored and has a strong religious component.

The double standard is striking: the Templars cannot take drugs, and yet they run one of the biggest methamphetamines traffic corridors to the United States.

The Knights Templar appeared to be successfully usurping La Familia's turf. As a result, Mexican army and police commanders made a promised to take them down with the same energy they summoned to destroy La Familia. But it was not easy, the Knights did not go quietly due to the cartel's structure, wealth, and size. It was perhaps the second most notorious Mexican cartel in terms of killing methods, the most vicious one, second only to the Zetas, is a group formed by Mexican army special forces in the 90s.

Not long after I stopped reporting on Borderland Beat did the Autodefensas or self-defenders organized in Tierra

Caliente. They were sometimes called Policia Comunitaria or Community Police and became vigilantes to fight against the cartels. Initially the Mexican government/military allowed them to operate, but eventually they attempted to stop them and resulted in the arrest of a few of their leaders.

The King of Crystal

Ignacio "Nacho" Coronel Villarreal did not know that they were coming for him until he had the military on top of him.

Literally.

The Mexican military elite group arrived by air and lined up in "single column," as the military refers to a particular formation. When he reacted, Colonel broke a window and tried to flee through the garden of his safe house, where he had been hiding for at least two weeks, afraid of being apprehended. He knew, that the fence working against him was too far away, was not coming to him fast enough.

Iran Francisco Quiñones Gastélum, the only man who accompanied the capo, and the physiotherapist who had provided him with a massage minutes before the military assault, made their way out through the broken glass, but were immediately stopped on the grass. Nacho Colonel turned back on his steps and went back inside his home. He ran up some stairs that lead to a corridor on the left to the main bedroom and on to the right was the living room.

He didn't get anywhere. He turned toward the soldiers coming up and fired five or six shots with an M-16 assault style rifle, caliber 5.56, that killed one soldier and wounded another. A few steps later he ran into a 12mm Mossberg shotgun. Nacho took two gunshots from the shotgun center mass, one in the abdomen and one in the thorax from a soldier at no more than four meters away. The pellets entered from his left side, almost on his back. The shot, at a wide range did not spread much. Nacho Colonel was dead.

Killed at the age of 55 years of age Nacho had been considered number three of the Sinaola Cartel behind only to Joaquín "El Chapo" Guzmán and Ismael "Mayo" Zambada.

A video seemed to confirm a different version that in the first contact with Colonel he had received several shots.

Details of the scene of his death, his body laid on the stairs with blood coming from his mouth, a hemorrhage. Near a plant you could see his favorite handgun with a diamond-covered grip. The military had said that Colonel fired at them with an M-16 rifle, which is not visible in the video or pictures taken of the scene. They say that the shotgun that killed Ignacio Coronel was usually used to force open doors.

During the years when the El Cártel del Pacífico was consolidated as the most violent and powerful criminal group (Sinaloa had been a part), an organization with the greatest capacity for the cultivation of heroin, as well as the trafficking of cocaine from South America, Colonel Villarreal was an important piece of the puzzle.

Nacho Colonel bought tons of cocaine from the Colombian cartels and was responsible for the production of large quantities of methamphetamines in clandestine laboratories. That earned him the nickname "The King of the Crystal."

"The King of Crystal" began his criminal career working next to "The Lord of the Skies," Amado Carrillo Fuentes. Carrillo "turned over" Nacho Coronel to the authorities in 1993, but the Sinaloa Cartel helped him to obtain his freedom.

After the escape of El Chapo from the prison Federal Center for Social Readaptation 2, West, in Puente Grande, Jalisco, the organization known as the Sinaloa Cartel was divided among Nacho Coronel, Ismael El Mayo Zambada and Juan José Esparragoza Moreno, El Azul.

Nacho became the right hand of Joaquín "El Chapo" Guzmán, someone that he had the most confidence to operate Jalisco, Colima and Nayarit. These areas that had been for the most part kept away from cartel violence. Especially the out of control violence that resulted from conflicts between Joaquín "El Chapo" Guzmán and the Beltrán Leyva brothers, that brought a series of murders along the Pacific coast and beyond.

The Beltrán Leyva brothers allied themselves with Los Zetas to face the powerful Sinaloa Cartel and its main leaders: El Chapo, El Azul, El Mayo and El Nacho.

The Beltrán Leyva Organization (BLO) and Los Zetas kidnapped and murdered the son of Colonel, Alejandro Coronel who was only 16 years of age. This heightened the violence and forced Nacho to enter the conflict against the BLO. Nacho responded to the death of his son by kidnapping the wife of Héctor "El Hache" Beltran Leyva, whom he soon released with a message: "I give you your wife back, healthy and unharmed so you can see and learn that for us the family is sacred."

In his thirst for revenge, "Nacho" Colonel was located by elements of the Mexican Marines. After they had located his whereabouts, an operation was launched to capture Nacho at his residence in the Colinas de San Javier community, in Zapopan, Jalisco.

The death of the Colonel left a power vacuum in the synthetic drug trafficking, which Nemesio Oseguera Cervantes aka "El Mencho" took advantage to create the Jalisco New Generation Cartel (JNGC) and dominate the west of the country after winning the battle against Ramiro Pozos González, aka 'El Molca', leader of La Resistencia.

The death of nacho was indeed a heavy loss for the Pacific Cartel operation, but El Chapo Guzmán already had the support of a cousin of Nacho Colonel. It was Inés Coronel Barreras, who eventually also became his father-in-law.

Colonel Barreras and his children, Inés Omar and Édgar Coronel Aispuro were operators of El Chapo Guzmán, for the Durango and Chihuahua region.

But El Chapo Guzmán became interested in Emma, the youngest daughter of Colonel Barreras, who in 2007 was the queen of the Guava and Coffee Fair in Canelas, Durango, where the entire Colonel's family originated. On July 2, 2008 the wedding was held in a ranch located in La Angostura, in the Golden Triangle area, in the limits of the states of Durango, Sinaloa and Chihuahua.

There were rumors that El Chapo Guzman made an agreement with the cabinet of President Felipe Calderon to give up Nacho Colonel to make it seem like the Mexican government was also hitting the Sinaloa Cartel. The Felipe Calderon was under fire that they were not targeting the high leadership of the Sinaloa enterprise.

In Mexico there has been just two known narcocorridos to Nacho's name, a kind of musical subgenre that feeds the ego of Mexican traffickers. One of them portraits "Nacho" Colonel a brave warrior who does not hesitate to challenge and engage the military in combat.

The Golden Triangle

Another region was the "Golden Triangle" that is primarily controlled by the Sinaloa Cartel while to some extend it also includes the Juarez Cartel, Tijuana Cartel and the Beltran Leyva Organization. The Golden Triangle is located in the states of Sinaloa, Durango, and Chihuahua. The region is mostly the mountain range of the Sierra Madre Occidental (western range of the Sierra Madre) that is used by the Sinaloa cartel to cultivate Mexican opium and marijuana.

This was the exact area where we use to ride the remote mountains on our motorcycles during the Christmas break. For some time, I had no clue to what extent the narco influence pervaded the region and made it dangerous if you found yourself involved directly or indirectly by accident.

Young sicarios driving late model luxurious pickup trucks and almost all of them carrying long rifles, guard the region to keep out rival cartels. This region is a main corridor for the trafficking of drugs targeted for the US. Two Sinaloa cell groups that control the mountains are "Los Salgueiro" and "Los Chavez Matamoros" This area is commanded by Sinaloa bosses Joaquin "El Chapo" Guzman Loera and Ismael "El Mayo" Zambada. There is a huge presence of members of the "Los Salgueiro" who can be found in villages like Batopilas around Guachochi and up to Creel. The vast majority of the municipal police provide support to most of the heavily armed sicarios in the region. Through the rugged mountain wilderness of Chihuahua, Sinaloa and Durango, the marijuana and opium poppy make its way to entry ports of Janos and Ojinaga.

It was not always like that, in 2008 Juarez Cartel controlled the region, where they charged "piso de plaza" or a toll for anyone wanting to do business in the region. It was the same year that a boss of the Juarez Cartel, Anicasio "El

Cacho" Cevallos was killed and violence spread from Guachochi to outlining areas of Sinaloa and Durango. Cevallo had been the one responsible for a massacre in Creel that killed 13. Sinaloa Cartel stopped the "cuotas" (protection money) and punished anyone who dare to betray the rules of Sinaloa Cartel. During this time Guachochi was a hot plaza, classified as the most violent in the world.

Like Pancho Villa did during the Mexican revolution, who hid in the Sierra Madres when he was pursued by US General Pershing, "El Chapo" Guzmán used the same mountains to hide. According to a federal report, Guzmán remained primarily inaccessible in the vast remote areas of the "Golden Triangle."

He was the barefoot son of a peasant who became one of the richest moguls in the world, a billionaire entrepreneur with a third-grade education. He controlled a vast drug distribution empire that spanned six continents, but he still carried his own AK-47. He was generous and feared, a mass murderer and a folk hero. He was a ghost who become a legend.

A general with an incorruptible reputation started to scale the highest peaks of the mountains that form El Triangulo Dorado, or the Golden Triangle. As a military commander of an elite Army unit, he was on a mission for one of the last hunts being undertaken by the government of Felipe Calderón that was seeking a trophy before the end of his failed administration in his drug war. The Mexican president was seeking the capture of El Chapo or El Mayo, the two leaders of the Sinaloa cartel, and they say, the world's most wanted. Any pacts or agreements made previously, did not mean much toward the end of his presidency. But it would not be easy, it would have to be an action of betrayal. He would use the same MO of the cartels themselves, not personal matter, just a business (political) decision.

It is the Sierra Madre mountains of Mexico that had exhausted the military, consumed the presidency of Felipe Calderon and left more than 43,000 dead in drug violence. In the Sierra Madre Joaquin "El Chapo" Guzman, the founder of the Sinaloa cartel, reigns supreme.

El Chapo Reigns; Supreme Capo

During my time reporting on Borderland Beat (from 2008 through 2013), Joaquín Archivaldo Guzmán Loera otherwise known as El Chapo remained at large. He had escaped from a maximum-security prison, Puente Grande in Jalisco, Mexico on January 19, 2001, in a laundry cart. The planned escape required bribes and cooperation allegedly costing him $2.5 million dollars.

He had obtained the nickname of El Chapo (Shorty) because of his 5 feet, 6 inches in height. Born in Sinaloa, Guzmán came from a poor farming family and was constantly physically abused by his father. As a child, he sold oranges and dropped out of school in third grade to work with his father. Through his father, Guzmán entered the drug trade, helping him cultivate marijuana and opium poppy for local dealers during his early adulthood.

After the fall of the Guadalajara Cartel, a summit took place in Acapulco and the group agreed to divide the territory in different organizations.

The Arellano Félix brothers formed the Tijuana Cartel, which controlled the Tijuana corridor and parts of Baja California. In Chihuahua state, a group controlled by the Carrillo Fuentes family formed the Juárez Cartel. The remaining region of Sinaloa and the Pacific Coast was formed as the Sinaloa Cartel under Ismael "El Mayo" Zambada and El Chapo Guzmán.

Guzmán always wanted to take control of Ciudad Juárez, a major drug crossing point, which was in the hands of the Carrillo Fuentes family of the Juárez Cartel. Guzmán convened a meeting in Monterrey with Ismael Zambada García ("El Mayo"), Juan José Esparragoza Moreno ("El Azul") and Arturo Beltrán Leyva. In this meeting, they discussed killing Rodolfo Carrillo Fuentes, who was in charge of the Juárez Cartel at the time.

On September 11, 2004, Rodolfo, his wife and two young children were visiting a Culiacán shopping mall. While leaving the mall, escorted by police commander Pedro Pérez López, the family was ambushed by members of Los Negros, assassins for the Sinaloa Cartel. Rodolfo and his wife were killed.

Ciudad Juárez found itself in the front line of the Mexican Drug War and would see homicides skyrocket as Sinaloa and Juarez fought for control. El Chapo would be the first drug lord to break the nonaggression "pact" the major cartels had agreed to, setting in motion a fighting between both cartels for drug routes that has claimed thousands of lives.

Mexican President Felipe Calderón took office in December 2006 and started to go to war against the cartels using the Mexican military and federal police, this was an attempt to stem the increase of violence. After four years in office, Calderon failed to slowed down the flow of drugs or the killings tied to the drug war. Of the 53,000 arrests made from 2010 to 2014, only 1,000 involved members of the Sinaloa Cartel, which led to suspect that Calderón was intentionally allowing Sinaloa to win the drug war. El Chapo's rival cartel leaders were suddenly being killed and their structure dismantled by the Calderon war on drugs, but the Sinaloa cartel was relatively unaffected. This allowed the Sinaloa to take over other rival's plazas as Tijuana, but also included the coveted Ciudad Juárez-El Paso corridor.

In a Newsweek investigation, it was alleged that in order for El Chapo to maintaining his dominance among rival cartels, he filtered information to the DEA and U.S. Immigration and Customs Enforcement that led to the arrests of his adversaries in the Juárez Cartel.

El Chapo is alleged to have also filtered information that led to the arrests of some of his top Sinaloa leaders. It is speculated that these arrests of his people were part of a deal Guzmán made with Calderón in exchange for immunity from arrest and prosecution. This would give the perception that the Calderón's government was heavily pursuing the Sinaloa cartel during his presidential term in office. This was a key factor influencing the breakaway between the Sinaloa Cartel and the Beltrán Leyva brothers, five brothers who served as Guzmán's top lieutenants. The arrest of Alfredo "El Mochomo" Beltran Leyva was attributed to El Chapo. There was also the understanding that El Chapo played a significant role in the death of his top Sinaloa deputy "Nacho" Coronel by Mexican federal forces in Guerreo.

Guzmán was known among drug lords for his longevity and evasion of authorities, assisted by alleged bribes to high level federal authorities, along with state and local officials. The huge military and federal police presence in Sinaloa for the manhunt of El Chapo failed to capture him for years. His elusiveness from law enforcement made him a legendary figure in Mexico's narcotics folklore. Stories abounded that Guzmán sometimes strolled into restaurants, his bodyguards confiscating peoples' cellphones and after eating his meal, he left paying for everyone's tab. Rumors circulated of Guzmán being seen in different parts of Mexico and abroad.

We always wonder what he looked like, as the only pictures known of him were when he had been incarcerated in prison in 2001 or old ones from before. Borderland Beat posted a couple pictures that were exclusive of the supposed Capo, but it was very hard to verify the authenticity.

For more than thirteen years, Mexican security forces coordinated many operations to re-arrest him, but their efforts were largely in vain as Guzmán appeared to be steps ahead of them.

Although his whereabouts were unknown, the authorities suspected that he was likely hiding in the mountains of the "Golden Triangle" where he grew up. Guzmán reportedly commanded a sophisticated security circle of at least 300 informants and gunmen resembling the manpower equivalent to those of a head of state. His inner circle would help him move around through several isolated ranches in the mountainous area to avoid capture.

He would eventually be arrested, only after he made two key mistakes. One grave mistake he made was to finally go public after an infatuation with a Mexican actress from a narco novela (soap opera actress Kate del Castillo). His meeting with the Mexican actress and American actor Sean Penn, allowed the Mexican and US government to pinpoint the location of the capo. This brought attention to the Calderon administration and forced the Mexican government to really go after El Chapo.

Mistake number two was getting flushed out of the safety of the vast dense mountains of the Sierra Madres while being pursued. El Chapo was on the run around Culiacan and Mazatlan. He would eventually be cornered for the third time by Mexican authorities and he would be ultimately extradited to the US for trial, sealing his fate and no more able to bribe government official using his billions of dollars chest fund.

Ciudad Juarez Almost a Failed State

Reputed Sinaloa drug lord Joaquin "El Chapo" Guzman Loera, accompanied by an army of sicarios, strolled into Juárez one day claiming the city's lucrative smuggling corridor as his own, so the rumor goes.

Whether true or not, Juárez and other parts of the state of Chihuahua had become ground zero in a battle over drug-trafficking routes that had been under the control of the Carrillo Fuentes (Juarez Cartel) drug organization for more than a decade.

The animosity between El Chapo Guzman's Sinaloa Cartel and the Juárez Cartel was evident as the death toll mounted, including several bodies found with threatening notes aimed at Guzman's associates.

"This will happen to those who keep supporting El Chapo. From La Linea and those who follow it," stated a note found next to two men slain in the Loma Blanca area outside of Juárez.

The leader of the Juárez drug cartel was Vicente Carrillo Fuentes, who was believed to have taken control of the organization after the 1997 death of his brother, Amado Carrillo Fuentes, who was nicknamed the "Lord of the Skies" because of his use of airplanes to smuggle cocaine.

Vicente Carrillo Fuentes, 45, was indicted in 2000 by a U.S. federal grand jury on a long list of charges, including 10 counts of murder and the distribution of tons of cocaine and marijuana bound for New York, Chicago and other markets throughout the nation.

A Mexican federal police commander identification card bearing a photo of Vicente Carrillo Fuentes was recovered by the FBI from in a west El Paso home in 2000.

To survive the recent upheaval, Vicente Carrillo Fuentes allied himself with reputed drug trafficker Heriberto "Lazca" Lazcano, one of three leaders of the Zetas.

The violence in Juarez from organized drug organizations fighting for turf intensified by the months. It seemed like murder had become a common theme in Juarez with no end in sight. Drug thugs were killing in daylight, in front of police headquarters, in the centers among the public. The citizenship often times found themselves in the crossfire or were killed at random.

Every day we would hear of yet more bloodshed on the streets of Juarez and no one was ever brought to justice. More often, drug cartels killed at ease despite thousands of military and federal police in Juarez. As president Felipe Calderon attempted to stem the drug violence in Juarez, it was a futile struggle and it only produced ineffective results against a wave of increased violence.

Yes, this border city had become the battlefield for warring cartels armed with smuggled American guns and it did not appear it would slow down any time soon.

There was never a shortage of weapons for the cartels.

Approximately 75 to 95 percent of the conventional guns -- from AK-47s to .50 caliber rifles capable of penetrating body-type armor -- supplied to the Mexican drug cartels were traced to the United States.

Mexican drug cartels were at war with the Mexican government and each other over distribution of illegal narcotics into the United States and they needed guns from the U.S. to fight back.

The deaths were not limited to drug dealers. Businessmen, lawyers and others were also killed in mob-style hits carried out by armed commandos. In addition, nightclubs, car lots and factories were torched.

The foundation of the drug war in Mexico is a drug-trafficking problem, which grew in size, sophistication and ruthlessness over the decades, all while being funded by the multibillion-dollar U.S. drug market.

Former Mexican presidents Carlos Salinas de Gortari and Ernesto Zedillo allowed this problem to get worse and worse, and allowed these cartels to get more sophisticated and powerful over time. The number one problem in Mexico, even today, is corruption.

There are rumors of deep corruption within the political machine, judicial process and more importantly, the police institutions. Corruption has allowed drug traffickers to elude Mexican authorities.

The government could not possibly be blind to the corrupt police forces operating among the plazas in the light of day? I remember my experience back when I visited Copper Canyon and knew that intervention from within was necessary if anything was going to change. This not only required reforming the police institutions, especial the municipal police departments but a purge of the bad apples that were colluding openly with organized crime would obviously be necessary. Certainly, an intervention in Ciudad Juarez was needed to slow down the flow of violence that was spiraling out of control.

Some Tourists on Cartel's Cross Hair

One question we often got when I was involved with Borderland Beat was "is it safe to travel to Mexico or Ciudad Juarez."

Between 2008 through 2013 Ciudad Juarez had a lot of violence. One could then easily say that Juarez would have a higher risk than any other city in the US. But cartels typically did not go out of their way to target tourists without a reason. If it did happen, it was under indirect circumstances, such as getting caught up in the crossfire.

But if any American got involved in cartel activities in Mexico, specifically in Ciudad Juarez, or if an American associated themselves with people that had ties to drug cartels, the risk would rise tenfold.

As was the case one day afternoon in 2009 in Ciudad Juarez, Mexico. The cracking sound of gun fire was once again heard coming from a motel room of "La Cúpula," located in Paseo de la Victoria and Tapioca. A sound that was way too common on the streets of Juarez, a playground for the battling drug cartels. It was believed that organized crime was responsible in the slaughter of four people.

Again, another senseless execution happening in the daylight hours, in a very public place with many witnesses and in one of the most reputable motels of the city.

Government officials from both sides of the border have been warning tourists who visit Juarez to stay in public places, remain vigilant of their surroundings, choose the option to stay in their motels without having to walk the streets and lock their doors.

But these safety tips mean nothing in Juarez where anyone can kill you at any time, in any place and nothing ever happens.

The incident happened minutes before 6pm and was reported by employees of the establishment. The unofficial account was that two men and two women were the victims of a killing.

Police say a group of heavily armed men ordered employees behind the front desk into one room while they searched the hotel register for the two men and women they were looking for.

The armed men then went inside room number 27 and opened fire on the four people. The assailants were described as at least two hooded commandos who were traveling in a Suburban. At the scene authorities found at least 40 spent shell casings fired from assault weapons known in Spanish as "cuerno de chivo" or AK-47 style weapons.

At least three of the victims received a gunshot to the head at close range or as is known in Mexico, "tiro de gracia." At the scene officials also recovered a 2002 gray Honda car that had been reported stolen.

The victims were identified as Daniel Ivan Torres Gutierrez of 22 years of age, Jimmy Albert Moreno Macias of 21 years of age, Yolanda Torres Vanessa Fernandez of 23 years of age and Brenda Lissete Fernández Torres of 20 years of age. Both of the females appeared to be sisters. Through unconfirmed sources it was believed that the target of the attack was Ivan Daniel Torres Gutierrez, a Mexican national, who had been in the company of the three others who at this point appear to be US citizens. Both of the females were said to be from the state of New Mexico.

During the beginning of 2009, the number of Americans executed in Juarez related to drug trafficking soared.

US State Department records noted that the number of cases of this type of incident since May of 2008 when it first saw eight executions related to drug trafficking of U.S. citizens had seen a drastic increase. From 2002 to 2009

Ciudad Juarez and surrounding areas had register at least 72 murders of U.S citizens, of which about 47 or 65 percent were reported to be potentially executions linked to drug sales.

As President Felipe Calderon attempted to weed out police corruption and break down drug cartels, it created a power vacuum among narco traffickers - and thus creating a new wave of narco-violence in Mexico. In its travel warning of 2009, the State Department declared that "some recent Mexican army and police confrontations with drug cartels have taken on the characteristics of a small-unit combat." The reason for the rise in crime was the fragmentation of the large cartels into smaller factions fighting for dominance within the cartel. It's hard to measure the strategy of Calderon making the criminal syndicates smaller, but, it certainly did not stop the flow of narcotics through Mexico and has only fueled the violence. The chances of being an innocent bystander or witnessing something bad in Juarez were higher than ever.

People on both sides of the border started to take noticed and caused a sense of fear from insecurity. People in Juarez started to leave by the thousands and tourist from the US and abroad, started to avoid Juarez.

You know the old saying in Juarez, "drugs go north, guns come south." In the meantime, blood tarnished shell casings scattered on the ground from weapons smuggled in to Mexico from the US have caused the blood of US citizens to spill on Mexican soil. The decision to travel to Mexico is a personal one, that must be made in a measured way, taking all precautionary measures to be safe and feel safe. But not to worry, the La Cúpula hotel re-opened within hours of the massacre and were taking reservations, I hear they accept Visa or Mastercard.

The Sinaloa and Juarez Conflict

To curb the wave of violence in Ciudad Juarez, the government of Felipe Calderón had rehearsed everything: it had replaced the police with the military, it had reinforced local security with federal police, but no measure had been effective against the overwhelming power of the drug cartels.

In addition to the presumable police protection that the Juarez cartel had, it had always enjoyed the protection of the Army's high command. This was according to testimony by Vicente Carrillo Leyva, El Vicentillo, that he made on March 1, 2009 before the SIEDO.

An anecdote told by Carrillo Leyva, illustrated how military personnel protected the emblematic figures of the Juarez cartel:

"We arrived in Cozumel in a private plane, my father (Amado Carrillo) and I, and immediately the military surrounded the plane. When they opened the doors, they greeted us very kindly telling us that they came from orders of General Curiel. The soldiers escorted us to our hotel. They did it in official vehicles that, I remember, were a Jeep and a Suburban.

We settled in the hotel.

In the afternoon General Curiel arrived, he was in company of dozens of high military commanders and they all put themselves under our orders."

Vicente Carrillo Fuentes inherited the Juarez Cartel from his brother Amado Carrillo Fuentes, "El Señor de Los Cielos" or "The Lord of the Skies." He had earned that nickname because of his large fleet of jets that he used to transport drugs. Amado Fuentes died in July 1997 during an extensive plastic surgery to change his appearance. Two of Amado's bodyguards were in the operating room during the procedure. On November 7, 1997, the two physicians who performed the surgery on Fuentes were found dead, encased in concrete inside steel drums, with their bodies showing signs of torture. That is how business was done in Juarez and that is how it has been done for a long time.

The death of Amado created a large power vacuum in the Mexican underworld.

Vicente was born in Sinaloa, the same state where Joaquin Guzman Loera, "El Chapo," leader of the Sinaloa Cartel, was from. The Juarez Cartel was once an ally of the Sinaloa Cartel. All that changed when El Chapo ordered the execution Of Rodolfo Carrillo Fuentes, "El Nino de Oro." Ismael El Mayo Zambada Garcia was in possession of the body when he received a phone call from Vicente who was aware that El Mayo was providing security for El Chapo.

It was at that moment that Carrillo asked him directly: Are you with me? Or are you against me? Zambada answered: "I'm with you, of course." It was then that Carrillo demanded El Mayo bring him the head of El Chapo. Of course, that never happened and the war between the Sinaloa and Juarez Cartels began.

Vicente retaliated by ordering the assassinating of El Chapo's brother in prison. This created a very dangerous feud between both cartel leaders.

It was Vicente's character and demeanor that drove the associates of his brother Amado, like El Mayo Zambada and Juan José Esparragoza Moreno, "El Azul" away from the Juarez cartel. This left the Juarez cartel isolated and fighting on its own. It was during this time that El Mayo and company had decided to take over operations in Juarez, and this intensified after the first escape from prison by El Chapo.

There is a story about a meeting that took place in Monterrey by numerous powerful capos that had planned a consolidation of resources to make Sinaloa the most powerful cartel in Mexico and they talked about conducting several executions to open the way to carry out their plan. It was said that they had the full support of the federal political establishment, at the time Vicente Fox was the Mexican President.

The meeting apparently took place in the city of Monterrey, Nuevo Leon, between several leaders of organized crime. Among the notable attendants were Ismael 'El Mayo' Zambada, Joaquín 'El Chapo' Guzmán, Juan José Esparragoza Moreno, alias 'El Azul', and Arturo Beltrán."

This was the initial alliance to take over the operations of the once powerful Juarez Cartel.

Despite fighting alone, Vicente started seeking help from other cartels and acquire political influence in the state of Chihuahua. It was said that he had the support of the then governor of Chihuahua, Patricio Martinez and forged alliances with the Tijuana Cartel, the Beltran Layva brothers (after the broke away from the Sinaloa Cartel) and Los Zetas. Vicente also started to strengthen his organization by creating his armed wing known as "La Linea" and coordinated cooperation from street gangs such as Barrio Azteca in Ciudad Juarez, El Paso, Dallas and Austin, Texas.

The war for control for the Juarez plaza was on.

During the years I was reporting on the cartels on BB, the violence by Sinaloa and Juarez cartels intensified between 2008 and 2011 reaching the highest levels in Ciudad Juarez that placed the city as the most violent in the world, with 9,000 executions in little more than two years.

The Sinaloa and Juarez cartels had a strong presence in the whole state of Chihuahua, in each and every one of the towns, one or the other was in control. Although the state of Chihuaha had always belonged to the Juarez cartel, the Sinaloa had the most presence in the state.

Despite the separation of Mayo Zambada, El Azul and other emblematic figures from the Juarez cartel, Vicente

Carrillo knew how to infiltrate the political structure in Chihuahua. With the help of Governor Patricio Martinez, the Juarez cartel reached its peak, it controlled all the state police and had in its pocket even the state attorney, Jesus Chito Solis, who was investigated by the SIEDO for alleged links to the drug traffickers.

Vicente Carrillo Fuentes had full control of the Chihuahua region since 2007, but the Sinaloa cartel started to move in to the state starting in 2010. This shift in power was led by Joaquín Guzmán Loera, El Chapo, who's cartel entered the state of Chihuahua from the south taking control of the towns of Guadalupe, Calvo and Guachochi, until seizing the towns of Ascensión, Parral, Jiménez, Camargo and Delicias.

In the middle of the state, Guzmán Loera also retained control of Benito Juárez and Villa Ahumada, which are a strategic trafficking points of drugs into the US within the state of Chihuahua. Chihuahua had more than 300 border breaches that facilitated the clandestine trafficking of illicit drugs into the US. After the arrest of Pedro Sánchez, third in command of the Juarez cartel, the area fell to the control of the Sinaloa cartel led by José Antonio Torres Marrufo.

In the north, after the arrest of José Rodolfo Escajeda, El Rikín, the Sinaloa cartel took possession of the Guadalupe Bravo District, Práxedis G. Guerrero and Ascensión, municipalities bordering the United States.

This forced the people of Vicente to retreat to the west, to towns of Cuauhtémoc, Madera, San Buenaventura, Galeana, Nuevo Casa Grandes and Casas Grandes.

The Sinaloa cartel was able to penetrate Ciudad Juarez but was not able displaced the Juarez cartel, creating Juarez into a deadly battle ground for both cartels. In the city of Chihuahua there was the presence of both cartels, but the violence was contained.

The Juarez Cartel

The Juarez cartel, through its armed branch of La Línea, participated in criminal activities such as drug trafficking, arms trafficking, money laundering, auto theft, kidnappings, extortions and executions.

Under the command of Vicente Carrillo Fuentes was José Luis Ledesma or Pablo Ríos Rodríguez, El JL, who was the main operator in the state of Chihuahua. El JL had under his command Luis Guillermo Carrillo Rubio, El Pariente, who led a group of sicarios from La Línea and who operated in some of the plazas in the state.

Juan Pablo Guijarro Fragoso, El Mónico, was plaza boss in the city of Chihuahua, Puerto Palomas, Ascensión, Nuevo Casas Grandes, Janos and Puerto San Luis. El Monico took command after the arrest of Carlos Vázquez Barragán, El 20, by federal police on July 25, 2010.

The towns of Creel, Cuauhtémoc and Batopilas were under the control of Hernán or Germán García Loya, El Gaviota, who had Misael Loya Caraveo as his lieutenant. The towns of Delicias, Ciudad Jiménez, Camargo, Parral and Balleza were under the control of Evaristo Rentaría, who now lives in the United States as a protected witness for the DEA and the FBI.

Ciudad Juárez was run by Juan Díaz, El Leopardo or El Rojo, who had Antonio Acosta, El Diego or El 10, who was head of La Linea. El Makarfi headed the drug distribution in the six districts of the Juarez city police, who was also assisted by El Mandis or El Gordo.

The operators of the cells of sicarios in the police districts of Ciudad Juarez had a group of 10 sicarios who were characterized as "bloodthirsty." Their ages range from 20 to 30 years of age and almost all of them came from Sinaloa. Some were former police or military members. In Juarez, one of the groups of gang bangers known as Los Aztecas, were commanded by El 51, who in turn was under the orders of El

JL. They operated under the control of El Diego, who personally ran the cell of Los Linces.

Diego also commanded the six cells in the Ciudad Juárez police stations. The head of each cell had five to eight sicarios.

90% of the members of the Juarez cartel dedicated themselves to drug dealing within the city, and the rest to drug trafficking in to the United States. The Juarez cartel also charged other cartels a 25% fee of any proceeds from drugs or human smuggling that crossed the border, this was also known as "derecho de piso." This was in essence a fee assessed to other cartels to use the plaza to cross dope or people in to the US.

The Sinaloa Cartel

At the same time, the groups and cells of the Sinaloa cartel, which were advancing to take control of the state of Chihuahua, functioned in a similar manner as the Juarez cartel. The leadership in the state was Noel Salgueiro Nevárez, El Flaco Salgueiro.

Their groups of sicarios were known as la Gente Nueva. They were mostly from Sinaloa, Michoacán and Guerrero and were responsible for eliminating the members of the local Juarez cartel, La Línea.

The plaza boss in Chihuahua, El Señor Delgado, was a direct subordinate of Salgueiro, who previously had Elizabeth Rodríguez Griego, La Doña, who was killed on August of 2010. La Doña previously had two cells of sicarios who were former military and cocaine dealers.

The municipalities of Ascensión, Puerto Palomas and Janos were under the control of Mario Amaya, El 11, who replaced Fernando Arámbula, who was in custody in the United States. From El Porvenir to Ojinaga, El Gavilán was in control. Nuevo Casas Grandes and Madera were under the command of Daniel Leo Pérez, El 16. In the city of Parral, El

R-3 was in charge and controlled several cells of sicarios that operated in Cuauhtémoc, Delicias, Camargo and Ojinaga.

In Ciudad Juárez, the main operator was José Antonio Torres Marrufo, El Jaguar, who worked alongside of Mario Núñez Meza El Mayito or El M-10. The Valle de Juárez was controlled by Gabino Salas Valenciano, El Ingeniero, who lived in Durango and had under his command two cells of sicarios, as well as the control of the trafficking of drugs into the United States.

El Jaguar had met with "El Chapo" and with Ismael "El Mayo" Zambada to join their cartel and confront the Juarez Cartel.

But why did Torres Marrufo decided to join the Sinaloa Cartel and betray the Carrillo Fuentes?

El Jaguar had been kidnapped years before by a man identified as "JL", who was a trusted man of the Carrillo Fuentes.

Torres Marrufo wanted revenge, it was personal, just as it was for "El Chapo" who wanted to steal Ciudad Juarez.

Thus, El Jaguar founded, along with Noel Salgueiro Nevárez, "El Flaco", the criminal cell group of "Gente Nueva", which served as the armed wing of the Sinaloa Cartel.

Torres Marrufo also controlled the street gangs of Los Mexicles and Los Artistas Asesinos(AA).

For the government of the United States, "El Jaguar" was identified as one of those responsible for the acts of violence in Ciudad Juárez and as one of the men closest to "El Chapo" in the state of Chihuahua and Durango. Torres Marrufo was arrested in 2012. He was extradited to the US at the request of a Texas Court order for the murder of two US citizens.

The name of El Jaguar reappeared in the trial of "El Chapo" in Brooklyn, in New York in 2019. Edgar Iván Galván, alias "El Negro", a man of low rank within the

Sinaloa Cartel, testified about his enlistment into the Sinaloa Cartel with the help of Torres Marrufo.

Torres Marrufo and Gabino Salas were the ones responsible for the increase in violence and insecurity in Ciudad Juárez due to the constant confrontation they had with La Línea.

The Sinaloa cartel dedicated 90% of their activities to drug trafficking to the US and 10% to local drug dealing in Ciudad Juarez. Mainly, the sale of narcotics was made in the state and municipal penitentiaries. It also obtained financial resources from kidnappings, robberies, extortions, assaults on shops and banks, executions, contraband, piracy, human trafficking, and arms trafficking.

El JL, who commanded Los Aztecas, had a presence in Rancho Anapra, Ladrillera, Popular, Altavista, Barrio Alto, Centro, Azteca, División del Norte, Partido Romero and Barreal.

Through Los Mexicles, Guzmán Loera controlled the communities of Nuevo México, Chavena, Juárez, Obrera and Pradera.

The role of Los Aztecas and Los Mexicles was to prevent the incursion of rival cartels, to protect the points of entry of drugs into the United States, to recruit members and to control the drug dealing in the more than 6,000 distribution points in the city.

In the end, according to reports from the Federal Bureau of Investigation of the United States (FBI), Carrillo's organization lost the war to the Sinaloa cartel in Ciudad Juarez. Despite this, the Juarez cartel remained active and continued operating in Juarez at a minimal level.

In October 9, 2014 Vicente, El Viceroy, Carrillo Fuentes was arrested. It was just a matter of time. Fausto Isidro, of the Beltrán Leyva cartel, tried to move in to be the new leader for the Juarez cartel. He felt he who could very easily occupy the place that was once held by the Carrillo Fuentes dynasty.

Attorney Interrogated and Executed

In October 2010 attorney Mario González Rodríguez was abducted by armed sicaros presumed members of the Sinaloa cartel, in the city of Chihuahua. Mario González was the brother of the former attorney general of Chihuahua Patricia González Rodríguez. A video uploaded on Youtube by a user named "quitapuercos" showed the abducted Mario González accusing his sister Patricia González of having ties to narco cartels.

In the video, Mario González, is seated and handcuffed while being held at gunpoint by five sicarios dress in military fatigues. The gunmen appeared to have professional training. Their AK-47s have two magazines taped together for quick reload. At the end of the video, one of the gunmen standing right behind Mario González approaches him, and it sounds as if he triggers his gun, but the rifle does not fire.

He is questioned and says that his sister Patricia González was protecting members of the Juárez drug cartel. When questioned, he also said she ordered the murders of two journalists, as well as Mormon community members in the Colonia LeBaron in northwest of Chihuahua.

Patricia González denied the claims her brother made. She said police officers working for the Sinaloa drug cartel were behind the video. She claimed they were seeking revenge for her cracking down on some of their cartel members.

Mario González answered questions from a man off-camera about high-profile killings and kidnappings supposedly carried out by La Línea, or the Juárez drug cartel.

Some of the armed sicarios seen in the video behind Mario González would eventually be arrested.

In November of 2010 eight alleged kidnappers linked to the Sinaloa Cartel were arrested during a confrontation with government officials. During the police action, police rescued two people who had been abducted. Police seized 12 long guns, four handguns, six vehicles, various magazines of different calibers, radio equipment and fake uniforms of different police agencies.

Among the eight detainees were three people who participated in the interrogation in the video and the subsequent murder of Mario González, while the masterminds of the events and three other sicarios who were in the interrogation, including the one who is asking the questions, managed to get away.

One of the detainees was identified as Luis Miguel Ibarra Castellanos, alias "El Cora," who provided authorities the location of where Mario González had been murdered and buried. El Cora also gave details of the abduction perpetrated in October 21, 2010 in the capital of Chihuahua. He added that the kidnapping and homicide was committed by orders of a person identified only as "El Buitre" and a municipal policeman named Adrián Orozco, aka "El M1", who worked directly for the plaza boss Noel Salgueiro Nevarez, alias "El Flaco" and was the leader of the group known as "Gente Nueva," an organization that is at the service of the Sinaloa Cartel.

Among those detained was Jorge "El Chuleton" Gutiérrez Corral who was the operational coordinator Cipol (state police) at a time when Raul Grajeda Domínguez was the State Secretary of Public Security.

Authorities were also investigating whether some of the individuals arrested were in fact active municipal police officers.

El Cora also revealed an interesting fact by saying that José Luis Ledesma , El JL, the Juarez cartel boss for the whole state of Chihuahua, had been killed. El JL was only second to Vicente Carrillo Fuentes, supreme leader of the Juarez cartel. El Chapo had put a bounty on JL and hated the man with a passion. No one had been able to confirm any information of El JL, if he was captured or killed, but rumors abound, as is customary in the Mexican culture.

It is known that this criminal group operated under the command of Noel Salgueiro Nevarez along with Antonio Torres Marrufo, El Jaguar and Gabino Salas Valenciano, El Ingeniero.

El Cora told police that they went to the legal office of González Rodríguez that day and ordered the people who were there to lay on the floor. Then they asked the secretary behind the desk where was Mario González, as they had his name written on a piece of paper. The secretary informed them that Mario González was on the second floor of the building, where they handcuffed him and took him to a safe house.

El Cora gave details about the torture of Mario González who was forced to implicate his sister, the former deputy prosecutor Patricia González Rodríguez, saying that she was protecting the Juárez Cartel and La Línea.

In a video released by the Federal Public Security Secretariat (SSP), El Cora explained how and why they killed Mario González Rodríguez.

El Cora said that during the recording of the video, a person arrived from the state of Durango who was present to coordinate the interview with El Buitre and the editing of the video. El Cora said the person was identified by the name of Charly.

He said that they used two memory cards for recording the interrogation of the attorney that would eventually be uploaded to YouTube. On the first he answered the questions freely but on the second one he was pressured to read from some placards.

El Cora said that the brother of the former Attorney General of Chihuahua, Patricia Gonzalez, was abducted because he was in charge of making deals with the organization "La Linea" on behalf of the former Attorney General.

"All the questions from the first recording he answered on his own, we never put anything ... In the second recording there were other questions, put there in order to incriminate, or I do not know the reason," El Cora said.

The video of a press conference released by the SSP showed the other seven detainees, who were wearing the same military uniforms as in the previous Youtube video of the interrogation of Mario González and who claimed to belong to the Sinaloa cartel.

El Cora did not specify what questions Mario González answered on his own. He said that they tortured him by beating him only on the soles of the feet and legs to avoid showing any physical sign of tortured on the video. Mario González was assassinated the next day.

The group was instructed to dig a grave in a vacant lot. "At six o'clock in the afternoon we were ordered to bury him. We killed him at that moment at the same house of the interview between all of us," El Cora said. El Cora said they used a rope and a piece of wood to apply a tourniquet to his neck in order to strangulate him. Immediately after killing him, they put him in a gray Dodge Nitro truck and moved him to the place where they had dug the grave to bury him.

Eventually, the mayor of a municipality of Chihuahua, Marco Quezada, confirmed that the police officers who were arrested in connection with the disappearance and subsequent torture and death of Mario González Rodríguez, brother of former state prosecutor, Patricia González were set free.

The mayor said that at the moment, there was not enough evidence to hold these officers on the charges of kidnapping and murder. Since the 60 days of arraignment were up, their rights must be respected, and they were allowed to continue working in the police department if they chose to do so.

According to a U.S. congressional report the Firearms confiscated during the death of Mario González Rodríguez were traced to the Operation Fast and Furious.

Mexican officials submitted information about the weapons to the ATF's e-trace system, and the ATF traced two of the AK-47s to Operation Fast and Furious. The congressional report said that an ATF email indicated that ATF officials in Phoenix who knew the two assault rifles came from the controversial operation withheld the information from Mexican officials.

In congressional testimony, Carlos Canino, the ATF's acting U.S. attaché in Mexico, said he was the one who finally notified Mexican federal Attorney General Marisela Morales about the weapons-tracing and their link to the death of Mario González Rodríguez.

Canino feared an international incident might break out with Mexico if the information leaked out to the news media instead of being sent through government channels. He told U.S. lawmakers that he did not want to undermine the trust that U.S. law enforcement had developed with their Mexican counterparts in the war against the drug cartels.

Ricardo Alday, spokesman for the Mexican Embassy in Washington, D.C., said in response to the U.S. congressional report's findings that "the government of Mexico had not granted, nor will they grant, under any circumstance, tacit or explicit authorization for the deliberate walking of arms into Mexico."

The ATF released a report that said 68,000 weapons recovered in Mexico between 2007 and 2011 were traced back to U.S. sources. That report does not mention which of the weapons were part of the undercover Operation Fast and Furious.

Weapons traced back to the operation have been recovered in eight Mexican states and in Mexico City, and most of them were destined for the Sinaloa drug cartel led by Joaquin "El Chapo" Guzmán, the congressional report said. At least eight Fast and Furious-connected weapons were recovered at crime scenes in Juárez and four in Chihuahua City between 2010 and 2011.

ATF officials launched Operation Fast and Furious in 2009 in Phoenix in an attempt to identify high-level arms traffickers who were supplying the Mexican drug cartels with weapons. The operation allowed weapons purchased in the United States to cross (walk) the border into Mexico.

ATF shut down the operation about a month after Border Patrol Agent Brian Terry was found murdered in the Arizona desert in December 2010. Two AK-47s, originally purchased as semiautomatics and connected to Fast and Furious, were found near Terry's body.

The number of weapons submitted for e-trace was 17,352 in 2007; 21,555 in 2009; 8,338 in 2010; and 20,335 in 2011.

From the al-Qaida Playbook

At around 7:30pm on July 15, 2010 two vehicles stopped in the middle of the streets of Bolivia and 16 de Septiembre, in downtown Ciudad Juarez. This area is always congested with commuters and people shopping. It is also close to the tourist district of the city.

This day it was busy as usual. Several people got out of the vehicles and placed a man on his knees in the middle of the street who was wearing a Juarez police uniform. The man had his hands tied behind his back and was already injured from a gunshot.

This caught the attention of the many people that were on foot on the sidewalk and vehicles in the heavy traffic on the street. Suddenly, while the man in policeman uniform was placed on his knees, they shot him in the head while everyone looked in horror. The men then drove away in one of the vehicles while leaving the other behind at the scene.

They also left the dead policeman in the middle of the street after taking several gunshots at close range to his head. Some people rushed to the scene, this included a doctor who happened to be in the area.

This resulted in a heavy response from the federal police and rescue personnel. Moments after the federal police arrived to investigate, a bomb detonated on the vehicle that had been left behind. The blast killed the doctor instantly who got the full force of the bomb, a civilian who was a musician that happened to be at the wrong place at the wrong time. Also killed in the blast was a federal police officer that was inspecting the car with the explosives. Several people were injured including a cameraman form Channel 2 that captured the explosion on video. The vehicle with the explosives appeared to be a Ford Taurus. Inside the vehicle there were traces of C-4 explosives and a cellular that was apparently used as a trigger.

It turned out that the police officer that had been executed in the middle of the road was not a police officer after all. They had dressed a man in police uniform and executed the man to lure the federal police officers to the proximity to the car bomb. The Mayor of Cuidad Juarez, José Reyes Ferriz, confirmed that the execution of the man dressed in police uniform was merely a ploy to lure federal police officers to the location of the car bomb.

"The person they placed there to attract the federal police was a man dressed in a municipal police uniform but was not a police officer. Since yesterday when we made the initial analysis, we saw that he had a normal civilian belt that is not part of the uniform, did not have any of the equipment, badge or other police insignia" said Reyes Ferriz.

There was a rumor that the bomb attack was in retaliation for the arrest of Jesus Armando Acosta Guerrero, "El 35, who was a Lieutenant of La Linea. Armando Acosta worked right under Jose Antonio Hernandez, "El Diego," and Juan Ledesma, "El JL," who were second in command next to Vicente Carrillo Fuentes.

This was to be the first successful car bombing that brought a new dynamic of how cartels operated in Mexico. This was reminiscence of an al-Qaida playbook. People were getting acclimated to the regular beheading, street shootout, or people hanging from bridges and this was just another method to instill fear and terror to the people of Mexico. This would start a conversation about how this could be classified as a terrorist attack. ATF assisting in the investigation and had been helping Mexican authorities in other cases were IEDs had been found on crime scenes.

A week later there as a written message on a wall warning US authority that if they did not arrest corrupt federal police officers, another car bomb would be detonated.

"If in 15 days, there is no response with the detention of corrupt federales, we will put a car with 100 kilos of C4," the message read.

Composite 4, or C-4, was the plastic explosive used for the attack that killed the three people in Downtown Juárez.

"Unfortunately, these drug cartels, they have an enormous amount of resources at their disposal. They can buy any kind of capability they want. But we are determined, working with Mexico, to do everything in our power to reduce this violence that affects not only the Mexican people, but our own," said U.S. State Department spokesman P.J. Crowley.

The Real Test of Confidence

On September 29, 2009 a post on Borderland Beat talked about the lie detector test administered to the Ciudad Juarez police officers and hundreds were terminated for untruthfulness results.

The majority of the 334 Juarez police officers that were dismissed after failing "confidence exams" left the city but a few have remained. These exams consisted of some sort of polygraph examination to weed out those who were questionable as having ties to organize crime. Most of these police officers that were suspected of being dirty and subsequently terminated have been tracked by the Juarez Municipal Police and the multi task force conducting an operation known as "Operación Conjunto Chihuahua", said Ciudad Juarez Mayor José Reyes Ferriz.

These are a lot of officers suddenly without a job and on the streets of Juarez desperate for a source of income. It's not easy finding a good paying job for anyone, yet alone for a police officer with specific skill set not common in most professions.

"Most of the policemen who were terminated for failing the confidence exams left the city, but those who remained behind, have been monitored tracking their activities," said Mayor Ferriz.

Many of the media community were concerned that these unemployed police officers would find themselves working for the drug cartels that are more than happy to snatch corrupt officers to use in their battle against each other. This is a legitimate concern as it is widely known that the drug cartels are constantly recruiting police or military personnel because of their training, knowledge and expertise in the use of firearms.

In the northern part of the state of Michoacan the Mexican police arrested a former police officer Marcos Arturo Juárez Cruz, aka "El Chamuco" or otherwise "The Demon," who formed part of the drug cartel known as, "La Familia." "El Chamuco" was a state police officer between 2001 and 2007, a time in which the Secretary of federal Public Security (SSP) said that he provided support to the well-armed Gulf cartel, and a group of assassins (sicarios) known as Los Zetas.

At that time the Gulf cartel was allied with "La Familia" in operations in Michoacan, but later they broke off their relationship and are now rivals.

According to the SSP, "El Chamuco" was recruited to "La Familia" and quickly rose through the ranks within the drug cartel for his "discipline, relationship with ranking officers and his negotiating skills. His salary was estimated to be 50,000 pesos per month (nearly $3,700 US dollars) plus expenses, a lot more of the basic salary of a Mexican police officer.

The SSP emphasizes that despite his youth, "El Chamuco" was well respected within the organization for his violent temper and coolness when killing his rivals.

"La Familia" is one of the most powerful cartels in Mexico, an organization that has forced the Mexican Government to deploy a total offensive in recent months. That is the primary reason why these cartels seek members who have tactical police/military experience and also members that have relationships with police and military organizations.

Mayor Ferriz said that the "Operación Conjunto Chihuahua" does a good job keeping track of police officers that have been given their termination papers after failing the reliability tests.

"We will continue to purge the bad elements from within the police department, and obviously, we will provide all pertinent data of these people to the "Operación Conjunto

Chihuahua" to enable them to follow up on these people, as has been done since October 17 when we terminated 334 members from the police department," said the mayor.

Yes, it is agreed that it's essential to remove the corrupt elements from within the police ranks as soon as possible, otherwise any significant result in controlling this wave of violence and mayhem in the streets of Juarez will be a total failure. Results from these initiatives are slow coming and in the mean time we continue to see the slaughtered of human bodies dumped on the city streets at a record number.

The only key element overlooked by Mexican President Felipe Calderon and Juarez Mayor Jose Reyes Ferriz, who are supposedly attempting to wage a war against the organized crime, is the corrupt political machine that protects the criminal structure from top to bottom. That is truly what is needed for any meaningful eradication of the carnage that has been engrained way too long in the very fabric of the social norm in Mexico.

Ciudad Juárez is in the grip of the most violent drug war the nation has ever seen. President Felipe Calderón has sent in the army to take on the Juarez cartel and a few too many corrupt police elements. The army is fighting the cartels, the cartels are fighting each other and honest cops are in short supply. Nowhere else has anyone suffered more than the people in Juárez.

The results have been nothing short of chaos.

On a daily basis, bodies are spotted on roadsides, down alleys, in public dumps and perched in public plazas. Bodies have been found handcuffed together, bearing the marks of vicious beatings. Severed heads have been dumped in cooler boxes and there are reports of torture videos posted on YouTube to include Borderland Beat. A local paper claimed one cartel hired a musician to play victims their favorite ballads during their executions.

The cartels act like they're untouchable. They pass lists of names to local police, telling them who they'll be killing in the weeks to come. One note was left at a monument to fallen officers. It listed 22 police officers who had resisted the corrupting efforts of the cartels.

So, Juarez was attempting to revamp its police forces with better training and a force possessing a degree of integrity. This required the cleansing of the Juarez police forces in order to eradicate the corruption from the drug cartels. Juarez was attempting to fill the void of hundreds of officers who have been fired for failing "confidentiality tests " or police officers who have quit for fear of being executed by the ruthless cartels.

Despite all this, life goes on in Juarez and people try to retain some trust in their government. It is obvious more police are needed and more training is necessary. Juárez was still looking to recruit 1,400 more officers as the city deals with a crime wave that began in 2008. This task will not be easy, especially when you are a cop in one of the most dangerous cities in Mexico.

The Mexican Drug War's Collateral Damage

President Felipe Calderon had to initially rely solely on the military to take on the cartels in the streets of Mexico while he revamped his federal police from the ground up. He had in mind to create a federal police force adequately equipped to take on the cartels in a tactical perspective. When you deploy military forces upon your community of civilians it poses some problems. The military function under different rules of engagements as oppose to police forces. The problems soon became obvious and caused negative controversy in the deployment of military among the civilian populace.

The Mexico conflict has three fronts:
1. Intra-cartel: Internal struggles and the elimination of "traitors" within an organization.
2. Inter-cartel: Fighting between different organizations.
3. Government vs. cartels: The military and law enforcement's fight against drug organizations.

The drug war waged in the streets of Mexico between cartel against cartel or cartel against military can be intense. Very often we saw that high caliber assault weapons in full auto (point and spray) method of operation are used. We saw many instances where innocent people that were caught in the crossfire were killed, too often - too many.

On March 28, 2010, I posted an article on the problem with what the military classified as collateral damage titled "The Mexican Drug War's Collateral Damage."

Mexican President Felipe Calderon declared war against various drug cartels around Mexico. The bloody confrontation between the Zetas against the Gulf cartel, which appears to be assisted by the Sinaloa cartel and La

Familia Michoacana, was spilling blood all over the streets of northeastern Mexico.

The victims of the massacre were primarily rival sicarios and in certain instances police officers and military personnel.

What is troubling is that too many innocent bystanders were getting killed when bullets found them when getting caught in the crossfire. What was more troubling was that in some cases, the innocent victims that were getting shot, were getting shot by the armed forces that were supposed to protect them in the first place.

Some would argue that a huge militarization of forces deployed in the streets of Mexico with almost daily firefights was bound to produce collateral damage. But we had seen in certain cases a military that was bent on responding to the attacks from sicarios almost in a blind, uncontrolled manner, where it almost appears that they kill anything that moves.

Consider that incident that occurred on March 19, 2010 at the prestigious Institute of Technology in Monterrey. Official statement from the Mexican Army and state government had mentioned that two gunmen were killed during a gunfight after they tried to evade the military. This would indicate that the people killed were running away. However, the two people killed were not involved in any criminal activity but were merely innocent students with excellent academic records at the institute.

They were Jorge Antonio Mercado Alonso, 23, studying a Master's degree and Javier Arredondo Verdugo, 24, studying a PhD. Monterrey Tech rector Rafael Rangel said in a news release that both students had scholarships for academic excellence.

If the rector had not corrected the official statement it would have stood that both victims were sicarios as initially reported by the military and state government. The mainstream media also did not break the story other than a brief coverage of the press conference by the rector Rangel. We didn't hear any more of it, other than a brief apology from one of the President's Secretary Cabinet member's weeks later.

It is hard to believe that while the media having access to witnesses and personnel involved, they could not know that innocent people were killed and that the official statement was not credible. The reason we question this is because not long after several incidents we started to receive e-mails from people who were reporting that innocent people had been killed in some shootouts that were reported to the contrary by the military. The majority of reporting of these events came from social media such as Facebook, Twitter and blogs.

The family of the victims and the people of Mexico have a right to know exactly how these shooting unfolded.

Borderland Beat also reported on a shootout in Anahuac on March 6, 2010 where ten sicarios were reported killed. The military reported two separate confrontations between soldiers and sicarios in the town of Anahuac that left a toll of ten dead, eight of whom were sicarios and two were military. What we found rare was that one of the supposedly heavily armed sicarios was a woman.

A couple of days later we received several anonymous photographs of the alleged sicarios dead on the streets with weapons next to them. Upon close examination of the position of the bodies and the weapons, it just did not look right, while looking at it in a law enforcement perspective.

The weapons were still in the hands of the dead alleged sicarios and the placement of some of the weapons did not seem natural after engaging in a supposed firefight. You can look at the pictures yourselves and be the judge, it's so obvious that you don't even have to be experienced law enforcement to know that things just don't add up. Even a "common citizen" who e-mailed us noticed that on the pictures next to the woman and man, there were no spent casings.

Well it turns out that a male and female killed were in fact not sicarios but innocent bystanders. There was a brief coverage of a press conference by the mayor of Anahuac.

"Two of the six people killed in a confrontation between sicarios and elements of the Mexican Army a few weeks ago at the town of Anahuac were innocent and had nothing to do with the shootout," said the mayor of the municipality, Santos Javier Garza.

The Mayor said that Rocío Elías Garza and Juan Carlos Peña who died in the incident had no link to organized crime and their unfortunate death was because they were caught in the middle of the confrontation.

"They were employees of the maquiladora and apparently were caught by surprise during the gunfire, but they had nothing to do with the acts," said the mayor.

So, this is the same almost identical example from the two students killed in Monterrey, they were killed while either running or walking away and reported to be sicarios by the government until another person with "standing" spoke for them. It wasn't like the media figured it out or anything.

What is troubling is that the two of the innocent bystander victims had weapons placed next to them. The man in the middle of the street had what appeared to be an AK-47 not far from his hand and the female appeared to have a weapon underneath her. If they were not involved in the shooting, but were merely innocent bystanders running away, why were they photographed with weapons?

We are certain that we could find other examples where the military or police forces have killed innocent bystander in the name of the drug war and have attempted to cover it up or reported different to the willing media.

As the confrontations between heavily armed sicarios and Mexican military forces intensified in the populated areas of town and cities, the safety of innocent people must be paramount. If the military is going to incur collateral damage in fighting the sicarios, the Mexican people are no better off than when they are picked off by the drug cartels.

This is problematic for two reasons. One; when we see one of these instances occur, impunity usually always prevails. We see nothing done about it. No investigation, no correction in tactics, no retraining, no policy change, nothing. Second the media itself covers very little of the actual discrepancies after the fact.

Why?

The answer might be that some news reporters have been found executed or threatened for snooping around and some media outlets are afraid to ask too many questions.

There has been reports for a while now that there is almost a news blackout in the northeastern part of Mexico. Granted a lot of reporters continue to attempt to report while risking their lives every day. The case of the mysterious disappearance of Borderland Beat reporter Iliana comes to mind.

Recently, a crew from Belo Television and a reporter for The Dallas Morning News were working in Reynosa. A stranger in jeans and a white and blue shirt approached the reporter and said: "You have no permission to report here. It's best you leave now."

The only entity, the media, that could make a difference in reshaping policy and assuring transparency for whatever reason are not reporting from an impartial standpoint. The Mexican government appears to have imposed a media blackout on coverage of cartel-on-cartel violence and operations in the Tamaulipas border region. Bits of coverage in the traditional Mexican media have misrepresented the degree of military involvement.

What is the U.S. responsibility?

We took note when U.S. Secretary of State Hillary Rodham Clinton said during a recent visit to Mexico, "The grim truth is that these murders are part of a much larger cycle of violence and crime that have impacted communities on both sides of the border."

The US taxpayer is already forking out $1.6 billion in an aid package in the Merida Initiative to the Mexican government. Any pledge by the US for economic aid to help battle the cartels must have assurances from Mexico that part of the core strategy is grounded by strict accountability measures to ensure those funds are being used effectively and responsibly.

We should all support an aggressive front to stop the wave of violence and not allow the cartels to continue to control of a whole nation, but at the same time, the Mexican government must do everything to protect its citizens from the cartels and the too often "friendly fire." The military must know that they are in the middle of populated neighborhoods and they must possess the training and will power to exercise restraint and discipline in the heat of battle. The people who they are sworn to protect depend on it.

El Hummer

Jaime González Durán, El Hummer was an elite Mexican soldier of the "Grupo Aeromóvil de Fuerzas Especiales" (GAFE), a group of military special forces trained in counterinsurgency, intelligence and the tactical apprehension of drug cartel members. El Hummer deserted from the military in the 1990s and became one of the 30 original founding members of the organization known as Los Zetas and third-in-command of that criminal.

At age 27, El Hummer deserted the army to join Los Zetas with Heriberto Lazcano Lazcano and Arturo Guzmán Tens, a former member of the Federal Judicial Police who had a police radio code of Z1. Together, with the 30 other members, he formed part of the personal escort of the leader of the Gulf cartel, Osiel Cárdenas Guillén and they all became the armed wing of the Gulf cartel, the elite group of military deserters that would be known as Los Zetas.

For nine years El Hummer would serve as a sicario for the Gulf cartel under the orders of Heriberto Lazcano, that combined a very violent presence and who used some of the most bloodthirsty acts to reign control. This violent nature of El Hummer opened the doors for him to become the boss of the plaza in Reynosa, Tamaulipas, where he controlled criminal activities for Los Zetas in at least five cities, including his native San Luis Potosi.

El Hummer was suspected of numerous executions, including his alleged involvement in the murder of regional music singer Valentín Elizalde Valencia.

It is said that a song was the cause for the execution of the singer in 2006.

The song was titled "A mis enemigos" or "To my enemies," one of Valentín's most emblematic musical themes. It is presumed that the song was written in honor of the leader of the Cartel de Sinaloa, Joaquín El Chapo Guzmán, and some of the lyrics gave a warning to the adversaries of El Chapo. This angered El Hummer and it became personal.

El Hummer always felt that the only safe place for him was in Reynosa, a region under his control and Los Zetas. Reynosa would be the place where he was captured by federal forces. Reynosa was a place where he never expected an operation of federal agents to surround his house in the Las Quintas subdivision. The operation came to him as such a surprise that the most feared sicario to other cartels and government forces, could only manage to hide under the bed.

Within 12 hours after he was arrested in Reynosa, El Hummer talked with federal prosecutors of the office of the Attorney General known as the Office for Specialized Investigation in Organized Crime (SIEDO).

"I was alone at my home. It was just before noon, when I looked out the window. I noticed that there were federals around my house, and they began to yell, but at that moment I hid under my bed," testified El Hummer after his capture.

"They forced open the front door and they went inside my house, yelling at me to give up. They entered my bedroom and shouted at me: 'come out of there, surrender' and I came out from under the bed. They started hitting me and asking where the weapons and the drugs were located," El Hummer said.

"I told them," he added, "that I did not have any weapons or drugs, I only had a Super 380 caliber pistol. It was then when they saw a safe and they ordered me to open it. I opened it and surrendered 25 or 30 bags with approximately $800,000 in dollars. I also gave them a briefcase that was in my car with $100,000 more."

"They then took me away in one of their vans straight to the airport. The money was supposed to be delivered to El Cos as profits from the sale of marijuana that he had made into the United States, specifically in McAllen, Texas," Said El Hummer.

An armed commando tried to rescue El Hummer when he was being transported to the airport where he would be taken to Mexico City. As El Hummer was being transported to the airport with a full police and military escort, but an armed commando, presumably Los Zetas, intercepted the escort of security forces and a gunfight ensued. The federal police and military were able to repel the attack and some of the sicarios fled, eventually allowing the transport of El Hummer.

A young lady, by the name of Gloria Garcia, said she managed to survive the shootout while she was at a drive through of a restaurant waiting for her order.

"Soldiers ran from one place to another while other vehicles were moving at high rate of speed shooting at the military forces. Suddenly I turned around and saw that the military was firing at a truck that was next to me. I turned around to tried to flee the place when two men arrived firing toward the military soldiers. I was frozen in fear and all I could do was pray to God for my safety.

She ducked inside her vehicle and could hear a barrage of gun fire, and felt several rounds impact her vehicle. After a few minutes the gunfire stopped and she tried to get out of her car, but a soldier told her to remain inside, as it was not safe yet. She said that after a couple of hours, she took cover inside a nearby bank. Her vehicle sustained numerous impacts from rounds, huge holes were visible all over her vehicle.

After the dust settled there was maroon Gran Cherokee riddled with bullet holes and two sicarios on the ground that had surrendered. Other vehicles with armed sicarios managed to escape after the shootout.

El Hummer would eventually be transported to Mexico City where he was presented to the media during a press conference. Also presented were large amounts of US currency and a large arsenal of weapons.

According to El Hummer, Osiel Cárdenas Guillén was still in charge of the Gulf cartel even from the US prison where he was confined.

El Hummer gave details of how the Gulf cartel was restructured, expanded and operated in several states, mainly in Oaxaca and Veracruz. The leadership of the Cartel del Golfo went to Jorge Costilla Sánchez, El Cos or La Sombra, alongside with Heriberto Lazcano Lazcano, El Lazca, the boss of Los Zetas.

El Hummer explained that Cárdenas Guillén sends all his orders through his lawyers who defend him, who pass the information to El Cos and El Lazca who are responsible for executing them. This has been done like this since Cárdenas Guillén was arrested on March 14, 2003 in the city of Matamoros.

The arrest of Cárdenas Guillén had not slowed down operations. The installation of plaza bosses in numerous cities in the Gulf coast ensured the smooth operation of drug trafficking and cartel operations.

For example, in Veracruz the plaza boss was El Gonzo, another of the founders of sicarios of Los Zetas. El Gonzo reported directly to the head of the state who was Miguel Treviño, El 40. The entire state police in these cities are said to be involved in the protection of Gulf cartel and operations of Los Zetas.

Lazca's Affiliation

Lazcano joined the Mexican GAFE, the Mexican Army special forces. During his tenure in the Mexican Army, Lazcano reportedly received military training from the Israeli Defense Forces and the United States Army, but eventually deserted in 1998, after eight years of service. Upon his desertion, he was recruited by Gulf Cartel bosses Osiel Cárdenas Guillén with around 30 other soldiers to work as the enforcers of the Gulf Cartel, forming the paramilitary group known as Los Zetas.

The thirty deserters were to become Guillén personal bodyguards, and later, as his mercenary wing. These deserters were enticed with salaries much higher than what they were paid by the military. Some of these former GAFE members reportedly received training in commando and urban warfare from the Israeli and U.S. Special Forces.

From time to time, I would get messages from active military US soldiers talking about how these elite Mexican soldiers had dishonored the Especial Forces military code, that was recognized universally. This was one of them:

"This is not to disrespect current honorable members of the Mexican Special Operations Forces.

The Gafes are supposed to be the elite of the Mex Armed Forces. Supposedly some former members have chosen to dishonor the brotherhood of sec-ops worlwide by utilizing their acquired skill set to promote criminality and create chaos against the populace and civilians of the country of Mexico. Many descriptions are used to describe their skill set. I can confirm what they can and cannot do.

1. Reconnaissance
2. Jungle Operations
3. Communications both LOS and BLOS

4. Urban Operations which has morphed into what is called FISH and CHIPS (Fighting In Someone's House and Causing Havoc In Peoples Streets).

5. Military Intelligence and Analysis.

6. Small unit Operations (Patrolling-Ambush-Counter Ambush Mostly Balanced and Combined).

7. Airborne and Air Assault.

8. General Weapons Familiarization

These are the basic skillsets as taught to their officers and senior NCO's. The purpose for this instruction is not only for their own National defense, but also to allow some sort of standard for integration in a major conflict with other NATO forces.

As it stands from investigations and information gleaned from various sources including this website, it appears that very few GAFE trained ZETAS remain. The bulk of the work is being accomplished by untrained or poorly trained individuals who have the basic rudiments of warfare but are very clearly not well rehearsed.

It's very easy to overwhelm an enemy with numbers or terrorize an unarmed population with a show of force. It is another when met with equal numbers or a smaller highly trained unit as evidenced by the news stories of the DTO's being thrashed rather soundly by Mexico's heroic Marine Infantry and on occasion Mexico's Army Infantry units. These are the "non-elite" units but with sound fundamentals, fire and maneuver, good communication and field leadership the good guys typically prevail.

That being said, here in the US many of us in my particular military unit keep our finger on the pulse of what's going on down in Mexico. You have no idea how many of us are just itching at the chance to avenge the deaths of all those innocent people and children, to restore peace and hope in the people of Mexico and to end the scourge of the indiscriminate assaults, shakedowns and kidnappings on the population. We consistently and independently prepare daily sitreps on the happenings and truly pray that we are given the green light soon.

Not one more citizen Mexican or American should live in fear of these amateurs. We live and train to fight every day perfecting our craft and I would gladly give my life to ensure true freedom and prosperity to the REAL honest hardworking citizens of Mexico. I took an oath several years ago to defend my country from ALL enemies foreign and domestic and right now every DTO member is a foreign enemy to me and my unit. Godspeed to the people of Mexico and you are not alone.

Anxiously awaiting the greenlight.

Sua Sponte

SSG M. Dietrich

3rd Bn 75th Ranger Regiment"

One of the GAFE that deserted the military to join Los Zetas that he was talking about was Lazcano who had a weakness for blonde women, a passion for horse racing and in the last five years, he had been passionate about another sport: the hunting of gazelles, zebras and exotic animals in reserves in Coahuila and San Luis Potosí.

He was born in 1974 in Apan, Hidalgo, a place that is famous for its pulque (a Mexican alcoholic drink made by fermenting sap from the maguey). He had planned to make the army a career, but a former soldier convinced him to become a bodyguard and lured him to leave the military armed forces to join another force, a criminal organization known as Los Zetas. That was pivotal point in his life, it was 1998.

His name was Heriberto Lazcano Lazcano, they call him "El Verdugo" (The Executioner) or "El Lazca." He managed the forces of more than 400 criminal elements in 18 states of the Republic that dedicated themselves to abductions, extortions, homicides and the sale of illicit drugs.

That is why he was number one in the organization of "Los Zetas."

This was the origin of "Los Zetas", which owes its name to the color blue zeta, the color of the uniforms of Army officers.

Second Lieutenant Alejandro Lucio Morales Betancourt "Z-2" was a boss of the criminal group until his arrest on November 17, 2001. The first task entrusted to Los Zetas was the elimination of the Gulf cartel's adversaries.

And from that moment on, Lazcano distinguished himself from the others.

In February 1999 Osiel Cárdenas Guillén met Arturo Guzmán Decena "Z-1" in a house in Reynosa and ordered him to gather 20 gunmen to assassinate Rolando López Salinas "El Rolys."

They arrived at a house in Miguel Aleman but failed to achieve their goal because Arturo Guzmán and Lazcano were the only one who assaulted the house firing gunshots but were met with heavy gunfire from the people inside.

Lazcano fired a gas grenade inside the house causing an explosion and everyone ran out causing various casualties in the house. The Ministerial Police was responsible for covering up the crime scene so that no one knew who the killers were.

At that time, in March 2002, Decena and Lazcano were "hunting" 4 police officers of the Nuevo Laredo Municipal Police. They were following them and the police officers noticed they were being followed. The officers were abducted, tortured and made them confess that they worked for the rival gang of Dionisio Román García "El Chacho," operator of "El Chapo" Guzmán.

The police officers were killed by Guzmán Decena, Lazcano, "El Caris" and Leopoldo Flores Soto. The bodies were incinerated inside a 200-liter metal drum, until they were completely consumed.

Then it was the turn of "Chacho" himself, whom "Los Zetas" executed on May 13, 2002.

Between 1997 and 2002, Osiel Cárdenas implemented an internal investment to expand his organization.

They called it "la polla" and it consisted of giving each new soldier that deserted and any civilian who joined their ranks a sum of 3 thousand dollars.

With the money, they were to buy cocaine, cross it to the United States, place it in the market and make contacts for distribution.

Everyone bought the cocaine from the Colombians Vicente and Camilo, who were contacted in Coatzacoalcos. As they made profits, each Zeta reinvested them in more coke and were able to grow their quantities of drugs from various transactions.

Heriberto Lazcano Lazcano with the code "Z-3," bought 18 kilos of cocaine.

The reproduction of the criminal enterprise was moving fast and up until then, there were no information or records from the PGR, that the Zetas were dedicated to the criminal activities of drug trafficking. Everything would change in a short period of time.

Various investigations of the ministerial department and federal files in Mexico as well as in the United States closely followed "El Lazca." He had managed to maintain his leadership role in the organization through his brutal methods in counteracting with his enemies and establishing his regime of internal discipline: any "Zetas" that violated the code or betrayed the organization were executed, tortured or punished.

Even if it was a friend. Lazcano always separated his businesses from his personal relationships. That was very well known by Alfredo Rangel Buendía "El Chicles", one of his most trusted men, who one day borrowed money form Lazca but did not pay him back in the time agreed.

"Lazcano ordered all of the sicarios from the Gulf Cartel to kill El Chicles. The plan was for Iván Velásquez Caballero "El Talibán" or "L-50 " to tell him to come to a central point in Colonia Madero in Nuevo Laredo. When El Chicles arrived, they were to intercept him, abduct him and kill him.

Instead El Taliban convinced Lazcano to just punish him instead and that he himself will get his money back. Lazcano hesitantly agreed, ordering El Taliban to just tie him up and sequester him for a month. To give him a little bit of water and food a day so that he did not need to go to the bathroom too often. This was related by a protected witness named "Karen."

Since the capture of Osiel Cárdenas in 2003, Lazca directed "Los Zetas" from drug trafficking to other crimes, established new operations similar to the military that included sicarios from the "Kaibiles" of Guatemala. He would deploy spectacular tactical assaults in operations to rescue some of his accomplices.

The Kaibiles were a special operations wing of the Armed Forces of Guatemala. They specialize in jungle warfare tactics and counter-insurgency operations.

His gunmen claim to be part of "La Compañía" and Lazcano had been responsible for making them feel that way. Every end of the year, he would organize narco parties (posadas) in Matamoros with their plaza bosses and, they would make plans for operations and assignments.

On January 14, 2002, the Army arrested Rubén Sauceda Rivera "El Cacahuate", the treasurer of the organization, and on November 21 of the same year, the historical leader of Los Zetas, Arturo Guzmán Decena "El Z1", was killed in a confrontation with the military in Matamoros.

The final climate came on March 14, 2003, when Osiel Cárdenas was arrested in a military operation.

In 14 months, the Army left the Gulf Cartel without its leader, without their finance chief and without the head of its armed wing Los Zetas. Coincidentally, at the same time a new external front was waged when Joaquín "El Chapo" Guzmán and partner Arturo Beltrán Leyva "El Barbas", then partners, decided to invade and steal the plaza of Nuevo Laredo from Los Zetas, when they invaded with 200 sicarios Sinaloenses (from Sinaloa).

The Zetas found themselves in a fierce war that they had to face with very little finances and without leadership.

One day in late 2009, Zeta bosses Heriberto "El Lazca" Lazcano and Miguel Angel "El40" Treviño called a meeting of top Zetas in Matamoros, where they voted to split from the Gulf Cartel. After the split, Los Zetas and Gulf cartel began to secretly arm themselves in anticipation of conflict. By February 2010, the Gulf Cartel and Los Zetas began a bloody war in northern Tamaulipas for the main drug trafficking routes into South Texas.

By late 2010 the tensions between the Gulf cartel and Los Zetas boiled over into open war in the country's east, with the Gulf cartel reaching out to its former rivals in Sinaloa as well as La Familia Michoacána to align under the name "New Federation" and pushing Los Zetas from one of their traditional strongholds, Reynosa, though not out of Nuevo Laredo or Monterrey. In its weakened state, Los Zetas began increasing operations outside the normal scope of drug trafficking, such as kidnapping for ransom. Cartel-related violence in the country reached new heights, with more than 11,000 deaths on record.

Violence continued to rise in all parts of the country. The Sinaloa Federation continued to expand its territory north and east, taking over areas formerly under the influence of the

Carrillo Fuentes Organization (Juarez Cartel) and the Arellano Felix Organization (Tijuana Cartel). With the help of Sinaloa, the Gulf cartel had been able to repel offenses from Los Zetas in Reynosa and Matamoros, though the Zetas proved to be very resilient.

Mateo Díaz López "El Comandante Mateo" or "Z-10" testified on July 17, that everything changed when Lazcano emerged as the new leader.

His first action was to employ "Kaibiles" from Guatemala and capitalize on the abductions, extortions and homicides inside and outside of Tamaulipas, to have financial resources that this war demanded.

When Osiel was arrested, there were many problems within the organization, as their main leaders such as Eduardo Costilla and Gregorio Sauceda became disorganized and wanted to hide, but Lazcano took control of the organization and tried to bring calm.

In order to sustain an organization with different operations, Lazcano created a new structure divided into regional specialized cells that dedicated themselves in criminal activities; "estacas" or groups of people that operated at the municipal level; "halcones" or lookouts, and auditors who reviewed the whole operation from time to time.

For El Lazca it was important to have basic rules regarding communications between members of the Cartel.

The number of Nextel cell phones belonging to Lazcano were identified by the letters MD, but every time they would arrest a member of the organization, all cellular phones would be destroyed and new ones bought along with the radios.

Along with being coerced to participate in the reunions (posadas) at the end of the year, there was also incentives. The reunions were held so that everyone who worked for Los Zetas got to know each other. At those meetings bonuses were paid, raffles were held to give away houses and cars. And in those reunions was when Heriberto Lazcano Lazcano decided what sicarios were going to go with them to the different places they had at their command, including Mexico City, all under the command of "El Rex." This was testified by protected witness "Karen" on June 24, 2007.

Thus, the Zetas resisted.

Lazcano would eventually be killed in a shootout with the Mexican Marines on October 7, 2012. After his death, his body was stolen from the funeral home by armed sicarios.

Alliances or agreements between drug cartels were shown to be fragile, tense and temporary. Since February 2010, the major cartels had aligned in two factions, one integrated by the Juárez Cartel, Tijuana Cartel, Los Zetas Cartel and the Beltrán-Leyva Cartel; the other faction integrated by the Gulf Cartel, Sinaloa Cartel and La Familia Cartel.

There were few publicly available details regarding the history and earlier organization of the Cartel del Pacifico (CPS), which was formerly known as the Beltran Leyva Organization (BLO). The cartel's leadership was comprised of five brothers, the top lieutenants, and the organization was based out of Sinaloa state. The CPS used to maintain operations on both Mexican coasts and its northern and southern borders, which moved significant quantities of cocaine into the US.

The dynamics of how the cartels were fragmented had a lot to do on how the federal government deploy their offensive. The Calderon regime had taken on the cartels, but some were hit more than others and then there was the other thing that not many were talking about, corruption at the highest level.

The Allende Massacre

From March 18 through March 20, 2011, Coahuila lived one of its bloodiest chapters in recent history, the massacre and mass disappearance of people in Ciudad Allende, that also extended to other towns north of Allende.

Los Zetas had established a strong hold in the north part of Coahuila when they advanced on that territory for the Gulf Cartel (CDG) to take Piedras Negras. Mellado Galindo Cruz, Commander Mellado or Z-10 , had led about 100 gunmen who threatened all drug traffickers in that border to join them or be killed.

Before they arrive, Hector Moreno smuggled narcotics on his own along with US citizen Alfonso "Poncho" Cuellar and José Luis Garza Gaytan. Another independent drug trafficker was Efren Tavira, who operated with a group of "narco juniors".

They decided to join Los Zetas.

Miguel Treviño Morales Z-40 and his brother Omar Treviño Morales Z-42 decided to use the experience of those drug traffickers and put them in front of their cocaine smuggling operation to the United States.

To protect their illegal activities, they bought protection from the Army, Federal Police, delegates from the PGR and state officials, especially the attorney general department.

The leader in the Piedras Negras plaza was reported to be Raul Lucio Hernandez Lechuga "El Lucky."

Lucio Hernandez was the owner of several businesses using assumed names, among them the Black City Mall and Mario's Steakhouse. Adriana Monserrat Cardenas, an associate and lover of el Lucky, was managing several of his business interests in Piedras Negras, along with other members of her family.

Under Lucio Hernandez hierarchy in the plaza was Mario Alfonso "Poncho" Cuellar, an ex-officer with the defunct Policia Federal de Caminos (federal transit police). Poncho Cuéllar was initially recruited and mentored by the late Tony Tormenta. Cuéllar was known to be a close friend and associate of Z-40.

The DEA had found $802,000 dollars in cash vacuum-packed and hidden in the gas tank of a pickup. The driver said he worked for a guy he knew only as "El Diablo."

After more arrests, DEA Agent Richard Martinez and Assistant U.S. Attorney Ernest Gonzalez determined that El Diablo was Jose Vasquez who was now the leading Zetas cocaine distributor in east Texas, moving truckloads of drugs, guns and money each month. Cuéllar and Vasquez were moving between 500 and 800 kilos of cocaine per month across the border.

As they prepared to arrest him, Vasquez slipped across the border to Ciudad Allende, Coahuila, Mexico where he sought protection from members of the Zeta's inner circle.

But Martinez and Gonzalez saw an opportunity in his escape. If they could persuade Vasquez to cooperate, it would give them rare access to the senior ranks of the notoriously impenetrable cartel and a chance to capture its leaders, particularly the Treviño brothers, Z-40 and Z-42.

DEA Agent Martinez persuaded Vasquez, a member of los Zetas, to give him the traceable identification numbers of the cell phones of Miguel Ángel Treviño Z-40 and his brother Omar Z-42, both leaders of Los Zetas.

What Assistant U.S. Attorney Martinez wanted was the trackable personal identification numbers of the Treviños' cellular phones. Vasquez had good reason to cooperate with the US agents, his wife and mother were still living in Texas.

Under pressure to get the PINs, Vasquez turned to Hector Moreno, by using some leverage he had of his own.

Gilberto Moreno was Hector Moreno's brother who had been caught driving the truck with the $802,000 in the gas tank.

Facing 20 years in prison, Gilberto had confessed that he was working for Los Zetas and that the cash belonged to the Treviño brothers.

Mario Alfonso "Poncho" Cuéllar was the man responsible of getting new cell phones every three or four weeks for his bosses. Cuéllar assigned that task to his right-hand man, Héctor "El Negro" Moreno. The Zeta who would end up giving the numbers to the DEA was José Vásquez, a native of Dallas and one of the largest cocaine movers in Texas.

Vasquez got all the numbers, including the ones for Z-40, and Z-42. Vasquez didn't know what the DEA was going to do with them. He thought they were going to try to wiretap them or something to that effect. Vasquez never thought they were going to send the numbers back to Mexico. He warned them not to do that, because it was going to get a lot of people killed. They promised they wouldn't. DEA Agent Martinez told Vasquez he had to trust him.

However, the DEA made a huge mistake of sharing the information with an agency of the Mexican police despite the warning. The chilling reports that would eventually come out about the horrific massacre in Allende made the US authorities realize the grave mistake that had triggered a leak by Mexican authorities. After Martinez gave the intelligence information to his superior, it was passed to a DEA supervisor in Mexico City. He then, in turn, shared them with a Mexican federal police unit that had been specially created to conduct operations under the DEA's direction.

The confidential information on the PIN cell numbers was leaked to Z-40, warning him that someone in his organization had betrayed him.

Most members of the Mexican Federal Police Unit received mandatory training and vetting by the DEA. But despite that vetting, most Mexican police units had a poor record of keeping information out of the hands of criminals. It was revealed that a supervisor with the Mexican federal police had leaked the information of the cellular PIN numbers to Los Zetas.

Vasquez had been given the cellular IDs by Héctor Moreno, a lieutenant under Mario Alfonso Cuéllar, who was the main operator of Los Zetas in Coahuila. The cellular PIN numbers were shared with the DEA and were used by Mexican intelligence to attempt to trace the location of the top bosses.

It was not difficult for the Zetas leaders to narrow down the list of people under suspicion, very few people had access to their PIN numbers. It didn't take long for the Zeta bosses to find out exactly who had betrayed them. They knew exactly who they needed to get revenge from. As soon as they found out who it was, the certain death of the traitors was assured.

Cuéllar said that Z-40 contacted him and told him to turn in any drugs he may have on his possession. Cuéllar knew that in the past when a member was going to be executed, they got all their drugs back first. This worried Cuéllar. Z-40 asked Cuéllar where he was going to be later in the day, he told him he was going to be at the racetrack. He never went because he was afraid. The sicarios of Z-40 went looking for him at the racetrack and became upset when they did not find him there. They sent Cuéllar a message that Z-40 wanted to talk to him. Cuéllar knew he was a target for execution and knew he had to get out of dodge ASAP.

Mario Alfonso "Poncho" Cuéllar, Héctor "El Negro" Moreno and José "La Güiche" Luis Garza (whose family's ranch was the scene of many of the killings) betrayed the criminal organization and were forced to flee the state of Coahuila to the United States. In their hands they allegedly carried 5 to 10 million dollars from profits of drug trafficking and an accounting book from the criminal organization.

Z-40 became enraged and wanted to punish all who dared to betray the Zeta organization. Z-40 warned the men to return the money or else they would kill all their family and friends.

The men knew they were dead men either way if caught by Los Zetas, so they men ignored the demand.

This would initiate the reign of terror in "Los Cinco Manantiales", (five springs) in the northern part of Coahuila. Los Cinco Manantiales are the towns of Allende, Morelos, Zaragoza, Villa Union and Nava,

Cuéllar and Moreno who had fled to the United States became protected witnesses of the DEA. Before leaving Coahuila, Cuéllar had warned those who worked for him to flee or hide, as their lives were in danger. Both agreed to cooperate with US law enforcement in exchange for clemency.

The massacre was set off by the corruption of an agent of the Mexican Federal Police who knew that the DEA had received the PIN numbers.

The families of Cuéllar and Moreno, for the most part, lived in the region of Allende, an area along the way to Piedras Negras, a border town with the United States. Only 40 miles separate Allende from the US border. This set of event would unleashed the monster, that would target whole towns and their people.

On the afternoon of March 18, 2011, a caravan of 50 late model trucks with dozens of Zeta gunmen onboard entered Ciudad Allende. They blocked the roads to the entrance of the town. They started knocking down doors from homes, killing people and making them disappear. Men, elderly, women, children, it did not matter to them, they were all the same.

Whole families were kidnapped or killed, including infants and children. Even servants of the families were made to "disappear." Many of those taken had the misfortune to simply have the same last names as the people in the hit list.

Horrific things began happening in the evening. Armed men began arriving. They were going house to house, looking for family and friends of the people who had done them wrong. At 11 at night there was no traffic on the streets. There was no movement of any kind. Everyone was in lockdown in their homes, terrified and not daring to even look out the windows of their homes. But it was not totally quiet, every so often they could hear screaming and gunfire. People in their homes were trying to reach anyone on the phone or on social media that could help them, but no one came.

A flame was set at blaze, and it would not be stopped.

The day they drove in to town, they started shooting at homes and abducting anyone seen in public that at one point it included four older women and two children. The next day, they went to the house of a person with the name of Garza, where they abducted a man, his wife and their young son.

The Zetas put them all in police cars of the Allende police department and transported them to one of the ranches where they were holding many people from during the weekend. When night came, it was the end for them. They were taken out to be executed.

The Zeta attack provided evidence of collusion with the local authorities. The 20 municipal police officers of Allende were instructed not go out on patrol, not to respond to calls for help and to detain anyone with the names of their traitors, so they could be turned over to Los Zetas.

The hitmen went to the mayor's office and demanded the home addresses from the property tax records of all the properties of the traitors and their families. The mayor of

Allende, Sergio Lozano, and his municipal police cooperated with Los Zetas, to include saying nothing about the disappearances and taking no action to stop it. Some of the police officers actually participated in rounding up people to turn over to Los Zetas.

Los Zetas destroyed and burned everything in their path; houses, ranches, businesses. For Allende and its residents, it was converted into an apocalypse scene, all in the name of hatred and revenge.

They killed and killed, and like cattle they loaded the bodies on the back of trucks.

A dozen Allende municipal police officers led various groups of assassins to the houses that had been located by the sicarios.

In one of the residences of the Garza Gaytan family, the Zetas were fired upon and three gunmen fell. In the end though, the man who dared to shoot at them in an act of self-protection, along with several of his relatives, were killed by the gunmen.

A few miles outside of town, the gunmen descended on several neighboring ranches along a dimly lit two-lane highway. The properties belonged to one of Allende's oldest clans, the Garzas. The family mostly raised livestock and did odd contracting jobs, including coal mining. But according to family members, some of them also worked for the cartel.

Now those connections were proving to be deadly. Among those the Zetas suspected of being a snitch was José Luis Garza, a relatively low-level cartel operative, whose father, Luis, owned one of the ranches. It was payday, and several workers had gone to the ranch to pick up their money. When the gunmen showed up, they rounded up everyone they could find and took them hostage, never to be seen again. After nightfall, flames began rising from one of the ranch's large cinder-block storage sheds. Los Zetas had begun burning the bodies of some of those they'd killed.

That weekend of March 18 through the 20, 2011, Los Zetas attacked 32 houses and seven ranches in Allende, in order to take revenge on Alfonso Cuéllar, Héctor Moreno and José Luis Garza. When they could, they would demolished dwellings and residences with heavy machinery.

On Saturday, March 19, the gunmen summoned several heavy-equipment operators and ordered them to tear down dozens of houses and businesses across the region. Many of the properties were in busy, well-to-do neighborhoods within sight or earshot of not only passersby but also of government offices, police stations and military outposts. The gunmen invited townspeople to take whatever they wanted, triggering a free-for-all of looting.

Allende was transformed into a post-apocalyptic scene, full of destruction and desertion.

From Allende the gunmen moved north along the dry, flat landscape, rounding up people as they covered the 35 miles to the city of Piedras Negras, a grimy sprawl of assembly factories on the Rio Grande. The attackers drove many of their victims to one of the Garza ranches, including Gerardo Heath, a 15-year-old high school football player, and Edgar Ávila, a 36-year-old factory engineer. Neither had anything to do with the cartel or with those the cartel believed were working with the DEA. They just happened to be in the way.

You could see the signs that something unspeakable happened in Allende, a quiet ranching town of about 23,000, just a 40-minute drive from Eagle Pass, Texas. Entire blocks of some of the town's busiest streets were left in ruins. Once garish mansions were now crumbling shells, with gaping holes on the walls, charred ceilings, cracked marble countertops and toppled columns. Strewn among the rubble were tattered, mud-covered remnants of lives torn apart.

In the ranch Los Garza, Los the Zetas brought in a truck with metal drums of gasoline.

They drenched bodies with fuel they had piled up against the walls in a warehouse and set them ablaze. They shot anyone they found still alive. To make some of the remains disappear, they dug narco graves.

In another place in the ranch Los Tres Hermanos (municipality of Zaragoza) they killed and burned people, using another procedure: they brought in drums, made holes in the bottom and sides. Then they put one body in each drum. Then they poured fuel on the bodies and set them on fire. After five or six hours the bodies were completely burned to ashes. They threw the remains in a ditch and in a well so that they could not be found.

In the Piedras Negras prison, which served as a den of the Zetas, Los Zetas forced 40 people to kneel and shot them in the city of Piedras Negras. This was according to testimony given by Adolfo Efrén Tavira to the Human Rights office in the University of Texas.

In Monclova, the night of March 18, 2011 a "surgical" operation was carried out by Los Zetas to kidnapped 7 bookkeepers and as many members of Los Zetas who were under the command of Poncho Cuellar.

The same happened in the coalfield municipalities as well as in Nava, Zaragoza, Morelos and other towns of Cinco Manantiales, where they kidnapped dozens of people.

In Piedras Negras, gunmen located and kidnapped 41 relatives and friends of Cuellar, who were taken away to an area in Pico del Águila to face the Trevino Morales brothers in person. They were all killed.

Among those arrested was Efren Tavira. He was saved from being killed because his Zeta friends told Z-40 that since Poncho fled he could worked for them.

Before leaving the area, Efren Tavira would witness when Z-40, Z-42 and other gunmen peppered Poncho's 40 friends with bullets.

Borderland Beat reporters Chivis and DD were boots on the ground in the northern part of Coahuila during the massacre of Allende. Chivis found herself in the area at the same time the attack on Allende was taking place:

"We could see the smoke from afar, yet the news was void of reports. I along with everyone else in the area could see what was happening with our own eyes, yet nothing was reported. Residents were left with no news or alerts on the streets, Coahuila was a narco news blackout state.

On March 18, 2011 we were driving from Monterrey, Nuevo Leon on Hwy 57, when we saw the smoke ahead. We saw a narco convoy and first responders but as in many other incidents of violence, the fire department were warned not to intervene. Residents flooded the emergency center with pleas for help, but help never arrived.

We decided to turn around and go through Tamaulipas and up through Texas and across to Del Rio and into Mexico that way.

I was scared far more than I ever had been while in Mexico, yet strangely residents didn't share the same level of fear as I. For example, on the second day we had a function at a school in Piedras Negras but traveling there was dangerous. I didn't want us to go. My staff said in the daytime it would be ok. They went, I didn't. They teased me for being afraid, I scolded them for their lack of fear.

In 2010 Tamaulipas became a blackout narco news state. Coahuila was even a blackout state even prior to 2010. In 2010 the SDR tuitero (Twitter) movement began with #ReynosaFollow leading the way. This movement filled the vacuum created by the conventional blackout media. By using social media, these warriors were able to send out warnings and reports of situations at risk in Tamaulipas, and joining states such as Coahuila, of narco roadblocks, shoot-outs, and other dangerous situations. This was a very perilous endeavor that cost the lives of Tamaulipas bloggers, some decapitated, hanged, and one, a doctor, abducted, made to "confess" on her twitter account and killed.

These brave citizen reporters have saved countless of lives. One of our reporters at BB joined the group in Tamaulipas who created a manifesto that was published to the world. The word and warnings on the street became news of information on social media.

And this was how we were able to receive any reports of what was happening in Allende.

We have had the best ongoing coverage anywhere. During the massacre, residents from Allende and Piedras Negras wrote to BB giving their accounts.

We covered the trial of the Zetas in Texas that allowed us direct reporting in court, especially when Cuellar took the stand.

For me it was difficult to know when to stop writing my post as there was an astronomical amount of more information.

There was much more happening in the surrounding cities, including military clashes, killings, destruction. It was not only Allende," recounted Chivis.

There was little or no press coverage except for Borderland Beat that published the first story on the massacre on March 26, 2011, just days after the terror ended. But no one paid attention. The story basically remained hidden (except to BB readers).

State emergency response authorities took some 250 calls from people reporting general disorder, fires, fights and home invasions throughout the region. But numerous people interviewed said no one came to help. The police emergency line 089 received 26 calls from Allende and 1,200 from Piedras Negras between March 18 and March 22, 2011.

Of the calls, 100 were to report 42 different fires in Piedras Negras, and nine in Allende.

Despite the calls. No authority responded. No municipal, state nor federal authorities. Due to the inaction of the authorities, there were no apprehensions for the horrific acts.

The police recorded emergency calls for help.

"Help! They are burning! They are burning houses!"

Nothing happened, there was no response. The government allowed the town of Allende to burn and their residents to be massacred.

There was a recorded emergency call from a female frantic reporting on the incidents; "Allende is a town without law, burning houses, the abduction of many people, there are many people missing, the Zetas they took them. I think someone betrayed the cartel because there is a brutal, horrible disorder. Please there are too many people missing, there are looting homes. This has been occurring since Friday afternoon and it's going on every night." The caller then hung up.

Almost all Borderland Beat contributors at the time were getting messages on social media of people frantically pleading for help.

Months later the Governor Rubén Moreira set up an operation consisting of hundreds of state and federal police, that also included military to conduct a thorough investigation of the massacre. Between January 26 and February 5, 2014, they searched for traces of missing people.

They found many narco graves and perforated metal drums where the bodies were supposedly burned with fuel. They found bone fragments. In total, 66 bone fragments were found along with 68 dental fragments.

The massacre was so brutal that there were no clear numbers of how many victims actually died.

The government of Coahuila estimated that 28 people had disappeared. However other media sources estimated the number to be more around 42 to 60 disappearances who were believed to be dead. Other sources, specially witnesses on the ground, said that the real number was around 300 people that were missing and probably dead.

Of the missing 20 were relatives of Garza, countless friends and family of Cuéllar and 40 workers and friends of Moreno.

A couple of people connected to criminal activities from the incident were arrested but not directly charged for the massacre. It included mostly former local police and low level cartel members who were just following orders. No one really was charged for the massacre.

A criminal judge of Piedras Negras issued formal arrest for the former mayor of Allende, Sergio Alonso Rodriguez Lozano, for crimes committed in the Zetas slaughter that occurred in Allende on March 2011.

The former mayor was charged with aggravated kidnapping and complicity in the massive disappearance of residents in Allende.

He was also charged with having knowledge of the crimes that Los Zetas were going to commit in later days, as he and another official attended a meeting with Los Zetas and agreed not to intervene to allow Los Zetas to operate freely.

The Mexican federal authorities question the role of the US authorities and pointed out the failure of the DEA to be transparent hindering the investigation to find the truth of what really happened. The Mexican government maintained that the DEA held important information needed to understand what role people played in events leading to the massacre. The Coahuila prosecutor's office had not been able to extradite or obtain information from the "main players" of the massacre that were in custody in the United States, for at least two of them were protected witnesses in the US.

The Mexican government would eventually apologize to the community of Allende for having failed them in protecting them and holding people accountable.

El Zeta 40

Miguel Ángel Treviño Morales, El Z-40 was born in 1973, in Nuevo Laredo, Tamaulipas, part of a poor large family consisting of six brothers and six sisters. El Z-40, grew up near the border with the United States. In his youth he was part of a gang known as "Los Tejas," in Dallas, Texas. The gang dedicated themselves to stealing cars and the sale of street drugs. They were part of the network of the Gulf cartel operating in the United States. In 1993 at the age of 23 he was arrested in Dallas on minor charges and for resisting arrest.

He would eventually become judicial police in Matamoros, Tamaulipas. In 1999 at the age of 27 years of age he would join the armed wing of the Gulf Cartel, known as Los Zetas. Los Zetas was mainly composed of former military deserters and at the time, were led by Arturo Guzmán Decena, Z-1, under the orders of Osiel Cárdenas Guillén.

They essentially formed Mexico's first narco-army. Many of the soldiers came from impoverished backgrounds. The army had offered jobs but the cartels offered money and power. The three most trusted men within the Zetas were Guzmán Decena (Z-1), Rogelio González Pizaña (Z-2), and Heriberto Lazcano (Z-3); the Zs were code names denoting their ranking and seniority in the organization.

These three men, along with new recruit Treviño Morales (Z-40), embarked on secret missions into cities and towns across Tamaulipas, including Nuevo Laredo. This was Treviño Morales's hometown, and he knew the targets intimately. He gained the reputation of a traitor. They were there to execute members rivals of the Gulf cartel and ensure that the gulf cartel remained the most powerful drug-trafficking organization in the gulf coast.

They suddenly found themselves rolling up into Nuevo Laredo sporting powerful military-style weapons, some smuggled by veterans of the Gulf War, like AR-15s and .50-caliber machine guns. People were paralyzed.

Z-40 reached the top spot position among Los Zetas becoming a plaza boss for the Gulf Cartel, in Nuevo Laredo, Tamaulipas. His job was to prevent the penetration of the Sinaloa Cartel in to the Gulf region. It was then that Z-40 began to create his bloodthirsty reputation by orchestrating dozens of brutal executions of members from rival criminal groups. On one occasion, to send a message to some of the street drug dealers that they were stealing part of his profits, he personally turned a man into pulp that made the victim unrecognizable after pounding him with a sledge hammer and another occasion he opened the chest of a man with a butcher's knife while still alive.

The message was clear, don't ever think about trying to conduct business in Zetas turf.

The cruel methods of Z40 are part of the new folklore of the narco violence in Mexico, as well as their ability to escape unscathed from authorities from their attacks and shootings against rival cartels.

Z-40 had a fundamental difference with the members of Los Zetas, he was not a military man. El Z-40 did not have a military career as was the case with all of the other 30 original members of Los Zetas.

He was recruited by Osiel Cárdenas Guillen when he was one of his main messengers. His main valuable skill in the organization was that he spoke English, a skill that helped Osiel to conduct business in the United States. Z-40 climbed the structure and positions of the narco syndicate to become the leader of the zetas, despite the fact that at one point in his life he was washing cars to earn a living. Osiel, then top boss of the Gulf, formed Los Zetas to be his own personal bodyguards. After the creation of Los Zetas, Osiel decided to appoint Z-40 as right hand of Heriberto Lazcano Lazcano, El

Lazca. Various reports and analysts indicated that z-40 would become even more violent than El Lazca.

When Z-40 was starting out in the trafficking business in Texas he met another US trafficker by the name of Mario Alvarado while deer hunting. Z-40 and Alvarado would eventually start working together, moving kilos of cocaine across the border. Some of the dope entrusted to Alvarado was seized and Alavarado ended up owing Z-40 around $500.000. Alavarado was brought in to Nuevo Laredo by Omar Trevino El 42 (brother of Z-40) and was held captive until his people in the US were able to pay most of the debt.

Z-40 had stash houses all along the border and the trafficking business for him was flourishing. Two men who had been recruited into the Zetas as sicarios, Wenceslao Tovar and Gabriel Cardona, witnessed Z-40 beheading victims on several occasions. They claim to have attended training camps in San Fernando where Zeta recruits were forced to kill men with machetes and sledgehammers. Z-40 sent crews to Laredo, Texas that included US citizens like Cardona along with Mexican nationals.

Z-40 had a hit list of people, some that had been already executed and some of the people who were targeted for execution. His number one target was Texas Syndicate gang member Jesus Maria Chuy Resendez. Resendez managed to escape death several times, but a lot of his people around him, that included a Nuevo Laredo cop were not so lucky. On April 2006 Resendez and his nephew were executed, it was said that they were shot about 100 times.

After the death of Z1 in November of 2002, and the arrest and extradition to the United States of Osiel Cárdenas Guillén, El Lazca, would take command of Los Zetas. El Lazca would take control of the old trafficking routes and plazas that were once under the command of the Gulf cartel. When tensions between the Gulf Cartel and Los Zetas erupted leading to the breakup of both criminal organizations in March of 2010, Z-40 chose to go with Los Zetas.

After the death of Lazca, Z-40 took command of Los Zetas extending its operations to San Luis Potosí, Durango and the Gulf coast in Veracruz, Quintana Roo and Tabasco.

With his new power of the Zetas, Z-40 openly declared war on Joaquin "El Chapo" Guzman, for the control of plazas further west of Mexico.

In May of 2012, the US Department of Justice indicted Z-40 of money laundering from drug trafficking, through the sale of racehorses. On September 5, 2013 a judge in the state of Texas, sentenced José Treviño Morales brother of Z-40, for investing 16 million dollars of drug money in the purchase and training of racehorses, as well as participating in quarter-mile races, in which they made bets. These horse races and bets were carried out throughout the southwestern United States.

Z-40 belonged to the list of 37 most wanted criminals by the government of Felipe Calderón, had 7 arrest warrants against him and was involved in at least 12 previous investigations. He was accused of organized crime, homicide, crimes against health, torture, money laundering, carrying a firearm that was only allowed to be used exclusively by the military armed forces and police.

Z-40 was known to be a lot more cautious than El Lazca, who, when he was killed by Mexican Marines, was guarded by only two bodyguards. Z40 was known to be super cautious, he had several security details in addition to his own personal bodyguard made up of several military experienced Zetas. Z40 had his bodyguards in the same way that Osial Cardenas wanted the Zetas to be his personal security. Except that was not the case on that day he was captured by the military.

Francisco Dair Montalvo Recio, El Rocky, that was detained in December of 2012 in Nuevo Laredo, was a key figure in the capture of Z-40. El Rocky cooperated with Mexican authorities. This helped Marine intelligence greatly in operations against Z-40. Mainly regarding the identification of movements of Los Zetas, Z-40 in particular. The Mexican Marines obtained important information on Z-40's schedules, his routes he used regularly, addresses he frequented, the location of other members of his inner group, the number of guards he used, as well as the license plate numbers of his vehicles. El Rocky gave up important detailed information in the state of Coahuila, where many of Z-40 operatives were located.

Following the leads provided by El Rocky, the Marines also managed to find the address of a safe house where Los Zetas kept migrants that had been abducted.

Using a Black Hawk helicopter, Marines came upon the safe house where they found 104 migrants (91 men and 13 women) from Honduras and El Salvador, who had been ordered kidnapped apparently by people under the command of Z-40.

To capture Z-40, elements of the Navy (Semar) had support from a "avión no tripulado" (better known as a drone), owned by U.S. agencies who had been operating these flying objects since 2004 on the border with Mexico.

The military intelligence had precise details of Z-40 using wiretapping equipment and tracking software, called Finfisher/Finspy, and Hunter Punta Tracking/Locksys.

The DEA provided information to the Mexican government that could establish the areas of Z-40's operations and learn about his group in areas such as Nuevo Leon, Coahuila and Tamaulipas, while the U.S. Immigration and Customs Enforcement (ICE) lent one of their drones, which monitors and collects data which is then processed in databases in California, Arizona and Texas.

In the early hours of July 15, 2013, El Z-40 was arrested by elements of the Mexican military during an operation in the outskirts of Nuevo Laredo, Tamaulipas. He was travelling on a four-wheel drive pickup truck on rough terrain when he was intercepted by military backed up by a helicopter. He was taken in custody without any rounds being fired. At the time of his arrest he was only with two men, his bodyguard and his accountant. At the time of his arrest, the military seized two million dollars in cash, eight long rifles and some 500 fully loaded magazines of ammunition of various calibers.

The day of his arrest, Z-40 was shown on video walking freely among the military without any restrains, walking tall and proud as if he was still supreme boss of a military commando, a commando that he had commanded, Los Zetas.

While looking at the steely eyes of Z-40 of his mug shot, it said it all. This was the face of a man who had set the standard on the extent of violence in Mexico.

The images forever embedded in people's minds; bodies hanging from bridges like piñatas, heads rolling next to mutilated arms, legs and bodies parts strewn on highways, discarded like trash, some etched with the letter Z and videotape of tortured sessions. One video went on for nearly an hour and showed a man pleading for his life as a knife cuts his head open and eventually uploaded to YouTube. Other victims were thrown into barrels of acid and dissolved into stew, menudo as some called it. And then there are the mass graves containing the remains of migrants who died with dreams of finding a better life north of the border.

He was a madman. His pep talk consisted of one line: "If you don't kill someone every day, you're not doing your job." He'd rather be feared than respected.

The Political Factor

It is easy for us to be judgmental when politicians or law enforcement collude with organized crime in Mexico. But imagine when brutal Mexican cartels threatened your family if you do not take a bribe or agree to look the other way or participate directly or indirectly with criminal elements. The "settling of scores" (executions for business reasons) could happen without notice at the blink of an eye.

On September of 2009 José Francisco Fuentes Esperón, a legislative candidate in the southeastern state of Tabasco, and his family were murdered in an apparent drug cartel hit as reported by Marc Lacey for the New York Times:

"Mr. Fuentes Esperón was shot in the neck, local news media reported, while his wife, Lilián Argüelles Beltrán, was shot in the head. Their two sons, ages 8 and 10, were asphyxiated. Mexico's violent drug cartels have increasingly taken aim at public officials. On August 20, the president of the legislature in the state of Guerrero was murdered. Last Wednesday, gunmen killed the undersecretary of public security in the state of Michoacán."

CNN reports that "the weekend slaying was not the first time an entire family has been killed in Tabasco":

"In February, a Tabasco police official who had arrested a drug trafficker a week earlier was killed together with his mother, wife, children and nieces and nephews. His brother, also a state police officer, was wounded, as were two others."

Many of the politician are either executed for not playing nice or are on the payroll. Just read the Borderland Beat blog, you will find tons of examples of incidents that proves the point.

Yes, there is a political factor. We will bust it open as we explore in more detail on the operations of the drug lords and cartels. The billions of dollars earned from trafficking drugs to the US corrupts all, from the lowest levels of government to the highest, the very top. Why water it down? There is plenty of evidence that can be traced, it always leads to some local police commander, or politician, all one has to do is just follow the money.

The Link of García Luna with "El Mayo"

Is it possible that the head of the Secretariat of Public Security for the federal government in Mexico, Genaro García Luna, considered untouchable and a favorite cabinet member of Mexican President Felipe Calderón, kept very close in his circle many officials accused of having links to drug trafficking, in particular that of El Mayo Zambada?

With his powerful tentacles and his ability to corrupt and infiltrate police institutions who are supposed to be responsible for combating drug trafficking, including the Ministry of National Defense, Ismael Zambada García, El Mayo, had extensive control within the Ministry of Public Security (SSP) headed by Genaro García Luna. Some of these main collaborators were accused of being in the service of the man who is considered the top capo of the Sinaloa cartel.

Owner of farms and haciendas, untouchable in Sinaloa, Zambada García had extensive networks of complicity in the most important areas of the PGR, as well as SIEDO, and in the SSP, where several governmental officials from the top level were being investigated for colluding with the capo.

García Luna did not seem to be able to escape from the networks laid out in the SSP by both Zambada García and the Beltrán Leyva brothers. These two capos broke up after the arrest of Alfredo Beltrán, El Mochomo.

This is how it's told through an investigation into the alleged links between García Luna and the cells of Zambada García and Arturo Beltrán Leyva, that was carried out by law enforcement officers who are not happy with the federal government to unify federal agencies (the decentralization of federal divisions).

Through a field investigation and also confirmed with background information in revelations allegedly made by Garcia Luna's own escort, police agents were able to clarify an

234

incident that occurred on October 19, 2008 in the state of Morelos. The investigation is narrated in a letter sent to the legislators of the Senate in order to exposed what they say is how dangerous it is to grant more power to the SSP, because a good portion of the high level officials are at the service of drug traffickers.

The document details:

On October 19, 2008, the current secretary of Federal Public Security, Genaro García Luna and his escort, composed of approximately 27 armed body guards travelling on a highway from Cuernavaca to Tepoztlán were intercepted by a top capo from a criminal cartel that was reinforced by a heavily armed commando travelling in approximately 10 armored Suburban vehicles. The escort of García Luna did nothing to repel the violent intrusion by order of García Luna himself.

The letter adds that the security detail that was escorting García Luna were stripped of their weapons and were blindfolded for approximately four hours.

The agents who told about the incident and whose names were omitted for fear of reprisals, maintain in the document that the voice from the top-level capo told García Luna:

"This is the first and last warning, so that you know that we can reach you anytime we want if you do not comply with the mutual agreement." It has been rumored that the capo was none other than Arturo Beltran Leyva, but this has not been confirmed. The letter states that after the words from el capo, García Luna left with the capo abandoning his escorts to their fate, without them knowing where he went and what he did during those four long hours.

When García Luna returned with the Capo, the sicarios returned the weapons to the bodyguards and they proceeded with the escort of García Luna. Most of the official government bodyguards, that were professionally trained to protect dignitaries and high-level politicians, felt humiliated and were not happy with how they were treated, while García Luna was complicit with the sicarios.

And, in another point, the letter states:

It should not go unnoticed that the secretary in question is an expert actor of deception, one should remember an incident that occurred previously that became a circus around a kidnapping of a French woman who was supposedly involved in the town of Ajusco, DF.

This generated a mass media attention where he was able to manipulate his entire escort, making them believe that what happened was an abduction (levantón) by some drug lord, and what actually happened was a concerted meeting with that supposed capo."

According to the investigations carried out by the Office of the Assistant Attorney General for Specialized Investigation in Organized Crime (SIEDO), many of the officials closest to García Luna seem to be corrupted by drug traffickers. All the way from the time of Vicente Fox's administration and now with the Calderon administration, evidence has emerged that the SSP is one of the institutions most infiltrated by the Sinaloa cartel and other criminal organizations.

For example, Édgar Enrique Bayardo del Villar, former inspector assigned to the Operations Section of the Federal Preventive Police, was presented with charges by SIEDO for allegedly colluding with Zambada García. A man who was very close to García Luna and with a salary of more than twenty thousand pesos a month ($1,000 in dollars), Enrique Bayardo went from poverty to an unprecedented wealth.

According to the investigation of the events, where PFP agents Jorge Cruz Méndez and Fidel Hernández are also implicated, Bayardo del Villar now has two residences with a joint value of close to 4.6 million dollars.

From one day to the next, he suddenly broke the retrains of his economic limitations and bought many luxurious cars like BMW, Mercedes Benz and an armored Cherokee. He spent 6.2 million dollars purchasing these vehicles and residences, all in cash.

Another piece of this network that presumably is at the service of the brothers Jesus and Ismael El Mayo Zambada, in the first circle of trust of Genaro García Luna is Gerardo Garay Cadena, ex-Commissioner of the PFP, who on November 1, 2008 resigned his position to voluntarily put himself "at the disposal of the authorities", although he was immediately arraigned by the SIEDO.

Investigators also center towards other officials linked to Garay Cadena.

One of them is Francisco Navarro, head of Special Operations of the SSP, with extensive controls at the International Airport of Mexico City, recognized as one of the largest centers of operations for the import of drugs and the export of money from drug trafficking.

Also, inside this group that according to the PGR provided protection to Mayo Zambada, is Luis Cárdenas Palominos, the right arm of García Luna, who was not arraigned but continues to be summoned to testify in front of the SIEDO. Other senior officers of the SSP and the PFP under arraignment are agents Jorge Cruz Méndez and Fidel Hernández García.

In the complaint delivered to the Mexican Congress, in particular to the Security and Justice commissions, where the process to unify the federal police is being considered, it affirms that it will be solved within a year. Agents of the AFI assure that García Luna is incorporating the PFP and the SSP that is suspected to have criminal history and links to organized crime.

In their complaint, the agents also address the corruption and disorder that deprive the dependency controlled by García Luna. They say that the personnel being requested to be moved from the AFI and join the Federal Police had not even served four years in their police positions and that favoritism was given to friends and personal relationship with high level officials.

Several of the complaints and warnings of the agents can be confirmed even in documented events. For example, two days after the resignation of Gerardo Garay, on November 3, 2018, García Luna appointed Rodrigo Esparza Cisterna as interim PFP commissioner, whose history is as long as it is murky.

In 1993, when Rodrigo Esparza was a delegate of the PGR in Sinaloa, the first rumors surfaced over his presumed relationship with Joaquín Guzmán Loera, El Chapo, then a bitter rival of the Arellano Félix brothers, heads of the Tijuana cartel.

According to an official case dated August 12, 2005, that had been obtained through an information request to the Federal Institute of Access to Information (folio 0001700181305), Esparza was accused of acting against the administration of justice. Despite this background, Rodrigo Esparza is the right arm of García Luna in the PFP.

In 2010 Zambada did an interview with Julio Scherer Garcia of Proceso Magazine. He criticized the government's effort to take him down, saying it was a little too late, if the goal was to hurt the drug trade.

"The problem with the narco business is that it involves millions of dollars. How do you dominate that?" Zambada said. "As for the bosses, locked up, dead or extradited, their replacements are already standing by."

"The government's drug war," he said, "is lost." Why lost? "The narcotics trade and everything that goes along with it,"

Zambada responded, "are inside the society, as deeply rooted as the corruption."

A Portrait of Power

Ismael "El Mayo" Zambada has historically worked closely with the Juárez Cartel and the Carrillo Fuentes family, while maintaining independent ties to Colombian cocaine suppliers. El Mayo is the last powerful boss of the old guard. All the others have either died or are in prison. Zambada headed the Sinaloa Cartel in partnership with Joaquín "El Chapo" Guzmán, until 2016 when El Chapo was captured. Zambada has now possibly assumed full command of the Sinaloa Cartel.

On October 20, 2008, some of his relatives were arrested in Mexico City on drug trafficking charges. Ismael's brother, Jesus "El Rey" Zambada, along with Ismael's son and nephew. His son, Ismael "Mayito" Zambada Jr. has been sought for conspiracy to distribute a controlled substance in the United States. His other son, Vicente Zambada Niebla, was arrested by the Mexican Army on March 18, 2009.

There are not many pictures that have been made public of Mayo Zambada. It is known that he was plump and chubby, but one day Vicente and Amado Carrillo, who underwent plastic surgery at the Santa Monica clinic in Mexico City, the same hospital where Amado Carrillo died in 1997, suggested that he change his appearance.

Zambada did.

Zambada lost weight and thinned out his cheeks, so that his face became stiff and a little elongated by the facelift. When José Luis Santiago Vasconcelos was the man in charge of SIEDO, federal authorities took possession of a photograph during a search warrant in one of his multiple properties. The photograph was of Zambada García who looked a lot younger and slender. The photo was kept in the files related to the Juarez cartel, the organization to which El Mayo belonged.

The man has been untouchable for decades. Ismael Zambada has shown his power and ability to infiltrate institutions, increasingly more during the six years of Ernesto Zedillo, Vicente Fox and Felipe Calderón: more than 35 agents of the Federal Public Ministry assigned to the SIEDO were his employees, and each one received between 350 and 400 thousand dollars a month for filtering information about consigned files and previous investigations in progress against members of his organization.

In the government of Vicente Fox, the Sinaloa cartel reached the Secretariat of National Defense (Sedena), where through Arturo González Hernández, El Chaky, several high-ranking Army commanders operating the telecommunication systems were found to be corrupt. They warned the cartel in advance what days and hours the military would be conducting operations.

In addition, El Mayo Zambada was in control of the Sinaloa police, and senior military officers looked after his physical integrity and his businesses. His impunity and his power were of such magnitude that, in December of 2005, in the ranch El Mezquite, they organized a party (narco posada) that included the popular musical group Illusion. Zambada García arrived at the party. A lot of alcohol flowed, heavy doses of cocaine were distributed and gunshots were fired into the air in celebration.

This attracted the attention of a sector of the Mexican Army stationed in Sinaloa and they requested a search warrant to enter the ranch. Because, these request for an order takes hours, Zambada García had time to leave protected by municipal police officers and go quietly to his hiding place, a walled fortress whose accesses and sidewalks are permanently guarded by his people.

In May 2007, the Office for the Control of Foreign Properties of the US Department of the Treasury reported that six companies and 12 people in Mexico were part of the financial network of Ismael El Mayo Zambada.

The US report indicated that Zambada's ex-wife, Rosario Niebla Cardoza, as well as her four daughters; Maria Teresa, Miriam Patricia, Mónica del Rosario and Modesta Zambada Niebla, play a key role in the dirty businesses of El Mayo, since they fulfill a function key in the ownership and control of companies of the capo.

After the breakup between the brothers Beltrán Leyva and El Chapo Guzmán, the Sinaloa cartel, perhaps at its moment of splendor, the most powerful criminal enterprise in Latin America, suffered a decline in its power, but it was not dead.

According to data from the SSP and the PGR, the Beltrán extended their tentacles: they penetrated the SIEDO, the PGR and a large part of the Army's regional commanders, in addition to allying with Los Zetas and the Juarez cartel, whose chief was Vicente Carrillo.

Zambada García and Joaquín Guzmán remained united along with Ignacio Nacho Coronel and the Cázares Salazar brothers who formed part of that group.

This clan of drug traffickers suffered big blow when Jesus Zambada Garcia, El Rey, brother of El Mayo was arrested in Mexico City who had a reputation of not being very discreet with his wealth.

Until 2007, Jesús Zambada was not considered to be a major capo by Mexico intelligence or by the intelligence agencies of the United States, but after his arrest, attorney general Eduardo Medina Mora labeled him as one of the most important heads in the network of money laundering, money belonging to El Mayo Zambada.

Another fact alluded to the true power of El Rey Zambada. In Culiacán, Sinaloa, a narco manta or narco banner bearing a message was placed near the state congress that discounted the notion that Jesús Zambada García was a minor operator. The banner read:

"Chapo Guzmán, they killed your son and you are still a friend of the murderers. You have no shame, how Nachito Coronel has changed you, he moves you at his whim and everything because he owns you. Smart is Rey Zambada: you are killing municipal, state and ministerial police, while El Rey is loading ephedrine and cocaine in the airport of Mexico City."

In October of 2008, the month in which García Luna was allegedly intercepted in Morelos, the blows against the structure of El Mayo Zambada intensified.

The ranches La Quinta La Paloma and Los Alpes, located in Acaxochitlán, Hidalgo, were subject of search warrants by federal police. The property of the facilities was tied to El Rey Zambada by SIEDO.

Mayo Zambada had been hit on September 18, 2018 with a financial blow to his empire with the seizure of 26 million dollars, money that he had kept in a safe house and perfectly organized in boxes of eggs.

Despite the blows received by the Sinaloa cartel and despite the division it suffered with the separation of the Beltrán brothers, the organization continued flourish in the drug trafficking business. It controlled ports and airports, and maintained allies at high levels of the SSP that, according to the letter sent by the federal police to Congress, "they are committed to comply with the agreements, that had been agreed upon."

If in doubt, ask García Luna.

They Killed El Ondeado

For Manuel Torres Félix , "Manuelon", "El Ondeado" or "El M1", the insomnia ended. In the early dawn on Saturday, October 12, 2012, he died during a confrontation with Mexican Army special forces.

They hunted him down like the wildcat that he was. Spotlighted at night on a road close to Oso Viejo, Quila, he wasn't able to get away this time like he did so many other times when, by blood and fire, he was able to flee only to hide in his dens in the hills.

Manuel Torres, accompanied by a strong group of bodyguards, met up with federal forces in Valle de San Lorenzo and tried to evade them. But they had him surrounded. For several days, special forces, supported by the 9th Military Zone, had embedded military personnel throughout the area. At dawn that day, a contingent of soldiers came in through Tacuichamona headed towards Oso Viejo, and a similar force came down from Quila, forming an impassable perimeter, even though Torres knew the terrain like the palm of his hand.

At the moment they got in a battle, Manuel Torres got out of the vehicle he was riding and tried to flee through the hills. But he was hit by a volley of gunfire. He fell on the spot.

Another version of the incident, that has been denied by the military, was that Manuel Torres stood his ground and with his gunmen they killed 11 soldiers, and even brought down a helicopter.

After his death, The military found Manuel Torres armed with a .38 Super handgun loaded with seven rounds, plus several loaded magazines. Manuel Torres had in his possession $9,980 dollars and 23,500 pesos (equivalent to $1,232.00 in dollars), plus several baggies of a white powder substance, apparently cocaine. There were several people detained and arrested.

Sinaloa had never know such a bloodthirsty drug trafficking sicario. He came from a family with criminal backgrounds; his brother Javier Torres was in prison in the United States where was serving a sentence for drug trafficking. Javier Torres had also confronted Mexican military forces where one soldier lost his life. After that incident, his own bosses gave him up to the authorities and he was eventually extradited to the U.S.

Javier Torres was one of Ismael Zambada Garcia, El Mayo's, top lieutenants. Although Manuel Torres never attained the same standing in the Sinaloa rank structure, he was a key player in the organization after the war broke out with the Sinaloa cartel against the Beltran Leyva brothers. Manuel Torres did not hesitate to confront the new enemies of Zambada and Joaquin Guzman.

Born in a small town in the state of Sinaloa, Manuel Torres began working for the Sinaloa Cartel in the 1990s and later ascended to the apex of the cartel after his brother Javier Torres Félix was arrested in 2004. He then began to work with Ovidio Guzmán López, the son of Joaquín Guzmán Loera, Mexico's most-wanted man, and oversaw drug trafficking shipments coming in from South America into Mexico under the tutelage of Ismael Zambada García.

He lived in the hills, in the valleys and rarely came down to the city. He mistrusted even his shadow. He would go two, three nights without sleep, always alert.

Hundreds of deaths were attributed to commandos led by Manuel Torres, who rightly earned the pseudonym of "El Ondeado" because of his lack of emotional stability.

He didn't discriminate. It was all about taking care of the plaza for El Chapo, and he acted without any consideration. Police officers from various agencies were targeted, and even some military personnel who dared invade his territory, losses that the Army never reported.

From the start of the war in 2008, the Torres (brothers) were the target of attacks from their enemies, largely by a group known as "Los Charritos," who were linked to the Araujo family, whose principal pillar of support was Gonzalo, "El Chalo" Araujo.

On April 4, battles were starting to take place and young Joel Torres Jimenez, son of "El JT," was attacked outside a pool hall located in the Colonia Guadalupe Victoria. He was 19 years old but managed to survive.

A few weeks later, on April 18, another Torres, this one the son of Manuel, Atanasio Torres Acosta, "El Tachio", was murdered by rival members of the Beltrán-Leyva Cartel. During the ambush attack Manuel Torres' daughter Alondra (aged 4) was injured along with his sister-in-law Sandra Rivas Heredia. This happened right next to the building of the Health Ministry, in the Montebello residential district.

Police located one of the vehicles apparently used by the gunmen. A red Tsuru (Mexico's version of the Nissan Sentra), where they found AK-47 rifles with a message: "On behalf of your friend [Arturo] and his buddies Los Zetas. So you can remember, Manuel Torres."

Manuel Torres went crazy with the death of his son, whose wake was held in one of his houses in the valley. That same night and the next day while they were keeping vigil over Atanasio's body, Manuel Torres was taking his revenge on young men that his gunmen were picking up and taking to his home for him to torture. The death of Anastasio marked the beginning of the cartel war in the state of Sinaloa. Manuel Torres became one of the most dangerous drug traffickers in Sinaloa where hundreds of deaths were attributed to his commandos.

Nothing stopped him. All over the city, headless bodies started to appear, mutilated, with messages alluding to Tachio's murder. No death, no limit, could contain his thirst for vengeance until his death.

The cartels were at war, but he was fighting his own war in the name of his son and the pain he had suffered.

At the place where his son was murdered, they started throwing decapitated bodies, one of them that of Barcelo Villagran, who had been the commander of the Ministerial Police and chief of the Centauro Group. They cut off both legs, decapitated him and cut open his back with a knife while he was still alive.

On the morning of October 16, 2012, three days after the death of Manuel Torres, at least three "narcomantas" (narcobanners) appeared throughout the city of Culiacán denouncing Ismael Zambada García of betraying and setting up Maneul Torres to be killed by the Mexican military.

Manuel Torres Felix was not even in the files of the PGR, much less in those of the State Department of Justice. In September 2008 under the Operation Sinaloa, the Mexican military located a safe house owned by Manuel Torres, where they confiscated several firearms, narcotics, radio communications equipment, and an armored vehicle.

The Mexican military also found a photo of Manuel Torres accompanied by Misael Torres Urrea, nicknamed El M2, his nephew and son of Javier Torres Félix. Manuel Torres was placed on the most wanted drug traffickers list under the Foreign Narcotics Kingpin Designation Act by the U.S. government on June 1, 2011, along with Gonzalo Inzunza Inzunza (a.k.a. El Macho Prieto), another high-ranking lieutenant of the Sinaloa cartel.

A narcocorrido of the Movimiento Alterado subgenere, sung by the musical groups Bukanas De Culiacan, El Komander, Los Buitres de Culiacan, Los Buchones de

Culiacan, Rogelio Martinez el RM, Los Nuevos Elegantes, Noel Torres, Erik Estrada, Oscar Garcia, and Los 2 Primos and titled Sanguinarios del M1 on YouTube ("The Bloodthirsty of M1") exalts Torres Félix for leaving decapitated and mutilated bodies in the trunk of cars as a message to his rivals. The lyrics of the song dedicated to Torres Félix start with the following:

With an AK-47 and a bazooka on our heads

cutting off heads that cross our path

We're bloodthirsty and crazy – We love to kill

Bullets fired and extortions carried out, just like the best of us

Always in a convoy of armored cars, wearing bullet-proof vests and ready to execute people.

Black Hawks Over Rocky Point

On December 18, 2013 Mexican special military naval forces surrounded a conglomerate community of condominiums by land and air that overlooked the beach in Las Palomas, in Puerto Peñasco, Sonora.

Puerto Peñasco or Rocky Point is located in the northern state of Sonora and is a popular vacationing spot among American tourists.

The objective was very clear, to capture, Gonzalo Izunza Izunza, "El Macho Prieto," dead or alive. Macho Prieto was one of the main operators of the Sinaloa Cartel in the region, along with Luis Fernando Castro Villa "El Checo."

The information about where the drug trafficker was hiding was not as a result of intelligence work, but of a betrayal from a top boss, Ismael "El Mayo" Zambada, of the powerful Sinaloa Cartel he worked for.

El Macho Prieto was a hindrance to the cartel because he was killing other members from within the same organization to expand his power in the region.

He was operating against the rules of the cartel.

This is how military forces "hunted" the drug trafficker in the luxurious area of Puerto Peñasco in that day that resulted in a toll of five dead sicarios, one being the operator of El Mayo Zambada, Macho Prieto, whose body was picked up by a team of sicarios before police could secure the scene.

What caused the betrayal?

On December 12, 2010 on the Sonoyta-Puerto Peñasco highway, El Macho Prieto murdered or ordered killed Paulo Osorio Payón, El Pablo. El Pablo was a personal friend of José Manuel Torres Félix, El Ondeado, a criminal boss of the Sinaloan cartel and an operator for El Mayo. Manuel Torres had ordered the execution of Izunza.

Aware of the hit, El Macho Prieto started massing weapons that he purchased from the United States to face Manuel Torres. However, Manuel Torres was himself killed on October 2012 in a confrontation with forces of the Mexican military.

With that matter cleared up, El Macho Prieto returned to his base of operations in Puerto Peñasco, where he continued to invade territories of other criminal cells within his own organization and kill his own criminal partners for control of their plazas.

Considered by his own partners as a violent person, Macho Prieto was accused of more than 80 executions. He came to the attention of the US government, who placed him on the list of the most dangerous capos. El Macho Prieto then began to become a liability and a problem by his own bosses who betrayed him by giving information to the federal authorities about his location.

Throughout that area and surrounding communities, the dreaded sicario, drug trafficker and a plaza boss of the Sinaloa cartel had "halcones" (Lookouts) and controlled a multi-million dollar criminal business with the complicity with senior officials from the Mexico State Attorney General's Office.

He controlled the sale of drugs and theft of cars in a very organized way and in concert with corrupt authorities of the different police agencies in the state of Sinaloa.

Macho Prieto travelled in convoys of four to ten vehicles like late model Suburbans and always wore his bulletproof vest and police badges. In addition, he and his people were always armed with high-powered rifles and grenade launchers.

Local authorities blame him for the violence generated between San Luis, the valley and Mexicali, this as a result of his internal fights with the cell leaders of the group known as "Los Garibay."

On October 2011, real estate agent Martha Fernandez Maldonado was executed in Mexicali. She was killed as a vengeance from some drug dealers after several homes rented from her were raided by the Army. A former member of the Army´s GAFE (Airmobile Special Forces Group) was arrested after her murder by local police; his last name was Parra Camargo, his brother being a Ministerial Police agent in Mexicali, and according to local intelligence, close friend and bodyguard of "Macho Prieto."

On January 2012, Jesus Daniel Samaniego, member of the Mexicali municipal police was shot on broad daylight just outside the main campus of Baja California´s Autonomous University. Unofficial reports mention the officer was executed in retaliation for stealing drugs from a group of narco traffickers under the leadership of Gonzalo Inzunza Inzunza.

Inzunza had a well-established criminal network that allows him to smuggle drugs into the US using three routes: Venezuela, Honduras, Costa Rica, Sinaloa; Chiapas, Acapulco, Mexico City, Jalisco and from there to the US; and the final route, from Sinaloa to Sonora, Mexicali, Tijuana, and finally, The US.

His criminal associates were identified as: Abraham Inzunza Inzunza aka "El Peque", Ismael Bernal aka "El Mongolo," and Jorge Avalos Meza aka "Yucateco."

About 15 days before the shooting at the Sonoran port, a federal agent infiltrated the Bella Sirena, set to become the shadow of El Macho Prieto, spying on him day and night. The mysterious federal agent rented a villa, as part of the strategy to arrest Macho Prieto. Stuck in the mouth of the Wolf, this agent almost didn't sleep.

People didn't pay attention to him and the staff looked at his "eccentricities" as rare behaviors of someone who "came to relax, to forget about all the stress.

He slept in the open or behind a glass door, where everything could be seen. The trap was set, the stage was ready for action.

In the morning of December 18, 2013 special naval forces arrived at Las Palomas and started to secure the area, setting up a perimeter, evacuating civilians and readying their weapons on lock and load.

The shooting began immediately. The response of El Macho Prieto's bodyguards was so violent that the element of surprise was lost. The intervention of two American manufactured Black Hawk helicopters was necessary, whose .50 caliber weapons wreaked havoc on the cars of the sicarios.

Immediately several vehicles attempted to flee at high speed but were fired upon from one of the helicopters causing the truck to catch on fire and crash in a small gazebo located at the exit of the condominiums. There were two casualties, one near the truck, another on the sidewalk. Federal Police would report that two Blackhawk helicopters fired at least 10 vehicles. The burned vehicles from the firepower of the two helicopters could be seen outside the condominium complex.

Simultaneously, at the entrance of the condominiums there was another confrontation, that resulted in one sicario being killed found lying on the ground next to a AK-47 at his side that was equipped with a high capacity drum magazine.

There were more shots fired at the entrance to the hall of the condominiums, the walls of the building were left with bullet holes from bursts of gunfire and blood splattered on the walls and in the ground.

Inside the rooms the battle lasted a long time, at least two hours. Afterwards reinforcements of El Macho Prieto began arriving, and federal forces tried to stop them from reaching the Bella Sirena.

Two cars blocked the entrance so more cars with El Macho Prieto's reinforcements could not enter.

The other two bodies were left on the ground in the middle of the round-abound circle of the street, without police securing the scene, not even the yellow tape that is typically used to protect a crime scene. For hours, residents of Peñasco drove by the crime scene, took pictures and video with their cellular phones of the bodies and burned vehicles, and uploaded them on to social media.

One of the victims on the ground was none other than El Macho Prieto, except that his body was taken away by his people before police secured the scene. Manuel Mondragon, national commissioner, while talking about the shootout in Sonora told the press that Inzunza´s men stole his body from the crime scene, although he was unsure if in fact the body was taken. He went on to say that DNA tests were being conducted on the blood left at the scene to make sure it was Inzunza Inzunza.

According to witnesses there were a total of five men dead. According to Mondragon's version, only four bodies were recovered by the authorities because the fifth was stolen.

A federal official, not authorized to be identified for security reasons, said two police officers were injured in the armed confrontation.

Police at the scene would eventually recover, in addition to the four bodies, 14 assault rifles, four handguns, five grenades, more than 2,000 rounds of ammunition and 16 vehicles.

La Gente Nueva and R5

"Mira bien Mencho… te puedo matar a la verga… nada más para que veas quien es la mera R5."

Translation: "Listen good Mencho, I can kill you, fuck, just so you can see who is the real R5," can be heard a little boy saying while he manipulates an AK-47.

These were the words posted on Youtube by a little boy. It was 22 seconds that got into the skin of millions. It was a video of a child, perhaps 8 years. He was in the passenger seat of a truck while holding a high caliber rifle, an AK-47. The child recited a rant full of obscenities common to what sicarios say when they threaten their rivals to death. The message is to the leader of the Jalisco Nueva Generación Cartel (CJNG), Nemesio Oseguera, El Mencho. The fable it is said; the child's bravado is protected at his young age by R-5.

El Mencho is not one to talk bad about on social media. He is one not to take things like this lightly. He has killed many who have invoked his name in ways he did not like. El Mencho is a powerful druglord that is a psychopath, but is a psychopath that has immense power, wealth and resources.

The video generated reactions of outrage, but few have tried to understand that child and his context. Its reality so alien to ours. To understand him, you have to start with the key he offers: his ultimate hero is R-5, a demon whose baptismal act is signed by the devil in the north of the country, a man by the name of Jesus Gregorio Villanueva Rodríguez, "El R5."

Jesús Gregorio's story is typical of a young capo: he was born poor and grew ambitious in a barren land of opportunities. In this case, the Sonoran Desert, a territory that has been under control of the Sinaloa Cartel for decades. He started selling drugs and moved on to become the small, dusty and hot towns chief in the north of the state, which would be insignificant if it were not because the polleros who cross migrants across the border and drugs to Arizona must pay a fee for each undocumented and each house of security and the torture that takes place there.

R5 became leader of the Nueva Gente (GN) when his brothers and founders of the GN were arrested. People like Noel Salgueiro Nevarez, "El Flaco" captured in 2011, then followed by his two other brothers; José Salgueiro Nevarez arrested in 2012 and Heriberto Salgueiro Nevarez arrested in February 2015. The last brother, allegedly killed in 2013 was El R5, who originated from Caitime Sinaloa and considered the top leader of the group of the sicarios of La Gente Nueva (NG). There are rumors and versions floating around that suggest that R5 is still alive and operating in command of the GN, a cell of sicarios for the Sinaloa Cartel. But the claims have been proven to be false, R5 only lives in the minds and dreams of young children in Sinaloa, Chihuahua and Sonora.

Another leader of GN was José Antonio Torres Marrufo that went by the names of El Jaguar, El Toñin, El Marrufo and El Catorce. He was originally responsible for helping El Chapo take on the forces of the La Línea, the armed wing of the Juarez cartel. El Jaguar has a striking set of scars running horizontal to his forehead, as well as others upon his cheeks which indicate being cut by knives at one point in his life. Scars inflicted by a capo from the Juarez cartel, that is why he went to the side of El Chapo and by helping El Chapo to defeat La Línea, he achieved revenge.

To truly learn about R5, one must learn about La Gente Nueva or GN.

The sicarios of la Gente Nueva (GN) operate in the region of the so-called Golden Triangle that comprises the regions of the states of Sinaloa, Durango and Chihuahua, but also have a huge presence in the Sonora region. In Chihuahua they fought for the Ciudad Juarez plaza that was protected by La Linea of the Juarez cartel. In 2012, US intelligence reported that the Sinaloa cartel with their armed wing of La Gente Nueva had emerged victorious in capturing the plaza of Juarez and relegated the Juarez cartel to second in power. The El Paso-Juárez corridor is a lucrative route for drug traffickers. The DEA estimated that around 70% of the total cocaine that enters the United States flows through El Paso-Juárez border.

GN also protects the operations of the cartel in the mountains of the Golden Triangle where there are large cultivations of Marijuana, heroin, as well as the production of methamphetamines. The sicarios of La Genete Nueva are responsible for the safeguard of these clandestine operations and fight off the incursion of rival cartels such as Los Zetas and of the people of Chapo Isidro. The sicarios of La GN receive better training and are more fit for battle than the other group of sicarios such as the "Anthrax." The Anthrax are famous due to the larger number of narco corridos that musicians have composed about them but they mostly operate in the Sinaloa region, mainly in Culiacán. Some people falsely believe that the NG is a group that has ceased to exist, but it is known that Antrax were born out of the NG. The truth is that GN still operate following the orders of Ivan and Alfredo Guzmán and their mission had been to protect and prevent the capture of Joaquín El Chapo Guzmán.

The GN is made up of at least 5,000 elements throughout the country in Mexico that were trained as military, federal police, ministerial police, Kaibiles (elite soldiers from Guatemala) and private security agents who resigned law enforcement agencies or deserted from the military to join the criminal side.

They are young people between 20 and 30 years old, bloodthirsty, brutal with no conscience for the pain of others and deeply loyal to the boss. In the past they have been trained in Veracruz, at least in their origins, but it is believed that they now train in the mountains of Sinaloa, Durango and Chihuahua to learn armed tactics and be able to fight with Los Zetas, La Línea and Los Aztecas.

They wear military uniforms, they cover their faces with balaclavas, they are armed with high-caliber weapons and they travel aboard armored SUV and trucks that are marked with the letter "X." Sometimes they paint the name of GN on the doors and show off their long rifles in public display.

The founder of GN is Noel Salguiero Nevarez, aka "El Flaco", who began as an apprentice of El Chapo in 1995 in the mountains of Chihuahua, where he was responsible for the operations of drug trafficking in to the United States. His efficiency for the business and his ruthless actions towards the enemies made him rise quickly within the organization of the cartel. He soon took control of most of the operations in the region from the US border to Sinaloa and became a direct lieutenant for man itself, El Chapo.

His leadership consisted of being a brutal killer, so much that in 2008 it cost the lives of more than 1,500 Mexicans in Ciudad Juárez alone, where the people of El Chapo fought for la plaza against the Gulf Cartel/Los Zetas when they were a single group. They beheaded victims and left messages about the power of El Chapo in the plazas throughout the state of Chihuahua.

On October 5, 2011 in Culiacán, Sinalona, "El Flaco" was arrested by Mexican military. Federal Government had a bounty for him for 3 million pesos ($254,000 dollars) for tips leading to his capture. At that time, the government of then President Felipe Calderón celebrated his detention as if it were the end of this organization. But his brothers were waiting in line.

Although Noel Salguiero is currently being held in a maximum-security prison in Jalisco, GN continued as an ascending criminal group in the national territory to control Sinaloa, Chihuahua and Durango. They also had a presence in Tamaulipas, Veracruz and Jalisco. In these regions they were dedicated to drug trafficking via Tamaulipas. To pass drugs through Tamaulipas it was necessary to take escorts to protect the cargo. That was the task of GN, to ensure that the drugs reached its destination due to the strong control that the zetas and the CDG had in Tamaulipas.

R5 was head sicario of Gente Nueva in Aguas Prieta Sonora under orders from Marco Antonio Paredes El M100 who reported directly to el Chapo. His job was to repel the excursion of the offensive by the Beltrans Layvas (BLO) and their allies the Zetas in the state of Sonora.

Atypical is what happened next. R5 seemed destined for mediocrity until a shooting made him an idol for children. This fray is known as The Battle of Tubutama and until 2010 was the confrontation between two more deadly cartels during the war on drug trafficking.

That July 1, 2010 Jesus Gregorio (R5), was waiting for an unusual day. He would leave in a convoy of 20 trucks from the US border and would cross the municipalities of Oquitoa, Altar and Atil. In his convoy of 20 trucks he had a commando of 50 heavily armed sicarios. His goal was to reach the municipality of Tubutama, where a cell of the Beltrán Leyva cartel (BLO) was revolting. The mission was to annihilate the BLO at midnight. But minutes before, 6 kilometers from Tubutama, R5 knew that someone inside his organization had betrayed him by giving his planned route to his rivals the BLO.

When passing through a tight strip of road, just between two boulders of brick-colored earth, dozens of sicarios appeared at the top and opened fire at them. It was the BLO. They threw grenades, rockets and sprayed them with high caliber gun fire. R5 called on to his entire troop and answered the aggression with the rage of rabid dogs. But it was a slaughter. The BLO was able to pick them out like sitting ducks. Municipal police said that the shooting lasted for about 9 hours and that there were more than 200 dead, but since the drug traffickers collect the bodies of their companions, the official number of murders was reported to be 28, something that caused the villagers to make fun of the low number.

One of the few survivors was R5, this to everyone's surprise. The children of Sonora and Sinaloa began to fantasize about being like that sicario renamed the R5.

His fame spread through corridos and stories told time and time again in all parts of northern Mexico. Corridos of R5 started to play in the radio and concerts. The narco band Traviezos de la Zierra wrote a famous narcocorrido that talks about how he was accompanied by very small soldiers and how he used fame among the children of northeastern Mexico.

One of the verses says:

"I looked for plebes (children) with guts/ to form my convoy/ and as Pancho Villa said/ I have my crew ready for the Revolution."

But in December 11, 2013 his luck ran out. R-5 was killed in Sonora. The Sinaloa Cartel lieutenant who had overseen the Hermosillo operations was killed. It was hard to believe.

He was traveling in a 2012 Passat Volkswagen with Sonora license plates, in the community of Hermosillo at around midnight when the shooting occurred.

He was with his 16-year-old girlfriend, Karely Inzunza Aguilar, who suffered two gun shots wounds that were none-life threatening. They were in the middle of buying fast-food when they were confronted by unknown assailants.

According to Karely, Jesus was buying fast food and at the exact same time he attempted to board his vehicle, he was attacked by numerous armed sicarios in several vehicles. After seeing the aggression, Karely got behind cover that ultimately saved her life. The two were transported to the hospital where within one hour the 33-year-old Villanueva or R5 was pronounced dead.

His death only increased his myth. More corridos flourished. Some of his followers say that he faked his death and that he still defends the lands of Chapo Guzmán accompanied by an army of children. His enemies, now the Jalisco Cartel (CJNG), swear that it is only a memory in the minds of some children who invoke his name.

Too many young lives have been lost, fighting for a cartel that only brings death or imprisonment. They are children, many as young as 8 years old are indoctrinated to be brutal killers without a conscience, many under the eye of their own parents.

The boy who for 22 seconds says he is the people of the R5, of course, he does not understand that he is actually speaking of a bloodthirsty criminal who has used children like him as human shields. The little boy speaks with naive falsehood of an idol, a legend, a longing that gave birth to a country that for years glorified its bosses.

The Pact Between BLO and the Zetas

The Attorney General's Office (PGR) learned through various investigations that the Beltran Layva brothers and the leaders of the Gulf cartel started to negotiate and build a powerful alliance in the narco trafficking business. This is evident in the large volume of cocaine they were moving.

In the file of Operation "Limpienza" or "cleanliness" it was learned that it was Sergio Villarreal "El Grande" and Heriberto Lazcano Lazcano "El Lazca" who formed a pact in 2007 between the BLO and the Gulf Cartel. In the investigation, PGR discovered that this alliance was formed by the owners of the two largest drug seizures in the history of Mexico: 23.5 tons of pure cocaine seized at the customs in Manzanillo and 11.7 tons of cocaine seized at the customs of Altamira, both in October of 2007.

Operation Cleanliness gave an insight on how "El Grande" managed to formulate a truce of peace on behalf of the Beltrán Leyva clan.

"El Grande" is a former Durango policeman whom the PGR considered the BLO's main operator in the heart of the country, while Heriberto Lazcano was considered the main leader of "Los Zetas", the armed wing of the Gulf Cartel.

A person in the witness protection program only known as "David" provided information about a secret meeting in a place just south of Mexico City that had been attended by José Antonio Cueto y Roberto "El 19" who was an operator for Beltrán, along with "El Grande." It told how they achieved the pact.

"The first time I spoke with "El Grande" he confided in me that he had been in charge of making a truce with El Lazca, to avoid further conflict and for the time being everyone would be at peace.

With the arrest of El Mochomo, El 19 told us, that the Beltrán Leyva brothers were very upset with the people of El Chapo Guzmán because they had learned that he had given up El Mochomo and the Beltrán Leyva brothers wanted to take revenge by looking for El Chapo Guzmán, Mayo Zambada, Rey Zambada and Nacho Coronel."

From previous investigations the PGR had already learned of the pact between the Beltrán's and the Gulf cartel.

The investigation into the shipment of the 23.5 tons of cocaine that had been intercepted in Manzanillo showed that Arturo Beltran had been the owner and that he was looking for support from Miguel Treviño Morales El 40, then one of the operators of the Gulf Cartel, to assist him to move the cargo to the US.

Of the cargo that was seized in Altamira, the investigation revealed that the recipient of the cargo had been intended for "El 40." The two large cargos were being transported to a temporary destination in Mexico City where the companies responsible for transporting the cargo were located.

The two shipments, according to the PGR, were from the same providers: two Colombian drug traffickers who were partners and who were identified as Claudia "El Mono" and a person by the name of Valenciano, nicknamed "El Jugador" or "El Futbolista".

The investigations indicate that the company Chatzi de México, S.A. de C.V., located in Mexico City, was responsible for putting together the import operation of the 23.5 tons of cocaine that had been seized on October 30, 2007 in the customs of Manzanillo.

As transport provider "Ocean Trading Limited" had locations in Barranquilla, Colombia and Guayaquil, Ecuador. This company was the one that sent the containers CMAU515156-0 and CMAU501629-9 in the ship

"Esmeralda," from Columbia. The paperwork said that the cargo was toilet and soap.

The protected witness said that the ship arrived in Colima on October 15 and that on the 28th of the same month - two days before the shipment was seized - almost at midnight, "El 40" was in Tamaulipas and was in communication via nextel with Arturo Beltrán Leyva.

Arturo Beltrán was asking Miguel Treviño if he had a way to talk to the people of Manzanillo, referring to whether he had a contact with customs.

"El 40" replied that he did know someone, but that he did not dare to operate Manzanillo because he knew that it was the plaza of the Sinaloa Cartel.

He told him that his Cartel tried to negotiate with an official of customs in Manzanillo, but since he did not accept the bribe, he was told that they were going to execute him. Immediately after hearing this, they protected the seizure.

After this incident, El 40 received a call from 'El Camello' to collect the money for the drug that was seized the Army on October 5, 2007 in the warehouse of Tampico. El 40 asked him how things were going, and he responded that he lamented another loss with the seizure of the two containers with 23 tons of cocaine in Manzanillo.

El Grande Dispensing Violence

Sergio Villarreal Barragán, "El Grande", one of the operators of the Beltrán Lyva Organization (BLO) in Mexico City and Morelos, did not tolerate other criminals to operate in the territories under his control. These criminals typically dedicate themselves to activities such as robberies and assaults.

Just in the month of November 2009, 40 people had been executed in Morelos, Guerrero and Mexico City, plazas controlled by BLO. Several of the victims were found with messages signed by "El Jefe de Jefes" or "The Chief of Chiefs" (Title given to Arturo Betran Leyva), that said that the victims were "adversaries, thieves and kidnappers ".

Some federal and local authorities had suspected that several of these executions could have been attributed to Arturo Beltrán Leyva himself.

On the matter of "El Grande", SIEDO had obtained testimony from former members of the cartel and also from some protected witnesses who described El Grande as a man that was better at conducting executions rather than being a cartel negotiator. El Grande was known to vigorously pursue and eliminate his intended targets.

A protected witness known as "Mario", one of BLO's former sicarios gave testimony in the federal case that before reaching Morelos and the Mexico DF, "El Grande" eliminated several thieves in La Laguna, because they unnecessarily "heated the plaza" through their criminal activities and attracted the attention from authorities.

"Mario" pointed out that El Grande killed three people; Carlos Gavira, Gavira's lawyer and Gavira's sister because Gavira was a person who was engaged in raiding commercial establishments, and because he had relatives in the northeast of the country, Villarreal believed that he probably belonged to the group of Los Zetas.

"Additionally, Villarreal thought that the criminal activities by Gavira, was "heating up" the Plaza of Gómez Palacio.

In order to get rid of Gavira, "El Grande" first spoke with Antonio Tagle Gutiérrez, then commander of the Tactical Support Group of the Gómez Palacio Police Department, to plant some baggies of cocaine on Gavira and to arrest him to present charges with PGR for being a street drug dealer.

But according to "Mario," Gavira came out positive of being addicted to alkaloid and managed to obtain his freedom. It was then that "El Grande" sent his most trusted and violent sicario Claro Burciaga "El Claro" to target Gavira.

"When Gavira was leaving the Public Prosecutor's Office, along with his lawyer Élfego Rodríguez Galarza, aboard a Dodge Cirrus and being followed behind them by his sister Perla Karina Gavira, Claro Burciaga, along with another sicarios, open fire with assault weapons on Gavira and his attorney, killing them both, this according to "Mario."

"El Claro" then abducted Perla Karina and took her to a safe house in the city of Lerdo, where she was tortured and killed. The next day they threw her body in Matamoros, Coahuila.

Arturo Beltrán Leyva "El Jefe de Jefes" had taken trust of "El Grande" when he started as a cocaine dealer on the border with Guatemala, when in 2006 he took control of the drug traffic in La Laguna in less than a year. This was the exact way how Arturo conducted business while building his trafficking empire.

With a similar Zeta style tactics of assaulting plazas, planting fear and assaulting police commands, he was able to eliminate his competition.

El Grande was attempting to take control of the city of Gómez Palacio and made it a point to find out who was selling drugs outside of the organization. These were people were known as "Chapulines." This was when he found out that a person by the name of "El Cácher," was selling large quantities of drugs and was doing it freely because he had a relationship with the PGR.

This caused Villarreal along with his sicarios Claro Burciaga and Arturo Gorena to abduct "El Cácher," along with a companion, whom they later released. "El Cácher" was tortured and ultimately, Villarreal himself shot him in the head.

Villarreal called several people who were selling drugs in Gómez Palacio, and told them they had to buy his cocaine at $13,000 (dollars) a kilo. Once his will was put in place, about 37 kilos were distributed to street dealers of Gómez Palacio, this according to "Mario."

Beltran Leyva Organization (BLO)

The arrest of one of the five Beltran Leyva brothers, Alfredo Beltran, split the Beltran brothers from Sinaloa cartel forming the BLO.

Born in the Sinaloan countryside in the 1960s, the Beltrán Leyva brothers – Arturo, Carlos, Alfredo and Héctor – worked closely with Joaquín "El Chapo" Guzmán, the leader of the Sinaloa Cartel, during decades of smuggling.

In 2004 and 2005, Arturo Beltrán Leyva led powerful groups of assassins to fight for trade routes in northeastern Mexico for the Sinaloa Cartel. Through the use of corruption or intimidation, the Beltrán Leyva Cartel managed to infiltrate Mexico's political, judicial and police institutions to feed classified information about anti-drug operations, and was known to have infiltrated the Interpol office in Mexico.

In January 2008, Alfredo "El Mochomo" Beltran Leyva was arrested by the Mexican army. There is speculation that the intelligence leading to the arrest came from Sinaloa leader Joaquin "El Chapo" Guzmán Loera. The death of Edgar Guzmán Beltrán, Guzman Loera's son, was retribution for the arrest from the BLO. Alfredo had commanded two groups of hitmen for the BLO, and was allegedly in charge of transporting drugs, bribing officials, and laundering money for the Federation at the time.

Borderland Beat started to track executions attributed to the BLO around the states of Guerrero, Morelos, Puebla and Mexico DF. Executions in Guerrero state had been on the rise over the past three months starting in mid-2009 and getting worst toward the end of the year. Executions with notes accompanying the bodies signed by a mysterious new player on the drug scene, "El Jefe de Jefes."

It was not until the discovery Oct. 18 of five bodies accompanied by similar notes in the resort city of Acapulco,

Guerrero state, that "El Jefe de Jefes" was identified as the leader of the Beltran Leyva Organization (BLO), Arturo Beltran Leyva.

The notes read, "This is what happens to thieves, kidnappers and traitors. Be careful, Manuel Torres. Sincerely, Arturo Beltran Leyva, El Jefe de Jefes."

More than 30 executions had been claimed by El Jefe de Jefes in notes left on or near dead bodies in Acapulco and Guerrero state and had contributed to Guerrero state's becoming one of the most violent in all of Mexico at the time.

The BLO was known to have been very active in the Guerrero region and southwestern Mexico for some time since breaking away from the Sinaloa cartel and Joaquin "El Chapo" Guzman Loera in late 2007. The group had managed to maintain a relatively low profile since the beginning of 2009 after a very active 2008, when it organized a string of assassinations of high-ranking federal law enforcement officials in Mexico City in May 2008.

The BLO intelligence apparatus drew national and international attention when Mexican President Felipe Calderon launched Operacion Limpieza in August of 2008 and uncovered a vast network of federal officials who were on the BLO payroll for providing information regarding counter narcotics operations.

All of this occurred while the BLO methodically executed operatives and supporters of Guzman Loera in the Guerrero, Morelos and Mexico states in an attempt to weaken the Sinaloa cartel's grip in that region. It appeared that the rivalry had been renewed between the BLO and the Sinaloa cartel, only with a different member within the Sinaloa organization, Manuel Torres Felix.

Manuel Torres Felix was a high-ranking lieutenant under Sinaloa cartel leader Ismael "El Mayo" Zambada Garcia. Zambada Garcia and Guzman Loera were essentially partners in the Sinaloa cartel. Zambada Garcia's primary area of operations was the Pacific coast from Jalisco state down to Oaxaca, which included Guerrero state, so it would come as no surprise to find a high-ranking member of Zambada Garcia's network, like Felix, operating in this region.

Other organizations operated in the Guerrero region as well, such as La Familia and Los Zetas. One of these other organizations could be leaving the notes and attributing them to Arturo Beltran Leyva in a tactic known as "calentando la plaza" (heating up the BLO's town), but given the overlapping geography of the BLO and Zambada Garcia's operations and the bad blood between the two organizations, this is likely not the case (repercussions from posing as Arturo Beltran Leyva would be quite severe).

Given the violent nature of how the BLO pursued its campaign against Guzman Loera in 2008 and the body count in the current campaign, more notes, executions and overall violence would be expected in the Guerrero region. And further violence in and around Acapulco and Guerrero does not bode well for the struggling tourism-based economy.

The increase activities in the region of Gerrero was an indication of the desperate attempt to take control by the BLO and this put pressure on the high levels of the Mexican government to take some form of control of the situation.

One of the most notorious cases of corruption was that of Domingo González Díaz, who in 2003 served as head of the Federal Investigation Agency (AFI) and was close to Genaro Garcia Luna. In the preliminary investigation it is said that La Barbie paid Gonzalez Diaz a million dollars to provide protection to the Beltran Leyva brothers.

The cell of narco trafficking which consisted of the brothers Arturo, Héctor, Mario, Carlos and Alfredo Beltrán Leyva was one of the oldest in the drug business in Mexico. It emerged in to the public eye between the mid-eighties and early nineties, when Amado Carrillo Fuentes became the boss of the Juarez cartel.

The Beltran Leyva clan deployed its considerable economic power and deployed their armament to impose their will throughout the country. They had for a long time relied in a strong support from all segments of police agencies, it was so strong that in 2007, José Luis Santiago Vasconcelos, deputy attorney general who served as Legal and International Affairs of the PGR, publicly acknowledged in fear that a group of sicarios under the command of the Beltran had planned to execute him.

The Beltran Leyva's were originally from Sinaloa, where the majority of the school in drug trafficking would form in the history of Mexico's organized crime. The Beltran Leyva clan remained for several years as a major wing of the Juarez cartel, but after the death of Amado Carrillo, they decided to operate on their own, although in those years they had already maintained ties to Joaquin El Chapo Guzman, who eventually became their boss.

Following the escape of El Chapo in January 19, 2001 from the prison de Puente Grande, the Beltran Leyva had allied with him. There was more than one reason for the Sinaloa cartel chief to take them in: it was they who had protected him after a fight with Miguel Ángel Félix Gallardo, the boldest capo in recent history of Mexico and one who Guzman himself served as one of his lieutenants.

During the imprisonment of Joaquin Guzman in Almoloya de Juarez in Puente Grande, the Beltrans made sure to supplying him with money and everything the Sinaloa capo needed to live comfortably at the maximum security, ironically known as "La Puerta de Frente" the front door.

After the escape of Chapo, Beltran brothers took positions in the drug trafficking business. During the presidency of Vicente Fox, they built their power base to dominate a total of 11 states of the Republic, although their main strongholds were Sinaloa and Guerrero but later settled in Morelos.

According to documents from the PGR, the Beltran Leyva clan directed drug transport operations, money laundering, they sold protection and recruitment of hired assassins or sicarios.

From the official documents of the PGR inquiry and criminal cases 82/2001 and 125/2001, it revealed that Arturo Beltran Leyva, El Barbas, Hector Alfredo, El H, Mario Alberto, El General, and Carlos, went unchecked for a long time thanks to the protection of police, military and high level officials of the government of Vicente Fox.

These agreements allowed his drug business to rise quickly and his partner, El Chapo, to become the most powerful crime boss of the last nine years.

Reports from the Ministry of Public Security cited records that indicated this plan of operations included the District of Mexico for at least a decade. Other territories under their control were the States of Sonora, Guerrero, Chiapas, Querétaro, Sinaloa, Jalisco, Quintana Roo, Tamaulipas and Nuevo Leon.

The same reports indicate, that in addition to their drug trafficking activities, the Beltrans owned many businesses including a soccer team in Culiacan, Sinaloa, and owned various luxurious vacation homes in Acapulco, Guerrero and Sinaloa.

According to a report prepared by the PGR, the leader of the band was Arturo Beltran Leyva. None of the five brothers had been arrested but that changed when in January 21, 2008 the military stopped Alfredo Beltran in a residential area in the capital of Sinaloa.

The arrest of Alfredo Beltran was considered a big blow against the Sinaloa cartel. The Beltran brothers' broke ranks with El Chapo because of disagreements about how to run the business and the effects of the break up reached the high level of the SSP, which was mismanaged by Genaro Garcia Luna, who has been mentioned publicly in the investigation as the alleged protector of the Beltran brothers.

The various members of the Sinaloa cartel, the most organized of all drug cartels, at least before the arrest of Alfredo Beltran were not only partners in the drug business but there were lines of kinship. Arturo Beltran Leyva is a distant cousin of El Chapo who really perfected the cocaine trade in Mexico.

Another partner of Beltran, Juan Jose Esparragoza Moreno, El Azul is married to a niece of Arturo Beltran. Not much is known of El Azul, but it is rumored that he died of a heart attack.

The powers of Arturo Beltran in the drug trade allowed him to murder, corrupt and buy senior members of various federal agencies without any interruption form anyone. He is credited for example in the murder of Edgar Millan, the Federal Police chief assassinated in 2008. He is also responsible for corrupting Igor Labastida, another officer linked with the head of the SSP Genaro Garcia Luna.

Information on reports collected on the system of protection for Beltran Leyva, specifically testimony from various witnesses who had been detained by the federal police and federal prosecutors, confirmed that within the criminal cell there were a network of contacts from the Mexican military who were actively participating in providing information to the cell about operations and other acts of intelligence, including the locations of checkpoints or roadblocks. The report does not mention any names of these alleged "contacts"

Within the group of protection that fell to the operation of the infantry of the Navy of Mexico, there were also active police officers who with the backing of their superior officers were directly responsible to provide protection to the houses of cartel members, to be bodyguards for cartel leaders or to be guides for different groups sicarios living in other states.

The document details how the agents were paid 2,000 dollars a month and their mission was to report any operation against the cartel, rescue or assist those members of the cartel that might get arrested, to report all suspicious vehicles or even serve as a "wall of protection" in ensuring the success of actions perpetuated by sicarios or executioners of the organization.

The large numbers of Halcones (lookouts) that dedicated itself to conducting runs throughout the state capital had private vehicles to carry out surveillance, while alone or in pairs and sometimes even in teams of four.

The document revealed that the Halcones were usually equipped cell phones or radios, but were not armed. Their primary mission was to report the movements of the Army, federal and state police, in addition to the presence of suspicious vehicles in each of their perspective areas.

The sicarios called Zafiros, who received the information from the Halcones, were in charged with alerting the cartel leaders of any threat.

Arturo Beltran Leyva, who is best described by all his nicknames: "La Muerte," "El Barbas," "El jefe de jefes" or "El botas blancas" made the lists of the most wanted drug traffickers in the world for his power and influence stretching from Columbia to the United States.

During his criminal career, he bought the same officials that were supposed to apprehend him and executed those who stood in the way of his operations.

El Grande

Sergio Enrique Villarreal Barragán, a.k.a. El Grande, is a former Mexican federal police officer who worked as a lieutenant for Arturo Beltrán Leyva of the criminal organization called the Beltrán Leyva Organization (BLO). He got his name El Grande ("The Big One") because he is 6 feet 7 inches tall.

El Grande was born in Torreón, Coahuila on September 21, 1969. He began his criminal career as a car thief in the state of Coahuila, and in 1990 at age 20, he was joined the Coahuila Judicial Police. He later joined the Federal Police and was stationed at Nuevo Laredo. El Grande was also stationed in Reynosa, Tamaulipas, where he worked until 1996. There he established a relationship with the Juárez Cartel. Between the years 2007 and 2010, Villarreal Barragán left the Juárez cartel to work along with the Gulf Cartel and Los Zetas. He later joined the Sinaloa Cartel, commanding a criminal cell of the Beltrán Leyva Organization (BLO).

The war started on a Monday, January 21, 2008. On board Hummer vehicles, and with heavy artillery, more than 300 elements of the Special Forces Aeromobile Group (GAFE) of the Mexican Army, positioned themselves in the area of a residence located in the Burócratas community in Culiacán. According to the Ministry of Defense, an anonymous call had told them that the youngest of the Beltrán brothers, Alfredo, alias El Mochomo, was waiting at that address for a shipment of money on an outstanding settlement from some of his Colombian associates. According to the statement from a drug trafficker known as El 19 - who had joined the witness protection program and went by the name of "Jennifer," the army had obtained the location of El Mochomo through confidential information from a soldier that had managed to infiltrate El Mochomo's inner circle, and who was known as

275

El Chamaco. El Chamaco managed to call the GAFE to provide the exact location and minimal amount of security they had.

The military had to postpone the operation for 10 hours, because they detected some men on the roof of the house. Near dawn, the gate opened. A white BMW van came out with four men on board. A team of elite military commandos blocked their way. The men in the vehicle surrendered without firing a single shot. Inside the house they recovered $900,000 in dollars, 11 expensive watches, an AK-47 and eight handguns. A narco corrido announced the event the following day:

"El Mochomo was a man of confidence
that the cartel needed
but on January 21 his career was cut short."

The news of the arrest of Alfredo Beltrán Leyva, one of the leaders of the Sinaloa cartel, that was led by Joaquín El Chapo Guzmán and Ismael El Mayo Zambada, was presented as the most important arrest carried out by the government in the war against drug trafficking that Felipe Calderón had carried out. In the Office of the Attorney General of the Republic, and specifically in the Office of the Assistant Attorney General for Specialized Investigation in Organized Crime, SIEDO, this arrest caused immediate panic. The cartel cell led by the brothers of Héctor, Alfredo and Arturo Beltrán Leyva had corrupted the highest level of that federal institution by paying monthly bribes of between $150,000 and $450,000 in dollars, as it was later discovered through the Operation Cleanup: Officials of the highest level of the SIEDO carried out arrests, searches and provided leaks of sensitive information to the BLO.

That day of El Mochomo arrest, several public officials were very nervous. They had received reports that El Mochomo was going to be arrested, but in the SIEDO they could do nothing to avoid it. They expected the leadership of Arturo Beltrán to call them to explained why Alfredo was arrested.

Hector Beltra leyva alias "El Hache," a top capo of the BLO, was upset with El Grande over the arrest of his brother Alfredo Beltran Leyva.

Although El Grande was not directly responsible for the security of El Mochomo, he was in charge of the cartel relationship with the federal government and the arrest caused suspicion for El Grande.

Hector Beltran was resting at his home in Morelos when he was told about the arrest of Alfredo Beltran and became so upset that he took out a firearm from inside his waist and started shooting up to the ceiling while his escort looked on very nervous. He smashed a bottle of wine that was on top of a table against a European table that had been a gift from the Panista governor Marco Antonio Adame Castillo. Hector Beltran requested the immediate presence of his most trusted man, El Grande. He was brought in all the way from Puebla in a helicopter from the state police of Morelos.

With his eyes red from anger and anguish, Hector Beltran Leyva requested a quick explanation why his brother was arrested. He reminded El Grande about the millions of dollars in bribes that the cartel paid to ensure the protection of his family from many levels of the government. There was a clear understanding that his family would not be touched. Hector Beltran requested that El Grande conduct a complete thorough investigation to find out who they have to kill.

The meeting lasted about ten minutes.

El Grande started making phone calls to his contacts with the PGR. It was later learned that he spoke with the Captain Fernando Rivera of the PGR. He arranged for a meeting in the city of Mexico to get the information on the arrest Alfredo Beltran Leyva in Culiacan. According to a statement from Rivera that was given at a later date when he became a protected witness, under the name of "Moisés," El Grande told them that Arturo Beltrán Leyva was pissed. Captain Rivera promised to give him a detailed report of the operation no later than the next day.

The next day the Captain Rivera met with El Grande in a restaurant on Avenida Reforma and the captain was also in company of commanders Menton Silia and Roberto Garcia, who Rivera ordered to gather the information immediately in less than 24 hours.

El Grande immediately got the names of the "snitches." It turned out to be two agents of the ministerial police of Sinaloa. Their prompt death was surely assured.

Rivera told El Grande that from 11 o'clock onwards, the special forces of the army would no longer be present, and that only 11 agents of the Federal Investigation Agency, AFI, would remain on scene to provide security. He told El Grande that with the delivery of one million pesos for the AFIS, as well as three million that would be to pay off Fernando Rivera and his people, it would be possible to get the cooperation of the security detail and allow an armored truck to break in to the gate to give them access to the SIEDO facility.

After El Grande gave the information to his boss, about the progress of his investigation, Hector Beltran ordered El Grande to take immediate action to rescue his detained brother. El Grande gathered about 100 men, that came from different parts of the country to the city of Mexico, to carry out an assault of the headquarters of SIEDO. The then allied leaders of the Beltran Leyva clan; Joaquin Guzman Loera, El Chapo and Ismael El Mayo Zambada refused to cooperate in the rescue attempt. The assault was planned for midnight on January 24th but in the end, it did not take place because El

Mochomo was transferred 7 days before to the federal prison Puente Grande.

The refusal of El Chapo and El Mayo to help secure the freedom of Alfredo Beltran prompted bad blood between the Beltran brothers. This caused the breakup of the two factions. This would be the start of the war between the Beltran Leyva Organization and the Sinaloa Cartel. Hector Beltran broke the alliance with the Sinaloa cartel that for many years had remained intact in the world of narco trafficking. Hector Beltran Layva never forgave El Grande that had allowed the arrest of his younger brother. Hector Beltran brought it up every time they saw each other. That is when El Grande brought up the notion that perhaps the people responsible for the arrest of El Chomo was attributed to El Chapo Guzman and Mayo Zambada.

Another version points out that Arturo Beltrán met with El Chapo Guzmán and El Mayo Zambada to ask them to help him rescue his brother. The leaders of the Sinaloa cartel asked him for more time, but in a second meeting they explained that the conditions were not right for a rescue attempt. They explained that Mochomo would have to be sacrificed.

It is believed that in the drug trafficking business where there is a blood alliance, it is virtually indestructible. El Mochomo was married to a cousin of El Chapo. Arturo Beltrán, however, left that meeting with the idea that the blood alliance had been broken. From now on he was going to have to be killed or arrested, for he did not care anymore of the consequences. El Chapo and El Mayo knew that this would result in a war with the Beltran clan but they accepted the risk. They just wanted to move on and allow things to remain the way they were without intervention from the powerful Sinaloa cartel. They either did not want to bring heat from the federal government or perhaps they were working another angle with the top levels of the federal government, or both.

Then, there was the rumor that the El Chapo had made a deal with the highest levels of the federal government that he would deliver El Mochomo in exchange for the release of his son, El Chapito.

At the end of April 2008, the same month that El Chapito was released, a shootout occurred in Culiacán. A house which allegedly belonged to the children of Arturo Beltrán, was targeted by elements of the Federal Police, supported by municipal police. Five sicarios and two ministerial police agents were killed during a fierce battle. Arturo Beltrán accused the feds of serving as an armed wing for El Chapo and ordered his people to kill any police officer wherever they may be found. He placed narcomantas in which he wrote: "Policemen, soldiers, so that it is clear to you, El Mochomo continues to reign. Atte. Arturo Beltrán Leyva." And also: "Warrying Soldiers, little federal police forces, this place is the territory of Arturo Beltrán."

One day after the shooting in Culiacán where Arturo Beltran lost five of his sicarios, four officers of the Federal Preventive Police (PFP) were killed when they were patrolling downtown Culiacán. In Imala, two municipal police officers were executed. All across the city, attacks against local police were taking place. The PFP gathered about 800 police elements to reinforce the Plaza of Sinaloa.

By the end of April of 2008 there was blood running down the street of Culiacan after the demons were unleashed, causing a string of confrontations that in that month alone resulted in 1,156 executions.

On May 7, 2008 a Federal Police checkpoint was installed at kilometer 95 of the highway del Sol. The PFP had just received information leaked by El Mayo Zambada. A convoy where Arturo Beltrán was traveling would cross at any time through that location. The official in charge of coordinating the capture was the regional director of the PFP, Édgar Eusebio Millán. The tip that had been provided by Zambada was good. Five suspicious luxurious SUVs left the motel Rosales, where Arturo Beltrán had just had a meeting. The police agents attempted to make a traffic stop. The sicarios from the convoy responded by opening fire. This started a pursuit that ended in Xoxocotla, with several cars destroyed and the arrest of nine sicarios along with two federal police agents killed. The truck in which Arturo Beltrán was traveling managed to evade the siege: one of his escorts crashed his vehicle in to a patrol car to make way for his boss.

Mayo Zambada, however, had contemplated the possibility that Arturo Beltran might escape capture. The information that had been leaked to the PFP also included addresses in the state of Morelos where Beltrán Leyva might seek refuge. The inspector of operations Edgar Enrique Bayardo, who was the official who had received the information and had direct contact with El Mayo relayed the information to the PFP. He had made contact with the anti-drug chief of the agency, Gerardo Garay. He told Garay that they had located several addresses in Morelos where Arturo might be located. Bayardo told Garay that they were in place and ready to make entry.

Chief Garay stopped the whole operation dead in its tracks, he instructed them to stop everything and return to Mexico City immediately.

This was similar to an event five months earlier. The PFP, through Director Roberto Velasco, had intercepted a telephone conversation where they had found the location of Arturo Beltrán in a mansion in Pedregal de San Ángel.

Velasco told chief Garay that he had agents already in place along strategic points and requested the green light to start the operation for an arrest. Garay refused to give the order by telling them to stand fast and wait for another time.

According a testimony from a protected witness, Fidel Hernández, who was a former agent of the Anti-Drug Division, said that the motives of Garay were criticized by his subordinates. They plead with him that they had evidence of the whereabouts of Arturo Beltrán, but Garay ordered them to dismantle the operation.

Édgar Millán, the same man who had previously attempted to apprehend Arturo Beltrán on the road to Xoxocotla, was executed hours after that operation. Millán was ambushed and killed when he arrived at his parents' house in a building located in a community in Guerrero. Although only a handful of people had access to the itinerary of Millán, the information was leaked from within the PFP to the BLO. Police agent José Antonio Montes Garfias gave the information of the location of Millán to the Beltran clan. Arturo Beltran did not hesitate to give the order to eliminate Millán at any cost. Millán had also been instrumental in the arrest of Alfredo Beltran.

Agent Montes Garfias removed a pair of keys from the drawer to Millán's desk and made a duplicate key. The keys were of the house where the parents of Millan lived. Garfias turned over the duplicate of the keys, 40,000 pesos and 75 grams of cocaine to a low-level gunman, Alejandro Ramírez Báez, who had a commando made up of five people. The sicarios waited for Millán in the garage of the building. They had turned off the lights. When Millán crossed the gate on foot of the courtyard, he took 11 direct gun shots to his body. The alleged shooter, Ramírez Báez, was subdued by Millán's escorts, and the federal authorities managed to get a confession of the plot.

The real revenge of Arturo Beltrán came 24 hours after the shooting in Xoxocotla. It happened on the other side of the country, on May 8, 2008. That night five SUVs loaded with sicarios surrounded the vehicle carrying Edgar Guzman, another son of El Chapo, in a parking lot in the of Culiacán, Sinaloa.

Edgar Guzman was executed. Five hundred gunshots were fired along with a grenade deployed from a grenade launcher. The burst of gun fire destroyed walls, glass and vehicles. In addition to the execution of El Chapo's son, a nephew of the drug trafficker, César Loera, was also killed.

In Culiacán the evil rage was unleashed. The local media did not dare to report the news. They only did it two days later, attributing the information to newspapers and news agencies in Mexico City. Borderland Beat was the place where some information could be obtained. The blood of the son of El Chapo was still fresh on the ground when the cries from the leader of the Sinaloa Cartel pledged that he would erase the name of Arturo Beltrán from the face of the earth.

In less than a month, however, El Chapo took two more blows. Filtrations from the BLO intelligence led to the arrest of one of his cousins, Alfonso Gutiérrez, and of a nephew, Isaí Martínez after a bloody shooting in a community of Culiacán.

The murder of El Chapo's son was part of the same MO that killed the police chiefs Millán and Velasco.

Millan, the commander that was executed while trying to visit his parents, had been the "brain" of the secretary of Public Security, Genaro García Luna, in many anti-drug operations. His death caused a change in the upper level of the structure of the PFP. Genaro García Luna replaced Millan with an old friend and companion of the Cisen, with whom he had collaborated closely while working with the AFI, it was Gerardo Garay, the anti-drug chief who had stopped two operations to capture Beltrán Leyva.

But as things happen in Mexico at the time, Garay only lasted a few months in that position.

Commissioner Garay was accused of serving two masters: the Beltrán Cartel and that of El Mayo Zambada. A judge ordered him to be formally apprehended in October 2008.

Inspector Edgar Enrique Bayardo was killed at a Starbucks in Mexico City after he had confessed of colluding with organized crime by allow infiltrations to the agency, tapping telephone calls to benefit particular cartels, allowing cartel operators to interrogate captured adversaries, and then presenting the arrestees as "as achievements of the PFP."

El Grande is Arrested

On September 12, 2010, El Grande was arrested in a raid by Mexican Marines in the central state of Puebla. Villarreal was charged with multiple murders and other crimes.

While in prison, El Grande told people that the arrest of Alfredo Beltran was the result of a deal that was made by El Chapo Guzman with the federal government in exchange for the release of his son Yvan Archivaldo. That is why he refused to send people to help with the rescue of El Mochomo. While making his claim loud and clear within the halls in the prison of Puente Grande, this made El Grande to be hated by all the convicts in the prison. Without thinking of the consequences, he started to plot against El Chapo Guzman. If at any place El Chapo Guzman was popular, it was in the prison of Puente Grande.

Soon many of the prisoners were attempting to kill El Grande but no one was able to touch a hair of his. At most, they would spit at his face, curse at him, and at other times, threw excrement at him when he walked the narrow corridor between the cells.

El Grande would laugh and make fun of the prisoners in the cells that were trying to degrade him. The prisoners would kick the bars of their cells in frustration that they could not put their hand on El Grande. They wanted more than anything to reclaim the honor of El Chapo.

On a certain occasion, a prisoner that they named "El Manita" managed to pull in El Grande by his shirt when he went by his cell, while the guards that were supposed to be escorting him were not paying attention. While talking about some of the officials of the PGR, El Manita grabbed him, pulled him in against the cell bars and started chocking him. El Manita used the bars as leverage and was able to get a good hold on the giant against the cell. El Grande attempted to free himself, trying to get air and trying to scream for help. His escorts quickly intervened to save the life of El Grande who was being chocked to death. The guards opened the cell of El Manitas and sprayed his face with chemical gas directly to his face. They sounded the code red that is sounded when someone tries to escape and a group of other guards started beating up El Manitas. His body was dragged away on the corridor. Two days later, it was learned that El Manitas had died. His family claimed the body and were told that Jose Manuel Hernandez, El Manitas had died of a heart attack.

El Grande warned all the other prisoners that the same would happen to them if they tried to attack him again. It was rumored the El Grande had a good relationship with the Mexican president. From then on the protocol of the prisoners changed. Every time El Grande walked the corridor between the cells, the prisoners had to move away from the bars, lay down face down and put their hands-on top of their head.

Up until the first of 2011, some of the supervisor of the guards, warned the prisoners that if they attacked El Grande, they would be killed.

The Fall of the Boss of Bosses

Borderland Beat continued to track the attacks from Arturo Beltran Leyva "Jefe de Jefes" and had been continuing up until the month of December 2009. Arturo continued to execute any adversary foe without blinking an eye. He seemed to be out of control. The arrest of his little brother, El Mochomo and the betrayal from El Chapo blinded him to focus on only revenge.

With the discovery of two more bodies in September 2009 in Guerrero attributed to BLO, the trail of deaths had not stopped.

* On December 10, 2009 four bodies were found in the center of Chilpancingo. Two were completely dismembered, with a message attributing the deaths to the "jefe de jefes". The term "El Jefe de Jefes" has been tied to the leader of the Beltran Leyva Organization (BLO), Arturo Beltran Leyva.

* On December 7, 2009 in the community of La Calera, Petatlan state police found the body of a man of approximately 48 of age, who had been killed with a gunshot to the head. Unlike other cases, the death was "for talking to adversaries," it was written in cardboard and left with the body.

* On December 5th two bodies were found in the road that leads to the village of Villa Lucerna of Chilpancingo. The bodies bore signs of torture, a black bag on their head and a message that accused them of being "kidnappers, thieves and extortionists".

* On December 2, 2009 police discovered a handcuffed body in the street Las Plazuelas in Acapulco. the body had a narco sign as is customary and the person had been shot (preferred method of execution of the cartel) The message warned people that this would happen to all the kidnappers. On the same day and in the same road that leads Tuncingo,

police discovered another body with the same message and also with a gunshot wound to the head.

In early December of 2009 DEA and FBI agents received information about Arturo Beltran Leyva's whereabouts in the city of Puebla, southeast of Mexico City, and shared it with Mexican naval officials. But Beltran Leyva and his bodyguards escaped a navy raid in Puebla.

The following day, Mexican forces raided a Christmas party in the picturesque southern Mexico City suburb of Tepoztlan in search for cartel members.

That night a narco party was being held by Artuto Beltran who had with him his main bosses, Edgar Valdés Villarreal "La Barbie" and Sergio Villarreal "El Grande." Arturo Beltran was in a festive mood and was welcoming guest that were arriving.

Arturo was behind a coffee table, on one side he had his gold-plated AK-47 and on the other side was Osmayda Nalleli Casarrubias, the woman who he relied to look after his health. La Barbie was on one of side dressed in a navy-blue suit while "El Grande" was on the other side wearing a denim, gray plaid shirt, baseball cap and an AK-47 hanging over his shoulder.

The musicians Los Cadets of Linares, Torrente and Ramón Ayala and his Bravos del Norte, were all lined up in a hall to wait for their turn to play in front of Arturo.

In the living room there were four armchairs, one for Arturo and the rest for the girls that were brought in from Acapulco. The first seven Acapulqueñas, of the 24 that would be at the party, arrived around 9:00 p.m. and were kindly received by Arturo each with a kiss. Arturo welcomed the girls and fondling some of the girls while asking them to take off their clothes. Most of the girls started dancing in their underwear.

Arturo started throwing money at the girls, all $100 dollar bills, while about twenty naked women were scrambling on the floor to grab the bills, as if they were picking up candy from a broken pinata. Ramón Ayala continued playing music while the women took off their clothes and were dancing with fist full of bills.

That night there was a grill in the garden with a table next to it, where Atanasio Reyes Vizcarra, the head chef of Arturo, who charged $2,000 to prepare meals for special events such as the one of that night.

Arturo whispered at La Barbie about his concern that he heard Joaquín "El Chapo" Guzmán was moving in to Puebla. Arturo told La Barbie that El Chapo and Mayo Zambada were moving in and they had already bought most of the police and military in Puebla. La Barbie reassured Arturo, "let them try to enter Cuernavaca, I will take care of them myself.

"They were eating taquitos of beef and, drinking beer, whiskey and tequila," said Antonio Ruiz González "El Tony", one of the kitchen helpers.

While the party was in full swing there was a loud knock on the door. Who is it?" Asked the gunmen guarding the front door of the residence. "We came to the party," said one of the newcomers.

As they opened the door the group that was dancing to norteña music asked, "are we expecting anyone else?"

"No, no, we got everybody!" Shouted someone from inside.

With those words, a shooting broke out targeting the visitors outside the front door, who were actually members of the Marine special forces of Mexico dressed in civilian clothes.

"Flee, patron! flee!" The gunmen shouted.

Suddenly El Barbie grabbed Arturo and said, "let's go, let's go boss, they are here!" He moved fast toward the rear exit of the house with Arturo and immediately they began to hear gunfire coming from the front of the house.

"La Barbie" and "El Grande" took Arturo Beltrán outside from the back of the house. His golden golden AK-47 on the couch was the only thing he managed to take.

"La Barbie" and "El Grande" took Beltrán to the rear parking lot outside where there was a black Suburban, a gray Pick Up and a gray Cherokee.

Also outside was a white GLI Bora and a silver Dodge loaded with sicarios that were there to engage the military forces to allow Arturo to escape.

They chose the gray truck and took off.

The sound of fully automatic gunfire put a sudden silence to the music of Ramon Ayala, who was playing his music for those who were attending the narcoposada (narco party). Suddenly numerous gunmen appeared from inside the house located on Paseo de los Naranjos, to confront the soldiers who retreated against the walls of the residence to engage the drug traffickers.

Amid the gunfire, a gray Toyota truck suddenly sped off away from the building.

According to unofficial sources, the goal of the operation had been to capture Edgar Valdes Villarreal, "La Barbie," Chief sicario of the criminal organization. Initially, they did not know that Arturo was also present at the party.

They arrested dozens of attendees and entertainers, including Latin Grammy-winning accordionist and singer Ramon Ayala.

According to statements from neighbors of the subdivision, located in the town of Ahuatepec, in the north part of Cuernavaca, the confrontation between the armed forces and the drug traffickers resulted in three deaths; two gunmen and an innocent woman that was caught in the cross fire who was identified as Patricia Terroba.

According to unofficial reports the woman is said to have resided near where the offenders had organized the party. The victim was considered collateral damage by the government.

A version of the incident had the Beltran Leyva brothers fleeing aboard a gray truck bearing the plates of 102WPH, which was later located at the corner of Teopanzolco and Rio Mayo, a highway that led to the Mexico-Cuernavaca or Cuernavaca-Acapulco. The vehicle was found with the doors open and blood stains in the interior, this was according to statements from the State Police.

According to locals, the confrontation between soldiers and drug traffickers lasted for about two hours, and detonations of grenades could be heard.

Before the armed confrontation, the clamor of the party was heard along the streets played by Ramon Ayala and his band Los Bravos del Norte.

Ramon Ayala 'El Rey del Acordeón" and members of Cadetes de Linares along with the Grupo Torrente had been detained and transported to the federal police headquarters in Mexico City. Eleven suspected members of the Beltran Leyva cartel were also detained.

Ayala's attorney said the musicians were hired to play at the party but didn't know their clients were suspected members of the Beltran Levya Cartel. Mexican norteno bands often sing about drug trafficking, violence and many have been rumored to perform at drug traffickers' weddings or other narco parties, but few have been caught.

Days later, residents in nearby Cuernavaca reported the presence of heavily armed men in their neighborhood. DEA officials said U.S. and Mexican agents received information that the Beltran Leyva group had fled to a Cuernavaca high-rise building.

Inside the building, a meal was being prepared in apartment number 201, one of the five residential towers called Altitude, located in the Lomas de la Selva, in Cuernavaca, Morelos, where el capo Arturo Beltran Leyva was residing.

The protection system of Arturo Beltran Leyva cartel included informants within the military, ministerial and municipal police forces along with watchmen designated under the key names of Zafiros and Halcones who moved around in vehicles or taxis throughout the city.

His inner circle of security that escorted him was composed of the most hardened sicarios who always guarded him. He was in company of five of his most trusted men, including Edgar Valdez Villarreal, La Barbie, the leader of his sicarios.

Inside the safety of his bunker of the building, Beltran received constant reports of gunmen who formed part the three levels of security guarding the condominium and movements out in the streets.

Arturo Beltran had already been told that his system of intelligence had observed suspicious movements outside his apartment, but he relied on his people to take care of matters, thinking that everything would be resolved and under control as usual.

Meanwhile the Arturo Beltran was having a conversation with Valdez Villarreal and other members of his entourage. They were fine tuning the details to receive a special guest who had agreed to have dinner with Beltran. It was General Leopoldo Díaz Pérez, head of the Military Zone 24, headquartered in Morelos.

According to statements from suspects that had been arrested on December 11th in the narco party (posada) in Tepoztlan, in Morelos, also attending the meeting were supposed to be a Major and Captain from the same military unit.

There was testimony from a person that would be eventually arrested that was only identified as "El Cocinero," who might be the actual chef. El Cocinero said that Valdez Villarreal was also supposed to be present but at the end he was not to be found. There was speculation that when the operation began to take place, he fled as he observed military commandos surrounding the building. There has been a lot of talk that La Barbie provided information to the Mexican military command of the exact location of Arturo Beltran and he attempted to became an informant to try to save himself from apprehension. This has not been confirmed, but was more of a rumor that was circulating on several media sources.

From noon until shortly before 5 pm on Wednesday 16, more than 200 commandos of the Navy/Marines of Mexico started to do surveillance of the facility and quietly started to evacuate the occupants of the apartments Elbus. The goal was clear: to corner Arturo Beltran Leyva, one of the most wanted drug lords in the last decade - and five of his bodyguards who accompanied him.

Mexican forces moved residents, including teens at a party, to a gym in the complex. All this movement occurred between 1 am through 4 pm and before the actual entry into the facility of Altitude, all in order to capture Beltran.

Soon thereafter, the military enter the high rise and the assault began.

Helicopters circled low.

Mexican Navy/Marines that stormed the upscale apartment complex provoked a ferocious gun battle that lasted for at least two hours. Witnesses said the raid began when marines rappelled down ropes onto the roofs of some of the apartment buildings at dusk. The Marines continued with their operation equipped with heavy artillery, tanks and armored vehicles, including helicopters hovering overhead.

When the security levels or "belts" of protection of Arturo Beltrán Leyva had been clearly defeated, and when the Marines felt they had the situation under their control, the members of the Special Forces were greeted with gunfire. Cartel gunmen hurled grenades that killed one marine and wounded two others.

This generated a heavy gunfight with high caliber weaponry. From their armored vehicles, the Marines triggered 7.62 caliber machine guns and assault rifles AR-15s, while another elite military commando from the helicopter rappelled down on top of the condominium where Arturo Beltran was located.

According to the versions that was disseminated by the Secretary of the Navy, they did not have it easy. Beltran Leyva's group of sicarios responded with dozens of fragmentation grenades and bursts of firepower from fully automatic AK-47 and AR-15 through the windows of department 201, located on the second floor of the 15-story luxurious building.

Other sicarios who were part of the security belt of protection of Arturo began firing at the Marines who were on the ground floor, but According to official reports, the counter did not work as a burst of gunfire took them out immediately.

"What an experience," one resident told Mexican television. "Explosions! Grenades! Machine guns! I would never have imagined something like this happening in Mexico City, and much less Cuernavaca."

As the hours pass (five in total) since taking the building, the sicarios were running out of grenades. No longer capable of an offensive, three of the five sicarios who were defending Beltran were shot dead in middle of the floor of the apartment. According to the official version, another sicario shot himself with one gunshot.

The same version says that one more desperate sicario decided to commit suicide by jumping out the window, but when he was freefalling a bullet penetrated his back. His body lying on his back was photographed on the garden of an apartment downstairs.

Arturo made one last call, to the main leader of his security escort, Edgar Valdez Villarreal, El Barbie. Arturo was requesting reinforcements, but La Barbie told him it was impossible to intervene. According to La Barbie, he told Arturo to surrender but that Arturo told him he was going to fight it out.

According to the press release of the Marines, it was about nine o'clock at night when Arturo Beltran, no longer having the protection of his gunmen, opened the door of his apartment. Apparently, he intended to flee through the elevator. Once outside, he engaged the Marines in a gunfight who were just outside by the door, but was shot down by the firepower of a group of Marines that were moving up the stairs.

The body of the one who was named El Jefe de Jefes, who had managed to live for two decades in the shadows of first, Amado Carrillo, and then of Joaquin "El Chapo" Guzman, had collapsed against the door with several expanding bullets shattering his chest, abdomen and head. Arturo was dead, killed in a gunfight with military forces.

Reporters were briefly allowed inside the apartment where Arturo's body still lay; his skull and one arm were mangled by bullet wounds, and in one hand he clutched a large gold-colored medallion. It was there that the body of Arturo Beltran Leyva was captured by various digital photographs and video. It was also the same spot where his body was staged in a humiliating display to the press.

The images of the body of Arturo Beltran made international news and angered some people who saw the display of his body as disrespectful. It was the method in which the military decided to show dismay for the capo, in how his body was presented for the world to see. Many times, the cartels pull down the pants of men left on the street after being executed, a sign of disrespect. Just like Arturo had done during some of his executions he conducted, the Mexican authorities had done the same to him; pulled down his pants and placed the contents from his pocket over his body. Mexican and US bills soaked in blood were seen blanketing his body in a display of trophy of some kind.

"First they were ordered to surrender, but they refused and then they opened fire at us," said one of the ski-masked Marines who participated in the raid.

The last meal of El Jefe de Jefes, the man who bought favors in exchange for millions of dollars and trafficked cargoes of drugs that were measured in kilos, the man with the jewels, the exotic animals, the ranches, the palaces, the planes; was eating eggs with ham that he had sipped in a plastic bottle of Coke.

He had called two masseurs, one of 18 and the other of 44, with whom he spent his last hours.

The first photos show him not at the door of the apartment, but inside it, with an energy drink next to his hands. According to the official version, the Marines found him with his pants to his knees and his shirt lifted to his chest. "I think he fell wounded and perhaps his clothes were loosened, he was pulled and he was left in that position, he was already in this position," exclaimed Admiral José Luis Vergara when questioned about the body of Arturo.

Except that a photo shows three civilians dressed in sweatshirts and red latex gloves, lowering the pants of Arturo down to his knees, and placing the body on a white sheet. In a third photo, those same civilians begin to place jewelry and bloody bills on the body.

No official explanation was offered about the humiliation of the body.

Admiral Vergara maintained that the objective of the marines was to capture the criminal alive, "but he resisted any attempted to be captured alive."

Testimony given to the ministerial agency by the masseurs gave a different version that official authorities did not disclosed. The two masseurs said that Arturo Beltrán had surrendered, that he had placed his hands up in a sign of surrender, before he was shot dead by the military.

President Felipe Calderon, speaking from the Copenhagen climate summit, said "this operation represents an important achievement for the government and people of Mexico, and a resounding blow against one of the most dangerous criminal organizations in Mexico, and on the continent."

Arturo Beltran Leyva was the highest-ranking figure killed under Calderon, who had deployed more than 45,000 troops across Mexico to crush the cartels since taking office in December 2006. Mexican Marines/Navy often had been used in these battles against heavily armed sicarios. The offensive earned Calderon praise from Washington even as 14,000 people had been killed in a wave of drug-related violence engulfing Mexico.

Not long after the death of Arturo Beltran Mexican authorities were wondering who would take over operations of the BLO. His death, as is common with the death of any top boss, very rarely slows down operations.

In fact, hitmen executed several members of the family of a dead marine that had participated in the operation that killed Arturo. Hours after the funeral of the marine who was killed in the raid that left Arturo Beltran Leyva dead, some of Leyva's allies invaded the marine's home and gunned down his mother, brother, sister and aunt.

The message couldn't have been clearer: Touch us, and your family will pay the price.

When the family of an ordinary marine is massacred because he took part in a raid against a cartel leader, it means two things: First, the cartels are raising the stakes as high as they can go. Second, the government is hitting them hard and hurting them badly. This had become a war of desperation on both sides, and America ought to be paying attention.

The family of Beltran claimed the body and held a funeral service in Culiacan, Sinaloa. It is said that the family bought all the white roses in the whole state of Sinaloa, to symbolize the white boots that Arturo often wore.

For more than two minutes "they killed him, they killed him" are the only words that are heard in a corrido dedicated to drug trafficker Arturo Beltrán Leyva. Another corrido warns President Felipe Calderón that "operatives like this do not do you a big favor" and one more even alludes to the burial in Durango. In total, eight videos of narcocorridos were written hours after the death of El Jefe de Jefes and could be seen on YouTube.

After the death of Arturo Beltran Leyva, the power of his criminal organization, one of the most powerful in the past 20 years, was put in the hands of Hector Beltran Leyva, one of the brothers who according to government official, is responsible for the laundering of money for the organization. Hector Beltran, El "H," would eventually be arrested by Mexican authorities and would die of a heart attack while in prison.

However, in the midst of internal realignment of forces, another name was mentioned as possible replacements; Edgar Valdez Villarreal, El Barbie, the leader of the sicarios under Arturo Beltran and one who had been marked as a traitor in the death of El Jefe de Jefes.

La Barbie

Edgar Valdez Villarreal (born August 11, 1973) also known as La Barbie, is a Mexican-American, born and raised in the United States.

In his initial stages Valdez Villarreal was a member of the Gulf cartel, responsible for coordinating all logistics of espionage in a large group of informants, known as Los Halcones.

He then left that criminal organization and became a key part of the Sinaloa cartel, when the brothers Arturo, Hector and Alfredo - known as "Three Caballeros" were part of what is now known as The Federation and that according to the PGR, were led by Ismael Zambada García El Mayo, and Joaquín Guzmán Loera, El Chapo.

Soon Barbie became leader of the group of Beltran's sicarios and was placed there specifically because he showed the ability to orchestrate the executions of rival members without blinking an eye. He is also distinguished himself by his ability to corrupt public officials.

According to some of the friends and foes of Edgar Valdez Villareal "La Barbie," they said that La Barbie was one of the most efficient hunters of Zetas.

La Barbie was once quoted as saying "Yes the Zetas are a danger, they do not respect anyone, because the truth is, they are filth, for not even their mother wants them."

La Barbie was described as a criminal master mind who had full control of airports and was also good in counterintelligence from within his criminal group to help him discredit public officials.

Those who knew him and later some who testified in legal proceedings with federal prosecutors of SIEDO gave information that sicarios under his leadership conducted routine executions, even of innocent people, without hesitation and some of which included the 24 farmers and masons from La Marquesa.

Mateo Díaz López, or "Comandante Mateo," a former military and a commander for Los Zetas that was arrested on July 2006 told SIEDO that "La Barbie" was responsible for filming the execution of four sicarios in Tamaulipas. This video was sent to The Dallas Morning News on December 1, 2005.

"I know that on that occasion the Preventive Police and the AFIs abducted nine members of my group (Zetas) in a nightclub in Zihuatanejo. These men were in that city in order to fight for control of the plaza," said Comandante Mateo.

Once abducted they took them to the city of Acapulco and there, they delivered them to La Barbie, who later released a video in which four of the men are seen being interviewed. Among them were "El Peterete," and Vizcarra, his cousin. According to Mateo Díaz, on the video these men said many things about Los Zetas. During the interrogation La Barbie forced the gunmen to say that Osiel was receiving protection from Santiago Vasconcelos, then head of SIEDO, with full intention to discredit him.

After interrogators, who are not seen on the video (one is alleged to be the actual Barbie) questioning the men, the video ends when a handgun enters the frame and shoots the man believed to be Vizcarra in the head.

Later on, the rest are also executed and their bodies were disposed to never be found. Also, in this video the captured Zetas say that the attorney Vasconcelos was involved with the Zetas. "this was not true, as this was only a strategy of La Barbie' to force the PGR to go after us," said Mateo Díaz.

La Barbie took control of illegal operations in the airports of Cancun and Toluca, through a partnership with federal agents José Antonio Rosales and Edgar Octavio Ramos Cervantes "El Chuta".

To gain their cooperation, La Barbie gave Rosales a BMW, $65,000 (dollars) and he also gave him the nickname "El buen hombre" or "The good man." He gave him that name because since 2008, he had provided access to move a cargo of cocaine in the airport of Cancun, according to the federal investigation and statements from the protected witness known only as "Jennifer."

"Rosales, apart from being in charge of operations at the Cancun airport, made sure that when we arrived, we were not inspected in the terminal," said "Jennifer" before the PGR.

La Barbie allegedly worked for several years as a cartel lieutenant before rising to a leadership position in an enforcement squad called Los Negros. Following the death of cartel boss Arturo Beltrán Leyva (BLO) in late 2009, Valdez was engaged in a bloody and protracted turf war for control of the BLO cartel, employing techniques such as videotaped tortures, decapitations of his adversaries, that resulted in over 150 deaths.

On August 30, 2010, La Barbie was arrested by the Mexican Federal Police near Mexico City on charges related to large scale drug trafficking with the Beltrán-Leyva Organization Cartel. He was facing charges in both Mexico and the United States.

Mexican authorities had been closing in La Barbie's allies in recent weeks. On July 10, 2010 marines raided a house in Acapulco and captured Gamaliel Aguirre Tavira, suspected regional chief of the Valdez faction.

Narcotics agents hunting "La Barbie" got a lucky break in a raid on August 9, in the elegant Bosques de las Lomas district of Mexico City, which turned up evidence leading them to the accused drug lord's mountain safe house in the region of Salazar.

A group of federal police officers encircled the rustic mountain house in Salazar, about 20 miles west of Mexico

City, where Valdez-Villarreal had holed up. Mobile phone service in the area was spotty, and the La Barbie along with six sicarios couldn't summon backup to fight their way out, he said. They were detained around 6:30 p.m. without a shot being fired.

The special unit that conducted the operation was highly qualified to operate in various types of terrain, as well as in the use of all kinds of weapons, thanks to extensive training both in Mexico and the U.S.

Another version of the capture of La Barbie is said that it did not happened in a spectacular police operation in Mexico as had been reported by Mexican authorities, but merely by chance.

Federal police on regular patrol on a highway in the state of Mexico were passed by three vehicles, a Chevrolet Cruze, a Chevrolet Malibu and a Ford Focus, traveling at a high rate of speed.

The police conducted a traffic stop and ordered the occupants through a police vehicle's loudspeaker to step out of their vehicles.

The first to get out was a white skinned man. The police officers did not know who he was at first, but later on they found out they had detained Édgar Valdez Villarreal, La Barbie.

The Federal Police requested his personal information and he told them that he was Édgar Valdez Villarreal, who is known by "La Barbie." He immediately told the police officers that he was a drug trafficker.

Based on the fact that his capture by Mexican federal police was completely without violence or casualties, there was a rumor that he made a deal to turn himself in and receive favorable treatment in exchange for providing intelligence information on his rival cartels.

In the U.S., when the police want to display a suspect for journalists and in front of a wider public, they commonly do a "perp walk," showing off the alleged perpetrator to the media as they walk him to the vehicle that is going to be transporting him to and from jail.

But not in Mexico, they truly know how to present their prized catch. Masked police paraded a handcuffed Edgar Valdez Villarreal before reporters during a press conference. Wearing a green polo shirt and jeans, the man nicknamed "La Barbie," named for his fair complexion, grinned openly as officials discussed his capture near Mexico City.

Mexico displayed one of its most violent drug lords that gave President Felipe Calderon hopes of a breakthrough in its campaign against the powerful drug cartels. Federal Police Commissioner Facundo Rosas said the capture of Valdez-Villarreal came after a yearlong hunt that involved as many as 1,200 law enforcement officers.

La Barbie had been labeled as one of the most powerful and bloodthirsty criminals in Mexico.

La Barbie showed no signs of ill treatment and had the chance to answer reporters' questions, but declined to do so without saying a word. Later on, Valdez would be allowed to be questioned by a reporter and the video was posted on the internet within minutes.

La Barbie was characterized by his enormous coldness. Maybe that's why he was seen laughing in front of the cameras and microphones when he was introduced by the federal authorities ... as if defying them.

"Are you really La Barbie?" a foreign correspondent asked in English.

"Is it true that you betrayed Arturo Beltrán Leyva?"

"Do you deny that? Do you deny it? " A journalist asked in Spanish.

Valdez Villarreal kept smiling.

"Do you want to be extradited to the United States or do not want to return there?" The foreign correspondent asked again in English.

La Barbie kept smiling.

"What are you laughing at?" A reporter asked.

The detainee turned to see her, but he did not answer.

Police confiscated two rifles, a grenade-launcher, nine packets of cocaine, computer and communications equipment and three vehicles.

Calderon confirmed the arrest in a short message on Twitter: "Federal police trapped 'La Barbie,' one of the most wanted criminals in Mexico and abroad." Government officials seemed to be seeking to regain support by offering abundant details about Valdez-Villarreal's background and capture.

"This is an extraordinary achievement," Felipe Gonzalez, head of the Senate commission on public security told Foro TV, "there was an air around this guy that he was untouchable, that he would never be caught."

The arrest was certain gave Calderon a boost in his campaign to confront drug traffickers, even at great human cost. The government was hoping that the arrest would give Felipe Calderon some positive attention since when he decided to declared war on drug cartels after taking office in late 2006. The death toll, which just in 2010 soared past 28,000 people, has upset many Mexicans on Calderon's tough drug enforcement policies. But the government maintains that the effort has produced some results, Valdez-Villarreal is the third top drug lord to be arrested or killed in nine months.

Less than a month ago before the arrest of La barbie, law enforcement agents in Guadalajara killed Ignacio "Nacho" Coronel, a drug lord in the Sinaloa Cartel who was considered the "king of crystal," or methamphetamine.

Certainly, this arrest dealt "a high impact blow to organized crime," said Alejandro Poire, a spokesman for Calderon's national security team. Poire said Valdez-Villarreal had ties to gangs operating in the United States, Central and South America.

It is unusual for an American to climb so high in the ranks of Mexican organized crime, but not unprecedented.

Texas-born Juan Garcia Abrego was captured in Mexico in the 1990s and sent to Houston, where he was convicted of drug-trafficking crimes as the head of the Gulf Cartel. He is now serving multiple life sentences.

"The operation that resulted in the arrest of la Barbie closes a chapter in drug trafficking in Mexico," said senior federal police official Facundo Rosas. Six other men, including another Texan, were arrested with Valdez, and police found weapons, late model trucks, cocaine and cellphones at a safe house guarded by cartel gunmen.

The capture of Edgar "La Barbie" Valdez, a Texas-born 37-year-old, may do little to halt the flow of drugs into the United States or staunch bloodshed in Mexico's most violent areas, many of them along the U.S. border.

But it's too early to celebrate, while La Barbie was in custody, cartel bosses were eager to replace him. His arrest has clearly left an opening for others to become the new kingpins.

The El Universal newspaper reported that Valdez-Villarreal has "one foot on a plane bound for the United States" to stand trial.

A federal indictment unsealed in Atlanta in June charged that Valdez-Villarreal, a U.S. citizen, imported tons of cocaine by tractor-trailer across the border at Laredo, Texas, and into the eastern United States between 2004 and 2006.

Valdez's Houston lawyer Kent Schaffer said his client has plenty of enemies in Mexico.

"I think he'd be much safer in an American facility," Schaffer said.

The Mexican magazine Proceso published a letter sent to journalist Anabel Hernández García by La Barbie while being held in the Altiplano maximum security prison. The journalist who had been threatened with death reported that a few days before the end of the Calderón administration in 2012, La Barbie sent her a letter from prison where he accused Calderon directly of protecting the Sinaloa Cartel.

La Barbie said that despite the rumors, he refused to participate in the witness protection program.

The letter says that "the war the Calderon administration started was to protect the Sinaloa Cartel and to take out the adversaries of El Chapo Guzmán."

In the letter, La Barbie announces that his arrest was due to "political persecution by Felipe Calderón," the former president of Mexico, because "the undersigned (La Barbie) refused to be part of the agreement that Calderón wanted have with the groups of organized crime." The letter went on to say that Calderón "personally held several meetings with criminal groups."

According to La Barbie, there were other meetings that included, on one side several high-ranking Mexican officials and military, and on the other side were leaders of Mexican cartels such as La Familia Michoacana, the Zetas, Beltrán Leyva Organization and El Chapo Guzmán.

"Calderón wanted agreements with all the cartels; the Zetas, Gulf cartel, Juarez Cartel, with Mayo Zambada, El Chapo and myself," Barbie said in the letter.

"I could have done what they wanted me to do, these public officials that I mentioned, are also part of the criminal structure of this country," La barbie said in the letter.

La Barbie said that the federal police had orders to kill him. He said that in fact when he was captured, he was moved from one location to another and when he was alone, the federal police officer that was escorting him told him to run so he could justify shooting him and say that he had resisted arrest.

On November 2010, the Mexican government agreed to extradite La Barbie to the US and was subsequently sentenced by the US government to 50 years in prison.

Today, Mexican drug cartels are splintered and spread out on a wider range as a result of infighting and a power vacuum left by arrested or killed drug lords.

Tony Tormenta

In 2006, when Mexican President Felipe Calderon took office, he had promised to fight back against the drug cartels. His first two years in office showed strong successes against the cartels, with large drug seizures and the capture of several organizations' leaders. One of the government's main target was the Gulf cartel, based in Matamoros, Tamaulipas, was one of the most powerful cartels in Mexico.

By late 2008, a two-year-long campaign by the Calderon government against the Gulf Cartel or Cartel del Golfo (CDG), it had left it crippled. The cartel's enforcement arm, Los Zetas, splintered off in spring 2008 and took control of much of what used to be Gulf territory. However, the government's success was a double-edged sword. The decline of the Gulf cartel left a large power vacuum, encouraging other organizations and factions within those organizations, particularly Los Zetas to fight to increase their influence.

Both groups engaged in widespread violence across several border cities of Tamaulipas state, turning several border towns into "ghost towns."

Borderland Beat continued to cover these conflicts and we continued getting execution videos, graphic pictures and news from anonymous sources. We started to get some information about events happening in the gulf. It was becoming very difficult to confirm a lot of the information as it was raw and not found in main stream media. One specific event that was unfolding in 2010 was related to "Tony Tormenta."

Antonio Ezequiel Cárdenas Guillén, commonly known as Tony Tormenta (Tony the Storm) was a Mexican cartel boss who was one of the leaders of the Gulf Cartel (Cartel del Golfo or CDG), a drug trafficking organization based in

Tamaulipas. He led the CDG along with Jorge Eduardo Costilla Sánchez.

Tony Tormenta was considered one of the most-wanted men by the Mexican government. Born in

Matamoros, Tamaulipas, Tony Tormenta had been a car washer at a local police station with his brother Osiel Cárdenas Guillén, the former leader of the CDG. By the late 1980s, Tony entered the drug trade, and later became the top cartel boss of Matamoros. Tony controlled all the drug trafficking shipments in Matamoros. Tony along with his brother Osiel formed the Zeta squad made up of military forces that had deserted the army.

Tony Tormenta was so powerful and bloodthirsty like his brother Osiel. He had the freedom of engaging in shootings and killings in and out of the state of Tamaulipas without being stopped by authorities. He was often seen in public places like Reynosa, Ciudad Victoria, Matamoros and other cities in Tamaulipas surrounded by state and municipal police officers, whose commanders remain loyal to his criminal organization, one of the oldest in the country that was formed over 50 years ago.

The US had an interest to capture Tony Tormenta primarily over an incident that happened back in 1998.

FBI agents acting on a tip raided Cardenas's home in Houston, according to the recently released records. They saw Cardenas leave the house, but, citing lack of resources, chose to execute a search warrant on the residence rather than follow him. The search yielded "cash, numerous vehicles, cocaine, marijuana, firearms and one 1996 Sea Doo Bombardier with expired Florida registration …"

According to the reports in the FBI files, investigators didn't know much about Cardenas or the organization with which he was working. Agents circulated information about him and his vehicle, but by then he had escaped. In a memo filed in December 1999, an FBI agent said Harris County prosecutors had indicted Cardenas on drug charges and wrote that the bureau would be closing its file.

Only a month earlier, the Cardenas name began to ring out along the Texas-Mexico border when Osiel and his sicarios forced a pair of U.S. agents off the road in Matamoros and threatened to kill them. The agents talked their way out and rescued the informant who had been showing them around the Gulf Cartel stronghold.

Osiel Cardenas was eventually arrested in Mexico in 2004 and extradited to the U.S. in 2007. In 2010, he was sentenced to 25 years in prison.

On September 17, 2010 I posted information that Tony Tormenta had been captured, this was confided to me by very reliable sources and confirmed by the main stream media in Mexico and the US.

"Ezequiel Cardenas Guillen, "Tony Tormenta", the main leader of the Gulf Cartel was arrested this afternoon amid heavy fighting that left many dead in Matamoros. This information was confirmed by reliable military sources in addition to the main stream media. La Reforma, and El Norte used unnamed law enforcement sources and witnesses to report on the outcome of the military operation.

In the firefight it is believed that "El Tyson" or "M3"

was also detained, he is the third in command of the Gulf Cartel who are currently waging a war against "Los Zetas" for control of the northeastern Mexican Border States. Lost Zetas are the former armed wing of the Gulf cartel.

The military operation was carried out by elements of the Mexican Naval Marines against sicarios of the Gulf cartel resulted in at least three separate shootouts in different parts of Matamoros this afternoon, as reported by the Daily Texan Brownsville Herald.

The newspaper reported that the first shootout took place in the district of Expo Fiesta Sur, where a commando of the Gulf Cartel attempted to raid a Zeta safe house.

This forced the marines to advance on the operation to arrest Tony Tormenta that had been scheduled for later in the afternoon.

A convoy of the marines came upon a heavily armed commando of the Gulf Cartel adjacent to the facilities of the Matamoros Municipal Police station.

According to witnesses this confrontation that would be reinforced by naval helicopters resulted in many casualties of sicarios and possibly military personnel.

The confrontation then turned in to a pursuit through the streets of the border town culminating in the exclusive neighborhood of Las Arboladas near the region of Playa Lauro Villar, very near to one of the international bridges in the area.

The confrontation in Las Arboladas was particularly violent, with a high number of casualties that included soldiers and sicarios of the Gulf Cartel.

"Eyewitnesses reported seeing dozens of bodies of both armed gunmen and Mexican soldiers," reported the Brownsville Herald.

The "M3" had arrived to reinforce and to strengthen the criminal organization with an undetermined number of armed sicarios named "Los Escorpiones". The marines also required and received reinforcement from additional military forces.

It was in Las Arbolada that Cardenas Guillen was arrested and was immediately transported to the facilities of the PGR in Mexico City.

M3 is said to have also been arrested but his current whereabouts are unknown.

"El Universal" had hinted that Tony Tormenta had been killed in a shootout, but that version is not panning out.

"Military forces engaged armed gunmen, killing one of them, in a confrontation after the military attempted to stop them. They have ruled that the dead victim, still unidentified, could be that of Tony Tormenta, brother of Osiel Cardenas Guillen," according to the news from El Universal."

A few days later I received information from anonymous sources that Tony Tormenta had been set free after he paid thousands of dollars in cash to high level members of the military. I was not able to confirm this, but I was getting this information from numerous sources. One thing was clear, Tony had eluded capture, despite the heavy presence of military and helicopters during the confrontation. I had to post a retraction on September 22, 2010.

"Last Friday I reported on the capture of Tony Tormenta based on official reports and anonymous information from reputable sources. I quickly jumped on the story wanting to bring our readers up to date information on a very important event. Well, it turns out, the information was incorrect. Tony Tormenta was at the scene of the conflict but managed to escape.

The information about the conflict remains sketchy at best. There are reports of sicarios that were allegedly captured at the scene but we have not seen anyone presented to the media (a press conference where arrested cartel bosses or sicarios are shown/presented to the media) or more detailed information coming out.

We apologize for the misinformation and any inconvenience this might have caused. We strive to bring you up to date and reliable information to the best of our ability. But I must agree that sometimes it is hard to do because the information coming out from Mexico at times is very hard to confirm."

I knew that the US played a huge role in providing intelligence information to Mexican authorities on Tony

Tormenta and I knew they were right behind his tail. I am not certain if the US had knowledge on exactly what happed when the military allegedly captured Tony and managed to escape. But not long after, Tony would be killed in a shootout with the military as reported by me on November 6, 2010.

Blog del Narco published two pictures, one of Tony Tormenta and the other of "El Tyson" or "M3" that showed them killed in the battle.

"A total of 660 members of the Navy of Mexico participated in the operation yesterday which resulted in the death of Ezequiel Cárdenas Guillén, alias "Tony Tormenta", a high-ranking kingpin of the Gulf Drug Cartel.

The Secretary of the Navy said in a statement that a total of 660 military marines were deployed in the operation,

and of these, 150 were in the first circle of action, supported by three helicopters and 17 armored vehicles.

Cartel gunmen used moving vehicles and sharpshooters positioned on rooftops to try to rescue Cardenas during the operation by Mexican Marines in the northeastern border city of Matamoros.

In the gunfight four gunmen were killed that allegedly belonged to the inner circle of protection to "Tony Tormenta." Also killed were three marines while four others were wounded, said the Navy said in a statement.

A source explained that Mexican authorities had been following the trail of "Tony Tormenta" for the last six months and on Friday they received his location in a downtown neighborhood of Matamoros, a city bordering the United States, but when the first group of marines arrived, they were met with automatic gunfire and grenades.

This conflict unleashed a fierce gun battle which lasted for more than two hours, until the capo "Tony Tormenta", a native of Matamoros and at the age 48, finally fell.

Friday's daylong gunfights throughout Matamoros between cartel hit men and Mexican soldiers and marines plunged the city into chaos and panic, witnesses said, as armed men plowed through streets on the backs of pickup trucks.

Residents rushed in helter-skelter traffic to get home; many remained trapped in their offices. Cellphone service went down, further stoking fears as bursts of high-caliber weaponry could be heard for hours.

The international bridges into Texas were closed for a time.

Most of the fighting barely made a ripple in national news here in Mexico because local reporters in Tamaulipas, out of fear or corruption, have been trained to ignore cartel activities. Only when a journalist for a Matamoros newspaper was killed in the gun battle did the news begin to trickle out."

The next day authorities found three banners (narcomantas) hanging on a bridge in the city of Nuevo Laredo by "UNIDAD ZTAS" or United Zetas.

The following content was written in each of the narcobanners:

"Once again it shows the fate of the traitors in the Gulf cartel (Las Golfas), who do not fit in anywhere, not even in hell, there they will find Los Zetas who went before us, to kill again. For all the traitors of the Gulf cartel bring out the school of the informant of Osiel, let's see where they go hide because they have nowhere to go, they are walking around in circles around the same frying pan ...

Sincerely Unidad ZTAS"

On November 10, 2010 Borderland Beat contributor RiseMakaveli posted some facts about Tony Tormenta in an article titled "Tony Tormenta : Story Behind His Death" As I had stated earlier, RiseMakaveli, or as he is known "Maka," was known to be a boot on the ground and had personal knowledge of Los Zetas and CDG. This is what he wrote:

"As you all know, Antonio Ezequiel Cardenas Guillen or Tony Tormenta, as many knew him by, was killed last Friday in a shootout against the Mexican military forces.

Over the last few months, a lot information has been flying around about the events leading to his ultimate death, I will try to share them with you guys here in this article. None of the information is being cemented as "facts", it's just simple information that's been received by several sources. I feel like I have to put this HUGE disclaimer before releasing this information due to the fact that in a recent article I wrote, I nearly got crucified for having an open mind. Anyways.

What I ask of you today before reading this is to keep an open mind, and remember, this was all information which was passed on to me by people who are somehow affiliated to the war. I do not paint this to be facts, I will only share with you my thoughts on this.

Ok, so here's the deal. Couple of months back I'm sure some of you guys heard about the huge shootout that broke out in Matamoros, where a picture flooded the internet claiming that it was possibly Tony. I quickly laughed at the idea and told you guys to ignore it. Well, what a lot of people don't know, even though he was not killed, he was actually captured. Now this is part of the story which I do back up and can almost swear by it.

Story is that Tony was involved in a shootout with Zetas and the military got involved, a huge chase and shootout eventually broke out. Story behind that, Tony was cornered and captured. Upon being captured there was an agreement with the "Commandante", Tony was to pay 3,000,000 dollars to be released.

Apparently, he was treated like shit and even smacked around by the marines, well none the less, story continue with Metro riding down to Matamoros to pay the ransom for Tormenta. It all sounded too Hollywood to be honest, I didn't really take much to it. It became a lot more noticeable after I was told this by more than three people, all stating the same story but adding a piece to it.

Apparently, word got out and the "Commandante" was charged and sent to Mexico D.F. for releasing Tormenta. I don't know if some of you guys remember reading it all over the place, newspapers printing "Confirmed by Credible Military Sources", meaning high ranking officers. Well, anyways, this guys will not just jump up on a speculation and print shit out like that, if that was published, it was published because it had a strong character backing up the claim. This was the first piece of the puzzle, story I heard weeks ago.

Well just yesterday I was told what appears to be the second part of the story. Apparently, after Tormenta was released, the man kidnapped 10 soldiers and called up the "Commandante" at the time (this is before he was prosecuted) and asked for a ransom. The Officer of course, did not give two cents, so Tormenta killed the soldiers and threw their bodies on the side of the road (I can't remember what road). Anyways, story continues. Apparently after the bodies were found, the Marines retaliated, they found out who his wife and family are and kidnap his wife and son.

Tony Tormenta is somehow contacted and alerted that they have his family, he completely disregards it by stating it is his sister and nephew, I guess to see if they would let them go or something, I don't know. Apparently, the Marines dismembered his son and badly beat up his wife, let her go only to go back and describe how they had murdered her son to Tormenta. At that moment, it clicked, weeks ago I had heard from a friend that Cardena's Sister had been kidnapped, that's when it kind of started to itch, you know. That certain situation where everything just seems to click.

'It's just a story and really, it's the first time I've heard it and nothing absolutely to back it up,' is what I thought. As the day went on I start reading my favorite website, borderlandbeat.com and I start reading my comrades coverage, when all of a sudden I remember, the story, and I think, "why not, let's just do a little research"

This is where it gets interesting.

Supposed Marines Kidnap Two In Tamaulipas.

Karla Elizabeth Cárdenas states a convoy of Marines broke into her house on Sunday and took her mother and brother.

That is an extract from this post in Spanish

I will not translate all of it, but it basically describes how Karla Elizabeth states that an alleged convoy of Marines broke into her house on Sunday. This article was published on the 29th of September, stating it happened on Sunday 26th. So far it fits, right, first shootout where tony was supposedly captured and released happened on the 18th of September I believe. So far it fits with the story right, but I mean, it could be anybody, just because her last name is Cardenas, does not mean she's related, right?

Until I found this other article.

'Tormenta's Body is returned to Wife and Daughter.'

Authorities informed that the body of Tormenta was turned over to his wife Hermelinda Rivera and daughter Carla Elizabeth Cárdenas Rivera.

Ok, well the name is spelled with a C instead of with a K like on the first link, but I'm pretty sure it's the same person.

I published this information to give you guys an opportunity to realize that the stuff that we see on TV is not all true, and that a lot of times information we think to be true, is really just a part of a bigger puzzle. It's not as simple as we all would like to think. Some of you guys where asking how Tormenta was still hanging around in Matamoros after how hot it was, would this be a good excuse? His son murdered and wife beat and probably raped.

I was told his son was kidnapped, and in the last article they mention wife and daughter, nothing about a son, although I know that Tormenta had a son. It all just seems to click, and I wanted to give you guys an opportunity to digest it.

My educated Guess....

-Maka"

La Pelirroja

Another interesting thing that happened toward the end of 2010 was a particular event when heavily armed sicarios rescued a female prisoner that was being transported from a prison to a hospital in the city of Monterrey. Ovemex posted a short piece on the story on December 29, 2010 in Borderland Beat that was titled "Kidnapper rescued from custody in Monterrey."

"Four guards were taking Gabriela Elizabeth Muñiz Tamez, known as "La Pelirroja" (The Redhead), from Topo Chico prison to Monterrey's University Hospital when they were intercepted on the road by some of the associates of the prisoner, who managed to free her without firing a single shot.

Muñiz Tamez, 31, and three accomplices had been arrested in July 2009 on charges of kidnapping and extorting shopkeepers in the southern part of Nuevo Leon state, whose capital is Monterrey.

The guards escorting her were held for questioning about the Monday night escape."

Then something happened, we got some messages about the incident.

On December 30, 2010 there was an email from anonymous source:

"Pinches pendejos, ustedes creen que rescatamos a la puta de la pelorojo? Cabrones vale de mierda, ahorita se la ensenamos para que dejen de reportar de cosas que no saben nada."

Translation: "You fucking assholes, do you think we rescued the little bitch the red head? Fucking worth a shit, in a while we will show her to you so you stop reporting about shit you don't know anything about."

We started getting information that "Pelirroja" was not rescued, but in fact had been abducted and would soon be tortured and executed. The body had not appeared anywhere and we were not able to confirm this claim. At least not until some time later when her body appeared hanging from a bridge.

The incident was reported in Borderland Beat by contributor "Smurf" on December 31, 2010 in an article titled "La Pelirroja Found Dead in Monterrey."

"A woman was found hanging this morning from an overpass that intersects with Gonzalitos avenue in colonia Mitras Norte. The body had a message that was written across her back and torso that read;

'Yair.'

She was identified as Gabriela Elizabeth Muñiz Tamez, nicknamed "La Pelirroja", who who had been abducted this past Monday by members of organized crime.

Initial reports had cast doubt this was 'La Pelirroja,' because the although the victim had a similar hairstyle, it was dyed blond.

However, after further investigation it has been confirmed that it was indeed the body of Gabriela Elizabeth.

On a side note, this story and events in Monterrey were being closely monitored by the staff here at Borderland Beat. Before this story broke, we were directed to comments and tweets from several well known narco blogs that indicated that there may be a split within "The Federation" of the Sinaloa, La Familia, and Gulf Cartels.

The specific letter mentioned that the people of this 'New Federation' did not agree with the policies of the old guard, whom they saw no difference between them and depravity of Los Zetas. The chilling effect was the fact that the comments seemed to predict that "La Pelirroja's" body would soon be found.

'La liberación de la Peliroja, la muy pendeja se creyó que la íbamos a liberar… (je) solo fue un ajuste de cuentas, pronto daremos la ubicación de su cuerpesito… (Solo le hicimos justicia al pueblo.'

Translation: 'The rescue of La Pelirroja, the stupid bitch actually thought we were going to set her free (ha) it was only a settling of accounts, you will soon find her little body (we were only bringing justice to the city)."

Sometimes the blogs would get the behind the scenes of events before they came up in public and eventually reported on main stream media. The hangings were another method of how organized crime sometimes executed people. It was a way to send a message in a very public way and spread terror in the communities. They would hang them from a bridge at night, and at day break, while heavy traffic filled the roads, the body was in display for everyone to see.

Bus Passengers Forced to Fight to Death

In 2011 I posted a very controversial post in BB that got a lot of attention. The Zetas were known of hijacking buses and executing the passengers. Police found hundreds of narco graves of people that had been executed and buried. Most of these deaths were people that had been abducted from buses.

This was happening in the so called "Highway of death,"

Highway 101 is in the state of Taumalipas. This highway travels from Cuidad Victoroa and Brownville, Texas, on the side of Mexico. The story started to make it's rounds on main stream media in both Mexico and the US.

Houston Chronicle's Dane Schiller described the chilling account of a member of the Zetas cartel who asked only to be referred by the apparent pseudonym "Juan" that combines Scarface, Saw and, unexpectedly, Gladiator.

This was published by the Houston Chronicle and Atlantic Wire

"Houston Chronicle's Dane Schiller points to Borderland Beat, a blog run by a former law enforcement officer in the Southwest United States, who published a more detailed account of the death battles in April. We talked to the blog's founder, Alejandro Marentes, who explained that a writer sent him the story which had been published on a blog in Spanish, and Marentes translated and republished it on Borderland Beat. After the post got some pickup on the internet, Marentes added this editor's note: "To this point we have not been able to confirm its validity, we publish it for information purposes and for you to formulate your own conclusions."

It's easy to see why some readers might find the story unbelievable.

"It's hard to get any type of confirmation from anything that's happening there," Marentes told The Atlantic Wire.

"We have some people in Mexico that have good contacts, but many times we have a hard time."

Marentes continued by describing a lack of journalists on the ground in the San Fernando area. Most journalists don't dare enter without police or military protection, but even then, many are threatened if not attacked. We contacted Dane Schiller, the Chronicle reporter, to find out more about how he found his source, he asked not to be interviewed. "I don't want to make the story about me and my efforts," Schiller said in an email.

However, the original report is written like fiction. Victims from bus kidnappings–many of whom are illegal immigrants passing through Mexico to the United States–have reportedly been rescued from gang members, but there's no indication that the post's author was one of them. (Besides the fact, that they survived the tell the tale, if it's true.)

We asked Marentes, who's been covering the cartel wars for years, his gut feeling on whether the reports of gladiatorlike battles could be true based on precedent in the Mexican drug wars. "The story's realistic," Marentes said. "All you've gotta do is look at what's going on with the brutality of the violence over there–I can see that happening very easily over there."

This is the story that was posted on April 18, 2011 titled "A Nightmare of the Massacre in San Fernando."

I put this disclaimer in the top of the story:

"***Editor Note:*** *Ok, for the readers who might be confused, this story is making its rounds around the internet. To this point we have not been able to confirm its validity, we publish it for information purposes and for you to formulate your own conclusions. I felt regardless if fiction or not, it has some value in light of all the atrocities we have seen in the last couple of months in the region.*"

This is the story:

"The bus of the ADO line was making its regular stop in the city of San Fernando, Tamaulipas on a destination to Reynosa. They arrived at the terminal unloading two people and boarding four, making a total of 15 passengers onboard the bus. The bus departed the terminal to follow the route; it was 8:30 in the evening of March 25, 2011. They quickly left the small village as they did not want to become victims of the criminals who operate in the city, however, that night would be the last they would fear, because they were already sitting in wait for them.

The streets in San Fernando empty at about 6 pm. The small town is a ghost town after dark, no one leaves their homes, and everyone protects themselves for fear of Los Zetas. Only the luxurious SUVs are seen travelling through the empty streets, no one wants to run into them.

The bus was just leaving the village when the driver saw a truck in the distance blocking the middle of the road and hooded men wielding AR-15s, at that moment he knew that all was over. The armed men ordered him to stop the bus; the driver was forced to stop. The men approached the bus pointing their long guns and shouting; "Open the door motherfucker, move it son of a bitch if you don't want me to shoot you in the fucking head." Shaking, the driver opened the door of the bus, and instantly the armed men boarded the bus, one of them struck the driver on the face with his rifle while the others went inside shouting at the passengers, "You all just got fucked mother fuckers." The passengers on board were terrified, the women were crying while the children were hugging their parents, and also crying. Everyone was in panic, they thought it was just a robbery, but it was not.

They ordered the driver to continue driving, taking him a several feet along the road until they reached a ditch, where they ordered him to get off the road there and go another 6 miles on a dirt road. This seemed to be the longest ride in the lives of the passengers. They reached a very wide open field in the middle of nowhere, a plot of some kind, it was very dark. At the location were approximately 20 luxury trucks, and 3 other buses from several different bus lines, some had visible bullet holes with flat tires and broken glass.

One of the armed men told the driver to stop the bus, then they separated the men and women and then they ordered all the men to get out of the bus. They forced about 8 men out of the bus who ranged from 15 to 50 years old. They lined them up next to the bus where several armed men approached them and they started to separate them again by removing the old or weak. They removed two old men and two others that looked sick. They tied their hands and feet, and took them to another group of men that also seem to be old and weak. The ones who remained back were told to remove their shirt and to wait there.

Some of the armed men went to one of the SUV's parked nearby and shouted "call the comandante." It is when the presence of this man was made known, who was dressed in all black commando style, wearing a bulletproof vest and pouches all over his clothes; they all called him "Comandante 40." The man approached the men without shirts that had been forced off the bus and told them in a loud military tone type of voice, "Let's see mother fuckers, who wants to live, tell me now," but no one dared to answer. Everyone was looking toward the ground; they were unable to look up frozen in fear.

A young man around 15 years of age urinated on his pants from the sheer fear while visibly trembling all over his body as if he was cold and a flood of tears ran down his cheeks. El 40 drew his handgun from his holster and without hesitation shot him in the forehead. The boy collapsed to the floor dead in an instant, while the other men also started to tremble in fear. "Who else is a fag here?" asked the El 40. No one dared to answer. "I will ask one last time mother fuckers, who wants to live?" This time he was yelling loud and clear, and suddenly all the men immediately raised their hands. "Good, we will give you a test to see how badass you all are, the ones who succeed will live, the ones who do not will get fuck." With that he ordered several of his men who were sitting inside another SUV to bring the sledgehammers and the men gave a sledgehammer to each man.

"Ok listen up assholes, the trick is this, we are going to pair you in twos, and you are going to fuck up each other with the sledgehammers, and the one who survives will join us in our work and you get to live, while the one who does not survive, well you get fucked," he said sarcastically making his men laugh out loud. The passengers were stunned by the instructions from a narco who resembled more a nazi than anything else, they could not believe this was happening to them. Everyone grabbed their sledgehammer and took their position with their pair. They stared at each other with a look of pure fear. "Ok, fuck each other up," ordered El 40.

One of the passengers came begging to him, saying, "Please sir, I do not want to do this, I will give all my money and my home if you let us go." El 40 looked at him straight in the eye, took his sledgehammer and said, "Okay fucking faggot, go." As soon as the man turned to leave El 40 hit the man in the head with the sledgehammer using brutal force. The man fell to the ground bathed in blood and El 40 just went crazy hitting the man on the head with the hammer until his head was smashed in to pieces. "This is what you all have to do son of a bitches, use your balls, anyone who does not want to do this tell me now and I will fuck you up," all men then began to fight against each other.

The bus driver was still inside the bus with the man who had intercepted them along with all the women and children. Several armed men got on the bus and forced all the women out of the bus who they felt were the prettiest. They were yelling at them; "Move whore," all crying and screaming as were the children. One of the armed men gave an ordered, "OK bitches, give me your young ones" and while weeping, the mothers took their children on their arms, which ranged from newborn to 8 years old. The children clung to their mothers while the sicarios snatched one at a time. They got everyone out of the bus and took them away, while some of the sicarios beat the women who remained on the bus.

The young women that had been forced off the bus were taken to a beat-up hut where other young women were waiting there. Inside it was dark and filthy, and one could hear screams and moans. There the sicarios tore the clothes off the women and began to rape them. Inside the hut were approximately 30 women being raped, others were torn up on the floor.

The children were taken to another location where there were tanks filled with acid, and there they threw them inside the tanks. Little by little the cries of terror began to fade in to the night. The only sound left was from the sicarios who were laughing out loud, one of them shouted to the others; "the soup is almost ready."

The armed man ordered the driver to turn on the bus, and directed him to drive the bus to the location where they had placed all the men who were old and weak, they were lying on the ground in a single line tied to their feet and hands. "Drive your bus over them," ordered the sicario to the driver. The driver looked at him stunned, he could not believe what he just ordered him to do. "I said drive your bus over them or I will place you along with them so you can get fucked too idiot," the sicario yelled at the driver who felt he had no other choice but to comply. While driving his bus, he could feel as if he was going over bumps, except the only difference was the screams from the people underneath. The women who remained inside the bus were crying uncontrollable after witnessing such horrible act. The sicarios inside the bus were just laughing. Not until he was finished driving over all of the bodies did, they order him to stop.

It was then that the sicario shot the driver in the head and began to shoot the women who were inside the bus. The sicarios got out of the bus and set it on fire.

Comandante 40 gathered all the Zetas and said, "that is all for fun and game for tonight cabrones. Bring me all the winners" and they brought all the men who had killed their partner with the sledgehammer and El 40 said," Welcome to the Special Forces of the Zeta, the other military."

This story was sent to me by someone anonymously and we were never able to confirm the validity of the story. It may not be true, or it may be. With enough horrific carnage we had been seen coming out of Tamaulipas, this did not seem far fetch.

Don Alejo, a True Hero

77 year old Don Alejo Garza Tamez had chosen his ranch named "San Jose Ranch" in the state of Tamaulipas very carefully. His ranch was about 9 miles from Ciudad Victoria. The ranch was next to lake Padilla along the Corona river. Ranching was his life and grew up in the region hunting and fishing, his favorite pass time. Don Alejo grew up in Allende, Nuevo Leon, about 50 miles from Monterrey, on the foothills of the Sierra Madre.

His ranch was in a perfect location, to do a lot of hunting and fishing in the beautiful back country. Don Alejo Garza Tamez was one of the founding members of the "Dr Maria Manuel Silva "Hunting, Shooting, and Fishing Club, located in Allende, Neuvo Leon. Growing up hunting Don Alejo had developed good marksmanship with firearms.

This area was also the heart of Zeta country. Zetas were notorious for evicting land owners by force and converting some of these secluded ranches as safe house, training camps and killing fields.

On November of 2013 a group of armed men suspected of being the feared Zetas came to visit Don Alejo. They wanted his ranch. They had a demand, give us your land, surrender it peacefully or they would take it by forced. The Zetas always got their way, and saw no reason why they could not this time. Do Alejo stood his ground, told them to take a hike and he would not be surrendering his land. They gave him 24 hours. They would come back and have him signed off the property to them or be killed. Don Alejo told them he would be waiting for them and they left after delivering their message.

What happened when the criminal came back after 24 hours? Ovemex explained it on a post on Borderland Beat:

"When Mexican Marines arrived at the San Jose Ranch, the scene was bleak. The austere main house was practically destroyed by grenades and heavy gunfire.

Outside of the home, they found four bodies. Cautiously, and with their weapons drawn, the troops continued inspecting the exterior and found two more gunmen, wounded and unconscious, but alive.

Inside the house only one body was found, riddled with bullets and with two weapons by its side. The body was identified as Don Alejo Garza Tamez, the owner of the ranch and a highly respected businessman in Nuevo Leon.

Upon further inspection of the interior, marines found weapons and ammunition at every window and door. This allowed them to reconstruct how, just hours prior, the battle had played out.

Marines searched for more bodies inside the house, but none were to be found. It seemed hard to believe that one person, armed only with hunting rifles, had caused so many casualties on the attackers.

Dozens of spent shells and the smell of gunpowder gave proof of the tenacity of the man who fought to the end in defense, of not only his ranch, but his dignity.

In the end, it was deduced the man had created his own defense strategy to fight alone, placing weapons at every door and window.

The story began that fateful Saturday morning, when a group of armed gunmen went to deliver an ultimatum to Don Alejo Garza Tamez: He had 24 hours to turn over his property or suffer the consequences.

Using the diplomacy, he had acquired over nearly eight decades of life, Don Alejo flatly announced that not only would he not be surrendering his property, but that he'd be waiting for them.

When the men had left, Don Alejo gathered his workers and ordered them to take the day off, he wanted to be alone.

He dedicated the rest of the day taking stock of his weapons and ammunition and creating a military fortress style defense strategy for his home.

The night of Saturday the thirteenth was long and restless, much like his past hunting adventures; Don Alejo woke up early. Shortly after 4 a.m. the motors of various trucks could be heard entering the property from a distance.

Marines who investigated the scene could only imagine how it was that morning. Armed men, their impunity secured, confident they'd soon be owners of yet another property. Nobody, or almost no one, could hold out against a group of heavily armed gunmen.

Only Don Alejo.

The trucks entered the ranch and took up positions surrounding the house. The gunmen got out of their trucks, fired shots in the air, and announced they came to take possession of the ranch. They were expecting the terrified occupants to run out, begging for mercy with their hands in the air.

Things didn't go as expected. Don Alejo welcomed them with bullets. The entire army of gunmen returned fire. Don Alejo seemed to multiply, he seemed to be everywhere. The minutes would have seemed endless to those who had seen him as easy prey. Various gunmen were killed on sight. The others, in rage and frustration, intensified the attack by swapping out their assault rifles for grenades.

When everything finally fell silent, the air was left heavy with gunpowder. The holes left in the walls and the windows attested to the violence of the attack. When they went in search of what they had assumed was a large contingent, they were surprised to find only one man, Don Alejo.

The surviving gunmen did not take over the ranch. Thinking the military would arrive at any moment, they decided to run. They left behind what they thought were six dead bodies, but two of their gunmen had survived.

Shortly after, the Marines arrived and methodically reconstructed the events. A lone rancher, a man who worked a lifetime to be able to enjoy the fruits of his labor such as his ranch, had defended it to his death.

In the last hunt of his life, Don Alejo surprised the group of assassins who wanted to impose the same law on his ranch that they had on the State, the law of the jungle.

The marines who were present will never forget the scene. A 77 year old man, who before death, took out four gunmen, fighting the same as any of the best trained soldiers, with dignity, courage, and honor.

Tracking El Lazca

As I had previously reported, Heriberto Lazcano Lazcano "El Lazca", top leader of Los Zetas was presumed to have been killed by the Mexican military on October 7, 2012. However, between 2008 through his capture in 212 there was a huge manhunt for El Lazca in the Gulf region of Mexico.

El Lazca was for the Federal Government the most difficult target to locate, one among a list of the most wanted criminals. On his long trips, he usually travelled alone, with a backpack on his shoulder and traveling by bus, avoiding airplanes. It was said that when Lazcano traveled alone, the only person that accompanied him was usually the most trusted Zeta named Pedro Vázquez Torres, aka El Perro. When arriving at a city under his control, he would use a public cellular to give notice of his arrival and immediately afterwards, El Perro would gather about 30 vehicles full of sicarios to provide El Lazca with escort all day and night.

He would use the cover among the masses of people to hide, but he also took the time to protect the air waves of his network of electronic communications, to prevent his immediate circle of people around him or other third parties from notifying authorities in real time of his location. In the investigation of Casino Royale, for example, it was learned that they acquired electronic devices to create static signal that blocked his communication for miles around.

Trust was huge thing for El Lazca and he did not tolerate any betrayal from any of his people under any circumstances.

"El Lazca has cost us more work in trying to locate his whereabout, it has been very difficult, even more than with El Chapo Guzmán," had said the head of SIEDO, Cuitláhuac Salinas, in an interview in 2008.

When Erick Cárdenas Guízar, "El Orejón", was arrested in Veracruz he told the PGR that El Lazca was very safe from rival cartels or authorities when he made public appearances. "El Lazca was always escorted by 30 suburban type vehicles and in each vehicle were about 5 heavily armed sicarios," El Orejón had said.

The first documented case of an attempt to capture El Lazca was on December 5, 2008, when Lazcano was at the ranch El Atorón in the Potosí municipality of Santa María del Río.

At 6:00 in the morning the Federal Police raided the ranch and captured two of the caretakers, as well as El Lazca's private secretary Víctor Hugo López Valdez, El Chiricuas, along with his assistant Pablo Gómez Solano, El Paguas, who had an arsenal of high caliber weapons in the courtyard of the main house.

El Paguas testified that he was brought in to the ranch because Lazcano wanted to see him. He was there with the people of El 40, Miguel Treviño, but he did not know why Lazcano wanted to see him. Lazcano had been at the ranch when El Paguas arrived.

According to police information, Lazcano managed to flee through the thick brush surrounding the ranch and survived three days without eating in the remote areas of the country, a practice that he would later employ in his paramilitary training centers in several states of the Northeast of the country.

After surviving, El Lazca ordered the execution of all those who had heard about their meeting at the ranch. He thought that someone that had knowledge of his movements had snitched the information to authorities. He disbanded his inner circle of trusted people, because he could no longer trust them. Authorities continued to track his locations. El Lazca was tracked in Monclova through intelligence from Mexico and the US and was suspected of living in the city of San Luis Potosí. He was tracked travelling constantly in the border of the state of Coahuila, many times to meet with Miguel Treviño Morales "El Z-40" where they would sometimes go hunting for deer.

But El Lazca remained elusive, always ahead of the authorities.

In Coahuila, more than in any other part of the Mexican region, Lazcano was being tracked since 2010. In the state of Coahuila, he would end up avoiding capture three other times. The first one occurred on February 16, 2010, when the Mexican Marines surrounded a house in Brisas del Valle, a residential neighborhood in the northern sector of the city of Monclova where El Lazca presumably owned a house. The military was unable to pinpoint the exact location of the house from the coordinates nor were they able to detain anyone.

The second time was on May 18, 2011, in a shootout between the military/federal police against armed men in the northern part of Monclova. Several buildings were damaged from gunfire during the confrontation with heavy weaponry. Casualties were reported but El Lazca managed to escape unharmed while his sicarios were engaging the military in the confrontation. El Perro was instrumental in numerous cases when he led his gunmen under his control to engage the military to facilitate the escape of El Lazca.

The last known time that El Lazca managed to escape from the authorities was at a party at a recreational center on Highway 57 north of the Monclova. El Lazca was there celebrating a woman's birthday, presumably his girlfriend. The popular band "Banda Jerez" was detained by the PGR along with waiters and other staff who had provided service at the party.

In August of 2011, two Cubans appeared before the cameras of Univision claiming that they had detained Lazcano on the high seas and that they handed him over to the DEA, an agency that did not want to pay them the 5 million dollars in reward. That was actually reported in some of the media in Mexico and in the US. that proved to be false.

Some police sources reported that El Lazca had some kind of unknown disease that had left him out of circulation for some time and that prevented him from moving more easily in order to control the daily tasks of his organization. There were also many reports in the media (US and Mexico) of rumors on the streets in the Gulf region that El Lazca was dead. Not until 2012 when he was actually killed after the military was finally able to track him down, catching him by surprise and killing him in a shootout. El Perro was not at his side, something that surprised a lot of people and started a rumor that perhaps El Perro was not the most trusted Zeta he had after all.

According to Mexican federal sources they had El Lazca's fingerprints on record because he had been detained in 1998 and was imprisoned in the Santa Adelaida Prison in Matamoros, where he was eventually released a short time after.

The body of El Lazca was stolen from the funeral home, never to be seen again. It was said that the body was stolen by orders from Miguel Treviño Morales, El 40, a good personal friend of El Lazca, although they had their differences toward the end of the Lazca's and El 40's regime of Los Zetas.

The name of El Perro, the one who had initially showed unwavering loyalty to El Lazca by protecting him and defending him with his own life, would come to my attention once again while reporting on the Borderland Beat blog.

Pedro

It was in the early part of October 2011 that I received an email on the address borderlandbeat@gmail.com.

"From: pedro
To: buggs2001@gmail.com
Date: Sat, Oct 1, 2011 at 2:08 PM
Subject: DEA fugitive
Buggs I have addresses cell numbers home numbers autos bus address hangout for above fugitive wanted by us marshal office if interested to speak with me email address is (removed). Home number (removed) ill be able to explain once we speak via phone. Pedro"

He went by the name of Pedro and he told me he had a lot of information about organized crime, including Mexican classified documents, pictures and telephone transcripts. I have a Google phone number that I ended up providing it to Pedro so we can talk on the telephone. Pedro wasted no time calling me. He told me he could send me a lot of information that might be useful to me in reporting about organized crime in Mexico. He told me that he needed to keep his identity secret for security reasons related to him, family and associates. Pedro told me I could use this information to share it on the Borderland Beat blog. I got tons of documents and photographs. Most were marked as classified from Mexican Naval Intelligence. Most of the documents I could not make any sense, I was not certain what they were, but I did notice some that peeked my interest. One was about someone that went by the name of "El Perro."

Date: Sat, 24 Jul 2010 13:13:00 -0500
Subject: El Perro Pedrito

To: NCAR23 <email removed>

El Perro, jefe de 20 escoltas del Lazca, primer cinturon de seguridad.

Pendientes."

"El Perro, boss of the 20 body guards of Lazca, first line of security."

The email included pictures, some were of military personnel that had deserted from the military and were marked as classified by Mexican Naval Intelligence. Looking at the documents it was concluded that El Perro was no other than Pedro Vasques Torres. It appeared to be a Mexican soldier that had apparently deserted the Mexican army and joined the forces of the Zetas under Heriberto Lazcano.

There was a certificate from the Secretaria de la Defensa Nacional (SEMAR) with Pedro Vazques Torrez' name and picture of him. The certificate stated: "For having completed the basic training of special forces, forming part of the 4/0 squadron, during the period from March 22 to May 1999 in the special forces training institute."

I was a little confused and just because of his name was Pedro I asked him if El Perro was him. Sometime people that have a name of Pedro are nicknamed Perro. Pedro respond that he was not the "Perro" in the documents.

"Date: Sun, Oct 9, 2011 at 3:01 AM

Subject: Re: VERY IMPORTANT INFO El Perro Pedrito

No buggs no its not me lol I happen to have many Mexican classified documents, lets talk via phone ill explain further just give me window time when to call.

pedro"

I was not certain if these documents were legitimate and was not sure what to do with them. It appeared that the

338

Mexican government knew more about Heriberto Lazcano Lazcano alias "Lazca" personal security detail and might be closing in on him. I spoke to Pedro and he confirmed my suspicion. He told me that the Mexican government, with the help of the US, was closing in on Lazca. His next correspondence led me believe that Mexico was very close to capturing Lazca.

Date: Fri, Oct 14, 2011 at 11:55 PM
Subject: LAZCA NEXTEL 10-15-11
"this is the ID number of the nextel radio of Lazca and his 25first belt of bodyguards. He is located right now in the mexican stateof San Luis Potosí. 52 * 135051 * 1 Lazca personal nextel id
52 * 135051 * 2 This is El Perro personal nextel id
" " 3
" " 4
" " 5
26
This kind of people changes very often his communication radios, so we have to move fast."

This appeared to be a conversation from agencies that had information on the whereabouts of El Lazca and were trying to expedite an operation. It included cellular frequencies and their location. Pedro kept updating me with the location of El Lazca and his personal escort El Perro, as he was moving from location to location. It was apparent that Mexican official with the help of the US were moving closer to him.

It was clear that someone close to the inner circle of El Lazca was filtering the ID numbers of the Nextel cellulars used by El Lazca and his inner circle. The Mexican and US authorities were tracking the locations of El Lazca using this information. There was no evidence that actual locations of El Lazca were leaked directly, but with this information related to the Nextel communication equipment, authorities (especially us intelligence) could very easily identified locations of the equipment.

This information gave me great concern, primarily because it dealt with a covert operation that dealt with extremely sensitive information related to the top capo of the Zeta Cartel. I was not sure if the information was legitimate, but I was curious to find out.

I had contacts in Monterrey and Matamoros who had sources in the Naval Intelligence, and I sent them the documents of Vasques Torres to confirm their validity. They got back to say that their sources who were in official governmental capacity could not confirm or deny their validity, but they were concern on how the documents were obtained. They indicated that some of the documents appeared to be official and classified documents, but would not be able to confirm their authenticity because they were classified documents. Both contacts became concerned for their safety and did not want to push matters further. This information was very important because it dealt with Heriberto Lazcano, the top boss of the Los Zetas.

I never acted on any of this information related to El Lazca that was obtained by Pedro in October of 2011 or posted anything about this on Borderland Beat. Frankly, I did not feel comfortable with this information, as it was based on an active operation. I did not want to be responsibility for what might happen if this information became public at this point in time. Later on, I discovered that Pedro was also providing this same information to other blogs and journalists. Much later, after I had moved on to other topics, this became apparent in an article published on Borderland

Beat by "Armchair" on February 26, 2013 titled "The Man who Turned on Lazca"

☐

By ACI - Borderland Beat

"In 2010 Heriberto Lazcano Lazcano was in San Luis Potosi, Mexico. His movements were being traced through a corrupted Nextel number. The only reason this is known is because of a man named Pedro Vazquez Torres ' el perro' or the dog. El Perro was part of Heriberto Lazcano Lazcano inner ring of security. It was said he rarely ever left Lazcano's side but on the day of his death El Perro was absent. While the accounts of what occurred that day differ widely, the following is what is believed to be true.

On October 7, 2012, Heriberto Lazcano Lazcano was attending a soccer game in the town of Progreso, Coahuila. As Lazca was watching the game he had little clue as to what was taking place around him. A contingent of Mexican Marines moved in on Lazca's location, surrounding the entire area.

The Mexican Government claimed someone had called in a tip about gunmen at a baseball game. This has been hard for many to believe. Some have speculated that perhaps he was set up by Z-40, another powerful leader of the group. While I cannot say for certain, I have confirmed what I believe is closest representation of the truth. Lazca was turned in by his inner ring of security, possibly with the green light from Los Zetas.

Heriberto Lazcano Lazcano was known to use several layers of security at any given moment. He was supposed to be alerted anytime anyone hostel was in the area. If the Military was moving anywhere in the state Lazcano should have gotten a phone call. The fact that Lazca was unaware of the military presence in the area suggests every layer of his security failed. He fell in a hail of bullets not far from the baseball field, shot by elements of the Mexican Miltary. He was killed with his lone body guard Mario Alberto Rodriguez Rodriguez.

There is very little information regarding Pedro Vazquez Torres. Most of the information presented in this story comes from a confidential

*file created by Secretaría de la Defensa Nacional or SEDENA. He
became part of Mexico's notorious Grupo Aeromóvil de Fuerzas
Especiales (GAFE) in 1999. The GAFE is a branch of
Mexico's Special Armed Forces. Los Zetas were originally founded by a
group of deserters who originated from GAFE. A Proceso article
mentioned his name incorrectly but did state he also worked on
communications for the group.*

What is known:

- *SEDENA had a file on el Perro since at least 2010*
- *In June of 2010 DEA had a working Nextel number for
Lazca*
- *In June 2010 Lazca was in San Louis Potosi, the DEA was
aware of this*
- *Lazca was killed in October 7, 2012 under suspicious
circumstances*
- *El Perro was not with Lazca when he died"*

It is worth noting that at the time the military had decided
to go to a place where El Lazca was located, El Perro was not
there.

El Perro was a military man considered one of the
quietest, reserved and most hardened of Los Zetas, that is
why he was recruited by Heriberto Lazcano Lazcano as part
of his personal escort. It was even said that El Perro always
watched the back of his boss.

El Perro became a man one hundred percent reliable,
because thanks to his military preparation, skills and "balls,"
he managed to get El Lazca out of truble many times.

An example was when in the beginning of 2008, a group
of soldiers in Tamaulipas ran into the convoy of El Lazca, so
El Perro confronted them without fear, proving that he could
cover the back of the boss in any situation.

Of course, the misfortune for El Lazca came in 2012
when he arrived to that soccer game in the state of Coahuila

without the company of El Perro and it was there that a contingent of the Marines caught up with him and shot him several times taking his life.

What caught everyone's attention was that the network of lookouts (halcones) failed him that day. For some reason, El Perro was not with him, which was are, as he was always with Lazca. This created suspicion that perhaps El Perro was the one filtering the information to the DEA, giving them his locations or providing the cellular telephone number of El Lazca, so they could trace his location. At the moment of the attempted capture of El Lazca, El Perro was given heads up to make himself invisible.

To date no one knows anything about what happened to El Perro after the death of El Lazca or his whereabouts. Some think that after the death of El Lazca he retired from the narco business or perhaps he is spending the 5 million dollars he got as a reward for providing the locations of his boss, an assumption that was never confirmed.

Later on, there would be more leaks of information on Lazca and Los Zetas, some was new information but most was the same information I already had. I had the impression Pedro did not have direct knowledge of what was happening with Lazca, but did have the classified information of operations and intelligence.

Pedro had also mentioned that he had information on Genaro Garcia Luna. He served as Secretary of Public Security in the federal cabinet of Mexican President Felipe Calderon. I wonder if it was the same information I already had of Garcia Luna or information that the government had not released. This is what Pedro sent me:

"Date: Fri, Oct 14, 2011 at 11:33 PM
Subject: GMAIL REF GENARA LUNA 10-15-11
USA dont have them because mexican goverment are very careful about that, usa know that mexico is a super

343

corrupt country, and President Calderon wants to keep in secret many internal things, but I have many documents, many my friend.

For example I have the file of Genaro Garcia Luna, the chief of the Mexican federal police, he is a fucking corrupt monster, this file is sealed and signed by the director of mexican CIA , CISEN"

I asked Pedro if he could provide me these documents for my review. He declined to do so, saying it was not safe for him or myself.

"DateFri, Oct 14, 2011 at 11:38 PM Subject: PGR CORRUPT 10-15-11

Another deal between you and me, never ask for a reward in PGR , means in Mexico, if you do that, I can tell you advance both of us will be dead soon, PGR is the most corrupt agency in Mexico, all of them works for drug lords, so be very very very careful. document from Mexican army intelligence, this document it's about he is a former special forces Mexican soldier, he is the personal bodyguard and gunman . I'm gonna send to you this email so you can see I can get top level confidential documents for my job, someday I will tell you how I can do that."

Mexico: Operation Salim

Although I did not act on the information I had obtained of Heriberto Lazcano Lazcano, Pedro continued to send me Mexican classified information. While getting information from Pedro this email peaked my interest.

"Date: Tue, Oct 11, 2011 at 7:18 PM
Subject: ADD'L DOCUMENTS #5
I sent 5 mails with different attachments. Please confirm receipt of same.
 Thank you
3 attachments — Download all attachments
HE STATES HE CAN GET DOCUMENTS AT HIGHEST LEVEL IN GOVT.wps
LAZCA, his name is Pedro, his aka El Perro The Dog.wps ROOM 12S AHMED SALIM EMAIL 4 OF 4 09.1.10.wps."

The documents of Ashmed Salim were ringing a bell. There were documents about a search warrant executed by the Mexican Navy/Marines and was titled "Operativo Salim." It had this notice:

"THIS TOP SECRET DOCUMENT IS ABOUT WHAT THE MEXICAN INTELLIGENCE NAVY FOUND INSIDE THE 12S ROOM, AND ABOUT AHMED FILE, LISTEN, NOBODY, NOBODY IN US GOVERMENT KNOWS ABOUT
THIS INF."

The classified documents stamped with "Confidential Naval Ministry" revealed information about the operation that included items found in the search warrant and identification of a suspect named Arturo Hernandez that appears to be the alleged Ahmed. Ahmed had ties to Al Shabaab with strong links to Al Qaeda and it was suspected that it was meant to be a plot to bomb the US embassy in Mexico City (DF). There was an article in 2010 about the search warrant in the publication Milenio.

Mexican media stories published in June 2010 mention that a bombing plot was foiled when Mexican Marines raided a residence in the Colonia Roma in Mexico City. Some published stories even mention that the raid by the Marines was based on information forwarded by the DEA to Mexican Naval intelligence that an Islamic terrorist named Salim or Saleem that had entered Mexico through the southern Guatemalan border.

According to the Milenio Weekly story, the DEA obtained the name of Salim during an investigation of Los Zetas weapons and explosives procurement networks.

The Milenio Weekly story and another one published in the MVS news agency describe how shortly after the raid in the Colonia Roma, the Naval Ministry issued a news release that it had arrested four suspects and seized 20 kilos of high explosives. Within several hours Mexico's Attorney General's Office (PGR), the federal organized crime task force (Siedo) and the Interior Ministry (Gobernacion, Segob) all issued a different version of the incident.

The official government version was that the four suspects were artists and the paraffin and pure glycerin were materials used in plastic artwork.

So here it was, possibly classified proof from the Mexican government themselves that perhaps the original story of an Islamic terrorist named Ahmed had indeed plotted bombings of the US embassy in Mexico City. I spoke with Borderland Beat contributors Gerardo and Ovemex about the information we had obtained and we agreed to do further research with the full intent to go public on Borderland Beat. With their contribution, we went public, posting the information on Borderland Beat on October 13, 2011 under the title "Mexico: Operativo Salim" We also shared all the classified documents and suspect information we had obtained from Pedro related to Operation Salim.

"A couple of days ago we received information from an anonymous person telling us about information that this person wanted to share with us. Without giving it any thought we agreed to get the information. We received some documents that appear to be official and did not appear to have been published anywhere else. One particular document that caught our attention was a Naval Ministry intelligence report stamped June 10, 2010.

In addition to the above described document, we also received a copy of an official voter ID with the name of Arturo Hernandez Hernandez that appears to be the alleged Ahmed described in the document.

First and foremost, we want to make it clear that we have no way to confirm the validity of these documents, but we present it for the content it represents, readers must form their own conclusion as to the validity of such document.

However, other documents stamped Confidential Naval Ministry that were received from the anonymous source were shown to a member of Mexico's security establishment who confirmed their validity.

As the Iranian backed plot to assassinate Saudi Arabia's Ambassador to the U.S. unfolds in the media we are faced with the question of what is the true level of risk that a terrorist attack by Islamic militants or contracted agents aimed at the United States would come from across our southern border.

According to the intelligence analysts at Stratfor, "The threat is much smaller than it might initially seem — in part because of close U.S.-Mexican cooperation and primarily because the threat of U.S. retaliation on any organization that participates in terrorist activities is extremely high."

However, the documents leaked by the anonymous source to Borderland Beat, together with ongoing criminal cases in the U.S. federal court system, paint a more complicated picture of what the risk may actually be.

In particular, the risk posed by the Somali based militant Islamic terrorist organization "Al Shabaab" (The Youth in Arabic) is highlighted.

Al Shabaab has strong links to Al Qaeda, and its latest suicide bombing in the Somali capital of Mogadishu resulted in the deaths of more than eighty people.

In July 2010, Al Shabab was responsible for the deaths of over eighty people in bombings at bars in the Kampala, Uganda as fans watched a World Cup match.

The documents posted are from a confidential report written by Mexican Naval intelligence and includes an analysis of evidence gathered in a raid between the days of June 7 and June 10, 2010 on a hotel room in Mexico City occupied by an individual identified as AHMED, allegedly a member of Al Shabaab.

Included in the report is a photograph of a Mexican voter's picture ID card identifying AHMED as Arturo Hernandez Hernandez, a Mexican citizen.

The translation of confidential Naval Ministry intelligence report stamped June 10, 2010 included the following:

Mexico D.F. June 10, 2010

Report of evidence in custody

In room #12S (128?)the following was found:

1-A cylinder shaped cardboard container holding 22.7 kilograms of high explosives and sealed with a paraffin compound. Two copper cables sheathed in plastic were inserted into the paraffin.

2-An orange colored thick fabric suitcase containing 2 Motorola c115 cellphones without batteries, 4 Motorola multichannel radios with chargers, 1 Radioshack frequency counter, latex gloves, 1 dark green notebook with Arabic and Spanish writing, 1 small prayer rug with Islamic motifs, 1 bar of body soap, 1 toothbrush, 1 sealed box of toothpaste, 1 liter of nitric acid, 5 liters of pure glycerin, 1 plastic bag containing 5 fuses (3 slow burn and 3 rapid burn), 1 kilogram of gunpowder containing aluminum, 10 meters of yellow/red colored detonation cord, 5 (illegible)__opines, 150 grams of mercury.

In the interior of the toothpaste box was a 2cm x 2cm piece of photographic paper imprinted with the logo of the armed Islamic extremist Islamic group AL SHABAB, attached with brown adhesive tape.

North American authorities informed us that intelligence agents attached to the Israeli embassy have been following the trail of the alleged terrorist of Somali nationality named AHMED, who allegedly belongs to the Islamic extremist organization mentioned above, and attached is a photograph and counterfeit credential. We also have information that the explosives were to be used in an attempt against the United States embassy in Mexico and also other objectives such as consulates.

Intelligence sources from the Israeli embassy in our country maintain that AHMED has been staying since Monday June 7th at the Hotel Puebla, located on the street of the same name Puebla and 1 and ½ blocks from the home of Merida #_2, as video from surveillance cameras within the hotel show.

Also included were photo ID of Ahmed/Arturo Hernandez Hernandez.

The documents posed many questions:

Are they valid? There is a possibility that they are although it is impossible to independently confirm their validity.

If this operation against Al Shabab did occur, who undertook it?

How did AHMED obtain the bomb making materials and a voter ID card? How well was his mission financed and planned?

What is the fate of AHMED?

The anonymous source's assertion that the U.S. Government had no knowledge of the operation seems improbable.

Mexico's security establishment is believed to be heavily infiltrated by U.S. intelligence agencies since the days of the Cold War. Although corrupt officials in government and law enforcement have often thwarted U.S. antidrug efforts, Mexico has always been a stalwart supporter of the U.S. against external enemies, from Communists to Islamic extremists.

Other aspects of Al Shabaab's presence in Mexico are highlighted in cases against U.S. citizens of Somali and non-Somali heritage, and resident Somali citizens in the U.S. federal court system.

To say that Mexico's drug cartels would police themselves and defer the hefty profits of smuggling these people into the U.S. should no longer be accepted as conventional wisdom. Even if they unwittingly smuggle potential terrorists into the U.S, the damage has already been done.

If these drug cartels have proven anything by their actions in Mexico, it is that financial gain will be obtained at almost any cost."

Needless to say, this post on Borderland Beat blog went viral in Mexico and started to make the rounds in main stream media in Mexico. Televisa had Millennuim news anchor

Joaquin Lopez Doriga report on television that the US government had actually leaked the information of "Operation Salim" and that it was confirmed to be false by the Mexican authorities. He failed to tell the truth, that in fact it had been exposed by Borderland Beat and the classified documents had been received by an anonymous person named Pedro as documented in the Borderland Beat Blog.

It also became a news topic in Notocias MVS with radio talk host Caremn Aristegui. A review of the topics that they covered were:

"1. On June 9, 2010, the Semar reported an operation in Merida 12, Colonia Roma. This is what authorities reported of the operation; "Over 20 kilograms of high explosive were recovered. The material is used in demolition and when applied directly to structures the velocity of the detonation along with the density of the blast is sufficient to demolish through steel." That night Televisa showed footage of the place and showed the materials described by the Navy.

2. On June 10, 2010 SIEDO corrects the Navy and reports: The official opinion is that chemicals found at the scene which included glycerin, nitric acid and paraffin ... do not correspond to any type of explosive material and in regards to the people detained, they were not under arrest, they were merely people presented.

3. In June 2010, Dolia Estévez, of MVS Mexican News confirms, with her sources in Washington that the original version of the Navy regarding the explosives was true and that the DEA was involved in the matter.

4. The 26, 30 and 31 of August 2010, Semar answers three requests for information by the media pursuant to the Transparency of Law. On the 26th they said that since the SIEDO determined that the substances that were seized were not found to be any type of explosive material, Semar

determines that their position is confirmation of the matter in question." On the 30th, they responded that "in their examination of the material using molecular detection equipment which has an effectively accuracy of 99.00% in determining explosives, the material examined in this specific case tested positive for explosives." Then on August 31 they said: "... Semar did not conduct an examination of the material since they do not possess any scientific means of examining chemicals or provide any conclusions to that end." They stress that SIEDO did determine that the material was in fact "paraffin, glycerin and nitric acid."

5. On June 17 the official website of the Navy removed the statement of the investigation 141/2010 where they revealed the discovery of the explosives.

6. On June 22, 2010 the Navy again gives access to their unchanged statement providing a description of explosive materials.

7. On August 31, 2010, PGR (The Attorney General Office) officially refuses to provide information on the matter claiming that it is of confidential information ... and may remain as such until a period of 12 years."

8. On October 13, 2011 the blog Borderland Beat that reports on the Mexican Cartel Drug War, that appear to be retired members of intelligence services in the United States, released a confidential document that is said to be originated by Semar entitled "Operation Salim." Dolia Estevez advises that it appears to be an official looking document, as well as the official seals and security marks on the paper.

The document provides details of the operation, its purpose and what they found. It states: "what was found inside the cardboard box that was taped with a brown sticker bearing the logo of the armed Islamic extremist group Al-Shabab." It also reports that: "U.S. officials informed us that intelligence officers assigned to the Embassy of Israel in

Mexico are the ones who have been tracking the alleged terrorist named Amhed who is said to be a Somali national. He allegedly belongs to the international armed Islamic extremist organization and whose photograph and a copy of his Mexican credentials has been falsified. There is also information that the explosives would be used to attack targets against the United States Embassy in Mexico, and other U.S. targets such as consulates."

9. On October 18, 2011. Semar rejects "categorically the authenticity of the documents." It claims that the documents are not legitimate however they say that they are not in any position to discuss the matter of the content."

10. On October 18 and 19 the journalist Joaquin Lopez Doriga of Millennium and Televisa says that the confidential document "Operation Salim" was leaked by the Government of the United States.

11. On June 20, 2010, journalist Jorge Alejandro Medellin published in the "Millennium Weekly" a report: "DEA and the Mexican Marines: how to hunt a terrorist" whose content coincides with the document attributed to the Navy. The story has never been officially rejected by the Mexican government. In the last paragraph it reads: "The man that the Mexican Marines and the DEA were looking for in the house of Mérida 12 had left the place three weeks before. In his room the fourth Special Forces of the Navy of Mexico found a copy of the Koran."

12. On September 9, 2011 Guillermo Valdés of CISEN said: "In Mexico some groups still operate that believe in violence as an instrument of change. We can never rule out the risk of the real possibility of the presence of Islamic terrorism in our country."

13. On October 20, 2011. MVS reporter Dolia Estevez said that according to her sources in the United States, their position is that it is very possible that the

confidential report "Operation Salim" may in fact not be a false document."

In one of the segments in discussions about Borderlan Beat with Caremn Aristegui and Washington DC reporter Dolia Estevez, they started to discuss who and what is Borderland Beat. I found it very interesting at best.

Caremn Aristegui: "Who is Borderland Beat, do you have any information who is behind this website, place where they receive documents like this and others."

Dolia Estévez: "They also show videos, yes."

Caremn Aristegui: "This report, well is not like "El Blog del Narco," let's say, it's another thing."

Dolia Estévez: "No, the founder, for starters all of them are anonymous, in other words they use nicknames, they don't give their information, and the founder is a person who worked 25 or 30 years in an agency of the Attorney General in the southern state of Texas, he calls himself buggs and for 8 years he was a member of the infantry of the Marines here in the US, of the navy, then one can easily say he is well prepared in the service of intelligence, I think he is retired has a pension. In 2009 they created this blog with the interest of reporting information, specially information related to the border because they operate primarily in the border of the US and Mexico, in Texas mainly, and they have an email address borderlandbeat@gmail.com where they request from their audience, public, society, from Mexico as well as the US to send them information, and they get a lot of information. For example they instantly posted the video that we also transmitted, Carmen, about the Matazetas. That is the kind of thing they do. and sometimes the post comments that in my opinion they are comments that are measured, they are not sensationalized, or exaggerated. They post a lot of photographs that are graphic, they have posted for example videos of people that are being decapitated that someone is filming in Mexico and they say that their interest is to keep the public informed of this threat that represents the narco trafficking in Mexico.

They don't appear to have any liberal affiliation or a position against the government of Mexico. Furthermore, they are not worried about the insecurity."

Caremn Aristegui: "Did you talk to them Dolia?"

Dolia Estévez: "No, I have not spoken to them, there is a telephone number that has an area code of 505 which I think is a telephone number in Texas."

Caremn Aristegui: "You have not spoken to them but they explain everything of what you are saying?"

Dolia Estévez: "Yes, the explanation is on the website, you open the website and you can see the first entry of October 19 "Mexico: Operativo Salim Update"

A lot of comments in the story posted on Borderland Beat discounted the events as false. Many stated that most Mexican cartel would never collude with Islamic terrorist. There were just too many coincidental facts in events that gave the plot more credibility.

Texcoco October 13, 2011: Honestly I don't believe this crap. "These are not organizations looking to make easy money or engage in other violent political proclamations specially in other countries. The Mexican cartels already face their own problems, as the battles between them and against the Government. Any foray into international terrorism would be bad for business".

"What they want (the cartels) is to make their business in secret, not to do someone else's job," I might be wrong but this is what I think

Anonymous October 14, 2011: Pure and total B.S...You stupid daydreamers in the cia propaganda department are idiots! Plant your stupid propaganda cheap excuse for attacking Iran in the ny times...the readers there are idiots like you and cant think for themselves...DONT YOU STINKING GET IT FAGGOTS? WERE SICK OF YOUR WARS, TRAMPLING ON THE RIGHTS OF AMERICAN CITIZENS, ATTACKING MY RIGHT TO DEFEND MYSELF FROM YOU HIDEOUS MONSTERS, YOUR NOTHING BUT BLOOD SUCKING TICKS. WE DONT WANT YOUR ENDLESS WARS IN EVERY COUNTRY THAT HAS OIL OR OPIUM OR COCAINE. I CALL ON BB READERS TO DENOUNCE THIS FAIRYTALE, TO THE STAFF AT BB THANK YOU FOR BEING HONEST AND POSTING INFO BUT THESE CHUPACABRAS ARE USING YOU TO SPREAD TRASH.

Anonymous October 14, 2011: Don't confuse probability with possibility. Islamoterrorists don't care about consequences. They just want to strike at the U.S. The narcoterrorists have been known to strike at innocent people in an effort to propagandize. As long as the threat coming across our southern border is possible, it remains a threat. Let's hope that the possible does not become probable then inevitable. Contingency plans should not be solely reactionary. We need real border security.

clazy8October 14, 2011: "REgarding the fake voter ID: of COURSE it's fake. The guy's real name is supposed to be Ahmed.

As for the unlikelihood that drug cartels would jeopardize business by participating in an Iranian scheme to blow up the Saudi ambassador in Washington DC: absolutely, it's pretty far-fetched. But no one has mentioned something else that is just as far-fetched: that this Iranian guy goes looking for a bomber in Mexico and happens to get a US informant. That's pretty bad luck! What are the odds?

Commenters who see the CIA hiding behind every bush would say these problems prove the whole story is an invention, but there is another interpretation that is, if anything, more likely. Suppose the bomber contacted by this Iranian went to his cartel bosses. Would they settle for a pittance in cash for helping the Iranian? Or would they offer him to the US in exchange for only God knows what, but I'm sure you can come up with a few possibilities."

Pedro got defensive when he read all the comments claiming the information had to be false.

Pedro also got bothered that I had sent some documents to contacts in Mexico to verify authenticity with sources in the Mexican Naval Intelligence.

"date: Fri, Oct 14, 2011 at 8:24 PM
Subject: 10-14-11 MEXICOS SECURITY
However, other documents stamped Confidential Naval Ministry that were received from the anonymous source were shown to a member of Mexico's security establishment who confirmed their validity.
WERE THE DOCUMENTS CONFIRMED AUTHENTIC AS PER ABOVE SENTENCE AM I UNDERSTANDING IT CORRECTLY."
"date: Fri, Oct 14, 2011 at 8:43 PM Subject: MOSSAD FINGERPRINTS 10-14-11
Anonymous said...
And surprise he had an alshaabah sticker on his toothpaste box. How convenient! The only problem with that is the toothpaste box had mossad fingerprints all over it! BUGGS REMEMBER WHAT I TOLD YOU REFERENCE MOSSAD RETIRED AGENTS AS WAS RELATED TO ME BY FBI."
"date: Fri, Oct 14, 2011 at 11:31 PM Subject: G MAIL OF NAVY INTEL GUS 10-15-11
s2informacion@semar.gob.mx   gusfergom@gmail.com
gustavo fernandez 011 52 55 562 46500

BUGGS   HERE IS   OFFICIAL FROM THE NAVY INTELLIGENCE WHO CLAIMED AND STATED TO ME VIA

TELEPHONE   CONVERSATION   THAT THE AHMED AND NAVY 3 COPIES ARE NOT THEIRS OR THAT THEY

ARE REAL   KINDA LEFT IN THE AIR   GAVE ME A SNOW JOB ANSWER   HMMM WHO TO BELIEVE

YOUR SOURCE   OR THE ABOVE   I HAVE MANY EMAILS OF COMMUNICATIONS WITH HIM AND OTHERS."

Pedro went on to tell me "here is the only photo that the us government has about the terrorist Ahmed, and guess who was the one that was given to them? me , of course, now ask your friends if I am a liar"

He provided excerpts of an email from June 2010 relating with the subject "African."

Date: Wed, 2 Jun 2010 12:42:16 -0500 Subject: Africano, el TIO y su gente To: NCAR23

"This person supposedly had been abducted by the omega, but they made a mistake and they abducted the wrong person, he was born in Somalia, his name is Ahmed, he has more than a year in the df and is related to people who move currency of the Islamic extremist organization Al Shabaab, the ife credential is false. They are trying to locate him, he supposedly bought a lot of nitric acid apparently, that he speaks Spanish and English and that he moves fast all over the country. That he resides in cheap hotels and rents cheap apartments, and that he is fanatic of Islam and that he is getting ready to plan something."

Pedro would eventually get in contact with Dolia Estevez, the Washignton DC correspondent with MVS, information that he got from posts on Borderland Beat. Days later "Pedro" would also provide Dolia with further documents related to the Ahmed person.

Back Home

This "Project Salim" that was posted on Borderland Beat was all over Mexico, making national news, being talked about on social media and I am sure it got someone's attention here in the U.S. from the federal government. I was an active law enforcement officer with the City of Albuquerque, and I started to think that perhaps I should let my chain of command know what was going on.

I had confided much of the information to my work associate and close friend, Officer Neal, whom I trusted, although he did not have much interest in the matter. I decided to let my immediate supervisor know that an unknown source had been sending me Mexican classified information about cartel activity. He had no clue how to handle my disclosure. He was merely an online supervisor who spent all his time in the field dealing with police matters at the lowest level possible.

What do you do when your subordinate discloses to you that he is involved with sensitive classified information from Mexico that is all over the Mexican news? And even though I was anonymous, people in the right places could very easily figure it out? Media and federal government entities were starting to figure out the true identity of Buggs. All this sounded like some spy novel, and way beyond my sergeant's level of expertise and rank. Another question popped up, is it even legal? And the third:

"Fuck dude, do I even know you?" was all he could say about the matter when I told him about it.

He did feel that perhaps I should talk to the police department's head of Homeland Security. I spoke with Albuquerque Police Commander Banes, who also was not quite sure how to handle my disclosure. He requested that I give him the documents so that he could turn them over to the local federal task force in charge of such matters. APD had detectives assigned to a federal task force that included officers from other counties around the state, state police officers, FBI and even the CIA. I turned over a disk to him with all the information I had in my possession. A few days later I got a call from the FBI agent in charge in Albuquerque, asking if I could provide all the documents I had. I had officer Neal go with me to deliver the documents to the FBI office.

Around this time Pedro stopped corresponding with me.

A few days later I got a call at work from an FBI agent. He asked me to confirm my name and requested that I meet with him to talk about the documents I had been receiving. Point blank he asked me if I was one of the good guys or bad guys. I told him I was willing to cooperate with anything they needed.

He told me that they had an interest to talk to me. I asked if I should discuss this with my chain of command and he requested that I speak to no one about this. We set up a meeting at a restaurant during the weekday at daylight hours. I asked how I would know it was him, he said he would be the one holding a folded-up newspaper in his arm. I hung up the phone and I had this uneasy feeling in my stomach.

My police friend Neal had heard my conversation as he was sitting right next to me, and I told him that it appeared that members of the FBI/CIA wanted to chat with me.

"How do you know it's the FBI?" Neal asked.

"I don't, I guess not until I meet with them."

"What if it's the Mexican cartel?" Neal enquired while raising his eye brows in a questioning form.

For the first time since I had been reporting on the Mexican drug cartels I felt that this was too close to home. Most of my activities had been on the internet, or on the telephone, or in another place away from my backyard, but now it was here, right at home. My friend suggested that I take an old friend of mine who had been on the SWAT team and who would be nearby for in for case everything went to shit. I considered it, but I did not want to involve anyone else. So, I decided to go by myself, but I would be armed. After all, I was a law enforcement officer.

My decision to come out of my anonymity with my real name and reveal some personal information concerned me, but mostly what it did was to restrict my travel into Mexico for safety reasons. It was during this time that some of the threats we received took a different meaning. They were not only directed toward Borderland Beat or Buggs, but some where directed toward me personally. People now knew my name, my profession, the city where I lived and to extend, pictures of me on the internet.

One day while at home around 8 p.m. I was sitting in the living room of my home watching TV and reading a book (Mexican cartel related). I had a lamp on beside me to get enough light so I could see the book.

I looked down and distinctively saw a red laser dot on my chest. I immediately dropped to the floor and crawled to my bedroom to get my handgun and shotgun. I made my way back to the living room, turning off all lights inside the house. I looked outside and saw nothing.

I went outside by way of the back and around the front of the house and looked around.

There is a park in front of my house and I looked for any vehicles or people in the park. There was no one. I stood there for a while, on the side of my house looking very carefully.

I would watch cars pass by, or cars driving by the park, and try to see if anything looked out of place. I knew that it was very unlikely that a cartel would have a sniper, it was not their MO. Then I realized that I had armed myself with a Remington tactical pump shotgun with an extended magazine along with a 9mm Glock with at least 17 rounds. Was this the right combination of firearms for the situation?

Hell, who knows!

I knew that if it was the cartel, they would try to catch me by surprise and ambush me in some way. I also knew they were known to be armed with long guns, and I knew that if for some reason the time came, I would have to be ready. It would happen very fast and I would not have time to react to anything. The key to surviving a hit from a cartel was to be prepared beforehand, take all necessary precautions and be armed to the teeth for a massive counterattack. I also wondered if I was overreacting to things and if I was overthinking the situation.

This made me think of a situation that I came across in the desert of the west side of the city several years ago in a remote area known as Pajarito mesa.

This area is a popular place for people who dump trash and also, many people go there to target practice. I was driving around looking for interesting things to photograph. I could hear gunshots in the distance echoing in the canyon. I thought someone is target shooting. I thought, it might be a cool idea to photograph someone actually target shooting.

I drove to the sound of the gunfire. I saw two late model pickup trucks that were backed up against a hill and it appeared that three men were armed with long guns. They were shooting at some paper targets and bottles propped up on a wooden pallet.

I immediately noticed that the men were nicely dressed in western wear, similar to what I have seen from men that are from the northern part of Mexico (Sinaloa). Two of them had AK-47s. They saw me and smiled. They were Mexican nationals as they spoke to me in Spanish. They become nervous and they started putting their weapons away.

I did not even ask if I could photograph them, I just greeted them in a friendly way and drove away. The scene just did not seem right to me, but I could not pinpoint what seem out of place at the time. This was an area where people go shooting all the time and I had seen my share of people armed with long rifles, including AR-15s and such. This just seemed different, I just could not figure it out.

Later on, when I started to learn more about Mexican sicarios and cartel members from Sinaloa, I wonder if they were cartel members? This possibility is not farfetched considering the proximity to the border and the large amount of the Mexican community living in the state. Based on what they were wearing, the late model pickup trucks, Mexican nationals, the "cuernos de chivo" (AK-47, the preferred weapon of the Mexican cartels) and their behavior, just made me wonder.

Cartels would have no problem reaching out to me and touching me for sure.

The next day at work I asked Neal if he had played a trick on me last night by pointing a laser through my window. He is a jokester sometimes, but he gave a look of concern. He said he had not. I told my sergeant what had happened, and he thought the whole thing was funny and that I was being paranoid.

Apparently, I was, because for the next couple of weeks I hid guns all around my house, and after work I went through the routine of checking and clearing my own house like police do when clearing a high-risk dwelling that might have potential suspects.

I met with the federal agents in a restaurant near Montgomery and Juan Tabo streets in the northeast of Albuquerque. It was an Italian restaurant and the owner had opened it just for our meeting. There was no one else inside.

Three people showed up, all three had newspapers folded under their arms. I assumed all were agents, either CIA or FBI, or perhaps both. One agent opened a brief case and inside were copies of all the documents I had surrendered. A lot were pictures of people I didn't know and pictures of license plates. They went through each picture and asked me if I knew anything about the subjects. I thought I recognized a few people who were possibly politicians, or Mexican actors and actresses, but I could not say for certain.

One of the agents started to ask me about Pedro, if I knew who he was. I said I did not know and he asked if I wanted to know who he was.

I said yes.

He told me that he could tell me a little bit because they were going to ask me not to post any other document on Borderland Beat for the public to see. He said that Pedro was a person in the witness protection program. They said they were very confused about why Pedro—apparently is not his real name—was sending this type of information to media outlets. The agent went on to say that he did not know why Pedro had such information in his possession. The agents did not give me any other information other than to say that they appreciated all the work I did on Borderland Beat and that many people in law enforcement relied on Borderland Beat for a lot of information related to organized crime in Mexico. They also requested that, for security reasons, I not share any of the documents I received with anyone else.

That day I went home and started to rethink my involvement with Borderland Beat. I was still interested in reporting on Mexican drug cartels, but I did not want it to get this close to home.

I started to piece together the events surrounding "Pedro." Perhaps he had been a high-ranking member of the Mexican naval intelligence (SEMAR) and had been collaborating with the FBI, an informant if you will. Perhaps he was providing them with classified information related to organized crime. Something happened that prompted the FBI to pull him out of Mexico. Perhaps his cover was blown, who knows? They brought him to the U.S. with his immediate family. He was probably in the witness protection program, perhaps somewhere in Florida. His phone number when he had called me had a Florida area code. He was not happy, especially if he still had most of his family and friends in Mexico, and he was not allowed to have any contact with anyone there. He did not know many people in Florida, he felt isolated in a country he was not familiar with. Perhaps he had a meager job in Florida, but all his expertise and education from Mexico did not mean shit in the U.S. Perhaps he did keep contact with some of his work associates from Mexico, and perhaps he was not the only informant in SEMAR providing sensitive information to the U.S. government. Perhaps this associate that was providing information to the U.S. government was also providing the same information to Pedro, as a safeguard in case anything happened to him. Maybe Pedro, being disgruntled with his situation, decided to disrupt things by reaching out to the media so he could be taken seriously. Maybe he felt the government was neglecting him and forgetting about him.

At one point, months later, while a whole bunch of us police officers were riding back from Santa Fe after attending a police workshop I got a call from an FBI agent. He wanted to know if I would be willing to testify against Pedro, as they were thinking of bringing legal proceedings against him in federal court. I told him I had no interest in testifying for security reasons, and that, quite honestly, I had nothing to bring to the table that they could not bring up themselves. The agent said he understood my predicament and thanked me for everything.

It was an interesting time. Every once in a while, I would get calls, mostly from the FBI, requesting to talk to me about things, but I really had nothing more to share, as I had stopped collaborating with Borderland Beat all together. I retained ownership of the project, but I no longer collaborated directly.

My police department really never made an issue with me about the Borderland Beat Project. In fact, they even asked if I could brief some of the officers on the Mexican cartel activities in Mexico. I did. I put together a PowerPoint presentation that included the most recent events in cartel activity in Mexico, a short history of the Mexican cartels, how they evolved, the principal players and al lot of media material. A lot of the media material were pictures we had received, or material we got from online sources, but it also included cellular videos of executions we had received from unknown sources through email. These videos were extremely graphic and violent. I would start my presentation by giving a disclaimer and cautioning officers to be prepared for what was to come:

"Because crime in Mexico is extremely violent, this presentation depicts large amount of very graphic media material. If this material is offensive to you, it is advised that discretion be used when participating in all aspects of this program. The need to present graphic source material is vital in showing a true representation of the extent of violence generated by the Mexican drug cartels upon the people of Mexico and the US."

Most of these videos we did not publish on the BB blog, as they were all starting to look the same, unless of course they had news value. The videos were so brutal that when I started showing them, some police officers simply walked out of the room. I remember some of our tactical units standing up and walking around grimacing in disgust and shock. That is how I felt in the early stages of Borderland Beat while reviewing these videos, but with time I had learned to accept it, which is totally wrong. It is not healthy and it leaves a horrific long-lasting impression that is hard to escape from. I thought about all the contributors of BB. I think in a way we all wanted to escape, but I also knew that burying our heads in the sand would not make things go away, but it would keep our sanity.

US Impact

In my involvement with reporting about the crime and violence in Mexico perpetuated by the cartels, I knew that all of it had a direct impact here in the US. The US was definitely involved in some form or another, we like to admit it or not. Mexico expected assistance from the US to help them slow down the flow of drugs pouring into the US. The State Department plays a huge role and has a huge interest in what happens in Mexico. It could be the manufacture and trafficking of illicit drugs, the cartel violence, the large amount of revenue generated from drug trafficking and the constant flow of weapons making their way into Mexico.

An overwhelming majority of confiscated guns in Mexico (90%) that are traced actually originated from the United States. The ATF has reportedly traced 22,848 guns smuggled into Mexico from the United States since 2005, and it showed that between 2005 and 2008, Texas, Arizona and California are the three most prolific source states, respectively, for firearms illegally trafficked to Mexico. Mexican officials only submitted 32% of the guns they seized to the ATF for tracing, overall, 83% of the guns found at crime scenes in Mexico could not be traced.

"Project Gunrunner" deployed new teams of agents to the southwest border. The idea: to stop the flow of weapons from the US to Mexico's drug cartels. But in practice, ATF's actions had the opposite result. Starting in February 2008 under Project Gunrunner, Operations "Fast and Furious", "Too Hot to Handle", "Wide Receiver" and others (all together satirically dubbed "Operation Gunwalker"), have done the opposite by ATF permitting and facilitating 'straw purchase' of firearm sales to traffickers, and allowing the guns to 'walk' and be transported to Mexico.

Statements of ATF agents obtained by Senator Grassley show that the ATF Phoenix Field Division allowed and facilitated the sale of over 2,500 firearms (AK-47 rifles, FN 5.7mm pistols, AK-47 pistols, and .50 caliber rifles) in 'straw man purchases' destined for Mexico. Many of these same guns have now been recovered throughout Mexico, which is artificially inflating ATF's eTrace statistics of U.S. origin guns seized in Mexico.

There were plenty of cases that some of these firearms that were ultimately recovered and traced to the ATF's operations were used in homicides in Mexico and at times, they did spill over to the US. One specific gun, recovered at a scene on the US side of the border, is alleged to be the weapon used to murder Customs and Border Protection Agent Brian Terry on December 14, 2010.

A commando of five illegal immigrants armed with at least two ak-47s were on the Arizona-Mexico border. Two of the Mexcian carried their rifle at the "ready position" showing intent and willingness to engage anyone who dared to confront them.

The Mexicans had crossed into US territory at night fall and were patrolling the area in "single-file formation" on the border just north of Nogales. Border patrol agents observed the Mexicans through thermal binoculars approaching and were able to see that two of them were armed with long guns.

The agents challenged the Mexicans, identifying themselves as US border agents and ordered the Mexicans to drop their weapons. When the Mexicans refused to drop their weapons, the agents engaged them with shotguns loaded with less than lethal beanbag projectiles.

At least one of the Mexican returned fire with an ak-47 rifle fatally wounding Terry, a former US Marine. Terry died at the scene.

The agents opened fire with their side arms and the Mexicans fled into the night. Later during testimony, it was learned that all of the five Mexican were armed.

Two Romanian-built AK-47 assault rifles found at the scene were identified as having been purchased in a Glendale, Ariz., gun shop as part of the ATF's failed Fast and Furious investigation.

After around the year 2009 these guns that were allowed to walk by ATF, were being recovered in crime scenes all over Mexico.

On January 30, 2010, a commando of at least 20 sicarios parked themselves outside a birthday party of high school and college students in Villas de Salvarcar, Ciudad Juarez. Near midnight, the sicarios, later identified as hired guns for the Mexican cartel La Linea, broke into a one-story house and opened fire on a gathering of nearly 60 teenagers. Outside, lookouts gunned down a screaming neighbor and several students who had managed to escape. Fourteen young men and women were killed, and 12 more were wounded before the hit men finally fled.

Three of the high caliber weapons fired that night in Villas de Salvarcar were linked to a gun tracing operation run by the Bureau of Alcohol, Tobacco, Firearms and Explosives (ATF). There were at least 57 more previously unreported firearms that were bought by straw purchasers monitored by ATF during Operation Fast and Furious, and then recovered in Mexico in sites related to murders, kidnappings, and at least one other massacre.

In Mexico, the timing of the operation "Fast and Furious" coincided with an upsurge of violence in the war among the country's strongest cartels. In 2009, the northern Mexican states served as a battlefield for the Sinaloa and Juarez drug trafficking organizations, and as expansion territory for the increasingly powerful Zetas.

The murder of Special Agent Jaime Zapata and the shooting of his partner, another ICE agent on February 2011 provides a sad reminder of the dangers American law enforcement officers face every day while embedded in Mexico. The attack on Zapata occurred in the north-central state of San Luis Potosi, as the U.S. agents were driving between Mexico City and Monterrey. The agents were traveling on a well-traveled highway in an armored car with diplomatic plates on a well-traveled highway.

Jaime Jorge Zapata and Victor Avila were ICE Special Agents assigned to the attaché office in Mexico City. Zapata and Avila were consultants working with the Mexican government and traveling between Mexico City and Monterrey. Zapata was behind the wheel of black armored Chevrolet Suburban with U.S. diplomatic plates on Panamerican Highway 57 in San Luis Potosi, Mexico. His partner, Avila Jr. was in the passenger seat. Both agents were not armed, as it's not permitted in Mexican law for foreign law enforcement to be armed while operating in Mexican soil.

They had just stopped to eat at a Subway in san Luis Potosi. Both men noticed an SUV tailing them. Zapta tried to speed up but the vehicle from behind kept up with him. The SUV pulled beside him and four men in the SUV flashed long guns, while speeding up in front of him. At that point another SUV came up from behind him and they had him boxed in. While boxing him in from the front and behind, they slowed Zapata to a stop.

A group of armed men surrounded the US agents. They started screaming at them to get out. Zapata showed them his US diplomatic credentials, telling them they were federal agents. The gunmen refused to relent and kept trying to get the agents to come out of their vehicle. Zapata put his vehicle on park that automatically unlocked the doors. They tried to drag Zapata out, but he managed to close the door. Zapata cracked his window open and continued to try to negotiate with the aggressors at one point yelling, "We are Americans, we are diplomats."

One of the men stuck his AK-47 through the crack and began to shoot indiscriminately, striking Zapata several times in the abdomen and Avila twice in the leg. Mexican investigators would later recover 83 spent casings.

Zapata managed to put the vehicle in gear and accelerated ahead of the gunmen, stepping on the gas pedal. Not long after pulling away of the armed men, Zapata slumped on the steering wheel, and their SUV came to a stop. His partner Agent Avila was not able to physically remove the mortally wounded Zapata from the drivers seat in order to be able to speed off, so he began calling for assistance. The gunmen caught up to the agents and started shooting at passenger side of the armored SUV. The bullet proof glass held, saving Avila's life. The armored vehicle had withstood the attack and the barrage of rounds.

A Federal Police helicopter arrived shortly after the attack as did several federal units from nearby San Luis Potosi.

The attackers gravely wounded agent Zapata while agent Victor Avila Jr. was wounded but survived the attack.

Mexican and U.S. officials said the ambush was carried out by Los Zetas, one of the major criminal drug cartels operating in Mexico. San Luis Potosi is at the center of a power struggle between two rival drug gangs, the Zetas and the Gulf cartel. It is also on the route north used by migrants seeking to reach the United States, and officials say cartels have begun recruiting some migrants to work for the gangs.

Although it is illegal for U.S. law enforcement officials in Mexico to carry weapons, U.S. officials have not commented on any protection the two special agents might have had, or why they would be travelling in the area seemingly unprotected.

Federal investigators say the gun used to kill Zapata in Mexico had been traced to a Dallas-area man. Agents of the U.S. Bureau of ATF arrested the man and two other suspected gun smugglers in Lancaster, Texas, a southern Dallas suburb

The Mexican government would eventually detain a suspect in the killing of ICE Special Agent Jaime Jorge Zapata. Julian Zapata Espinoza, known as "El Piolin," was detained along with five other suspected members of a local cell of the Zetas organization.

The other members arrested of the Zetas were Armando Álvarez Saldaña, Mario Domínguez Realeo o Domingo Díaz Rosas, Jesús Iván Quezada Peña, Martin Bárcenas Tapia and Rubén Darío Venegas, who was said to be from Honduras.

The suspect told authorities that Zapata's SUV was attacked because it was mistaken for that of a rival drug organization. Some U.S. officials maintained the attack was an intentional ambush of the agents and said the gunmen made comments before they fired indicating they knew who their targets were.

Zapata Espinoza admitted that he and other "estacas" or "hit squads" armed with AK-47s, AR-15s and handguns, surrounded the armored vehicle in which Zapata and Avila were aboard. El Piolin stated he fired several shots in the air trying to get the agents to exit the vehicle. When they refused to do so, the "estacas" fired weapons at the vehicle, Espinoza Zapata said.

The purpose of "stopping the armored vehicle was to steal it," Espinoza Zapata said. In an initial statement to Mexican authorities, Zapata Espinoza said that agent Zapata's death was a case of mistaken identity. He and others believed the Suburban in which Zapata and Avila were riding belonged to a rival drug cartel. Zapata Espinoza said Zeta members had a "standing order from the Zetas leadership to steal vehicles deemed valuable to the cartel."

The death of Zapata and the attempted killing of Avila became an international incident that was discussed between President Barack Obama and Mexican President Felipe Calderón during a state visit.

Zapata's murder was the first slaying of a U.S. law enforcement agent since 1985, when Drug Enforcement Administration agent Enrique "Kike" Camarena was kidnapped, tortured and murdered.

In 2011, while speaking near the Juarez border wall, then President Obama remarked that "El Paso and other cities and towns along the border are consistently rated among the safest in the nation."

"Over the past two-and-a-half years, we've seized 31 percent more drugs, 75 percent more currency, and 64 percent more weapons than before," Obama said. "Even as we've stepped up patrols, apprehensions along the border have been cut by nearly 40 percent from two years ago – that means far fewer people are attempting to cross the border illegally."

The Obama administration sent National Guard troops to the border on Sept. 1, 2010. The 1,200 guardsmen were scheduled to leave on June 30 the following year. The National Guard troops assisted in seizing more than 14,000 pounds of drugs and apprehending 7,000 illegal aliens, according to the Department of Homeland Security (DHS).

Does illegal immigration facilitate drug trafficking to the US from Mexico? Are drug cartels members embedded in the millions of illegal Mexican immigrants in Mexico?

I feel comfortable when I say that the vast majority of illegal immigrants coming into the US are hardworking people with the only interest being to make a better life for themselves and their families. They, for the most part, are constructive members of society. There is a very small segment that have different motives.

Most of the violence remains firmly on the Mexican side of the border, but there is some evidence of increasingly violent attacks on US border patrol agents by drug traffickers. There has also been a reported rise in drug-related shootings and kidnappings in some US cities and towns, especially in the south-west.

A May 2010 report from the US National Drug Intelligence Center said that Mexican drug trafficking organizations "continue to represent the single greatest drug trafficking threat to the United States".

American border towns have not seen anything remotely approaching the blood-stained carnage of some north Mexican cities where rival drug cartels are in a high-stakes war that has killed thousands of people every year in the last decade, but that may change if the problems in Mexico spirals out of control. The links that U. S. gangs have with the Mexican cartels should be a concern. Gangs already control the distribution of the majority of illicit drugs in the streets of the U.S. The drug lords to the south can easily tap this ready-made criminal infrastructure for a range of nefarious purposes. We better read the writing on the wall because it already has.

American street gangs are known to have ties to Mexican cartels and help distribute drugs on streets. In Mexico drugs cartels, have been known to use street gangs to help them distribute drugs and be the street soldier.

One example of gang street influence in the cartel structure is the Juárez Cartel recruiting members of Barrio Azteca while the Sinaloa Cartel recruiting rival gangs as the Artist Assassins (Double A's) and Los Mexicles. A US Congress report drew on evidence from intelligence sources suggesting that Mexican cartels had forged closer links with established drug gangs inside the US. Gang members will do what is profitable. Hardened gangs are carving out turf on the border and beyond as part of a scramble to make money from the tons of illegal drugs pouring north from Mexico each month. There is an obstacle that traditional Mexican cartels have with the American street gangs.

Trust.

The cartels will deal with the U.S. gangs on some levels but there are clear lines in the sand. Business stays in the family.

The gangs are a resource for the drug cartels but not their primary resource. The Mexican drug dealer is a very parochial individual. He would rather deal with a family member than someone just entering the business.

For example, the Mexican drug lords will not entrust an American gang with the task of bringing large quantities of cash, the profits of their trade, back to Mexico. That means the cartels would have to have a Mexican presence in the US to coordinate and perform the more delicate operations of the drug trade.

Not all U.S. gangs that the Mexican cartels have allied with are the same. But examining how Barrio Azteca operates offered an insight into how other gangs — like the Latin Kings, the Texas Syndicate, the Sureños, outlaw motorcycle gangs, and transnational street gangs like MS-13 — operate in alliance with the cartels. This all shows that there is some sort of association between the US gangs and the Mexican cartels, to what extent remained unclear.

One thing is for certain, this alliance only makes things worst on both sides of the border. Despite efforts by both governments in the border to combat drug trafficking, it's still a big problem. It is found all along all the US states along the Mexican border and beyond.

Even in places like Albuquerque, New Mexico it is hard to gage the extent of the criminal level among the Mexican national community, primarily because many are afraid to report crime for fear of deportation.

According to an intelligence report, Mexican drug recently sent a team of 15 heavily armed hit men into the United States. Their job? To protect the flow of drugs and human smugglers and kill anyone who gets in their way. This is a larger national security threat facing America than anywhere in Iraq or Afghanistan or anywhere else in the world. Mexican cartel violence has spread to U.S. cities and suburban communities, particularly in the Southwest.

Mexican drug cartels are operating in more than 230 U.S. cities as they seek to spread their influence, a top State Department official said. According to the National Drug Intelligence Center estimates, criminals smuggle between $18 billion and $39 billion each year across the Southwest border alone. The cartels control the trafficking of drugs from South America to the US, a business that is worth an estimated $13 billion a year.

The National Drug Intelligence Center listed the cartels with the widest influence in the United States. It said the Sinaloa cartel is operating in 75 cities, followed by the Gulf cartel in 37 cities, the Zetas in 37, the Juarez in 33, the Beltran Leyva Organization in 30, La Familia in 27 and the Tijuana cartel in 21.

The Merida Initiative is a treaty under which the U.S. government pledged to contribute $1.5 billion, along with drug-fighting equipment and personnel, to Mexico.

The Hometown Influence

I was raised in Albuquerque, New Mexico. A crossroad between two major drug routes (I40 and I25) and geographically, not far from the US-Mexican border. The Mexican cartel influence is very subtle, it's does not stand out like in other border cities found in Texas and Arizona.

But it does exist.

Case and point; take just one incident that happened at the end of 2007 involving Danny Baca who was supposed to bring a load of drugs across the border for the Juarez cartel. He was to meet a connection in El Paso and go from there. But Baca instead decided to take the load to his hometown of Albuquerque and keep it for himself. He sold the load for $7,000. The cartel came looking for him. He was shot 22 times and his body left burning on the west side of Albuquerque in a place known as Pajarito Mesa. Cartels usually do not go to this extent for such small amount of money, but they seemed to think that a message had to be sent.

Then Bernalillo County Sheriff Darren White said that Baca "signed his own death warrant." when he and another man chose to betray a powerful cartel.

Three cartel-affiliated men -- Jaime Valeta, 25, and 26-year-old Mario Talavera and an unknown Hispanic male -- and another man, Gerardo Nunez, 27, had kidnapped Baca from his East Mountains after he refused to return the drugs or the car. That's the last time Baca was seen alive.

Nunez was taken in custody on charges of kidnapping, aggravated burglary evidence tampering and conspiracy. His bond was set at $1 million cash only. Valeta and Talavera face the same. Mario Talavera who is a US citizen was tracked down by US Marshals in Cuauhtémoc, Mexico. Talavera was deported by Mexican authorities and brought back to New Mexico to face federal charges of drug trafficking, murder and kidnapping.

Although the cartels have not declared open war on each other on the U.S. side of the border, they do have influence here, which often comes in the form of murders and bribing law enforcement. In 2007, the FBI discovered collaborators inside the drug task force. New Mexico State Police Officer Keith Salazar and former San Juan County Sheriff's Deputy Levi Countryman were feeding information to a drug cartel. Borderland Beat typically does not focus too much attention of what is happening in the US related to Mexican cartels, mostly because BB focuses on activities that are not being reported in the US, coming out of Mexico. If you look closely, you will find plenty of news related to Mexican cartels having direct influence in US soil.

As I mentioned previously, sicarios in Mexico most of the time are well trained men and are usually well armed with heavy weapons. Sicarios are paid professional men who many times are former or current police officers or men that have deserted from the military for better pay. We see this play out in Mexico every day, sometimes they are fighting other sicarios from rival cartels or fighting the federal police or Mexican military. Not a lot of spill over in to the US, but it does happen. We have seen sicarios in US soil protecting loads of narcotics entering the US or settling of scores from someone that "talked," or betrayed the organization.

An example of sicarios operating in the US was the incident that happened on November 2011 where a tractor trailer that was carrying a load of marijuana through the state of Texas. This was more than just the trafficking of drugs. Undercover officers were attempting to make a "controlled delivery," where they allow the drugs to reach their destination while covertly tracking (shadowing) the truck from a distance. While passing through the area of Harris County three sport utility vehicles intercepted the truck. They sprayed the truck with heavy gunfire, killing the driver, Lawrence Chapa, who was an informant.

A firefight ensued between the gunmen and lawmen. One gunman was killed while three were arrested. One sheriff deputy was wounded on the leg and made a full recovery.

The three gunmen that were captured had military style haircuts, no tattoos and seem to be able to use good tactics during the firefight. They were sicarios for the Zetas.

It seemed like a scene that takes place in Mexico every day where cartels regularly engage in firefights with military and federal police. The truck was carrying a load of 300 pounds of weed, not enough for a cartel to take such bold action on US soil.

Through the interrogation of the sicarios it was not clear on the motive of the attack. Some sicarios confessed that it was a hit on the driver, as they had learned he was an informant. But it was also thought that perhaps it was an attack to rip off the load thinking it was carrying more marijuana than it actually had. The motive is irrelevant, what is relevant is that such an attack by sicarios would take place on US soil.

When I had mentioned that Mexican cartels had the means to reach out and touch anyone in the US, it seemed incredible to some. After all, we had not seen the spillover from Mexico into the US at the level that we had seen in Mexico. In Mexico sicarios are heavily armed with high caliber weapons and kill with impunity. It happens regularly, on a daily basis, every day. We don't see the daily violence from Mexican cartels here in the US. So why would we think Mexican cartels would be operating in the US at the same level as in Mexico. People would simple suggest I was paranoid when I was concern about safety from cartel in the US. I was reminded, "it's just not happening here." But although in the surface it all seems normal, upon closer examination you can see cartel activity alive and well in the US and has the potential to rival the brutal violence seen in Mexico.

Take for instance an incident that happened in Albuquerque, my home of residence. In 2018 Bernalillo county deputies (BCSO) initiated a routine traffic stop of a vehicle that matched the description of one involved in a domestic disturbance call. The vehicle was pulled over after it swerved out of its lane of travel. There were three occupants inside the vehicle. Two of them were Mexican nationals and the other man, the driver, was native of Albuquerque, NM. What happened next was something that should give law enforcement reason to be concerned.

The deputy noticed that one of the men appeared to be wearing body armor, saw what appeared to be large amounts currency in the center console and upon further examination, noticed a large number of weapons in the back floorboard.

The deputies would eventually find eight rifles, six handguns, night vision goggles, multiple sets of body armor, ballistic helmets, more than $33,000 in cash, and a small amount of cocaine in the vehicle.

Looking at the equipment, these men were ready to engage other armed targets, while travelling within the US. These types of traffic stops are common and routinely seen in Mexico.

These men were better equipped than the patrol deputies that stopped them at the scene and could have caused some heavy damage if they had chosen to engage the deputies. For the most part US patrol officers only carry side arms on them when conducting routine traffic stops and the long rifles found in the vehicle of the suspects could easily penetrate the soft ballistic armor worn by patrol officers in the course of their duty.

Two of the rifles, including one fully automatic "machine gun" were confirmed to be stolen. The driver, Jesus Samaniego-Villa, and his two passengers were charged with possession of stolen firearms in state court, but the case was quickly handed over to federal prosecutors to avoid being botched up by the seemingly incompetent New Mexico state court system.

Federal prosecutors would eventually brought up charges against Daniel Landeros-Garcia, Sergio Samaniego-Villa, Jesus Samaniego-Villa, Jessica Moya and Christian Meza-Samaniego.

Jesus Samaniego-Villa and the two passengers were identified as belonging to a criminal organization ran by Jesus' brother, Sergio Samaniego-Villa, who the FBI had been buying heroin and crack from through informants to build a case against the group. It was said that they had ties to the Sinaloa Cartel.

Sergio was deported back in 2012 while facing pending drug charges. He and his wife were arrested again for drug trafficking in 2018, but posted bail and fled the state to California, where he continued to run the organization back in Albuquerque through surrogates like his brother Jesus.

This illustrates a small portion of what American law enforcement should expect to confront when coming in contact with Mexican cartel operatives and their drug trafficking activities in US soil. The Mexican drug cartels go through extensive means to protect their operations and sometimes will resort to violent means when they feel trapped in an attempt to escape justice.

One Last Incident

Back around 1992 or so I use to work the graveyard shift for the Albuquerque Police Department. I was assigned as a field Investigator. My job required me to be in uniform driving a marked police car, but my primary duty was forensics, which is the collections of physical evidence in the field. Most of my job consisted of lifting latent prints, collecting trace evidence, tagging items from crime scenes and taking photographs of crime scenes or events of significance importance. The job description required me to work in the field among the patrol officers and provide them support. I would assist the officer in the field by providing backup on calls or helping in situations where multiple officers were needed.

During this time there use to be a Mexican style nightclub called, I believe, the "Copa Cabana." It was on Central Avenue and catered to mostly Mexican clientele. Police would be called there often, and I would be called to assist for translation purposes. I got to know the club's owners, Alonso and Rosalba Ibarra. I also got to know the security guard working there, as I had to talk to him numerous times.

One day, as I was driving my unit in front of the club, the security guard flagged me down. He told me that there was a man who was trying to leave the parking lot in his truck and was extremely intoxicated. He pointed out a new silver Chevrolet truck that appeared to have a dead battery, as the vehicle was refusing to start. I noticed that it had a Texas license plate. I called it out and dispatch advised me that they would get me a backup as soon as one became available.

I made contact with the driver who attempting to start the truck. He was wearing a black cowboy hat and seem to be around 25 to 30 years of age. In Spanish, I instructed him to step out of the truck. The area where he was parked was dark

384

and I was having a hard time looking inside the vehicle, even with my flashlight. He told me to fuck off and that he was one I should not fuck with. The security guard came around to the passenger side and was looking in through the open passenger window. I became firmer in my commands and ordered him to place his hands on the steering wheel where I could see them, and to step out of the vehicle. He refused my instructions and was cursing at me. Later I found out he initially thought I was a security guard, as we both had dark uniforms.

I then noticed that the driver of the truck was attempting to reach behind his back to get something out. I continued to give him commands to put his hands on the steering wheel. Suddenly, the security guard yelled that the driver was trying to pull out a gun.

The man had a semi-automatic handgun inside the rear area of the waistband of his pants. He was having a hard time pulling the gun out because he was drunk, his pants were tight and he was pressing against the truck's seat. I pulled out my gun and placed it to his head, reminding him that I knew he had a handgun and not to pull it out. He continued to curse and attempt to pull the gun out. I had not actually seen the gun and was not ready to use lethal force on him, but I was very close. I thought to myself, "He knows that I know he has a gun and he was still trying to get it out, despite the fact that I just placed my gun to the side of his head."

I realized that this man intended to kill me. I then decide to pull hard on his left arm, which caused him to fall out of the truck. As he was falling, his gun came out and the security guard snatched it from his hand. After realizing that the driver no longer had his gun, I got into a struggle with him in an attempt to get him into custody. While fighting with him, his front shirt pocket tore off and money flew to the ground. I was able to get him secured and he was charged with felony aggravated assault on a police officer with a deadly weapon.

I later found out that the passenger door of his pickup truck had numerous bullet holes, shot from inside out. He had three driver's licenses from New Mexico, Texas and Arizona, all with the exact same personal information. When we towed his truck, we found three unopened boxes of clear zipper bags. A few day later I attended his arraignment and found out he had an attorney from Texas. He was released after paying a bond. I never heard from him or the case ever again.

I spoke with Alonso afterwards, and he told me that he knew the man from his hometown of Sinaloa and that he belonged to a Mexican cartel (most likely the Sinaloa cartel). Alonso had told me that the man had been buying drinks for everyone at the club and was asked to leave after he started a fight with another costumer. He said that this man had a reputation for killing cops in Mexico, and he told me he was glad nothing had happened to me.

Alonso himself would later be suspected of drug trafficking and ties to drugs cartels. He was also a suspect in at least one homicide in Albuquerque. His brother, Luis Ibarra, was executed along with six other people in El Paso, Texas, inside a club Luis owned. Rosalba had a husband serving time in a federal prison for drug trafficking. I remember Rosalba having diamonds on the silver-laced braces of her teeth. I made a comment about them to her once when I happened to be talking to her. She told me that when her husband was arrested for drug trafficking, the authorities had seized everything of value they owned. She told me if that ever happened again, at least they would not be able to take the diamonds on her teeth.

At the time, I did not know anything about drug cartels in Mexico. This was the closest I had come to knowing anything about organize crime, and I considered myself lucky to have survived the event to tell the story. But later in the years, I realized cartel incidents in the U.S. were alive and well, and apparently, it had been like that for a long time.

Although I no longer contribute to Borderland Beat, I still follow the Mexican drug cartels religiously. I read BB daily and make every attempt not to be lured back to the dark side of the drug cartels. I hear conversations about cartel activity or I watch the news about something cartel related, and it has my total interest, focus, like it did before, when I first started documenting stories myself. Things in the drug cartels have changed with time but at the same time, remain the same. Same story, just different place and people. Despite all the problems, violence and corruption, I still love Mexico. I love the places and people. I still travel to Mexico from time to time, I just don't publicize it. I keep it to myself, although it's hard at times.

I have left many things behind me, my law enforcement career and my involvement with reporting on the Mexican Drug War. Although, you can say both deal in negative terms. With police work, you deal with offenders, suspects, witnesses or victims of crime, it's really never a good thing. I have never pulled anyone over to give them a treat or say hello. It is the nature of the job. After a while, in time, it's just a job, an area of responsibility you have to get through with your sanity and life. The key word is longevity, surviving alive but also keeping your sanity. At the same time, reporting on drug violence is shocking at first, but you eventually settle down and realize it's really the same over and over again. Yet, both still remain in my heart, but I have learned to accept it and let go.

Mexican Cartel Structure

The Mexican drug cartel structure is constantly changing, everything in Mexico is so fluid. Just when one thinks one particular cartel has been dismantled, it emerges out of the ashes. Or new ones sprout like some menacing flowers in spring after a downpour.

No one knows who is who. Plaza bosses get promoted as soon as the old one is executed or captured. Keeping track is a nightmare, and very hard to confirm.

Alliances among cartels change constantly and cells breakaway or start working independently.

For a while I was attempting to update the current affairs of the Mexican drug war, but just when I have it settle some dispute over authenticity of fact derails any attempt to get the beat of the heart in the cartel structure.

So I was happy User G]-[057 in the Borderland Beat forum attempted to give it a go. I thought it looked good, although I am sure someone will dispute some or parts of it, but here it goes:

MAIN CARTELS:
Cartel de Sinaloa
Cartel de Juarez
Cartel del Golfo
Cartel de Tijuana
Cartel de Los Zetas
Cartel Beltran Leyva
Caballeros Templarios
Cartel de Sonora
Cartel de Guadalajara
Cartel Oaxaca o El Istmo
Cartel de Colima
Cartel del Milenio
Cartel de Nezia

OTHER SMALL CARTELS:
Cartel Jalisco Nueva Generacion
Cartel de Centro
Cartel Independencia de Acapulco
Cartel de la Sierra
La Familia
Cartel Pacifico del Sur
Cartel Los Pelones

ARMED GROUPS OPERATING FOR A CARTEL:
Los Teos
Guerreros Unidos
Comando del Diablo
La Barredora
Guradianes de Morelos
La Resistencia "CT"
Comando Negro "CAF"
Fuerzas Especiales Muletas
Fuerzas Especiales Koreano "CIDA"
Fuerzas Especiales Zetas
Grupo Operative Zetas
La Comania

SINALOA FEDERATION BEGINING:
Los Linces "JUAREZ"
Los M's "C.D.S OR JUAREZ" ???
La Linia "JUAREZ"
Los Tejas "C.D. "
Los Chachos "C.D.S OR JUAREZ"
La Gente Nueva "C.D.S"
Los Antrax "C.D.S"
Nueva Generacion del Chapo "C.D.S"
Los Aztecas "JUAREZ"

Los Triple A "CDS"
Comando X "C.D.S" mixture of G.N and Antrax i guess

BELTRANES FACTIONS SINCE BEGINING:
Los Mazatlecos "BELTRANES"
Los Negros "C.D.S AND BELTRANES"
Los Pelones "BELTRANES"
Los Tarascos "BELTRANES OR FAMILIA"
Los Numeros "BELTRANES"
LA MANO CON OJOS "BELTRANES"
Los Charritos "BELTRANES"
Los Gueros "BELTRANES"
Los Rojos "BELTRANES" they also had a group
Fuerzas Especiales de Arturo "BELTRANES"
Los Sultanes "BELTRANES"

Old school CDG 2003-2008 era some still exist. Back in the Day every border town had their own Nick Name of each CDG faction. I Just don't remember who was who. After the Separation of Zs and CDG, everyone scattered joining one side. Then the CDG internal war, separated them again. All them groups have songs, either by the Cartel rap singers or Beto Quintanilla and his Brother Chuy.

Los Arfiles "CDG"
Los Lobos "CDG"
Los Escorpios "CDG"
Los Kalimanes "CDG"
Los Rojos de Laredo "CDG"
Los Oriones "CDG"
Los Cobras "CDG"
Los Deltas "CDG"
Los Sierras "CDG"
Los Gammas "CDG"
Comando 7 "CDG"
Los Metros de Raynosa "CDG"

Los L's "CDG"

Los Ciclones "CDG"

Los Alacranes "CDG"

Los Tiburones "CDG"

Los XW "CDG"

Other groups that fall uncategorized:

La Gente Nueva (Nuevo Leon) not sure if it was a branch of the Sinaloas.

Carteles Unidos "The Modern Federation of Sinaloa??"

Fall of Guadalara – Chart

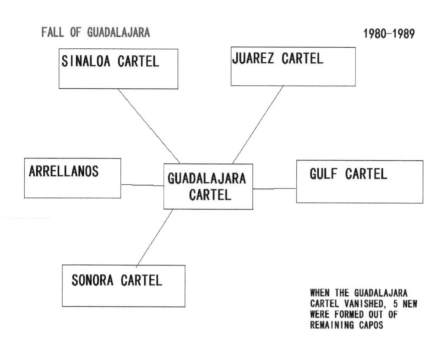

FALL OF GUADALAJARA   1980–1989

SINALOA CARTEL

JUAREZ CARTEL

ARRELLANOS

GUADALAJARA CARTEL

GULF CARTEL

SONORA CARTEL

WHEN THE GUADALAJARA
CARTEL VANISHED, 5 NEW
WERE FORMED OUT OF
REMAINING CAPOS

1989 to 1999 Rise of New Cartels Chart

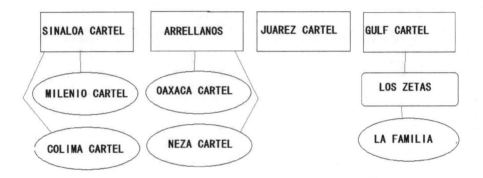

1989-1999
RISE OF NEW CARTELS

| SINALOA CARTEL | ARRELLANOS | JUAREZ CARTEL | GULF CARTEL |

MILENIO CARTEL   OAXACA CARTEL   LOS ZETAS

COLIMA CARTEL   NEZA CARTEL   LA FAMILIA

NEW CARTELS EMERGE, AND TAKE SIDES, THE
GULF CARTEL CREATES THE ZETAS AND LA
FAMILIA MICHOACANA TO EXPAND THE
TERRITORY.

ZETAS AND FAMILIA FIGHT OF MILENIO
CARTEL FROM MICHOACAN.

1999-2008
SHIFTING POWERS

SINALOA CARTEL

LA FAMILIA CARTEL

JUAREZ CARTEL

GULF CARTEL

BELTRAN LEYVA

ARRELLANOS CARTEL

LOS ZETAS

THE WEAKEST OF THE CARTELS, DISBAND OR JOINED SIDES WITH A MORE POWERFUL FACTION.

LA FAMILIA DECLARES WAR ON THE GULF CARTEL AND LOS ZETAS, FOR FORGING AN ALLIANCE WITH THE MILENIO CARTEL (ARCH ENEMIES OF THE FAMILIA)

BELTRAN LEYVAS, SPLINTER FROM SINALOA CARTEL AND FORGE AN ALLIANCE WITH SINALOA CARTEL ENEMIES.

MEMBERS OF THE OAXACA, NEZA, SONORA, MILENIO, ALL JOINED SIDES OF A STRONGER FACTION AND BECAME PART.

2009 to 2012 New Era - Chart

ERUPTION OF NEW CARTELS, SOME LASTED A COUPLE
OF MONTHS AND VANISHED OR JOINED THE STRONGEST
FACTIONS.

2009-2012
NEW ERA

LOS ZETAS BECOME INDEPENDENT CARTEL FROM THE
GULF, FORGE AN ALLIANCE WITH THE BELTRANES

SINALOA CARTEL	LA FAMILIA CARTEL	LOS ZETAS CARTEL	BELTRAN LEYVA	ARRELLANOS CARTEL	JUAREZ CARTEL

GULF CARTEL

AFTER LA FAMILIA SPLINTERED THIS GROUPS FORMED.

SPLINTERED GROUPS AFTER THE DEATH OF ARTURO BELTRAN

CARTEL JALISCO NUEVA GENERACION

CABALLEROS TEMPLARIOS	OPERATING	CARTEL PACF. SUR	SHORT-LIVED CARTEL

CARTEL DEL CENTRO	SHORT-LIVED CARTEL	CARTEL IND DE ACAPLCO	OPERATING INDEPENDENT

CARTEL DELA SIERRA — SHORT-LIVED CARTEL

CARTEL LOS PELONES — SHORT-LIVED CARTEL

ARELLANOS APPEAR WEAK SO DOES THE JUAREZ
CARTEL.

LA FAMILIA DISBANDS, AND FORMS LOS
CABALLEROS TEMPLARIOS AND A SMALLER
FACTION THAT WAS QUICKLY SHORT LIVED

Bio of Mexican cartel covered in this book

Mexican cartels that played key roles during the time lines covered in this book.

Guadalajara Cartel

The Guadalajara Cartel was a Mexican drug cartel which was formed in the 1980s by Rafael Caro Quintero, Miguel Ángel Félix Gallardo and Ernesto Fonseca Carrillo in order to ship heroin and marijuana to the United States. Among the first of the Mexican drug trafficking groups to work with the Colombian cocaine mafias, the Guadalajara cartel prospered from the cocaine trade.

After the arrest of Rafael Caro Quintero and Ernesto Fonseca Carrillo, Félix Gallardo kept a low profile and in 1987 he moved with his family Guadalajara city. "The Godfather" then decided to divide up the trade he controlled as it would be more efficient and less likely to be brought down in one law enforcement swoop. In a way, he was privatizing the Mexican drug business while sending it back underground, to be run by bosses who were less well known or not yet known by the DEA.

Félix Gallardo "The Godfather" convened the nation's top drug narcos at a house in the resort of Acapulco where he designated the plazas or territories. The Tijuana route would go to the Arellano Felix brothers. The Ciudad Juárez route would go to the Carrillo Fuentes family. Miguel Caro Quintero would run the Sonora corridor.

The control of the Matamoros, Tamaulipas corridor - then becoming the Gulf Cartel- would be left undisturbed to Juan García Abrego. Meanwhile, Joaquín Guzmán Loera and Ismael Zambada García would take over Pacific coast operations, becoming the Sinaloa Cartel. Guzmán and Zambada brought veteran Héctor Luis Palma Salazar back into the fold. Félix Gallardo still planned to oversee national operations, he had the contacts so he was still the top man, but he would no longer control all details of the business; he was arrested on April 8, 1989.

According to Peter Dale Scott, the Guadalajara Cartel, Mexico's most powerful drug-trafficking network in the early 1980s, prospered largely because it enjoyed the protection of the Dirección Federal de Seguridad, under its chief Miguel Nassar Haro, a CIA asset."

Sinaloa Cartel

The Sinaloa Cartel (Pacific Cartel, Guzmán-Loera Cartel) (Spanish: Cártel de Sinaloa) is a Mexican drug cartel primarily operating out of the states of Baja California, Sinaloa, Durango, Sonora and Chihuahua. The cartel is also known as the Guzmán-Loera Organization and the Pacific Cartel, the latter due to the coast of Mexico from which it originated, another name is the Federation. The 'Federation' was partially splintered when the Beltrán-Leyva brothers broke apart from the Sinaloa Cartel.

The Sinaloa Cartel is associated with the label "Golden Triangle" as the regions of Sinaloa, Durango, and Chihuahua in which they operate the most form a 'triangle' when their capital cities are looked at on a map. The region is a major producer of Mexican poppy and marijuana. This area is similar in the United States to the Emerald Triangle consisting of the three largest marijuana-producing counties in the US:

Mendocino, Humboldt, and Trinity in Northern California, United States.

According to the U.S. Attorney General, the Sinaloa Cartel is responsible for importing into the United States and distributing nearly 200 tons of cocaine and large amounts of heroin between 1990 and 2008.

Background

Pedro Avilés Pérez was a pioneer drug lord in the Mexican state of Sinaloa in the late 1960s. He is considered to be the first generation of major Mexican drug smugglers of marijuana who marked the birth of large-scale Mexican drug trafficking. He also pioneered the use of aircraft to smuggle drugs to the United States.

Second generation Sinaloan traffickers such as Rafael Caro Quintero, Ernesto Fonseca Carrillo, Miguel Ángel Félix Gallardo and Avilés Pérez' nephew Joaquín 'El Chapo'

Guzmán, would claim they learned all they knew about narcotrafficking while serving in the Avilés organization. Miguel Ángel Félix Gallardo, who eventually founded the Guadalajara Cartel was arrested in 1989. While incarcerated, he remained one of Mexico's major traffickers, maintaining his organization via mobile phone until he was transferred to a new maximum security prison in the 1990s. At that point, his old organization broke up into two factions: the Tijuana Cartel led by his nephews, the Arellano Félix brothers, and the Sinaloa Cartel, run by former lieutenants Héctor Luis Palma Salazar, Adrián Gómez González and Joaquín Guzmán Loera (El Chapo).

Leadership

Sinaloa Cartel hierarchy in early 2008The Sinaloa Cartel used to be known as La Alianza de Sangre (Blood Alliance). When Héctor Luis Palma Salazar (a.k.a: El Güero) was arrested on June 23, 1995, by elements of the Mexican Army, his partner Joaquín Guzmán Loera took leadership of the cartel. Guzmán was captured in Guatemala on June 9, 1993, and extradited to Mexico, where he was jailed in a maximum-security prison, but on Jan. 19, 2001, Guzmán escaped and resumed his command of the Sinaloa Cartel. Guzmán has two close associates, Ismael Zambada García and Ignacio Coronel Villareal. Guzman and

Zambada became Mexico's top drug kingpins in 2003, after the arrest of their rival Osiel Cardenas of the Gulf Cartel. Another close associate, Javier Torres Felix, was arrested and extradited to the U.S. in December 2006; so far, Guzmán and Zambada have evaded operations to capture them.

On July 29, 2010 Ignacio Coronel was killed in a shootout with the Mexican military in Zapopan, Jalisco.

Operations

The Sinaloa Cartel has a presence in 17 states, with important centers in Mexico City, Tepic, Toluca, Guadalajara, and most of the state of Sinaloa. The cartel is primarily involved in the smuggling and distribution of Colombian cocaine, Mexican marijuana, methamphetamine and Mexican and Southeast Asian heroin into the United States. It is believed that a group known as the Herrera Organization would transport multi-ton quantities of cocaine from South America to Guatemala on behalf of the Sinaloa Cartel. From there it is smuggled north to Mexico and later into the U.S. Other shipments of cocaine are believed to originate in Colombia from Cali and Medellín drug-trafficking groups from which the Sinaloa Cartel handle transportation across the U.S. border to distribution cells in Arizona, California, Texas, Chicago and New York.

Prior to his arrest, Vicente Zambada Niebla ("El Vicentillo"), son of Ismael Zambada García ("El Mayo"), played a key role in the Sinaloa Cartel. Vicente Zambada was responsible for coordinating multi-ton cocaine shipments from Central and South American countries, through Mexico, and into the United States for the Sinaloa Cartel. To accomplish this task, he used every means available: Boeing 747 cargo aircraft, narco submarines, container ships, go-fast boats, fishing vessels, buses, rail cars, tractor trailers and automobiles. He was arrested by the Mexican Army on March 18, 2009 and extradited on February 18, 2010 to Chicago to face federal charges.

In the late 1980s, the United States Drug Enforcement Administration believed the Sinaloa Cartel was the largest drug trafficking organization operating in Mexico. By the mid-1990s, according to one court opinion, it was believed to be the size of the Medellín Cartel during its prime. The Sinaloa Cartel was believed to be linked to the Juárez Cartel in a strategic alliance following the partnership of their rivals, the Gulf Cartel and Tijuana Cartel. Following the discovery of a tunnel system used to smuggle drugs across the Mexican/US border, the group has been associated with such means of trafficking.

By 2005, the Beltrán-Leyva brothers, who were formerly aligned with the Sinaloa Cartel, had come to dominate drug trafficking across the border with Arizona. By 2006, the Sinaloa Cartel had eliminated all competition across the 528 km of Arizona border, and it was suspected they had accomplished this by bribing state government officials. The Colima Cartel, Sonora Cartel, Milenio Cartel, Guadalajara Cartel and Sonora Cartel are now branches of the Sinaloa Cartel.

In January 2008, the cartel allegedly split into a number of warring factions, which is a major cause of the epidemic of drug violence Mexico has seen in the last year. Murders by the cartel often involve beheadings or bodies dissolved in vats of acid.

Atlanta has been used as a major U.S. distribution center and accounting hub, and the presence of the Sinaloa Cartel there has brought ruthless violence to that area.

Alliances

Since February 2010, the major cartels have aligned in two factions, one integrated by the Juárez Cartel, Tijuana Cartel, Los Zetas and the Beltrán-Leyva Cartel; the other faction integrated by the Gulf Cartel, Sinaloa Cartel and La Familia Cartel.

Allegations of collusion with Mexican federal government forces in May 2009, the U.S. National Public Radio (NPR) aired multiple reports alleging that the Mexican federal police and military were working in collusion with the Sinaloa Cartel. In particular, the report claimed the government was helping Sinaloa cartel to take control of the Juarez Valley area and destroy other cartels, especially the Juarez Cartel. NPR's reporters interviewed dozens of officials and ordinary people for the series. One report quotes a former Juarez police commander who claimed the entire department was working for the Sinaloa cartel and helping it to fight other groups. He also claimed that Sinaloa cartel had bribed the military. Also quoted was a Mexican reporter who claimed hearing numerous times from the public that the military had been involved in murders.

Another source in the story was the U.S. trial of Manuel Fierro-Mendez, an ex-Juarez police captain who admitted to working for Sinaloa cartel. He claimed that Sinaloa cartel influenced the Mexican government and military in order to gain control of the region. A U.S. Drug Enforcement Administration (DEA) agent in the same trial alleged that Fierro-Mendez had contacts with a Mexican military officer.

The report also alleged, with support from an anthropologist who studies drug trafficking, that data on the low arrest rate of Sinaloa cartel members (compared to other groups) was evidence of favoritism on the part of the authorities. A Mexican official denied the allegation of favoritism, and a DEA agent and a political scientist also had alternate explanations for the arrest data. Another report detailed numerous indications of corruption and influence that the cartel has within the Mexican government.

Battling the Tijuana Cartel

The Sinaloa Cartel has been waging a war against the Tijuana Cartel (Arellano-Félix Organization) over the Tijuana smuggling route to the border city of San Diego, California. The rivalry between the two cartels dates back to the Miguel Ángel Félix Gallardo setup of Palma's family. Félix Gallardo, following his imprisonment, bestowed the Guadalajara Cartel to his nephews in the Tijuana Cartel. On November 8, 1992 Palma struck out against the Tijuana Cartel at a disco in Puerto Vallarta, Jalisco, where eight Tijuana Cartel members were killed in the shootout, the Arellano-Félix brothers having successfully escaped from the location with the assistance of Logan Heights gangster David "D" Barron.

In retaliation, the Tijuana Cartel attempted to set up Guzmán at Guadalajara airport on May 24, 1993. In the shootout that followed, six civilians were killed by the hired gunmen from the Logan Heights, San Diego-based 30th Street gang. The deaths included that of Roman Catholic Cardinal Juan Jesús Posadas Ocampo. The church hierarchy originally believed Ocampo was targeted as revenge for his strong stance against the drug trade.

However, Mexican officials believe Ocampo just happened to be caught in cross fire. The Cardinal arrived at the airport in a white Mercury Grand Marquis town car, known to be popular amongst drug barons, making it a target. Intelligence received by Logan Heights gang leader David "D" Barron was that Guzmán would be arriving in a white Mercury Grand Marquis town car. This explanation, however, is often countered due to Ocampo having been wearing a long black cassock and large pectoral cross, as well as him sharing no similarity in appearance with Guzmán and having been gunned down from only two feet away.

Edgar Valdéz Villarreal

Edgar "La Barbie" Valdez Villarreal was a Sinaloa cartel lieutenant and the operator of its armed group known as Los Negros, formed by the Sinaloa Cartel to counter the operations of the rival Gulf Cartel's Los Zetas. Los Negros have been known to employ gangs such as the Mara Salvatrucha to carry out murders and other illegal activities. The group is involved in fighting in the Nuevo Laredo region for control of the drug trafficking corridor. Following the 2003 arrest of Gulf Cartel leader Osiel Cárdenas, it is believed the Sinaloa Cartel moved 200 men into the region to battle the Gulf Cartel for control. The Nuevo Laredo region is an important drug trafficking corridor into Laredo, Texas, where as much as 40% of all Mexican exports pass through into the U.S.

Following the 2002 assassination of journalist Roberto Javier Mora García from El Mañana newspaper, much of the local media has been cautious reporting the fighting. The cartels have pressured reporters to send messages and wage a media war. The drug war has spread to various regions of Mexico such as Guerrero, Mexico City, Michoacán, and Tamaulipas.

On 30 August 2010, Villarreal was captured by Mexican Federal Police.

El Chapo Timeline

- 1960s - Begins planting marijuana with his cousins.
- 1970s - Begins running drugs to major Mexican cities and the US border and working with major drug traffickers such as Miguel Angel Felix Gallardo, leader of the Guadalajara Cartel.
- 1980s - Member of the Guadalajara Cartel. After the arrest of Felix Gallardo, the cartel splits into factions. Guzmán becomes leader of the Sinaloa Cartel Pacific coast faction.
- February 1992 - Police find the bodies of six of Guzmán's top lieutenants dumped along Tijuana highways; the six men had been tortured and shot.
- November 1992 - Six people are gunned down at a discotheque in Puerto Vallarta by gunmen working for Guzmán, whose targets are traffickers in the Tijuana Cartel.
- May 1993 - Gunmen with the Tijuana Cartel attempt to assassinate Guzmán in retribution, firing upon a vehicle at an airport. Guzmán escapes unharmed, but Cardinal Archbishop of Guadalajara Juan Jesús Posadas Ocampa is killed accidentally, along with six others.
- June 9, 1993 - Wanted on charges of drug trafficking, murder and kidnapping, he is arrested in Guatemala and extradited to Mexico. Guzmán is subsequently sentenced to a minimum of 20 years in a maximum-security prison.
- Early 2000s - Violence across Mexico escalates as El Chapo's Sinaloa Cartel attempts to encroach upon Tijuana and Gulf Cartel territory.
- January 19, 2001 - Escapes the maximum-security Puente Grande prison in Jalisco, Mexico, in a laundry cart. The planned escape requires bribes and cooperation allegedly costing him $2.5 million, according to Malcolm Beith's book, "The Last Narco."

- 2004 - The US government announces a $5 million reward for information leading to Guzmán's arrest and conviction.
- May 2008 - Guzmán's son, Edgar, is murdered in a parking lot shootout near Culican, Mexico.
- 2009 - First appears on Forbes' billionaires list.
- 2009 - Guzmán and other cartel leaders are indicted on charges of conspiring to import more than 264,000 pounds of cocaine into the United States between 1990 and 2005.
- August 2011 - Guzmán's wife, Emma, who has dual US-Mexican citizenship, gives birth to twin girls in a hospital outside of Los Angeles.
- 2012 - The US Treasury Department uses the Foreign Narcotics Kingpin Designation Act to freeze the US assets of his relatives.
- February 22, 2014 - Guzmán is apprehended at a beach resort in Mazatlán, Mexico.
- July 11, 2015 - Escapes the maximum-security Altiplano Federal Prison near Toluca, Mexico, by crawling through an opening in the shower area of his cell block leading to a nearly mile-long tunnel.
- October 2015 - While on the run, he meets with movie star Sean Penn and Mexican actress Kate del Castillo. Penn's interview with Guzmán subsequently runs in Rolling Stone magazine. "I supply more heroin, methamphetamine, cocaine and marijuana than anybody else in the world," Guzmán is quoted in the interview. "I have a fleet of submarines, airplanes, trucks and boats."
- January 8, 2016 - Guzmán is recaptured by Mexican authorities in Los Mochis, Sinaloa, after a raid leads to a shootout in which five people connected to Guzmán are killed.
- May 9, 2016 - A judge in Mexico approves the United States' request to extradite Guzmán, who faces charges in

seven states. Once extradited, he will be sent to Brooklyn, New York, to stand trial on federal charges.

• January 19, 2017 - Mexico's Foreign Ministry turns Guzmán over to US authorities.

• January 20, 2017 - Enters a plea of not guilty at his arraignment in US District Court for the Eastern District of New York.

• November 13, 2018 - Guzmán's long-awaited criminal trial begins in a New York federal district court amid unprecedented security measures, including armed escorts for the anonymous and partly sequestered jurors, as well as heavily armed federal marshals and officers with bomb-sniffing dogs standing guard outside the courthouse.

• January 15, 2019 - Guzmán once paid a $100 million bribe to former Mexican President Enrique Peña Nieto, according to testimony given by a former close personal aide to Guzman during his trial. Peña Nieto's former chief of staff denies the allegation.

• February 12, 2019 - Guzmán is convicted of 10 counts, including engaging in a continuing criminal enterprise, conspiracy to launder narcotics proceeds, international distribution of cocaine, heroin, marijuana and other drugs, and use of firearms. He faces a mandatory life sentence without the possibility of parole for leading a continuing criminal enterprise, and a sentence of up to life imprisonment on the remaining drug counts. His attorneys say they plan to file an appeal on a number of issues.

Juárez Cartel

The Juárez Cartel (Spanish: Cártel de Juárez), also known as the Vicente Carrillo Fuentes Organization, is a Mexican drug cartel based in Ciudad Juárez, Chihuahua, Mexico, across the border from El Paso, Texas. The Juárez Cartel controls one of the primary transportation routes for billions of dollars worth of illegal drug shipments annually entering the United States from Mexico.

Drug lords from contiguous Mexican states have forged alliances in recent years creating a cartel that sometimes is referred to as 'The Golden Triangle Alliance' or 'La Alianza Triángulo de Oro' because of its three-state area of influence: Chihuahua, south of the U.S. state of Texas, Durango and Sinaloa. The Juarez Cartel is a ruthless, dangerous drug trafficking organization that has been known to decapitate their rivals and mutilate their corpses and dump them in public to instill fear not only to the general public but to local law enforcement and their rivals, the Sinaloa Cartel.

History

The cartel was founded in the 1970s by Rafael Aguilar Guajardo and handed down to Amado Carrillo Fuentes in 1993 under the tutelage of his uncle.

Amado brought his brothers in and later his son into the business. After Amado died in 1997 following complications from plastic surgery, a brief turf war erupted over the control of the cartel, where Amado's brother —Vicente Carrillo Fuentes— emerged as leader after defeating the Muñoz Talavera brothers.

Vicente Carrillo Fuentes, who still remains in control of the cartel, then formed a partnership with Juan

José Esparragoza Moreno, his brother Rodolfo Carrillo Fuentes, his nephew Vicente Carrillo Leyva,

Ricardo Garcia Urquiza, and formed an alliance with other drug lords such as Ismael "Mayo" Zambada in

Sinaloa and Baja California, the Beltrán Leyva brothers in Monterrey, and Joaquín "El Chapo" Guzmán in Nayarit, Sinaloa and Tamaulipas, according to sources in the FBI and the Mexican Attorney General's office. He also kept in service several lieutenants formally under his brother, such as "El Chacky" Hernandez.

When Vicente took control of the cartel, the organization was in flux. The death of Amado created a large power vacuum in the Mexican underworld. The Carrillo Fuentes brothers became the most powerful organization during the 1990s while Vicente was able to avoid direct conflict and increase the strength of the Juárez Cartel. The relationship between the Carrillo Fuentes clan and the other members of the organization grew unstable towards the end of the 1990s and into the 2000s.

In 2001 after Joaquín Guzmán Loera 'El Chapo' escaped from prison, many Juárez Cartel members defected to Guzmán Loera's Sinaloa Cartel. In 2004, Vicente's brother was killed allegedly by order of Guzmán Loera. Carrillo Fuentes responded by assassinating Guzmán Loera's brother in prison. This ignited a turf war between the two cartels, which was more or less put on hold from 2005-2006 because of the Sinaloa Cartel's war with the Gulf cartel.

As recently as November 2005, the Juárez Cartel was the dominant player in the center of the country, controlling a large percentage of the cocaine traffic from Mexico into the United States. The death of Amado Carrillo Fuentes in 1997, however, was the beginning of the decline of the Juárez cartel, as Carrillo relied on ties to Mexico's top-ranking drug interdiction officer, division general Jesús Gutiérrez Rebollo.

After the organization collapsed, some elements of it were absorbed into the Sinaloa Cartel, a relatively young and aggressive organization that has gobbled up much of the Juárez Cartel's former territory. The cartel has been able to either corrupt or intimidate high ranking officials in order to obtain information on law enforcement operatives and acquire protection from the police and judicial systems.

The Juárez cartel has been found in 21 Mexican states and its principal bases are Culiacán, Monterrey, Ciudad Juárez, Ojinaga, Mexico City, Guadalajara, Cuernavaca and Cancún. Vicente Carrillo Fuentes remains the leader of the cartel.

Since 2007, the Juárez Cartel has been locked in a vicious battle with its former partner, the Sinaloa Cartel, for control of Juárez. The fighting between them has left thousands of dead in Chihuahua state. The Juárez Cartel relies on two enforcement gangs to exercise control over both sides of the border: La Linea, a group of current and former Chihuahua police officers, is prevalent on the Mexican side, while the large street gang Barrio Azteca operates in Mexico and the U.S. in Texas cities such as El Paso, Dallas and Austin. as well as in New Mexico and Arizona.

On April 9, 2010, the Associated Press reported that the Sinaloa Cartel had won the Juarez turf war. Nevertheless, the Juarez Cartel has continued open confrontations with the Sinaloa Cartel and Mexican police forces. On July 15, 2010, the Juarez Cartel raised their attacks to a new level by using a car bomb to target federal police officers.

Members of the cartel were implicated in the serial murder site in Ciudad Juárez that was discovered in 2004 and has been dubbed the House of Death. The Juárez Cartel was featured battling the rival Tijuana Cartel in the 2000 motion picture Traffic. The Australian ABC documentary La Frontera (2010) described social impact of the cartel in the region.

Alliances

Since February 2010, the major cartels have aligned in two factions, one integrated by the Juárez Cartel, Tijuana Cartel,

Los Zetas and the Beltrán-Leyva Cartel; the other faction integrated by the Gulf Cartel, Sinaloa Cartel and La Familia Cartel.

Tijuana Cartel

The Tijuana Cartel (Spanish: Cártel de Tijuana or Arellano-Félix Organization) is a Mexican drug cartel based in Tijuana, Baja California. The cartel has been described as "one of the biggest and most violent criminal groups in Mexico". The Tijuana Cartel was featured battling the rival Juárez Cartel in the 2000 motion picture Traffic.

BackgroundMiguel Ángel Félix Gallardo, the founder of the Guadalajara Cartel was arrested in 1989. While incarcerated, he remained one of Mexico's major traffickers, maintaining his organization via mobile phone until he was transferred to a new maximum security prison in the 1990s. At that point, his old organization broke up into two factions: the Tijuana Cartel led by his nephews, the Arellano Félix brothers, and the Sinaloa Cartel, run by former lieutenants Héctor Luis Palma Salazar and Joaquín Guzmán Loera El Chapo.

Currently, the majority of Mexico's smuggling routes are controlled by three key cartels: Gulf, Sinaloa and Tijuana — though Tijuana is the least powerful. The Tijuana cartel was further weakened in August

2006 when its chief, Javier Arellano Félix, was arrested by the U.S. Coast Guard on a boat off the coast of Baja California. Mexican army troops also were sent to Tijuana in January 2007 in an operation to restore order to the border city and root out corrupt police officers, who mostly were cooperating with the Tijuana cartel. As a result of these efforts, the Tijuana cartel is unable to project much power outside of its base in Tijuana.

Organization

The Arellano Félix family was initially composed of seven brothers and four sisters, who inherited the organization from Miguel Ángel Félix Gallardo upon his incarceration in Mexico in 1989 for his complicity in the murder of DEA Special Agent Enrique Camarena. Although the subsequent brothers' arrest in the 1990s and 2000s are blows to the Arellano Felix cartel, it did not dismantle the organization which currently is led by the Arellano's nephew, Luis Fernando Sánchez Arellano.

The Tijuana Cartel has infiltrated the Mexican law enforcement and judicial systems and is directly involved in street-level trafficking within the United States. This criminal organization is responsible for the transportation, importation, and distribution of multi-ton quantities of cocaine and marijuana, as well as large quantities of heroin and methamphetamine.

The organization has a reputation for extreme violence. Ramón Arellano Félix ordered a hit which resulted in the mass murder of 18 people in Ensenada, Baja California, on September 17, 1998. Ramón was eventually killed in a gun battle with police at Mazatlán Sinaloa, on February 10, 2002.

The Arellano Félix family has seven brothers:

- Francisco Rafael Arellano Félix (born 24 October 1949) - Captured and released.
- Benjamín Arellano Félix (born 3 December 1952) – Captured.
- Carlos Arellano Félix (born 20 August 1955) - is not currently wanted.
- Eduardo Arellano Félix (born 11 October 1956), - Captured on October 26, 2008.
- Ramón Eduardo Arellano Félix (born 31 August 1964) - Deceased, shot by police in 2002.
- Luis Fernando Arellano Félix (believed to be born 26 January 1966) is not currently wanted.
- Francisco Javier Arellano Félix (born 11 December 1969) - Captured

They also have four sisters, where Alicia and Enedina are most active in the cartel's affairs. The family inherited the organization from Miguel Ángel Félix Gallardo upon his incarceration. Eduardo Arellano Félix was captured by the Mexican Army after a shootout in Tijuana, Baja California, on October 26, 2008; he had been the last of the Arellano Félix brothers at large. According to a Mexican official, Enedina's son, Luis Fernando Sánchez Arellano, has taken over the cartel's operations. His two top lieutenants are Armando Villareal Heredia and Edgardo Leyva Escandon.

Activities

The Tijuana cartel is present in at least 15 Mexican states with important areas of operation in Tijuana,

Mexicali, Tecate, and Ensenada in Baja California, in parts of Sinaloa and Zacatecas. After the death in 1997 of the Juárez Cartel's Amado Carrillo Fuentes, the Tijuana Cartel attempted to gain a foothold in Sonora. The Oaxaca Cartel reportedly joined forces with the Tijuana Cartel in 2003.

Fourteen Mexican drug gang members were killed and eight others were injured in a gun battle in Tijuana near the U.S. border on Saturday, April 26, 2008 that was one of the bloodiest shootouts in the narco-war between the Tijuana Cartel and the Sinaloa Cartel.

Captures and trial

In October 1997, a retired U.S. Air Force C-130A that was sold to the airline Aeropostal Cargo de México was seized by Mexican federal officials, who alleged that the aircraft had been used to haul drugs for the cartel up from Central and South America, as well as around the Mexican interior. Investigators had linked the airline's owner, Jesús Villegas Covallos, to Ramón Arellano Félix.

On August 14, 2006, Francisco Javier Arellano Félix was apprehended by the United States Coast Guard off the coast of Baja California Sur.

Alliances

Since February 2010, the major cartels have aligned in two factions, one integrated by the Juárez Cartel, Tijuana Cartel, Los Zetas and the Beltrán-Leyva Cartel; the other faction integrated by the Gulf Cartel, Sinaloa Cartel and La Familia Cartel.

Los Zetas Cartel

Los Zetas Cartel is a criminal organization in Mexico dedicated mostly to international illegal drug trade, assassinations, and other organized crime activities. This drug cartel was founded by a small group of Mexican Army Special Forces deserters and now includes corrupt former federal, state, and local police officers, as well as ex-Kaibiles from Guatemala.

This group of highly trained gunmen was first hired as a private mercenary army for Mexico's Gulf Cartel. After the arrest of the Gulf Cartel's leader, Osiel Cárdenas Guillen, as well as other events, the two entities became a combined trafficking force, with the Zetas taking a more active leadership role in drug trafficking. Since February 2010 Los Zetas have gone independent and became enemies of its former employer/partner, the Gulf Cartel.

Los Zetas are led by Heriberto "El Lazca" Lazcano and are considered by the Drug Enforcement Administration (DEA) as probably being the most violent paramilitary enforcement group in Mexico. Los Zetas have expanded their operations to Italy with the 'Ndrangheta.

Etymology

The group's name Los Zetas is given after its first leader, Lieutenant Arturo Guzmán Decena, whose

Federal Judicial Police radio code was "Z1", a code given to high-ranking officers. The radio code for

Commanding Federal Judicial Police Officers in México was "Y" and are nicknamed Yankees, for Federal

Judicial Police in charge of a city the radio code was "Z," and thus they were nicknamed as the letter in Spanish, "Zetas."

Los Zetas posting a recruiting poster for military or former military

History

In the late 1990s, the Gulf Cartel leader, Osiel Cárdenas Guillen, wanted to track down and kill rival cartel members as a form of protection. He began to recruit former Mexican Army's elite Grupo Aeromóvil de Fuerzas Especiales (GAFE) soldiers. It is argued that they received some of their specialized military training in counter-insurgency and locating and apprehending drug cartel members at the military School of the Americas in the United States, in Fort Benning, Georgia and by other foreign specialists of the United States, France and Israel.

They were trained in rapid deployment, aerial assaults, marksmanship, ambushes, small-group tactics, intelligence collection, counter-surveillance techniques, prisoner rescues and sophisticated communications. Military forces from around the world train at Fort Bragg, so there is nothing unique about Mexican operatives learning counter-insurgency tactics at the facility.

Cardenas Guillen's top recruit, lieutenant Arturo Guzmán Decena, brought with him approximately 30 other GAFE deserters enticed by salaries substantially higher than those paid by the Mexican government. The role of Los Zetas was soon expanded, collecting debts, securing cocaine supply and trafficking routes known as plazas (zones) and executing its foes, often with grotesque savagery.

Guzmán Decena (Z1) was killed by a rival cartel member on November 2002 in a restaurant, while he was dining, so Heriberto Lazcano (Z3) ascended to the leadership of the paramilitaries.

In response to such aggressive efforts on the part of the Zetas to defend and control its smuggling corridors to the United States, the rival Sinaloa Cartel established its own heavily armed enforcer gang, Los Negros. The group operated in a similar fashion to the Zetas, but with less complexity.

Upon the arrest of Gulf Cartel boss Osiel Cardenas Guillen in 2003, Los Zetas negotiated a collaboration pact with the Gulf Cartel and the Beltrán-Leyva Cartel to engage in their own drug shipments.

In February 2010, Los Zetas (and its ally, the Beltran Leyva Cartel) engaged in a violent turf war against its former employer/partner, the Gulf Cartel, in the border city of Reynosa, Tamaulipas, turning some border towns to "ghost towns". It was reported that a Gulf Cartel member killed a top Zeta lieutenant named Victor Mendoza. The Zetas demanded that the Gulf cartel turn over the killer. However, the Gulf Cartel refused and an all-out war has broken out between the two criminal organizations.

Alliances

Since February 2010, the major cartels have aligned in two factions, one integrated by the Juárez Cartel, Tijuana Cartel, Los Zetas and the Beltrán-Leyva Cartel; the other faction integrated by the Gulf Cartel, Sinaloa Cartel and La Familia Cartel.

Organization structure

Los Zetas have set up camps to train recruits as well as corrupt ex-federal, state, and local police officers. In September 2005, testimony to the Mexican Congress, then-Defense Secretary Clemente Vega indicated that the Zetas had also hired at least 30 former Kaibiles from Guatemala to train new recruits because the number of former Mexican special forces men in their ranks had shrunk. Los Zetas' training locations have been identified as containing the same items and setup as GAFE training facilities.

Los Zetas are primarily based in the border region of Nuevo Laredo, with hundreds more throughout the country. In Nuevo Laredo it is believed they have carved the city into territories, placing lookouts at arrival destinations such as airports, bus stations and main roads. In addition to conducting activities along the border, they are visible throughout the Gulf Coast region, in the Southern states of Tabasco,

Yucatan, Quintana Roo, and Chiapas, and in the Pacific Coast states of Guerrero, Oaxaca, and

Michoacán, as well as in Mexico City. Evidence also indicates that they may be active in Texas, other U.S. states and in Italy with the 'Ndrangheta.

The 30 original Zetas were former Mexican elite military soldiers that deserted to join the Gulf Cartel to form the para-military group known as Los Zetas.

Some of the original members were:

- Arturo Guzmán Decena (Z-1).
- Jesús Enrique Rejón Aguilar (Z-2).
- Heriberto Lazcano (Z-3)
- Carlos Vera Calva (Z-7).
- Galdindo Mellado Cruz (Z-9)
- Flavio Méndez Santiago (Z-10)
- Jaime González Durán,
- Rogelio González Pizaña
- Efraín Teodoro Torres
- Raúl Hernandez Barrón
- Óscar Guerrero Silva
- Luís Alberto Guerrero Reyes
- Mateo Díaz López
- Jorge López
- Daniel Peréz Rojas
- Sergio Enrique Ruiz Tlapanco
- Nabor Vargas García
- Ernesto Zatarín Beliz
- Eduardo Estrada González
- Prisciliano Ibarra Yepis

- Rogelio Guerra Ramírez
- Miguel Ángel Soto Parra
- Gonzalo Ceresano Escribano
- Daniel Enrique Márquez Aguilar
- Germán Torres Jiménez.

Over time, many of the original 30 have been killed or arrested, and a number of younger men have filled the vacant vacuum, forming something that resembles what Los Zetas used to be, but still far from the efficiency of the original Zetas.

Law enforcement raids

Following a joint investigation, titled Operation Black Jack, by the ATF, DEA, ICE and the United States Department of Homeland Security (DHS) through the FBI, two Zeta safe houses were identified and raided, recovering more than 40 kidnapped individuals.

On October 26, 2008, the Washington Times reported of an FBI warning that Los Zetas' cell in Texas were to engage law enforcement with a full tactical response should law enforcement attempt to intervene in their operations; their cell leader was identified as Jaime González Durán (The Hummer), who was later arrested on November 7, 2008, in the border city Reynosa, Tamaulipas. In this operation, three safehouses in Reynosa were raided by elements of the Mexican Federal Police and Mexican Army, yielding the largest weapon seizure in the history of Mexico; it included 540 rifles including 288 assault rifles and several .50-caliber rifles, 287 hand grenades, 2 M72 LAW anti-tank weapons, 500,000 rounds of ammunition, 67 ballistic vests and 14 sticks of dynamite.

In February 2009, Texas Governor Rick Perry announced a program called "Operation Border Star Contingency Plan" to safeguard the border if Zetas carry out their threats to attack U.S. safety officers. This project includes the use of tanks, airplanes and the National Guard "as a preventive measure upon the possible collapse of the Mexican State" to protect the border from the attack of the Zetas and receive an eventual exodus of Mexicans fleeing from the violence.

Gulf Cartel

The Gulf Cartel (Spanish: Cartel del Golfo) is a Mexican drug cartel based in Matamoros, Tamaulipas. The cartel is present in 13 states with important areas of operation in the cities of Nuevo Laredo, Miguel Alemán, Reynosa and Matamoros in the northern state of Tamaulipas; it also has important operations in the states of Nuevo León and in Michoacán. The Gulf Cartel traffics cocaine, marijuana, methamphetamine and heroin across the U.S.-Mexico border to major cities in the United States. The group is known for its violent methods and intimidation.

Aside from earning money from the sales of narcotics, the cartel also imposes "taxes" on anyone passing narcotics or aliens through Gulf Cartel territory. The cartel is also known to operate protection rackets, extorting money from local businesses and to kidnap for ransom money.

History

Foundation, 1970s – 1996 The Gulf Cartel was founded by Juan Nepomuceno Guerra in the 1970s. Nepomuceno Guerra was a notorious Mexican bootlegger who smuggled whiskey into the United States in the 1930s along the Gulf of Mexico. In the 1970s, he became politically active and began smuggling more contraband into the United States, including marijuana and heroin produced in Mexico. His nephew, Juan García Abrego, was born in a ranch called "La Puerta" in Matamoros, Tamaulipas.

He began slowly taking over day-to-day operations of what was now being called the Gulf Cartel. García Abrego expanded the business to include the more lucrative cocaine trade throughout the 1980s and 1990s, all with the assistance of the political connections that his uncle had fostered. Juan García Abrego became so powerful that he was placed on the FBI Ten Most Wanted

Fugitives in 1995. He was the first drug trafficker to ever be placed on that list. García Abrego was captured in 1996 and extradited to the United States. He is currently serving eleven life terms in a maximum security federal prison in Colorado, U.S.

Arrest of Abrego

Following Abrego's 1996 arrest by Mexican authorities and subsequent deportation to the United States, he was replaced by Oscar Malherbe De León, until his arrest a short time later, causing several cartel lieutenants to fight for the leadership. The next in line was Sergio "El Checko" Gomez, however, his leadership was short lived when he was assassinated in April 1996 by Salvador "Chava" Gómez. After this, Osiel Cárdenas Guillén took control of the Gulf Cartel in July 1999 after assassinating Salvador Gómez.

In 1999, Cárdenas learned that a Gulf Cartel informant was being transported through Matamoros, Tamaulipas, by the FBI and DEA. Cárdenas and his men intercepted and surrounded the vehicle on a public street and demanded the informant be released to him. The FBI and DEA agents refused to turn over their informant, and after a tense standoff they were released. As for Cárdenas, the damage had been done by taking on the U.S. government, which placed pressure on the Mexican government to apprehend Cárdenas. Cárdenas was arrested during a gun battle in Matamoros in March 2003 and sent to the Penal del Altiplano (formerly known as "La Palma"), a federal high security prison.

Since the arrest of Cárdenas Guillen, his two partners - Antonio Ezequiel Cardenas Guillen and Jorge Eduardo Costilla Sánchez- took control of the cartel, with the militant wing —Los Zetas— taking a leadership role; the two groups worked together for a few years, but Los Zetas no longer taking orders from Gulf Cartel.

Since the extradition of Cárdenas Guillen to the U.S., Los Zetas gradually took more control from the Gulf cartel and eventually broke away, formed their own cartel and made an alliance with the BeltránLeyva Cartel.

On September 17, 2008, United States Attorney General Michael Mukasey announced that 175 alleged Gulf cartel members were arrested in a crackdown on the cartel in the U.S. and in Italy.

In February 2010, Los Zetas engaged in a violent turf war against his former employer/partner, the Gulf Cartel, in the border city of Reynosa, Tamaulipas, rendering some border towns into "ghost towns".

Alliances

Alliances or agreements between drug cartels have been shown to be fragile, tense and temporary. In 2003, the Gulf Cartel joined in a temporary alliance with the remnants of the Arellano Félix Organization, also known as the Tijuana Cartel, based out of the state of Baja California. This was based primarily on prison negotiations between top leaders such as Benjamín Arellano Félix and Osiel Cárdenas. After a personal dispute between leaders, however, Osiel Cárdenas ordered Benjamín Arellano Félix beaten, and all alliances ceased at that point. It is reported that after the fallout, Cárdenas ordered the Zetas to Baja California to wipe out the Tijuana Cartel.

Since February 2010, the major cartels have aligned in two factions, one integrated by the Juárez Cartel, Tijuana Cartel, Los Zetas and the Beltrán-Leyva Cartel; the other faction integrated by the Gulf Cartel, Sinaloa Cartel and La Familia Cartel.

On November 5, 2010 Antonio Ezequiel Cardenas Guillen was gunned down by the Mexican Army in the earlier hours of the day leaving Jorge Eduardo Costilla Sánchez in charge of the Gulf Cartel.

Structure

On January 20, 2007 and after the extradition of Osiel Cárdenas Guillen to the U.S., the Gulf Cartel's leadership evolved into one with a decentralized structure, with two drug lords sharing control of the cartel: Jorge Eduardo Costilla Sánchez (a.k.a: El Coss) who maintains close contacts with Colombian narcotics suppliers, and Antonio Ezequiel Cárdenas Guillen, who was killed by the Mexican military on November 5, 2010 in the city of Matamoros, across the border from Brownsville in Texas.

The decentralized structure of the cartel differentiates it from other cartels, in that power is shared equally among a set of gatekeepers (plaza heads), each of whom is responsible for running different trafficking routes. Each gatekeeper is also responsible for security and the collection of 'taxes' for each plaza they are responsible for.

Transportation

According to the book "Drug Wars: Narco Warfare in the 21st Century" by Gary Fleming, there are many ways in which drugs enter the United States. Due to the Gulf Cartel's large amount of territory, the cartels utilize every way possible to get drugs into the United States. One avenue that they have implemented is to construct tunnels to get their product across the border.

By constructing a tunnel, the cartel is able to get their product across the border with minimal to no detection. The advantages of having a tunnel are tremendous, not only can they charge for smuggling illegal aliens but they can also use this for human trafficking as carriers of cartels. Each human can carry up to half a million dollars worth of drugs.

Another venture the cartels utilize are the many bus routes across the United States. With each instance of human trafficking, they can have people carry the product with them on a bus and deliver it to its destination. Main hubs for these bus routes include but are not limited to Los Angeles,

Chicago, Denver, and Dallas. The buses are a vital asset to the cartels because they often go without detection from devices or X-ray machines. The major highways accessed are I35 and I25 which are central highways for the drug trade. The cartel also implements the use of the train system to ship large quantities of illegal drugs.

A narco submarine seized in Ecuador on July 2010. Apart from using these common ways, once the product is across the border, common cars and trucks are utilized for faster distribution in different cities. In an effort to use the seas, the cartel also implemented the use of narco submarines.

Indictments

On July 21, 2009, the United States DEA announced coordinated actions against the Gulf Cartel and Los

Zetas drug trafficking organizations. Antonio Ezequiel Cárdenas Guillen, Jorge Eduardo Costilla Sánchez,

Heriberto Lazcano Lazcano and 15 of their top lieutenants, have been charged in U.S. federal courts with drug trafficking-related crimes, while the U.S. State Department announced rewards totaling $50 million USD for information leading to their capture.

La Familia Michoacana

La Familia Michoacana (English: The Michoacan Family) or La Familia (English: The Family) is a Mexican drug cartel and an organized crime syndicate based in the Mexican state of Michoacán. Formerly allied to the Gulf Cartel—as part of Los Zetas—it has split off as its own organization since 2006.

The cartel's recently deceased leader, Nazario Moreno González, known as El Más Loco (English: The Craziest One), preached his organization's divine right to eliminate enemies. He carried a "bible" of his own sayings and insisted that his army of traffickers and hitmen avoid using the narcotics they sell. Nazario Moreno's partners are José de Jesús Méndez Vargas, Servando Gómez Martínez and Dionicio Loya Plancarte, each of whom has a bounty of $2 million for his capture.

On July 2009 and on November 2010, La Familia Michoacana offered to retreat and even disband their cartel, "With the condition that both the Federal Government, and State and Federal Police commit to safeguarding the security of the state of Michoacán." However, President Felipe Calderón's government refuses to strike a deal with the cartel and rejected their calls for dialogue.

Background

Mexican analysts believe that La Familia formed in the 1980s with the stated purpose of bringing order to Michoacán, emphasizing help and protection for the poor. In its initial incarnation, La Familia formed as a group of vigilantes, spurred to power to counter interloping kidnappers and drug dealers, who were their stated enemies. Since then, La Familia has capitalized on its reputation, building its myth, power and reach to transition into a criminal gang itself.

La Familia emerged to the foreground in the 1990s as the Gulf Cartel's paramilitary group designed to seize control of the illegal drug trade in Michoacán state from rival drug cartels. Trained with Los Zetas, in 2006 the group splintered off into an independent drug trafficking operation. La Familia has a strong rivalry with both Los Zetas and the Beltrán-Leyva Cartel, but strong ties with the Sinaloa Cartel of Joaquin Guzman. La Familia Michoacana is one of the strongest and fastest growing cartel in Mexico.

References to religion

La Familia cartel is sometimes described as quasi-religious since its leaders, Moreno González and Méndez Vargas, refer to their assassinations and beheadings as "divine justice" and that they may have direct or indirect ties with devotees of the New Jerusalem religious movement, which is noted for its concern for justice issues.

La Familia's boss and spiritual leader Nazario Moreno González, (a.k.a.: El Más Loco or The Craziest One) has published his own 'bible', and a copy seized by Mexican federal agents reveals an ideology that mixes evangelical-style self help with insurgent peasant slogans. Moreno González, who was killed on 9 December 2010, seems to have based most of his doctrine on a work by Christian writer John Eldredge, using their own understanding of the idea in Eldredge's message that every man must have "a battle to fight, a beauty to rescue and an adventure to live."

The Mexican justice department stated in a report that Gonzalez Moreno has made Eldredge's book Salvaje de Corazón (Wild at Heart) required reading for La Familia gang members and has paid rural teachers and National Development Education (CONAFE) to circulate Eldredge's writings throughout the Michoacán countryside.

La Familia cartel emphasize religion and family values during recruitment and has placed banners in areas of operations claiming that it does not tolerate substance abuse or exploitation of women and children. According to Mexico

Public Safety Secretary Genaro Garcia Luna, it recruits members from drug rehabilitation clinics by helping addicts recover and then forcing them into service for the drug cartel or be killed. Advancement within the organization depends as much on regular attendance at prayer meetings as on target practice. The cartel gives loans to farmers, businesses, schools and churches, and it advertises its benevolence in local newspapers in order to gain social support.

On July 16, 2009, a man by the name of Servando Gómez Martínez (La Tuta) identified himself as the 'chief of operations' of the cartel when he contacted a local radio station. In his radio message, Gómez stated: "La Familia was created to look after the interests of our people and our family. We are a necessary evil," and when asked what La Familia really wanted, Gómez replied, "The only thing we want is peace and tranquility." President Felipe Calderón's government refuses to strike a deal with the cartel and rejected their calls for dialogue.

On April 20, 2009, about 400 Federal Police agents raided a christening party for a baby born to a cartel member. Among the 44 detained was Rafael Cedeño Hernández (El Cede), the gang's second in command and in charge of indoctrinating the new recruits in the cartel's religious values, morals and ethics.

Alliances

Since February 2010, the major cartels have aligned in two factions, one made up of the Juárez Cartel, Tijuana Cartel, Los Zetas and the Beltrán-Leyva Cartel; the other faction made up of the Gulf Cartel, Sinaloa Cartel and La Familia Michoacana, these last three now known as Carteles Unidos.

Operations

La Familia has been known to be unusually violent. Its members use murder and torture to quash rivals, while building a social base in the Mexican state of Michoacán. It is the fastest-growing cartel in the country's drug war and is a religious cult-like group that celebrates family values. In one incident in Uruapan in 2006, the cartel members tossed five decapitated heads onto the dance floor of the Sol y Sombra night club along with a message that read: "The Family doesn't kill for money. It doesn't kill women. It doesn't kill innocent people, only those who deserve to die. Know that this is divine justice."

The cartel has moved from smuggling and selling drugs and turned itself into a much more ambitious criminal organization which acts as a parallel state in much of Michoacán. It extorts "taxes" from businesses, pays for community projects, controls petty crime, and settles some local disputes. Despite its short history, it has emerged as Mexico's largest supplier of methamphetamines to the United States, with supply channels running deep into the Midwestern United States, and has increasingly become involved in the distribution of cocaine, marijuana, and other narcotics.

Michael Braun, former DEA chief of operations, states that it operates "superlabs" in Mexico capable of producing up to 100 pounds of meth in eight hours. However, according to DEA officials, it claims to oppose the sale of drugs to Mexicans. It also sells pirated DVDs, smuggles people to the United States, and runs a debt-collecting service by kidnapping defaulters. Because often times they use fake and sometimes original uniforms of several police agencies, most of their kidnap victims are stopped under false pretenses of routine inspections or report of stolen vehicles, and then taken hostage.

La Familia has also bought some local politicians. 20 municipal officials have been murdered in

Michoacán, including two mayors. Having established its authority, it then names local police chiefs. On May 2009, the

Mexican Federal Police detained 10 mayors of Michoacán and 20 other local officials suspected of being associated with the cartel.

On July 11, 2009, a cartel lieutenant— Arnoldo Rueda Medina —was arrested; La Familia members attacked the Federal Police station in Morelia to try to gain freedom for Rueda shortly after his arrest. During the attacks, two soldiers and three federal policemen were killed. When that failed, cartel members attacked Federal Police installations in at least a half-dozen Michoacán cities in retribution.

Three days later, on July 14, 2009, the cartel tortured and murdered twelve Mexican Federal Police agents and dumped their bodies along the side of a mountain highway along with a written message: "So that you come for another. We will be waiting for you here." The federal agents were investigating crime in Michoacán state; President Calderón, responded to the violence by dispatching additional 1,000 Federal Police officers to the area. The infusion, which more than tripled the number of Federal Police officers patrolling Michoacán, angered Michoacán Governor Leonel Godoy Rangel, who called it 'an occupation' and said he had not been consulted. Days later, 10 municipal police officers were arrested in connection with the slayings of the 12 federal agents.

The governor's half-brother Julio César Godoy Toscano, who was just elected July 5, 2009, to the lower house of Congress, was accused to be a top-ranking member of La Familia Michoacana drug cartel and of providing political protection for the cartel. Based on these charges, on 14 December 2010, Godoy Toscano was impeached from the lower house of Congress and therefore no longer enjoys immunity (Spanish: fuero).

President Calderón stated that the country's drug cartels had grown so powerful that they now posed a threat to the future of Mexican democracy. His strategy of direct confrontation and law enforcement is not popular with some segments of Mexican society, where battling violent drug gangs has brought out several human rights charges against the Mexican military.

Project Coronado

On October 22, 2009, U.S. federal authorities announced the results of a four-year investigation into the operations of La Familia Michoacana in the United States dubbed Project Coronado. It was the largest U.S. raid ever against Mexican drug cartels operating in the U.S. In 19 different states, 303 individuals were taken into custody in a coordinated effort by local, state, and federal law enforcement over a two day period. Seized during the arresting phase was over 62 kilograms (140 lb) of cocaine, 330 kilograms (730 lb.) of methamphetamine, 440 kilograms (970 lb) of marijuana, 144 weapons, 109 vehicles, and two clandestine drug laboratories.

Since the start of "Project Coronado", the investigation has led to the arrest of more than 1,186 people and the seizure of approximately $33 million. Overall, almost 2 metric tons (2.2 short tons) of cocaine, 1,240 kilograms (2,700 lb) of methamphetamine, 13 kilograms (29 lb) of heroin, 7,430 kilograms (16,400 lb) of marijuana, 389 weapons, 269 vehicles, and the two drug labs were seized.

"Multi-agency investigations such as Project Coronado are the key to disrupting the operations of complex criminal organizations like La Familia. Together—with the strong collaboration of our international, federal, state, and local partners—we have dealt a substantial blow to a group that has polluted our neighborhoods with illicit drugs and has terrorized Mexico with unimaginable violence", said FBI Director Mueller.

The investigative efforts in Project Coronado were coordinated by the multi-agency Special Operations

Division, comprising agents and analysts from the DEA, FBI, U.S. Immigration and Customs Enforcement, Internal Revenue Service, U.S. Customs and Border Protection, U.S. Marshals Service and ATF, as well as attorneys from the Criminal Division's Narcotic and Dangerous Drug Section. More than 300 federal, state, local and foreign law enforcement agencies contributed investigative and prosecutorial resources to Project Coronado through OCDETF.

Knights Templar - Caballeros Templarios

Crusaders of Meth: Mexico's Deadly Knights Templar

The Knights Templar cartel (Spanish: Caballeros Templarios) is a Mexican criminal organization and an offshoot of the La Familia Michoacana drug cartel based in the Mexican state of Michoacán.

Various objects seized by the police in the Mexican state of Michoacan, revealed that the mysterious 'Knights Templar" drug cartel is more bizarre than most people imagine.

There were four hooded tunics, with a red cross, a metal helmet, and a pamphlet or Templar rule book. This drug cartel claims to draw inspiration from the medieval Christian warriors who fought to protect Jerusalem and the Holy Grail.

The rules in the modern day 'templar bible' call for observance of 'gentleman' like behavior and respect for women – but also state that any disclosure of knights templar activities will result in the death of the person and his whole family, and confiscation by the cartel of the snitch's property.

The cartel is like a secret society.

After the death of Nazario Moreno González, leader of the La Familia Michoacana cartel, the other cartel co-founders, Enrique Plancarte Solís and Servando Gómez Martínez, formed an offshoot of La Familia calling itself Caballeros Templarios (or Knights Templar). Dionicio Loya Plancarte would also join.

The Knights were purportedly headed by an old lieutenant of Moreno's, Servando Gómez (now arrested), a former schoolteacher from Michoacán's rugged hills, where meth labs abound like hillbilly stills. Mexican police files show that both Moreno and Gómez converted to Evangelical Christianity when they were migrants in the U.S. in the 1990s. Returning to Mexico, they found that religious discipline was a useful tool to keep criminal troops in line.

Like La Familia, the Knights claim to be pious and patriotic protectors of the Michoacán community even as they traffic and murder. When they first announced themselves last spring, they hung more than 40 narcomanteles, or drug-cartel banners, across the state with a message promising security. "Our commitment is to safeguard order, avoid robberies, kidnapping, extortion, and to shield the state from rival organizations," they said. A week later, their first victim was hanged from an overpass with a note claiming that he was a kidnapper.

The Mexican Templars have an initiation ritual, which apparently includes dressing up like knights from the Middle Ages, and performing blood pacts.

The cartel recruits drug users and enrolls them in the organization's rehabilitation centers; the process is closely monitored and has a strong religious component.

The double standard is striking: the Templars cannot take drugs, and yet they run one of the biggest methamphetamines traffic corridors to the United States.

The Knights Templar appear to be successfully usurping La Familia's turf. As a result, Mexican army and police commanders have promised to take the new group down with the same energy they summoned to destroy La Familia. But it's unlikely that the Knights will go quietly due to the cartel's structure, wealth, and size. It is perhaps the second most notorious Mexican cartel in terms of killing methods, the most vicious one, the 'Zetas', is a group formed by Mexican army special forces in the 90s.

The cartel's armed wing is called La Resistencia. The Knights Templar cartel indoctrinate its operatives to "fight and die" for what they call "social justice".

Beltrán-Leyva Cartel

The Beltrán-Leyva Cartel (Spanish: Cártel de los Beltrán Leyva) is a Mexican drug cartel and organized crime syndicate founded by the four Beltrán Leyva brothers: Marcos Arturo, Carlos, Alfredo and Héctor.

The cartel is responsible for cocaine transportation and wholesaling, marijuana production and wholesaling, and heroin production and wholesaling, controls numerous drug trafficking corridors, and engages in human smuggling, money laundering, extortion, kidnapping, murder and gun-running. The Beltrán Leyva brothers, who were formerly aligned with the Sinaloa Cartel, are now allies of Los Zetas.

History

Born in the Sinaloan countryside in the 1960s, the Beltrán Leyva brothers – Marcos Arturo, Carlos, Alfredo and Héctor – worked closely with Joaquín "El Chapo" Guzmán, the leader of the Sinaloa Cartel, during decades of smuggling. Sensing a void in the rival Gulf Cartel after Osiel Cárdenas' arrest on March 14, 2003, the Sinaloa Cartel began to move into Gulf Cartel territory. Both gangs have been battling each other in northern Mexican cities since then, resulting in the deaths of hundreds of people including civilians, police and journalists. About 90% of the deaths are of drug traffickers.

In 2004 and 2005, Arturo Beltrán Leyva led powerful groups of assassins to fight for trade routes in northeastern Mexico for the Sinaloa Cartel. Through the use of corruption or intimidation, the Beltrán Leyva Cartel has been able to infiltrate Mexico's political, judicial and police institutions to feed classified information about anti-drug operations, and has even infiltrated the Interpol office in Mexico.

Switch of alliances

The arrest of Alfredo Beltrán Leyva (a.k.a.: El Mochomo) on January 20, 2008, was a huge blow to the Sinaloa Cartel, as he allegedly oversaw large-scale drug-smuggling operations and was a key money launderer for the cartel. In apparent revenge for the arrest of his brother Alfredo, Arturo ordered the assassination of the commissioner of the Federal Police, Édgar Eusebio Millán Gómez, and other top federal officials in the Mexican capital.[One group of these hit men was captured in a Mexico City house with dozens of assault rifles, pistols, grenade launchers, 30 hand grenades, and bullet-proof jackets bearing the legend FEDA — the Spanish acronym for 'Special Forces of Arturo'. Apparently, the Beltrán Leyva brothers blamed their boss Joaquin "Chapo" Guzmán for their brother's arrest, and ordered the assassination of Guzmán's son, 22 year old Édgar Guzmán López, which was carried out in a shopping center parking lot by at least 15 gunmen using assault rifles and grenade launchers.

The residual impact of Alfredo's arrest not only undermined long-term Sinaloa alliances, but resurrected animosities between rival cartel leaders Joaquin "El Chapo" Guzmán and Arturo's new allies, the Juárez Cartel, and provided the catalyst behind the bloodshed in Mexico's most-violent city: Ciudad Juárez. The Beltrán Leyva brothers, and those loyalists who departed the Sinaloa Cartel with them, have allied with Los Zetas, causing an escalation of conflict in strongholds shared uneasily by "old" Sinaloa leaders.

In February 2010, the Beltrán-Leyva Cartel and los Zetas engaged in a violent turf war against the new alliance integrated by the Gulf Cartel, Sinaloa Cartel and La Familia Cartel in the border city of Reynosa, Tamaulipas, rendering some border towns "ghost towns".

Official reports from early 2010 mention a current infighting for the control of the cartel and its territory. One faction is led by Liuetenants Édgar Valdez Villarreal and Gerardo Alvarez-Vazquez, while the other is led by Héctor Beltrán Leyva and his lieutenant Sergio Villarreal Barragán.

On April 2010 Héctor Beltrán Leyva created a cartel cell or branch in Morelos state named Cartel del Pacífico Sur (English: South Pacific Cartel) best known for having employed a 12-year-old gunman and executioner.

Since February 2010, the major cartels have aligned in two factions, one integrated by the Juárez Cartel, Tijuana Cartel, Los Zetas and the Beltrán-Leyva Cartel; the other faction integrated by the Gulf Cartel, Sinaloa Cartel and La Familia Cartel.

Assets

The cartel's assets include:

Dominance over drug and other illegal activities at airports in Mexico, Monterrey, Toluca, Cancún, and Acapulco;

Hotels and restaurants, constructed to launder money, in Cancún, Acapulco, Cozumel, and other resorts;

A working agreement with Los Zetas.

Supply corridors for moving marijuana, heroin, and methamphetamine from the Andes to the Arctic;

Capability to extort, launder money, run guns, smuggle humans, promote prostitution, and carry out kidnappings;

Operations in Mexico City, Chiapas, Guerrero Mexico State, Morelos, Nuevo León, Querétaro, Quintana Roo, Sinaloa, Sonora, and Tamaulipas, as well as in the United States and Canada;

Access to some high-ranking public figures and Army personnel whom they have bribed or intimidated.

Suppliers

The Beltrán Leyva brothers' Colombian cocaine supplier, Ever Villafane Martínez, was arrested in Morelos in August 2008. Since then, the organization has pursued a relationship with Víctor and Darío Espinoza Valencia of Colombia's Norte del Valle cartel.

Bounty

The United States is offering a US$5 million reward for information leading to the arrest and/or conviction of Héctor Beltrán Leyva, who now leads the drug cartel.

Captures

Alfredo Beltrán Leyva was captured on January 20, 2008, Arturo was killed by Mexican Marines in a shoot-out on December 16, 2009. Carlos Beltrán Leyva was captured by the Mexican Federal Police on December 30, 2009, in Culiacán, Sinaloa after showing authorities a fake driver's license. On April 22, 2010, a cartel lieutenant Gerardo Alvarez-Vazquez was captured on the outskirts of Mexico City; the U.S. had been offering a $2 million U.S. bounty for his arrest. Hector's rival, Edgar Valdez Villarreal, was arrested on August 30, 2010 outside Mexico City. On September 12, 2010 Sergio Villarreal Barragán was arrested in the city of Puebla, east of Mexico City. Héctor Beltrán Leyva, is still at large and considered to be the leader of what remains of the cartel (Arrested).

Narco Terms

Ajuste de cuentas (m): Settling a score. Getting even. Revenge. alt. ajusticimiento

ATF: Agency of Department of Justice— the Bureau of Alcohol, Tobacco, Firearms and Explosives.

Aztecas (los): Barrio Azteca. Narcomenudistas working for Juárez cartel. A steet gang with strong ties to El Paso and Ciudad Juarez. Controlled by La Linea.

Beltran Leyvas: brothers and childhood friends of Joaquin Guzman. Broke with him after the arrest of El Mochomo Beltran Leyva and engaged in a bloody dispute for territory. Relocated to Nuevo Leon in aftermath.

CT: Caballeros Templarios

Cartel: 9 organizations in Mexico are the Golfo, Sinaloa, Tijuana, Juarez, Beltran-Leyva, AmezcuaContreras, Los Zetas, Diaz-Parada, & La Familia Michoacana, Caballeros Templarios.

Cartel del Poniente: A place of the Sinaloa cartel usually found in Durango and Gomez Palacios C.D.G.: Gulf Drug Cartel

CECJUDE: Centro de Ejecución de las Consecuencias Jurídicas del Delito.

Chapos or Chaparrines: The troops of Joaquin Guzmán Loera's Sinaloa Cartel. Derived from Guzmán's nick name of "El Chapo."

Charoliar: Pretending to belong to a cartel and having a lot of inside knowledge of cartel activities.

CNDH: Comisión Nacional de los Derechos Humanos.

C.J.N.G: Enforcer group, Jalisco Cartel New Generation aka GN or GNX

C.N.G.T.: Cartel New Generation Tijuana, is an allied group with members of CAF and CJNG. The alliance was created to establish control of Baja and quell the Sinaloa Cartel, after CAF became weakened.

C.O.: Organized crime group

Coddehum: la Comisión de Defensa de los Derechos Humanos (Chihuahua).

Cortar cartuchos: armatillar. Ready to fire. to cock a weapon.

Cuerno de chivo: AK-47, the preferred weapon of drug cartels. Some (e.g. Roberto Saviano) have claimed that the AK-47 has been used to kill more people than any other weapon. 90% of arms used in Mexico originate from the United States and arms dealers in Arizona and Texas.

DTO: Drug trafficking organization.

El Señor de los Cielos: Amado Carrillo Fuentes, the Lord of the Skies who helped consolidate the Juárez cartel. He died in 1997 undergoing plastic surgery in Mexico City (Polanco).

Encajuelados: Victims found in the trunks of cars.

Encintados: Vicitims found bound and blindfolded with tape.

Encobijado: a common way that sicarios dispose of bodies — wrapped in a blanket, rug, or tarpaulin and taped.

Estacas: 3 or more armed persons in a vehicle patrolling their territory

Familia (also LFM or LF): 'de Michoacan'. DTO that specializes in synthetic drugs (crystal) and with a religious code. Extremely violent and unpredictable.

FFL: US legal term for federal firearms licensees. Approximately 6700 operate in American Southwest.

Foco: crystal meth.

Fuero (el): (jurisdicción) jurisdiction (privilegio, derecho) privilege;

GATE, GAFE, GOES: Are acronyms for Special State Police, names vary with states

Gente nueva (la): Chapo Guzman sicarios (Chihuahua).

Guachicol: oil product stolen from PEMEX and then sold back to business under duress. A practice common in Tamaulipas.

Halcon (los): There are two meanings here. In the border area, "halcones" are lookouts and street level informants (falcons) who warn the drug cartels about intrusions from other DTO's, police or army manoeuvers. Halcones are also an elite squad of commandos that have a notorious reputation for violation of civil rights and abuse.

Hormiga (el correo de..): an ant run. Big result of lots of little additions and purchases.

ICESI: Instituto ciudadano de estudios sobre la inseguridad.

IOI: US DOJ-ATF agents investigating gun movement. Industry Operations Investigators.

Jefe de Jefes: Capo de Capos. The name applied to the most prominent drug chief in Mexico. Most frequently is associated with Miguel Angel Felix Gallardo. Popular corrido of Los Tigres del Norte, although Miguel Felix Gallardo denies that the song is about him.

La Última Letra: Los Zetas (Last Letter)

Levantón (m): Abduction. Term used in northwest Mexico to describe forced seizure of a person. Most of the time, the "levantado" is never seen alive again. Secuestro is the term used more often to describe kidnapping.

Linces (los): a unit of sicarios employed by "El Viceroy" Vicente Carrilo-Fuentes and the Juárez cartel. May have evolved from "La Linea". This group is apparently composed of military deserters (like the Zetas) who are well trained, use military ordnance, uniforms and vehicles. The Mexican military argues that this group is responsible for most human right violations in Chihuahua. linea (la): sicarios in employ of Juarez DTO.

Los Viagras: Michocan cartel founded in 2014 by the Sierra Santana brothers. The first splinter group of Caballeros Templarios. Alliances are with Cartel Jalisco New Generation headed by El Mencho. Viagras were responsible for the creation of the H3 (Buenavista) the "fake" autodefensa group, headed by "El Americano".

Matapolicia (f): bullets of heavy calibre that can penetrate vests. Police killers — ordnance used when attacking police or members of the military.

Matazetas (los): a name used by a group that has executed members of Los Zetas. It's most likely that the matazetas are members of a rival cartel, but it's possible that they are actually an independent group.

Maña: a local name for cartels in Tamaulipas, most often used to refer to Los Zetas or other sicarios working for Gulf cartel.

Mota (f): marijuana.

Narco: General term for drug trafficker

Narcobloqueo: A barricade in the streets with vehicles that are carjacked to delay the arrival of the police or military.

Narcocorrido: a version of a corrido that deals with a drug theme. Some narcocorridos are commissioned by the drug dealers in order to "sing their praises", but others share much in common with morality plays because they sing about the negative consequences of drug dealing. See the excellent book by Elijah Wald describing narcocorridos.

Narcofosa: narco cemetery; body disposal place, usually clandestine and used for a period of time. Have been found in at least 8 Mexican states.

Narcomanta (f): a banner or a poster placed in a prominent location with a message. Most frequently, the messages seem to originate with the drug organizations, but the message may also be aimed at the drug trafficking organizations.

Narco tienditas or picaderos: Businesses where they traffic drugs.

Operation Coronado: The code term for the DEA/FBI/ICE coordinated arrest of La Famila de Michoacana members on Oct. 24 2009.

Pelones (los): sicarios that were originally assembled by the Beltran Leyva brothers for the Sinaloa Federation.

Perico (m): cocaine. A parrot. Nickname based on the idea that it "goes up the nose".

Pez gordo (m.): big fish, big boss.

PGR: La Procuraduria General de la Republica. The institutional agency of the Mexican Attorney General.

Pista (f): the 'game'. Literally, 'the track' as in racing. Refers to the business at hand.

Plaza (f): Territory, turf. Can also refer to the product being moved or in dispute. P.M.: Military Police.

Polizetas: Policemen at the service of the narcos. It originated from Nuevo leon, Tamaulipas region where the Zetas were deeply embedded with the Zetas.

Pozolero: A person within the cartel who has a knowledge of chemistry and disposes bodies.

PROCAMPO: Federal program to provide financial support for farmers and ejiditarios. Recent revelations indicate that it has been a cash-cow for agribusiness and PRI party members. Little of the original program (to provide irrigation etc.) has benefitted the poorest farmers.

Project Gunrunner: US DOJ and ATF plan to disrupt illegal flow of guns from US into Mexico.

Rematar: literally "to re-kill". the prefix re is used to indicate "once again" when it precedes a verb. rematar is used when a means of execution is especially brutal, and also used to mean "slaughter", "finish off."

S.D.R: Situation at Risk (violence erupted)

P.S.D.R. Possible situation at risk

Sicario (m): the word used to describe an "assassin" or hitman for the cartels. The word has roots back to Roman times. Sicarios are sometimes young and "throw-away" bodies recruited by the cartels, but can also be well-trained military deserters or police (e.g. Los Zetas).

Sistema SNSP: Sistema Nacional de Seguridad Pública.

SSP: Secretaria de Seguridad Publica.

Straw purchasers: surrogate purchasers of guns— someone who is licensed to purchase a gun but does so on behalf of someone who is not. Cartel sicarios have a system of straw purchasers.

T.C.O.: Transnational Criminal Organization Tiendita: Excact location where drugs are sold.

UIFA: Unidad de Inspección Fiscal y Aduanera.

WATCHIVATO: Mexican "narco artist" who has produced iconic images of Jesus Malverde. Artist images can be seen on BB.

Wathivato (El): Mexican artist famous for narco images — especially iconic images of Jesus Malverde. Artist on BBC site Narco Mexico.

Zetas, (los): now la Compañía. Paramilitary force formed by Gulf Cartel and now independent. Deserters from Mexican army GAFE unit; highly trained anti-terrorist unit.

Events of Organized Crime

2006

November 25 - Popular singer Valentín Elizalde is gunned down along with his manager (and best friend) Mario Mendoza Grajeda, and driver Reynaldo Ballesteros. In an ambush after a concert in the border city of Reynosa, across the border from McAllen, Texas in an apparent gangland style hit.

December 1 - President Felipe Calderón assumed office and declared war on drug traffickers. He also imposed a cap on salaries of high-ranking public servants and ordered a raise on the salaries of the Federal Police and the Mexican armed forces.

December 11 - Operation Michoacan is launched.

2007

January 2 - Operation Baja California is launched.

April 3 - Police arrest suspected drug lord Victor Magno Escobar in Tijuana.

March 17 - Zhenli Ye Gon, relieved of $213 million USD in Mexico City.

May 14 - Jorge Altriste, head of operations for Mexico's elite police force in Tijuana, was murdered.

May 16 - May 18: Battles in Cananea, Sonora, kill 15 gang members, five policemen, and two civilians.

August 26 - Trigo de Jesús son (and manager) of Popular singer Joan Sebastian is shot in the back of the head after one of Joan Sebastian's concert in Texas. Trigo was transported to the McAllen Medical Center where he was pronounced dead.

December 2 - Popular singer Sergio Gómez is kidnapped and killed.

December 8 - Gerardo García Pimentel, a crime reporter, was killed.

December 29 - The entire police force in the town of Playas de Rosarito, Baja California, is disarmed from their weapons after suspicion of collaborating with drug cartels.

2008

January 21 - Mexican security forces capture drug lord Alfredo Beltrán Leyva.

April 26 - 15 people are killed in a gun battle between the Arellano-Félix cartel and a rival gang.

May 8 - National Police Chief Édgar Eusebio Millán Gómez was gunned down in Mexico City. He was the highest-ranking Mexican official to be killed.

May 9 - Esteban Robles Espinosa, the commander of Mexico's investigative police force, was shot dead on a street in Mexico City.

May 17 - Presumed members of the Sinaloa Cartel attacked Villa Ahumada, Chihuahua, and killed the police chief, two officers, and three civilians, and kidnapped at least 10 additional people.

May 28 - Seven federal police agents die in a shootout in Culiacán, Sinaloa.

May 31 - The United States announces it is using a drug trafficking law to impose financial sanctions on Mexican drugs cartels, along with other non-state actors.

June 26 - Police commander Igor Labastida is shot dead in a restaurant in Mexico City.

August 27 - Police find three headless bodies in a rubbish dump in Tijuana, killed by drug cartels.

September 15 - 2008 Morelia grenade attacks: Grenades killed eight civilians and injured more than 100 in Morelia, Michoacán.

September 17 - Over 200 people across Mexico, Guatemala, Italy and the United States, including members of the Gulf cartel and the 'Ndrangheta are arrested in a major anti-drug trafficking operation, Operation Solare.

October 22 - Police capture boss Jesus Zambada of the Sinaloa cartel after a shootout in Mexico City.

October 24 - Mexican criminal investigator Andres Dimitriadis is shot dead by drug traffickers in his car on his way home.

October 26 - Colombian police seize a shipment of cocaine worth US$200m en route to Mexico.

October 26 - The Mexican army captures drug lord Eduardo Arellano Félix after a shootout in Tijuana.

November 2 - Senior Mexican police officer Víctor Gerardo Garay resigns amidst claims one of his aides was on the payroll of the Sinaloa cartel.

November 4 - 2008 Mexico City plane crash: Juan Camilo Mouriño, Secretary of the Interior of President

Felipe Calderón, dies when his Learjet crashes in Mexico City. Fourteen others die, including José Luis Santiago Vasconcelos, the former assistant attorney general. Authorities said there was no evidence of foul play, as both Mouriño and Vasconcelos were key figures in the drug war, and that the accident was caused by wake turbulence.

November 7 - The Policia Federal arrested Jaime González Durán in Tamaulipas who was a founding member of the original Los Zetas

November 19 - Mexican Interpol chief Ricardo Gutiérrez Vargas is arrested on suspicion of links with drug traffickers.

November 21 - Noé Ramírez Mandujano, ex-head of Mexico's anti-organized crime agency, is arrested on suspicion of links with drug traffickers.

November 28: Gunmen in Ciudad Juárez killed eight people at a restaurant.

November 30: Guatemalan and Mexican drug gangs clash on the two country's border, leaving 18 dead.

December 4: 13 bodies are found near a dirt road in Sinaloa.

December 8 - Ten suspected drug traffickers and one soldier are killed in a shootout in Guerrero, while another six people are killed when fire is opened on a pool hall in Ciudad Juárez.

December 10: Felix Batista, an American anti-kidnapping expert was kidnapped in Saltillo, Coahuila.

December 21: Seven off-duty soldiers and one police commander were kidnapped, tortured and decapitated.[34] Their heads were left at a shopping center with a threat note to the military.

Summary: For 2008 a record of 5,630 deaths was reached.
2009

January 2 - Mexican authorities arrested Alberto Espinoza Barrón (known as "La Fresa"), who is presumed to be one of the leaders of the Michoacán Drug Cartel (La Familia Michoacana).

January 6: Gunmen fired on and threw grenades at the Televisa TV station in Monterrey during a nightly newscast, causing no injuries. A note left on the scene read: "Stop reporting just on us. Report on the narco's political leaders."

January 19 - 21 police officers in Tijuana are arrested on suspicion of collaborating with drug cartels.

January 22 - Police arrest Santiago Meza, a man who allegedly dissolved 300 bodies of rival drug traffickers for his boss Teodoro García Simental, after he split from the Arellano Félix cartel.

February 3 - The body of retired General Mauro Enrique Tello Quiñónez, who had been appointed a special drugs consultant to the Benito Juárez municipality mayor, was found near Cancún along with the bodies of his aide and a driver.

February 5 - Police capture drug dealer Gerónimo Gámez García in Mexico City.

February 10 - Troops descended upon a police station in Cancún in connection with the torture and murder of former general Mauro Enrique Tello, who led an elite anti-drugs squad.

February 10 - Assailants kidnapped 9 people in Villa Ahumada, Chihuahua. They were then pursued by the Mexican military to a ranch located 12 km south of the Garita de Samalayuca, where at least 21 people were killed. The fatalities included one soldier, 6 of the 9 prisoners and 14 assailants that were killed by The Mexican army. This event shares much with the attack of May 17, 2008, and it is presumed that the attackers were members of the Sinaloa Cartel.

February 12 - Octavio Almanza, alleged head of Los Zetas in Cancún, is arrested.

February 12 - Gunmen assassinate Detective Ramón Jasso Rodríguez, the chief in charge of the homicide division for the state police of Nuevo León.

February 13 - A police patrol was ambushed in a grenade attack in Lázaro Cárdenas, Michoacán. Two municipality police officers were injured and evacuated to the hospital, they were reported to be in stable condition.

February 14 - In the municipality of Villa Ahumada, 125 kilometers south of Ciudad Juárez. troops on patrol fought a gun battle with cartel gunmen, leaving three assailants dead.

February 15 - Five people were killed by alleged narco assailants in Gómez Palacio, Durango.

The Mexican Navy, with the help of the United States Coast Guard, confiscated 7 tons of cocaine being transported on a fishing vessel in international waters in the Pacific Ocean.

Gunmen in Tabasco kill a policeman, ten members of his family, and another person.

February 16 - Seven people were killed by alleged narco assailants in Jalisco.

February 17 - A multiple-hour running gun battle between elements of the Mexican Army and unknown attackers (sicarios) has resulted in five dead soldiers and five dead assailants in a shopping district and several residential neighborhoods of Reynosa, Tamaulipas. Approximately 20 additional people were injured by gunfire and grenades.

February 20 - Ciudad Juárez Police Chief Robert Orduna announced his resignation after two police officers are killed. Drug traffickers had threatened to kill a police officer every 48 hours until the chief resigned.

February 22 - Five assailants attacked the convoy of Chihuahua governor, José Reyes Baeza, killing a bodyguard.

February 24 - Mexican authorities extradited Miguel Ángel Caro Quintero (the brother of Rafael Caro Quintero) to the U.S.

Heavily armed gunmen assassinated the Vista Hermosa Mayor in Michoacán.

February 25 - assailants attacked a police patrol with gunfire and fragmentation grenades in Zihuatanejo, Guerrero, killing four police officers.

American raids code-named Operation Xcellerator on the Sinaloa cartel in California, Minnesota and Maryland lead to 755 arrests, the discovery of a 'super meth lab' and laboratory equipment capable of producing 12,000 ecstasy pills an hour.

February 28 - Close to 1,800 Mexican troops arrived in Ciudad Juárez as part of a contingent of 5,000 Federal Police and troops.

March 4: 2009 Mexico prison riot leaves 20 dead.

March 9: French President Nicolas Sarkozy meets President Felipe Calderón in Mexico. Sarkozy discussed with his counterpart the fate of French national Florence Cassez who was sentenced to a 60-year jail term for being involved in kidnappings in Mexico. Cassez may ask to be returned to France to finish her sentence in her home country.

The Mexican Army confirmed the arrest of 26 members of the Arrellano Félix Cartel, including Ángel Jácome Gamboa (El Kaibil'), one state police officer, one municipal police officer, and other suspects.

March 10: The Mexican Ministry of Defense orders 6 Eurocopter EC 725 Helicopters from Eurocopter to transport soldiers in special operations. The deal was finalized behind closed doors between Felipe Calderón and French President Nicolas Sarkozy.

March 10: 5 human heads found in coolers in Jalisco. State Public Safety Secretary Luis Carlos Najera says threatening messages aimed at drug traffickers were found with the heads, which were covered with tape and discovered in individual coolers near the community of Ixtlahuacán del Río.

March 12: The United States Department of Homeland Security stated that it is considering using the National Guard as a last resort to counter the threat of drug violence in Mexico from spilling over the border into the US.

March 19: The Mexican Military captures alleged Sinaloa cartel drug trafficker Vicente Zambada Son of Imsael Zambada. Zambada's father, Ismael "El Mayo" Zambada, also is considered a top leader of the Sinaloa cartel and is among Mexico's most-wanted suspects.

March 22: Gunmen have killed a state police commander in charge of investigating kidnappings and extortion in the western state of Michoacán. Édgar Garcia was sitting at a red light in his car Sunday when two other vehicles pulled up and opened fire, the state government said in a communique late Sunday. He died at the scene. State police in a nearby patrol car chased the suspects. One of the cars went out of control and crashed into a university building, according to the statement. A gunman got out of the car and began shooting at police, injuring one officer. Police then shot the gunman dead while his partner fled with apparent gunshot wounds.

March 25: A battle took place between The PFP and members of a kidnapping gang linked to "La Familia" cartel. Two federal policemen were injured and 3 of the delinquents were captured.

Special Forces Unit captured one of Mexico's most-wanted drug smugglers, Héctor Huerta Ríos, whose nickname "la burra" — female donkey — belies his power as the alleged trafficker controlling drugs flowing through the northern city of Monterrey.

March 26: A US Marshal, Vincent Bustamante who was the subject of an arrest warrant, was found dead in Ciudad Juárez.

April 1: Three gunmen were killed by the Mexican army in a 10-minute gun battle.

April 2 - Vicente Carrillo Leyva, son of Amado Carrillo Fuentes, was arrested near Mexico City.

April 19 - Eight police officers are killed in an attack on a prison convoy transporting senior leaders of the Beltrán Leyva cartel cartel. Federal Police captured 44 members of "La Familia", including its chief Rafael Cedeño Hernández "El Cede".

April 22 - The bodies of two undercover government agents are found in Durango, 50 km south of Guanacevi, along with a note saying "Neither priests nor rulers will ever get El Chapo" (El Chapo referring to Joaquín Guzmán and with clear allusion to the comments of the Archbishop of Durango Héctor González Martínez)

April 30 - Gregorio Sauceda Gamboa, an influential figure in Los Zetas, was captured in the city of Matamoros.

May 17 - An armed gang linked to the Gulf cartel disguised as police officers break into a prison in Zacatecas and free 50 inmates.

May 27 - 27 high-ranking officials including 10 mayors and a judge in Michoacán suspected of collaboration with La Familia cartel.

June 6- 16 gunmen of a drug cartel and 2 Mexican Army soldiers are killed during a four hour shootout in Acapulco

June 15 - Juan Manuel Jurado Zarzoza of the Gulf Cartel is captured in Cancún.

June 26 - Federal police kill 12 members of Los Zetas in Apaseo el Alto.

Gunmen kill two assistants of Ernesto Cornejo, a Partido Acción Nacional candidate, in Sonora, but fail to kill him.

July 7 - Anti-crime activist Benjamin LeBaron and his brother-in-law Luis Widmar are murdered after armed men storm their house in Galeana, Chihuahua.

July 11 - Several Police headquarters are attacked by gunmen in Michoacán, leaving several injured, and 2 members of the Mexican Army dead.

July 14 - The organization tortured and murdered twelve Mexican federal agents and dumped the bodies along the side of a mountain highway. The agents were investigating crime in President Felipe Calderón's home state of Michoacán.

In a confrontation with Federal Police officers, two gunmen died in the state of Veracruz, no federal officers or soldiers were reported injured.

August 6 - A shootout between police and gunmen leaves over a dozen dead and 22 injured in Pachuca, the capital of the state of Hidalgo. Nine Mexican cartel suspects and three law enforcement officials were injured Thursday. Missing federal agents were found alive, however this discovery initiated simultaneous shootouts and grenade attacks on police installations around Mexico.

August 8 - Federal police arrest Manuel Invanovich Zambrano Flores, a top lieutenant of the Tijuana Cartel.

August 20 - Law enforcement officials, led by the U.S. Drug Enforcement Administration disrupted a massive drug operation by cutting off shipments of cocaine by the ton into Chicago and knocking out a major distribution network that operated out of the city. The drug operation allegedly brought 1,500 to 2,000 kilos of cocaine every month to Chicago from Mexico and shipped millions of dollars south of the border. At the top of the Chicago crew were 28-year-old twin brothers—Pedro and Margarito Flores— who controlled a group of underlings and headed up incoming drug shipments. They were also in charge of collecting, storing and shipping the cash and distributing the drugs around the country, authorities said. The Flores brothers were allegedly supplied by two warring cartel factions that have played a major role in the escalating drug violence in Mexico, including one reputedly led by Joaquín "el Chapo" Guzmán Loera, 54, and Ismael "el Mayo" Zambada García, 59, and another led by Arturo Beltrán Leyva, 47. The Flores brothers, who are in custody, had done business with each of the warring drug cartels, authorities say. Each cartel threatened the Flores brothers with violence if they did business with the other, according to the charges.

September 3 - Gunmen attack a drug clinic in Ciudad Juárez, lining up patients against a wall and killing at least 17.

September 6 - José Rodolfo Escajeda of the Juárez cartel is arrested in connection with the drug clinic massacre several days earlier.

September 16 - 10 people are killed in another gun attack on a drug clinic in Ciudad Juarez.

October 16 - One Federal Police officer was killed by gunmen while the officer was conducting a traffic stop, instead the men in the vehicle opened fired and killed officer

Valentin Manuel Gutierrez Heredia, 34, who was assigned to the Mazatlan sector. shortly after in the afternoon, Mexican troops conducted a raid in the residential zone of Mazatlan leading to a gun battle. One civilian was killed while one soldier and one police officer were injured. Unofficially, it was reported that the armed group is the same one that killed federal agent Valentin Gutierrez, Thursday night.

December 16 - A two hour shootout between 200 Mexican Marines and Beltrán-Leyva Cartel gunmen led to the death of Marcos Arturo Beltrán-Leyva the main head of the organization and his brother Mario Alberto Leyva, or Hector, in an upscale resort in Cuernavaca, also killed were four of his bodyguards, of which one committed suicide while surrounded by marines. Two marines were also injured and one other died, Navy 3rd Petty Officer Melquisedet Angulo Córdova died while being treated for his injuries.

December 22 - Only hours after the burial of 3rd Petty Officer Melquisedet Angulo Córdova, gunmen break into his family's house and kill Angulo's mother and three other relatives. The shooting was believed to be retaliation for the death of Marcos Arturo Beltrán-Leyva, as well as a warning against the military forces involved in President Felipe Calderón's war on Mexico's drug cartels.

2010

On January 2, Carlos Beltrán Leyva brother of Marcos Arturo Beltrán-Leyva was arrested by Federal Police officers in Culiacan, Sinaloa.

January 8, due to high crime rates in the munipality of Tancítaro, Michoacán its Municipal Police force have been disbanded. City officials will leave the Army and Policia Estatal (State Police) incharge of public security.

January 12, Federal Police arrested the leader of the Tijuana Cartel, Teodoro "El Teo" García Simental in La Paz, Baja California Sur.

January 31, Teenagers at a party in Ciudad Juarez are gunned down. At first the number of casualties was reported to be 14 but increased to 16 after two victims died in the hospital later on. Ten of the victims were between the ages of 13 and 19, according to the Chihuahua state prosecutor's office. Four ranged from ages 23 to 42, and two others were unidentified. The local police is investigating the possible causes but said that it is likely linked to a turf battle between rivaling Cartels. However only three of the victims could be linked to the drug trade so far.

February 8, Raydel Lopez Uriarte, known as El Muletas or Crutches, was arrested in the capital of La Paz. Raydel Lopez Uriarte was considered the leader of the criminal cell that had been previously led by "El Teo", who were engaged in a bloody dispute over turf with Francisco Sanchez Arellano (a) "El Ingeniero", the head of the Arellano Felix cartel.

February 22, Jose Vasquez Villagrana "El Jabali," 40, was arrested in his home town of Santa Ana, Sonora, which borders Arizona. Described as a key operator of the powerful Sinaloa cartel who served briefly in the U.S. army before taking on the trafficking of 2 tons of cocaine a month into the United States.

February 24, Osiel Cardenas, 42, is sentenced to 25 years in prison and made to forfeit $50 US million of his personal fortune by a federal court in Texas. Osiel formerly headed Mexico's notorious Gulf cartel, was arrested in Mexico in 2003 and extradited in 2007 to the US, where he has been held behind bars without parole.

March 1, The Gulf cartel declares war against Los Zetas. Los Zetas are pursued form Matamoros to Monterrey. La Familia sends re-enforcements to assist the Gulf cartel. It is believed that the Sinaloa cartel might also be helping the Gulf cartel attempt to eliminate Los Zetas. The northeast border of

Mexico becomes a battle ground in the escalating violence between rivals cartels, military and police officers.

March 15, Three people connected to the US consulate in the Mexican border city of Ciudad Juarez were killed. A U.S. consular employee and her husband were gunned down inside their SUV near the Santa Fe International Bridge. The husband of an employee of the U.S. Consulate is also executed within seconds. The executions are attributed to the Juarez cartel armed wing "La Linea" using street gangsters of Barrio Azteca with ties to El Paso and Ciudad Juarez.

March 17, President Felipe Calderon makes an unprecedented third visit to Ciudad Juarez within 33 days. The Mexican President was in Juarez to share his plan to quell violence and to analyze the comprehensive strategy on security. He was pushed to act by the Jan. 31 massacre of at least 15 mostly young people at a party and the slayings of three people attached to the U.S. Consulate. He promises that Juarez will not be forgotten and he promised to send economic and security support.

March 31, the slaying of an Arizona rancher Robert Krentz by a suspect who apparently fled to Mexico

April 20, The Hummer Sentenced to 16 Years.

April 23, Mexico Captures Indio.

April 29, Drug Lord Extradited to Texas.

April 29, Wife of "El H" Abducted and Set Free.

May 15, Former Mexico Presidential Candidate Missing.

June 28, PRI Gubernatorial Candidate Assassinated in Tamaulipas.

July 29, Nacho Coronel Killed in Zapopan, Jalisco.

August 17, Mayor Mayor Edelmiro Cavazos is abducted and killed.

August 26, Zetas Massacre 72 Illegal Immigrants in San Fernando, Tamaulipas.

August 30, La Barbie Arrested.

September 9 – Gunmen killed 25 people in a series of drug-related attacks in Ciudad Juárez, marking the deadliest day in more than two years for the Mexican border city. Two graffiti messages' appeared in Ciudad Juárez threatening the Sinaloa Cartel drug lord Joaquin Guzman. One message read: "You are killing our sons. You already did, and now we are going to kill your families."

September 10 – In the border city of Reynosa, across the border from McAllen, Texas, 85 inmates — 66 of whom were convicted or on trial for federal charges like weapons possession or drugs — scaled the Reynosa prison's 20-foot (6-meter) walls using ladders. Forty four prison guards and employees were under investigation. Two were missing. So far this year a total of 201 inmates have escaped from prisons in the Mexican state of Tamaulipas.

September 12 - Mexican marines arrest Sergio Villarreal Barragán, a lieutenant of the Beltrán-Leyva Cartel.

September 16 - In Matamoros, Tamaulipas, over 25 people were killed after a confrontation between the Gulf Cartel, Los Zetas, and elements of the Mexican Navy. This was during the eve celebration of the Mexican Independence Day.

October 18 – Mexican authorities seized 105 tons of marijuana bound for the U.S., representing the biggest bust in the history of the state of Baja California. Soldiers and police seized the drugs in predawn raids in three neighborhoods. The marijuana was found wrapped in 10,000 packages. The drug had an estimated street value in Mexico of 4.2 billion pesos, about $338 million.

October 22 – Gunmen kill 14 people at a boy's birthday party in Ciudad Juarez, Chihuahua.

October 24 – Gunmen in Tijuana kill 13 people at a drug rehab clinic.

October 27 – Gunmen kill 15 people at a car wash in Tepic, Nayarit.

November 4 – In Ciudad Mante, Tamaulipas, 8 beheaded corpses were found on the trunk of a pickup truck. On top of the corpses, a poster read the following: "This happens for supporting Los Zetas. Here are all your halcones (informants). Sincerely, the Gulf Cartel.

November 5 – Antonio Ezequiel Cárdenas Guillen, co-leader of the Gulf Cartel, was shot and killed during a gunbattle against Mexican authorities, along with more than 50 of his gunmen, in the border city of Matamoros, Tamaulipas. Although not confirmed, some local sources reveal that more than 100 people died that day in Matamoros.

November 9 – Customs authorities at the International Airport of Mexico City seized 113 kilos of cocaine and two thousand bottles of pills with Risperidone.

November 9 – Mayor Gregorio Barradas Miravete was found executed with a note left on him that read: "This is going to happen to all those who continue to support Los Zetas."

November 22 - In the rural outsides of Ciudad Victoria, Tamaulipas, drug cartel gunmen threatened a 77- year-old local entrepreneur, Don Alejo Garza Támez, to give away all his property. According to the report, they gave Don Alejo one day to leave his ranch before the gunmen arrived. If not, they threatened to kill him. Instead, Don Alejo made a fortress in his own ranch; setting up traps, and placing rifles on every house window, waiting for the arrival of the gunmen all by himself. When the gunmen arrived, Don Alejo shot and killed 4 of them, and gravely injured 2. Nevertheless, Don Alejo was killed, too, but he was commemorated for his heroic act.

December 3 - In Cuernavaca, Morelos, Mexican authorities capture Edgar Jiménez Lugo, alias "El Ponchis," a

14-year-old hitman from the South Pacific Cartel. He is the youngest sicario that there is register of in Mexico; "El Ponchis" is well-known for carrying out over 300 violent executions, most of them by mutilation, torture, and decapitation.

December 9 – La Familia Michoacana's drug lord, Nazario Moreno González, was killed in a shootout with the federal police.

December 18 – In Nuevo Laredo, Tamaulipas, 151 inmates escaped a federal prison—58 of them were high-profile criminals—and investigations mention that the convicts left through the front door, which implies that the director allowed them to escape.

December 19 - 2010 Puebla oil pipeline explosion: In the state of Puebla, a pipeline owned by PEMEX company exploded after thieves from Los Zetas attempted to siphon off the oil. The explosion killed 28 people, injured 52, and damaged over 115 homes.

December 28 – Around 60 gunmen stormed the small, indigenous town of Tierras Coloradas, Durango. The gunmen burned all the houses (40), cars (27), and an elementary school; over 200 natives had to flee the area, others were killed.

For 2010, the drug-related deaths reached 15,273.

2011

January 8 – 28 bodies were discovered in Acapulco, including the decapitated bodies of 15 young men, with the heads scattered around them, which were found outside the Plaza Sendero shopping center. Media reports say that three messages signed by Joaquin "El Chapo" Guzman, leader of the Sinaloa cartel, were found alongside the bodies. The other bodies include 6 found in a taxi behind a supermarket, 4 riddled with bullets in two residential neighborhoods and 3 others in other locations.

February 16 – In San Luis Potosí, the American ICE agent Jaime Zapata was ambushed, shot, and killed on a highway during his trajectory to Mexico City by a group of gunmen, later confirmed to be Los Zetas. The second agent, Victor Avila, was wounded, and is now in the United States. The gunmen involved in the shooting have been apprehended.

February 27 – Sergio Mora Cortes, aka "El Toto," is captured by Mexican Marines in Saltillo, Coahuila. Mora Cortes was a leader of Los Zetas in the state of San Luis Potosi, and he was wanted for the murder of the American ICE agent Jaime Zapata and for the murder of a Nuevo Laredo police chief.

February 28 – 7 bodies found hanging from bridges in Mazatlan, Sinaloa. Messages left with the corpses alleged that the dead were members of the South Pacific Cartel.

March 1 – A mass grave with over 20 bodies was uncovered in San Miguel Totolapan, Guerrero. Other sources, however, mention that more than 70 bodies were exhumed.

March 2 – A three-day shooting was registered between the Mexican Marines and Los Zetas in the city of Valle Hermoso, Tamaulipas. During these three days, all local businesses and schools closed; a convoy of 50 SUV's from Los Zetas was seen in the rural highway outside the city.

March 8 – 18 killed in gunfights in Abasolo, Tamaulipas. Most of the dead are believed to be operators for the warring Zetas and the Gulf Cartel. Mexican troops were deployed to restore order.

March 10 – Jorge Hernández Espinoza, the Director of Public Security for Santiago Tangamandapio, Michoacán, was found dead in his vehicle with one shot once in his head and three times in his chest.

March 29 - Police found the bodies of 6 men and 1 woman inside a car abandoned in an exclusive gated community near Cuernavaca.

April 2 - In Ciudad Juarez, a group of gunmen attacked two bars with fire bombs and shootings in less than forty-eight hours, killing over 15 people.

April 4 - A clash between the police and drug cartel gunmen left 7 dead and 6 people injured in

Acapulco, Guerrero. In addition, a whole shopping center was burned down by the gunmen, and a dozen of stores were left in ruins.

April 26 - 2011 Tamaulipas massacre: In San Fernando, Tamaulipas, after exhuming more than 40 mass graves, the final body count reached 193 corpses. Although not confirmed, some newspapers mention that the body count surpassed 500, but that the state government of Tamaulipas supposedly censored and prevented such publications.

May 1 - MEXICO CITY - The drug-war death toll for Mexico in April was 1,400, the highest of any month since the Mexican government began its war on illicit drug trade four years ago. The previous high was 1,322 in August 2010.

May 9 - The Mexican government, along with Sedena, disarm all police forces in the state of Tamaulipas, beginning with the cities of Matamoros and Reynosa.

May 14 - 2011 Durango massacres: In the state of Durango, 249 bodies were exhumed from numerous clandestine mass graves. Some sources, however, indicate that the actual body count reached 308 corpses.

May 16 – In Guatemala, 27 farmers were killed by Los Zetas; the majority of the victims presented signs of torture and decapitation.

May 20 - In Nuevo Laredo, Tamaulipas, directly across the border from Laredo, Texas, 31 people were killed in a 24-

hour span. In addition, more than 40 people were injured, and 196 drug cartel gunmen were detained.

May 27 - In Ruiz, Nayarit, a convoy from Los Zetas ambushed a group of gunmen of the Sinaloa Cartel; 29 gunmen were killed, 3 were found injured.

A confrontation between the Federal Police forces and La Familia Michoacana in a ranch at Jilotlán de los Dolores, in western Jalisco, left 11 La Familia gunmen killed and 36 arrested. More than 70 assault rifles were confiscated, along with 14 handguns, 3 grenades, 578 cartridges, 20,000 rounds of ammunition, and 40 bullet-proof vests. It was later discovered that La Familia Michoacana was planning a raid against the Knights Templar.

June 3 - In the state of Coahuila, 38 bodies were exhumed from clandestine mass graves.

June 9 - The United States government arrested 127 U.S. Customs and Border Protection agents who were collaborating with the Mexican drug cartels.

June 15 - A total of 34 people were killed in Monterrey, Nuevo León in a 24-hour span.

June 21 - José de Jesús Méndez Vargas 'El Chango', leader of La Familia Michoacana, was captured in Aguascalientes.

July 1 – In Fresnillo, Zacatecas, during a confrontation between Los Zetas and the Mexican forces, 15 Zeta gunmen were killed, and 17 were arrested; SEMAR notified that 6 marines were wounded.

Zacateca's Attorney General, Arturo Nahle García, confirmed that in Fresnillo, more than 250 Los Zetas gunmen confronted elements of the Mexican Navy throughout the whole city.

July 4 - Federal Police agents arrest Jesús Enrique Rejón Aguilar, one of the leaders and co-founders of the Los Zetas drug cartel.

July 8 - In the city of Monterrey, Nuevo León, a group of gunmen shot and killed 27 people, injured 7, and kidnapped 8 in 'Bar Sabino Gordo.' Presumably, this massacre was from the Gulf Cartel to their rival group Los Zetas.

July 9 - Fighting among Los Zetas and other drug cartels led to the deaths of more than 40 people whose bodies were found in three Mexican cities over a 24-hour span.

July 11 - Armando Villarreal Heredia, a U.S-born drug lieutenant of the Arellano-Felix drug cartel, is arrested by the Federal Police.

July 12 - In Ciudad Juarez, 21 people were killed in different parts of the city by gunmen. This marked the deadliest day for Ciudad Juarez in 2011.

July 14 - The Mexican Army discovers the largest marijuana plantation ever found in the country, 320 km (200 mi) south of San Diego, CA., in the Mexican state of Baja California; consisting of 120 hectares (300 acres) that would have yielded about 120 tons, and was worth about USD $160 million.

July 15 - In Nuevo Laredo, Tamaulipas, 66 inmates escaped a federal prison during a massive brawl, where 7 other inmates were found dead.

July 23 – The president of Mexico, Felipe Calderón Hinojosa, and peace and human rights activists, which included the poet Javier Sicilia, gathered in Chapultepec Castle to initiate a national aired discussion on Mexico's drug war violence and on the country's military-led strategy against the drug cartels.

Due to anonymous calls by civilians, the Mexican Army carried out an operation to crackdown operatives from Los Zetas in Pánuco, Veracruz; when the Mexican forces arrived at the place, the gunmen received them with shots, but the Army repelled the aggression and killed 10 Zetas.

July 24 - An unidentified group of gunmen disarmed 21 policemen in Michoacán. According to the information given, the gunmen carried out personal inspections to each police officer, disarming them one by one. The cops refused to defend themselves because the gunmen expressed high levels of anxiousness, and they were scared of being executed.

July 25 - Inside a prison in Ciudad Juárez, 17 inmates were shot and killed during a brawl between rival drug groups.

July 28 - Fortino Cortés Sandoval, the mayor of Florencia de Benito Juárez, Zacatecas, is found dead after a group of gunmen abducted him from his office.

July 31 - The Federal Police forces of Mexico captured José Antonio Acosta Hernández, nicknamed "El Diego," supreme leader of La Linea, the armed wing of the Juárez Cartel. According to government sources, "El Diego" had ordered more than 1,500 executions, some of them including government officials.

August 4 - The Secretariat of National Defense announced that after the initiation of the 'Operation Lince Norte', an operation focused primarily on destroying the financial and logistic sectors of Los Zetas, more than 500,000 pesos have been confiscated, and more than 30 'Zeta' gumnen killed.

August 12 - Óscar García Montoya, alias 'El Compayito', supreme leader of the criminal group La Mano con Ojos, was captured. He confessed to have killed over 300 people by himself, and ordered the execution of 300 more.

August 20 - In Torreon, Coahuila, a shooting was registered during a Mexican soccer match between Santos Laguna and Monarcas Morelia.

The mayor of Zacualpan, Mexico State, Jesús Eduviges Nava, was found dead after being kidnapped by gunmen who interrupted a meeting he was holding in his municipality.

August 25 - 2011 Monterrey casino attack: a well-armed group of gunmen massacred 52 people, and injured over a dozen, at Casino Royale. Although not confirmed, some sources mention that 61 were killed in the attack. This attack was the most violent and bloodiest in the history of Monterrey and of the whole state of Nuevo Leon. According to eyewitnesses, the gunmen quietly stormed the casino and immediately opened fire at the civilians, and then doused the casino entrances with gasoline and started a fire that trapped the people inside.

August 30 - In Acapulco, Guerrero, 140 elementary schools closed and over 600 teachers quit their jobs due to the money threats they have been receiving from the drug cartels. Over 75,000 kids are not attending school. One teacher confessed to have seen on a regular basis men in cars with assault rifles sticking out the windows, just outside school grounds.

September 14 - In the small town of Juchipila in the state of Zacatecas, over 80 gunmen—presumably from the Gulf Cartel—took control of the town, its jail, and its city hall for over five hours. They mentioned that their goal was to wipe out any presence of Los Zetas in the area.

September 17 - Moisés Villanueva de la Luz, a Mexican congressman, is found dead in Guerrero after being kidnapped for thirteen days.

September 20 - Two trucks containing 35 dead bodies are found in Boca del Río, Veracruz. Sources mention that all victims were linked to Los Zetas, and that the executions were performed by the Sinaloa Cartel's armed wing, Gente Nueva. Nevertheless, the criminal group Los Mata Zetas claimed responsibility for this massacre. In addition, 14 more bodies were found around Veracruz two days after this incident, summing up to 49 bodies found in public highways in the last forty-eight hours.

October 4 - The Mexican federal government launches the military-led project called Operación Veracruz Seguro to ensure tranquility in Veracruz. Reports mention that Los Zetas, the Gulf Cartel, and the Sinaloa Cartel are present in that state.

October 5 - In Culiacán, Sinaloa, Mexican authorities captured Noel Salgueiro Nevárez, the supreme leader of the Sinaloa Cartel's armed wing, Gente Nueva. In addition, they also captured Martín Rosales Magaña, one of the founders of La Familia Michoacana.

October 6 - In Boca del Río, Veracruz, a total of 36 bodies were found by Mexican authorities in three houses. Eight alleged perpetrators of the recent killings in Veracruz have been caught, including the leader of the group Los Mata Zetas. In addition, the Attorney General of Veracruz resigned from his position due to the increasing violence. A day after this incident, another 10 bodies were found across the state of Veracruz. The wave of violence has caused over 100 deaths in the past two weeks in Veracruz.

October 14 - Carlos Oliva Castillo alias "La Rana," third-in-command in Los Zetas organization and the mastermind of the 2011 Monterrey casino attack where 52 were killed, was captured in northern city of Saltillo, Coahuila.

November 11 – Francisco Blake Mora, Secretary of the Interior in the cabinet of Felipe Calderón, dies in a helicopter accident in foggy weather. Some sources speculate that his death was an assassination, though no concrete evidence suggests this.

November 23 – A total of 23 bodies—16 of them burned to death—were located in several abandoned vehicles in Sinaloa.

November 24 – Three trucks containing 26 bodies were found in an avenue at Guadalajara, Jalisco. All of them were male corpses. Reports mention that Los Zetas and the

Milenio Cartel are responsible for the massacre of these twenty-six alleged Sinaloa Cartel members.

December 14 – A convoy of U.S. military members was seen crossing the U.S-Mexico border from Brownsville, Texas into Matamoros, Tamaulipas. The U.S. soldiers were greeted by Mexican military officials at the international bridge, and were escorted to their meeting location south of Matamoros. Reports mention that the meeting between the two military units was to discuss "mutual security" concerns.

December 25 – The Mexican army announced that it had captured Guzmán's head of security. The arrest took place in Culiacan, the Sinaloa state capital.

2012

January 4 – In a prison brawl in Altamira, Tamaulipas, 31 inmates were killed. According to the witnesses, the brawl was between Gulf Cartel and Los Zetas.

January 7 – Mexican police in the northern city of Torreon found the severed heads of five people killed in a suspected outbreak of drug gang violence. Officials were still searching for the bodies. The heads were found in black bags in various parts of the city late on Friday, a spokesman for the ministry of public security in the state of Coahuila said on Saturday. Threatening messages were left with the severed heads – a common feature of killings by drug cartels in Mexico – that suggested the slayings were the result of feuding between local gangs, the spokesman said.

February 2 – Two U.S. missionaries from a Baptist Church were killed in Santiago, Nuevo León by drug cartel members.

February 19 – In Apodaca, Nuevo Leon, 44 inmates were killed in a prison riot, presumably caused by a brawl between the Gulf Cartel and Los Zetas.

March 19 – While conducting an investigation on the beheadings of ten other people, 12 policemen were ambushed and killed by gunmen in Teloloapan, Guerrero. Eleven other police officers were wounded.

March 23 – Thirteen people were killed in a wave of drug violence that swept Mexico a day before the Pope's visit. Seven men were found shot on the side of the road in Angostura, Sinaloa at a spot where locals often purchased contraband gasoline from the cartels. Four decapitated heads were found in an abandoned car in Acapulco. The body of a minor and a cab driver were also found in the town.

March 27 – Ten people were reported killed in a shootout in Temosachi in the Mexican border state of Chihuahua, where the Sinaloa and Juarez cartels have been fighting for control over drug smuggling routes into the U.S.

April 20 – Gunmen kill 16 people in a bar in the capital city of Chihuahua, Chihuahua. Two of those killed were journalists.

May 1 – Armed confrontations between the Mexican military and cartel members in Choix, Sinaloa left 27 people dead.

May 4 – In Nuevo Laredo, Tamaulipas, 23 corpses—14 of them decapitated and 9 of them hanged from a bridge—were found early in the morning.

May 9 – The chopped-up remains of 18 bodies were found inside two trucks near Chapala, Jalisco, just south of the city of Guadalajara.

May 13 – The Cadereyta Jiménez massacre occurred on the Mexican Federal Highway 40. The decapitated and dismembered bodies of 49 people were found in Cadereyta Jiménez. The remains were left along the road in Nuevo León state, between the cities of Monterrey and Reynosa. A message written on a wall nearby appeared to refer to Los Zetas drug cartel.

June 4 - In the Mexican city of Torreón, Coahuila, gunmen killed 11 people at a rehabilitation clinic.

August 12 - A total of 12 decomposing bodies are found inside an abandoned vehicle in Zacatecas.

August 14 - Members of the Gulf Cartel storm a bar in Monterrey and kill 10 people.

October 7 - Heriberto Lazcano Lazcano is killed by the Mexican Navy.

December 19 – A failed prison break and subsequent brawl between inmates leaves at least 23 dead in Gómez Palacio, Durango.

The Original Zetas

1. Arturo Guzman Decena, El Z-1, killed
2. Miguel Angel Soto Parra, El Parra, Arrested.
3. Daniel Perez Rojas, El Cachetes, arrested in Guatemala.
4. Jaime Gonzales Duran, El Hummer, arrested
5. Navor Vargas Garcia, El Debora, Arrested
6. Mateo Diaz Lopez, El Comandante Mateo, Arrested
7. Omar Lormendez Pitalua, El Pita, Z-10, Arrested
8. Eduardo Salvador Lopez Lara, La Chavita, El Z-48, arrested
9. Alfonso Lechuga Licona, el Cañas, Z-27 arrested
10. Isidro Lara Flores, El Colchon, arrested
11. Jose Ramon Davila Lopez, El Cholo, Arrested
12. Heriberto Lazcano Lazcano, El Lazca, killed
13. Jorge Lopez, El Chuta
14. Galindo Mellado Cruz, El Mellado Z-9, killed
15. Jesus Enrique Aguilar, El Mamito Z-8, arrested
16. Sergio Enrique Ruiz Tlapanco, El Tlapa, Z-44, arrested
17. Gonzalo Jerezano Escribano, El Cuije, El Z-18, arrested
18. Gustavo González Castro, El Erotico, at large
19. Flavio Mendez Santiago, El Amarillo, arrested
20. Carlos Vera Calva, El Vera Z-7, at large
21. Victor Nazario Castrejon Pena, at large
22. Braulio Arellano Dominguez, El Ganzo El Z-20, killed
23. Rogelio Guerra Ramirez, El Guerra, killed
24. Eduardo Estrada Gonzales, El Piti
25. Ernesto Zatarin Beliz, El Traca, killed
26. Raul Alberto Tejo Benavidez, El Alvin, killed
27. Luis Alberto Guerrero Reyes, El Rex, El Guerrero, Z-12 killed

28. Oscar Guerrero Silva, El Winnie Pooh, killed
29. Efrain Teodoro Torres, La Chispa, El Z-14, killed
30. Eduardo Costilla Sanchez, El Coss, arrested
31. Gregorio Saucedo, El Caramuela, arrested.

Known leaders of La Línea

- Vicente Carrillo Fuentes Viceroy Arrested 9 October 2014
- Juan Pablo Ledezma   El JL arrested
- Juan Pablo Guijarro El Mónico Arrested 3 January 3, 2010
- Luis Carlos Vázquez Barragán El 20 Arrested 26 July26, 2010
- Marco Antonio Guzmán Brad Pitt Arrested   17 June 2011
- José Guadalupe Rivas González El Zucaritas Arrested 18 June 2011
- José Antonio Acosta Hernández El Diego Arrested 29 July 2011
- Jesús Antonio Rincón Chavero El Tarzán Arrested 18 August 2011
- Luis Guillermo Castillo Rubio El Pariente Arrested 20 April 2012

The Bounty of Mexican Capos

1. Beltrán Leyva Arturo Beltrán Leyva El Barbas $30M Killed 2009-12-16
2. Beltrán Leyva Héctor Beltrán Leyva El General $30M Captured 2014-10-01 died in prison 2018-11-18
3. Beltrán Leyva Sergio Villarreal Barragán El Grande $30M Captured 2010-09-13
4. Beltrán Leyva Edgar Valdez Villareal La Barbie $30M Captured 2010-08-31
5. Beltrán Leyva Francisco Hernández García El 2000 $15M captured 2011-09-14
6. Beltrán Leyva Alberto Pineda Villa El Borrado $15M Killed 2009-09-12
7. Beltrán Leyva Marco Antonio Pineda Villa El MP $15M Killed 2009-09-12
8. Beltrán Leyva Héctor Huerta Ríos La Burra $15M Captured 2009-03-25
9. La Familia Michoacana Nazario Moreno González El Chayo $30M Killed 2010-12-09
10. La Familia Michoacana Servando Gómez Martínez El Profe $30M Captured 2015-02-27
11. La Familia Michoacana José de Jesús Méndez Vargas El Chango $30M Captured 2011-6-21
12. La Familia Michoacana Dionicio Loya Plancarte El Tío $30M Captured 2009-04-18
13. Los Zetas Heriberto Lazcano Lazcano El Lazca $30M Killed 2012-10-07
14. Gulf Cartel Jorge Eduardo Costilla Sánchez El Coss $30M Captured 2012-09-12
15. Gulf Cartel Ezequiel Cárdenas Guillén Tony Tormenta $30M Killed 2010-11-05

16. Los Zetas Miguel Angel Treviño Morales Comandante 40 $30M Captured 2013-07-15

17. Los Zetas Omar Treviño Morales L-42 $30M Captured 2015-03-23

18. Gulf Cartel Iván Velázquez Caballero L-50 $30M Captured 2012-09-26

19. Los Zetas Gregorio Sauceda Gamboa El Goyo $30M Captured 2009-04-30

20. Gulf Cartel Sigifredo Nájera Talamantes El Canicón $15M Captured 2009-03-23

21. Los Zetas Ricardo Almanza Morales El Gori $15M Allegedly killed 2012-11-11

22. Los Zetas Raymundo Almanza Morales El Gori $15M Captured 2009-05-22

23. Los Zetas Flavio Méndez Santiago El Amarillo $15M Captured 2011-01-18

24. Los Zetas Sergio Peña Solís El Concord $15M Captured in 2012

25. Los Zetas Raúl Lucio Fernández Lechuga El Lucky $15M Captured 2011-12

26. Gulf Cartel Sergio Enrique Ruiz Tlapanco El Tlapa $15M Captured 2009-11

27. Juárez Cartel Vicente Carrillo Fuentes El Viceroy $30M Captured 2014-10-09

28. Juárez Cartel Vicente Carrillo Leyva - $30M Captured 2009-04-03

29. Juárez Cartel Juan Pablo Ledesma El JL $15M Fugitive

30. Sinaloa Cartel Joaquín Guzmán Loera El Chapo $15M Captured 1993-06-09, escaped 2001-01-19, recaptured 2014-02-22, escaped 2015-07-11, recaptured 2016-01-08

31. Sinaloa Cartel Ismael Zambada García El Mayo Zambada $15M Fugitive

32. Sinaloa Cartel Ignacio Coronel Villarreal El Nacho Coronel $15M Killed 2010-07-29
33. Sinaloa Cartel Juan José Esparragoza Moreno El Azul $15M Allegedly died of heart attack 2014-06-07
34. Sinaloa Cartel Vicente Zambada Niebla El Vicentillo $15M Captured 2009-03-19
35. Tijuana Cartel Teodoro García Simental El Teo $15M Captured 2010-01-12
36. Tijuana Cartel Fernando Sánchez Arellano El Ingeniero $15M Captured 2014-06-23